Subject Access to Films & Videos

Subject Access to Films & Videos

SECOND EDITION

Sheila S. Intner, David P. Miller, Andrea Leigh,
and Bobby Ferguson

Edward Swanson, Contributing Editor

LIBRARIES UNLIMITED

AN IMPRINT OF ABC-CLIO, LLC
Santa Barbara, California • Denver, Colorado • Oxford, England

Library of Congress Cataloging-in-Publication Data

Subject access to films & videos. — 2nd ed. / Sheila S. Intner ... [et al.] ; Edward Swanson, contributing editor.
    p. cm.
    Rev. ed. of: Subject access to films and videos / by Sheila S. Intner and William E. Studwell ; with the assistance of Simone E. Blake and David P. Miller. 1992.
    Includes bibliographical references.
    ISBN 978–1–59158–937–2 (acid-free paper) 1. Cataloging of motion pictures. 2. Cataloging of video recordings. 3. Subject headings—Motion pictures. 4. Subject headings—Video recordings. 5. Motion pictures—Abstracting and indexing. 6. Video recordings–Abstracting and indexing. I. Intner, Sheila S. II. Swanson, Edward, 1941- III. Intner, Sheila S. Subject access to films and videos. IV. Title: Subject access to films and videos.
Z695.64.I55 2011
025.3′473—dc22   2010032375

ISBN: 978–1–59158–937–2

15 14 13 12 11   1 2 3 4 5

This book is also available on the World Wide Web as an eBook.
Visit www.abc-clio.com for details.

Libraries Unlimited
An Imprint of ABC-CLIO, LLC

ABC-CLIO, LLC
130 Cremona Drive, P.O. Box 1911
Santa Barbara, California 93116-1911

This book is printed on acid-free paper (∞)

Manufactured in the United States of America

Contents

Foreword

I cataloged motion pictures (and all other audiovisual/nonbook material) for 30 years for an academic library, and was well aware of the problems of cataloging this form of media—problems of descriptive cataloging, problems of classification, and problems of subject access.

As the publisher Soldier Creek Press, Sheila Intner approached me and proposed a book on subject access to this material. *Subject Access to Films and Videos*, by Sheila S. Intner and William E. Studwell with the assistance of Simone E. Blake and David P. Miller, was published by Soldier Creek Press in 1992, and was used by many catalogers around the world.

This work included chapters on (1) subject access to films and videos, (2) a comparison of *Moving Image Materials: Genre Terms*, and *Library of Congress Subject Headings*, (3) developing video collections, with (4) a bibliography of collection development sources, (5) a bibliography of useful sources for subject access, and extensive lists of (6) Library of Congress subject headings, with selected *Moving Image Materials* headings, (7) revised Library of Congress subject headings, and (8) LC Annotated Card Program descriptors.

The 1992 book is long out of print. Recently, librarians have made inquiries about the availability of a new edition. Because Soldier Creek Press no longer exists (except to publish the annual *Cataloging Service Bulletin Index*), I suggested Sheila contact Libraries Unlimited about publishing a new edition. She did, they agreed, and here is the result.

Nancy B. Olson
AV Cataloger, retired (Emeritus Professor)
Minnesota State University, Mankato

Preface to the
Second Edition

Subject Access to Films and Videos (*SAFV1*), published by Soldier Creek Press, appeared at the end of the 1980s—about 20 years ago—aiming to provide a complement to the numerous descriptive cataloging manuals that the Press was issuing for materials other than books. A short time after it came out, Nancy B. Olson wrote her own film and video cataloging manual, titled *Cataloging Motion Pictures and Videorecordings* (Soldier Creek Press 1991). Following a flurry of interest that included several very nice fan letters, the authors/compilers of the original volume (Sheila S. Intner and William E. Studwell, with the assistance of Simone Blake and David P. Miller) moved on to new projects and eventually forgot about *SAFV1*.

Film and video catalogers, however, continued to find *SAFV1* useful. It came as something as a surprise, however, in the middle of 2008, when a long-time user of *SAFV1* emailed me, asking if we were planning to update the book and publish a new edition. She had discovered the book was now out of print and, after two decades, probably also out of date, given how much the field had changed over the years.

The idea seemed sensible, but, alas, Nancy Olson, the founder of Soldier Creek Press had retired and closed Soldier Creek Press a few years earlier. Co-author Studwell was also retired for many years and had long ago moved on to write on other subjects. Olson immediately gave her blessing for us to proceed with the idea (see her foreword to this book). Miller was now a well-recognized scholar and prolific author on cataloging topics as well as head of Curry College's technical services department, and I was still writing and publishing, although I had retired from Simmons College in 2006. We needed to enlist the support of a new publisher, find a new partner willing to spend the long hours needed to compile the list of relevant *Library of Congress Subject Headings*, and invite someone knowledgeable about methods of providing subject access beyond LCSH and MARC to write an entirely new chapter about film and video metadata.

Always open to new ideas, editors at ABC-Clio/Libraries Unlimited encouraged me to work on the project. I contacted David Miller and he was ready to update his contribution. He also knew Andrea Leigh, LC's Moving Image Processing Unit Head, our metadata expert, and persuaded her to write a chapter on metadata for the new book. Having worked on a number of successful cataloging manual projects with Bobby Ferguson, author of the Blitz Cataloging Workbook series and recently retired, and knowing that she was never afraid of Big Projects, I invited her to be our new compiler. To my amazement, she agreed with her usual enthusiasm. Moreover, Edward Swanson, who also retired recently and was the editor of the first edition of this book, also agreed to edit the new compilation. Edwards' contribution is invaluable—he has completed more editorial work on cataloging manuals more brilliantly than anyone I know. This splendid team—David, Bobby, Andrea, and Edward—earned much more than my thanks—they have my heartfelt admiration.

Like its predecessor, *Subject Access to Films & Videos 2* is primarily a compilation of LCSH subject descriptors pertaining directly to materials in the media group that catalogers call moving image materials. Once, the group was limited to a few material types consisting of images showing motion, generally (though not exclusively) recorded on film (motion pictures) or magnetic tape (videorecordings). Today, there are many kinds of motion pictures and videorecordings as well as more carrier types, including crossovers that combine moving images with music (music videos, MTV), electronic resources (digital video), and more. Similarly, once there were only LCSH headings to consider. Today, there are genre headings, free-floating subdivisions, etc. These were included in the compilation as well.

It was not easy for the compiler to determine where the boundaries lay between "films and videos" and other media groups, such as recorded music and electronic resources. It was tempting to expand into those areas, but, ultimately, it would have overwhelmed the project. Every effort has been made to limit the compilation to descriptors representing topics pertinent to the worlds of film and video alone. Yes, something such as computer animation has a place in it, but only insofar as that process produces an intellectual product the world perceives as a "film"—something people go to see in a movie theater or on television, or buy as a videorecording on DVD, or that can be nominated for an Academy Award (think of *Avatar*, for example). When the fuzzy edges of the subject approached, the compiler's decisions were respected as final.

Rounding out the compilation of subject headings and furnishing a measure of guidance in the application of the subject headings in the compilation, I have updated my chapters on principles of subject cataloging as they apply to nonprint materials in general and films and videos in particular. They are now a single chapter, titled "Subject Cataloging for Films and Videos: Principles and Practice." David has revised and expanded his chapter on form and genre issues with regard to films and videos— an area of subject cataloging that has rightfully come into its own in recent years—titled "Genre/Form Headings: From the Margins to the Center." Andrea has provided an entirely new and well-written chapter on nonlibrary, nonMARC cataloging options, titled "Metadata for Subject Access." In addition, I have written an updated chapter about collecting film and video materials, titled "Developing Film and Video Collections." Finally, a section called "About the Contributors" furnishes brief descriptions of us who have labored on this book.

There you have it—the new, updated, twenty-first-century, second edition of *Subject Access to Films & Videos* (*SAFV2*). All of us who worked on the book hope SAFV2 aids librarians in enhancing the quality of film and video cataloging, thus enabling users of these collections to discover and locate what they want more quickly and effectively. At the end of the day, that is what good cataloging is all about: the best possible user service.

Sheila S. Intner
Principal Editor

1

Subject Cataloging for Films and Videos: Principles and Practice

Sheila S. Intner

An Introductory Word about Terminology

Many synonymous terms are in common use for films. They are variously called *movies*, *moving pictures*, *motion pictures*, *picture shows* and just plain *pictures* or just plain *shows*. (In the early days, they were also called *talkies* and *talking pictures*, but those terms are rarely heard today, except in reference to the earliest examples of films that included sound tracks as well as images.) To make matters worse, the word film has two meanings—it can mean the plastic material on which moving images are recorded as well as completed works consisting of filmed images. Nonetheless, film is in common usage and has the advantage of being one short word.

Videos also have language issues, though they are different. Television broadcasts were called *programs* or *shows*, similar to radio broadcasts. Radio never included images, so the term film or its synonyms were never applied to stories and factual presentations broadcast on radio. They were called radio plays if they were stories, or, if they were nonfiction offerings, programs or shows, sometimes qualified by the adjective educational. If a television broadcast was a film previously shown in theaters, it was not called a telemovie or telefilm, which would have made sense, although it sometimes was called a TV film. (The shorthand *TV* soon replaced the spelled out version of the word television much of the time.) Most of the time, a film shown on television was simply called a film or a movie. Perhaps, because television technical staff referred to TV sound and images as *audio* and *video*, television products began to be called *videos*. Eventually, anything packaged as a video recording began to be called a video.

Today, we have films-made-for-television and films made to be shown in theaters that are marketed simultaneously as videos. There are educational films (rarely called educational movies or educational motion pictures) and educational videos. And, of course, there are audiovisual aids, though that appellation has been avoided in this book.

Carriers for videos have changed over the years from videotape on cassettes to digital signals on optical discs. Digital video is now delivered to computers and other Internet-enabled devices. Development of new storage and delivery systems continues unabated. As a result, the terms films and videos adopted by the authors of *Subject Access to Films and Videos* (SAFV1) in the 1990s reflect only two of the many possibilities that could be used for moving image materials in the 2010s. Readers need to be aware of this situation. They should understand that this book employs the terms films and videos mainly to be consistent with the previous edition, not because they are the only terms or the best terms that could be used. In this chapter, however, *moving image materials* is preferred except when referring solely to moving images on film or moving images in a video recording, because it is a more generic term.

Underlying Assumptions

This compilation of a subset of *Library of Congress Subject Headings* (LCSH) relating to films and videos rests on a number of unspoken assumptions, among them the following:

1. Libraries of all kinds—public libraries, academic libraries, school library media centers, learning centers, information centers, etc.—can be expected to purchase, catalog, and circulate moving image materials, generally in the form of video recordings. In the 20-plus years since the first edition of this book was published, moving image materials have found a place in library collections, albeit in small numbers compared to books. Library users expect to see moving image materials on library shelves.

2. Librarians who read this book are committed to doing standard cataloging for their moving image materials. This means it is possible to merge the resulting records into an Online Public Access Catalog that contains cataloging for all the other types of materials in libraries' collections, although doing so is not required. Evidence for this assumption rests on the fact that LCSH is a cataloging standard and using it implies (although it does not guarantee) adherence to other standards as well.[1]

3. Subject headings from the LCSH list and related lists (genre terms, free-floating subdivisions) can be assigned to moving image materials even though the terms were not specifically designed for that purpose. For the most part, the headings were and still are intended for books about moving image materials, not the moving image materials themselves.

4. Cataloging tools and methods are equally applicable to all sorts of moving image materials no matter how they appear physically, such as on reels of film or magnetic tape, or as cassettes and cartridges containing magnetic tape, or optical discs or other digital media containing electronic signals.

The contents of the various containers (called "carriers" by catalogers) are intellectual/artistic works similar to the contents of books.

5. Carriers of moving image materials pose issues that subject catalogers must address apart from and in addition to the intellectual and artistic issues of their contents.

Assumption number 5 bears a little more attention. An important step in the development of cataloging rules has been the recognition that there are differences between works and their expressions, and between expressions of works and their manifestations. Is a video of a performance of William Shakespeare's *Hamlet* less of the work we know as *Hamlet* than a book containing only the words of the play in printed form? Or, by contrast, is a video of *Hamlet* something more than the play as printed? Or, perhaps, something different? The expressions differ and, indeed, the manifestations differ considerably, but if the words are the same, are these all not really alike? To a great extent, the answer to that question depends on whether the respondent is focused more on the object than its contents, or on the way the contents are expressed than what is being expressed. For moving image materials, therein lies the rub, as Shakespeare might have observed.

The assumptions previously listed spell out two important principles on which the balance of this chapter is based:

First, that moving image materials are essential parts of library collections.
Second, that moving image materials can be cataloged like all other library materials.

Cataloging Decisions

Three basic issues discussed at the start of SAFV1's counterpart of this chapter included the appropriate bibliographic unit for subject cataloging, the choice of a subject authority, and the balance between national and local subject cataloging policies. Several assumptions in the section above obviate the need to justify using LCSH as the subject authority for moving image materials. The assumption that libraries are committed to cataloging moving image materials the same way they catalog other materials also obviates the need to discuss summary-level subject cataloging versus deeper kinds of indexing. For better or worse, librarians do summary-level subject cataloging for their materials. Arguments that justify deeper indexing, should any emerge, are unlikely to change that stance. On the other hand, the trend toward listing tables of contents in contents notes continues to build, albeit slowly, which indicates that if it becomes a local policy, moving image materials will be treated that way also, as appropriate. Because contents notes are a source of subject-rich information, this trend might lead to added indexing.

The third issue, that of the balance between national and local policy, is less clear cut. Because the Library of Congress (LC) and its national library peers do not do as much moving image cataloging as Online Audiovisual Catalogers, Inc. (OLAC) member libraries, national policies do not play as strong a role as they might. On the other hand, national library cataloging represents a quality standard for all others. Professional groups such as OLAC, that lobby for quality cataloging for nonprint materials seem focused less on subject cataloging than on description, descriptive access, and MARC coding. Whether this is because subject access already is considered adequate and, thus, not a problem, or whether it is because subject heading assignment is less amenable to solutions involving rule changes, is hard to determine.

Some of the subject access issues debated in the 1980s and 1990s have been solved to a great extent by the development and application of form and genre terms. A number of LCSH subject headings are authorized both as topical and form-genre headings. David Miller discusses form and genre terms in chapter 2, so such headings are not covered here. It is enough to acknowledge them and point out that LC's recommendations are to assign form and genre terms. Libraries whose policies are to assign such terms as topical terms can continue to do so given their double authorization.

The next section describes the subject heading policies of the Library of Congress, which are basically the same as they were when the first edition of this book was published. The principal difference between the instructions discussed in the next section and those covered in chapter 1 of the first edition is that form and genre headings are treated separately from topical headings. The next section covers topical headings; chapter 2 covers form and genre headings.

How LC Does It

Heading Development

Development of all LCSH subject headings is governed generally by the principle of literary warrant. If material being cataloged requires a subject heading and no suitable term is present in LCSH, a new one is created. According to longstanding LC policies, the term chosen to represent the topic should be in current usage, have a clear and unambiguous definition, and represent the topic specifically, that is, not be broader or narrower than the topic.[2] Similarly, if an existing term does not adequately represent a topic because it is no longer in current usage or its definition changes, it can be changed or replaced by another term.

One of the drawbacks of following literary warrant, however, lies in the fact that creators of materials do not use language rigorously. As stated in a 2009 discussion paper on LCSH video headings, " . . . since authors are not always consistent in the terms they use, literary warrant can occasionally lead to inconsistencies within LCSH. One of the apparent inconsistencies dwells in the area of moving images. There are separate headings for genres of video recordings and genres of films. . . . If an author used the term 'videos,' a heading using that word was used or proposed. If on the other hand an author discussed 'films,' a film heading was used or proposed. However the use of the terms videos and films is very fluid in American usage. Every use of the word 'videos' does not refer to works originally recorded on videotape, and every use of the world 'films' does not refer to works originally recorded on motion picture film."[3]

The forgoing statement was made with regard to genre terms, not topical terms, but, despite serious efforts to exclude synonyms from the list, it applies to LCSH terminology more generally as well. Terms that appear discrete from a lexicographer's point of view may be used synonymously in practice and vice versa, the same term may be used for different topics. The terms *film* and *video* exhibit both of these undesirable properties. Sometimes, in conversation, they are used to refer to physical and/or literary form; other times (even in the same conversation) to content. One could argue that a film made for television is both a film and a video, especially if it was originally shot on videotape, which is likely. Therefore, LC's definition of films is of particular importance. It is: "the term films refers to works that are originally recorded and released on motion picture film, on video, or digitally."[4] Given the rapid changes in recording technologies, the word film may become technically obsolete. Digital cameras, whether used for still pictures or moving images, no longer employ the kinds of film that earlier cameras once used.

Another issue involves the distinction between topical headings and form-genre headings. Practically speaking, headings coded 650 in the MARC format are topical headings and headings coded 655 are genre headings. Extending this point to subdivisions: those coded $x are topical subdivisions and those coded $v are form/genre subdivisions. Intellectually speaking, however, some headings LC designates as topical headings actually refer to form or genre, such as **Internet videos** and **Podcasts**. LC acknowledges this, authorizing many headings for use as both topical and genre/form headings. It also makes the two aforementioned headings exceptions to the rule that eliminated separate topical headings for videos in favor of correlated topical headings for film genres or forms.[5] (The 15 terms that use the word *film* instead of *video* are considered topical terms and coded 650.) See chapter 2 for additional discussion of these matters.

Perhaps the trouble, as it has been so aptly phrased, lies not in our stars but in ourselves. People—catalogers included—tend to use language casually and ambiguously; thus, why should we expect subject heading terminology to be absolutely rigorous and crystal clear? Certainly, the pragmatic decision to use the word films for videos, while understandable, further muddies the waters.

Basic Guidance for Heading Assignment

A note at the start of instruction sheet H 2230 that provides guidance for assigning subject headings for motion pictures and video recordings[6] explains: "As used in this instruction sheet, the word film is understood to refer to any type of visual material."[7] The balance of this instruction sheet is divided into seven simple rules, some of which are followed by MARC encoded examples. The first six are:

1. Assign subject headings for all important topics mentioned in the summary statement (520 field). If a specific topic is emphasized in order to illustrate a more general concept, assign subject headings for both the specific and the general topics.
2. When a topic is discussed in conjunction with a particular place, make . . . a subject entry under both the topic and the place.
3. When a . . . person is treated as illustrative of a profession or activity, assign a heading for both the person and the field of endeavor. Do not . . . treat such materials as biographies.
4. Special topics of visual materials:
   a. Fiction films. Assign topical headings with the subdivision—**Drama** . . . Assign headings of this type to the same extent that such headings are assigned to individual dramas in book form.
   b. Foreign language teaching films. Assign the heading [. . .] **language— Films for [. . .] speakers** as the first heading and bring out any special

topics by assigning additional headings. [For example, **French language—Films for Greek speakers**.]

    c. Juvenile films. *See H 1690.* That instruction sheet directs catalogers to assign topical headings subdivided—**Juvenile films** as well as **Children's films** as a second heading for fictional films.

    d. Films for the hearing impaired and for people with disabilities. *See H 1913, sec. 1.e.* See chapter 2.

5. Moving image genre/form headings. *See H 1913.* See chapter 2.

6. Treatment of "editions":

    a. Audio or visual presentations of published works. If the contents of the printed edition and the . . . visual presentation are the same, the subject cataloging should match, even if it is necessary to assign new, more appropriate headings to the printed [materials].

    b. Identical works in different formats. A single work is sometimes issued in more than one format, for example, as a motion picture and as a video recording. . . . The subject headings for the work in all formats with records in MARC should match, even if it is necessary to correct the subject headings that were assigned when the work was originally cataloged in another format.[8]

The seventh rule instructs how to encode MARC field 043, which identifies the geographical focus of contents in coded form.

Two grassroots trends are addressed by LC's recommendations to subject catalogers: treat fiction materials with as much care and respect as you treat nonfiction materials; and harmonize the treatment of various expressions and manifestations of the same work. The instruction to add new subject headings to printed works in order that they match the subject headings assigned to film or video versions of the same works is a giant step in the quest for equal access to films and videos. While it is not a new instruction, its influence on practice has increased. Perhaps this is a byproduct of a larger trend to be more generous with access points than catalogers were in pre-computer days when added headings meant more typing and filing work, but the result is positive nevertheless.

Recognizing the informational value of fiction materials is a practical response to what is actually happening on the ground. People who use libraries often look to fiction to learn about a subject. Who can say that a well-researched story on film (or video) is necessarily less informative than a similar piece that does not tell a story and is marketed as an educational film? The former can sometimes provide as much or more information to its viewers as the latter, even though creators of works of imagination are not bound to be totally factual.

Stories have long been used to transmit knowledge. Unfortunately, it puts the burden on viewers to evaluate materials carefully and look for evidence and corroboration before accepting what they see and hear as the truth. This attitude would be an insurmountable problem for fictional materials except for the fact that educational materials purporting to be factual and accurate have been shown to contain errors and are, sometimes, not just inadvertently wrong but deliberately misleading. In the twenty-first century, "misinformation" and "disinformation" are used to influence people to such an extent that, at the end of the day, viewers must always be on their guard. With fiction, at least, viewers expect to encounter the taking of poetic license—fudging facts to make a good story better or altering the outcomes of stories to create happy endings—thus preparing them to be skeptical.

Though LC's instructions have not changed much since the first edition of this book, the way catalogs are used is not the same as it was in the 1990s and the differences have prompted more attention to subject cataloging. Libraries now serve increasing numbers of remote patrons—college students enrolled in online courses or at satellite campuses, residents of surrounding communities, and patrons of consortium libraries. These people consult Web-based catalogs to decide what to borrow from local libraries. Many own video equipment and want materials for their studies or entertainment.[9] They need (and expect to get) more subject access than was once provided, consulting the catalog to locate and select the films and other programs they want whether they plan to obtain them on interlibrary loan or by visiting library buildings after completing their catalog searches to pick them up in person.[10]

Subject searching, always a large proportion of all searching, has attained even greater importance for remote users who cannot simply browse shelves or amble over to a reader's advisor's desk for help. Catalog records must provide the answers to their questions and display the whole array of materials libraries have available for their use. Catalog records can no longer be the cryptic, greatly abbreviated little pointers that used to be printed on 3×5 cards. They must be satisfactory substitutes for the materials they represent, giving enough information about those materials to answer the questions searchers have in dealing with collections of millions of titles.

Progress and Problems

Subject cataloging for films and videos has come a long way since the days when a film lasting 40 minutes or more was assigned the heading **Feature film** and not much else and a film lasting less than 40 minutes was assigned the heading **Short film**. These form headings still are assigned as applicable, but now, more than ever, catalogers recognize the importance of first assigning relevant topical, geographical, and chronological subject headings and subdivisions to reveal the contents of films and videos. (A long time principle of subject heading assignment is topic before form, with some exceptions.) LC provides instructions on how to determine easily which subject headings to assign, employing a key element of descriptive cataloging—the summary note—for this purpose.

LC's basic rule—to assign a subject heading for all topics given in the summary note—mandates the creation of good summary notes for films and videos. Too often, summary notes, deemed optional by AACR2-2005, are either overlooked or written carelessly, quoting bits and pieces of the blurbs found on the boxes or jewel cases in which the materials are packaged. The blurbs are designed to excite interest and induce suspense that only viewing the whole content will satisfy, not to describe the contents objectively. They may save busy catalogers a few minutes thinking up a good way to phrase a plot summary, but they are unlikely to be sufficiently complete (without, of course, giving away surprise endings or whodunits) or sufficiently "objective" to satisfy AACR2's requirements. Nevertheless, such practices are a necessity sometimes, because neither the time nor the equipment is available for catalogers to view the films and videos before writing their summary notes.

Allowing these problems to persist inevitably leads to inferior public service. An important issue for policy makers in libraries that collect and catalog large numbers of films and videos should be finding a way to enable catalogers to view films and videos so they can write good summaries. One possible solution is to add the task of reviewing them to make purchasing decisions to the job descriptions of moving image catalogers. Another is making moving image catalogers the liaisons to departments that use the materials heavily, so reviewing new films is justifiable as part of the liaisonship. The fact that summary notes are the information source for subject cataloging is reason enough to find a way of allowing catalogers to view moving image materials, to say nothing of confirming the rest of the descriptive details, especially running times, which can vary from what is printed on containers. One can rightfully ask, why buy the materials if good cataloging is not provided for them? Not only do remote searchers need the information good cataloging provides, but onsite users often need it as well, because film and video stacks are closed and/or viewing facilities are not provided.

Conclusion

Film and video collections have been accepted as routine in libraries. After years of being handled as special materials requiring unique treatments, they are now mainstreamed in standard workflows. Unlike books, however, moving image materials still need a few special considerations, most importantly, the extra time it takes to view enough content to make writing good summary notes possible. LC subject cataloging policies for moving image materials state that summary notes should be consulted to select the headings to be assigned. How can this procedure work in practice if those doing the original cataloging have not seen the content and cannot write good summary notes? Perhaps, better methods of viewing moving image materials technically, akin to reading books technically to derive cataloging information, need to be developed.

Book catalogers also might do well to recognize the need for good summaries as a routine element of descriptive cataloging that benefits online catalog users. Why should children's books be the only ones receiving such treatment? Would not adults who rely on the catalog for enough information to select educational books—treatises, textbooks, research reports, introductions to a subject, etc.—find complete, objective summary notes useful? The new environment in which catalogs operate to reveal the contents of library collections begs for more and better information of all kinds in catalog records. Subject access—the key to contents—is a prime candidate for attention in this regard.

Notes

1. Back in 1980–1981, when the author was conducting her dissertation research, she learned that public librarians tended to think that nonprint materials contained good information, but that members of the public preferred books, which she reported in her book based on the study,

Access to Media: A Guide to Integrating and Computerizing Catalogs (New York: Neal-Schuman, 1984). An interesting discovery was that many of the responding libraries that did not follow standard descriptive cataloging rules or assign standard call numbers for these materials often assigned LCSH subject headings to them.

2. David Judson Haykin, *Subject Headings: A Practical Guide* (Washington, D.C.: Government Printing Office, 1951), pp. 7–11.

3. *Disposition of* LCSH *Video Recording Headings in the New Genre/Form Environment: Discussion Paper, May 11, 2009.* Available at http://www.loc.gov/catdir/cpso/videorecheadings.pdf (viewed February 7, 2010).

4. Library of Congress Policy and Standards Division, *Subject Headings Manual*, instruction sheet H 1913. Available in *Cataloger's Desktop* (viewed February 7, 2010).

5. *Decision Regarding the Final Disposition of LCSH Headings for Video Recordings, November 6, 2009.* Available at http://videorecheadings2.pdf (viewed February 7, 2010).

6. The choice of LC subject catalogers for the two word phrase, "video recordings" begs the question why they do not accept AACR2's spelling of the term as one word: "videorecordings." Even if the phrase is considered better orthographic practice, the mere fact that descriptive cataloging differs ought to exert enough persuasive pressure to conform to a single spelling. Persistence in the face of the potential confusion that different spellings might create seems counterproductive to this author.

7. Library of Congress, Policy and Standards Division, *Subject Headings Manual*, instruction sheet H 2230. Available in *Cataloger's Desktop* (viewed February 3, 2010).

8. Ibid.

9. A word about physical form of moving image materials in libraries: Although no study has documented it, the author believes that most libraries collect videos, not films as defined by H 2230. Motion pictures are primarily a public performance medium, although "home movies" played a role in private lives in the mid to late twentieth century. The rise of video camcorders made home movies obsolete. Libraries that once collected motion picture films, whether fiction or nonfiction, usually did so for presentation purposes in film series or classrooms, rather than for personal borrowing. As more materials originally created on film were also distributed on video, libraries were able to utilize the videos both for presentation and personal borrowing. Not only are the videocassettes and videodiscs less fragile than film reels, but the equipment needed to project them is simpler, easier to run, and less costly.

10. A recent OCLC study confirms the point. It is available at http://www.oclc.org/reports/onlinecatalogs/fullreport.pdf (viewed February 21, 2010).

2

Genre/Form Headings: From the Margins to the Center

David P. Miller

In 1992, when the first edition of this book was published, the provision of access to forms and genres represented by video and film materials was still very new. As cartographers of old did embellishing the empty spaces representing unknown territory, many catalogers thought *Here Be Monsters* when contemplating the absence of mainstream thesauri, application policies, and indexing standards. Although many individual Library of Congress (LC) subject headings, such as Feature films and Children's films, had in fact been established to provide form/genre access, the matter had not been systematically considered as separate from subject access. Most subject files (card and online) indiscriminately intermixed the two, and it was widely considered that this was not a problem worth solving. At the present time, the better part of two decades later, the situation has changed significantly. Following a review of the past, this chapter will discuss the new *status quo*, with references to some continuing issues and further developments.

In the early 1990s, there was one easily read thesaurus specifically developed for provision of genre access to video, film, and related materials. This was *Moving Image Materials: Genre Terms (MIM)*, compiled by Martha M. Yee.[1] *MIM* was developed by the National Moving Image Standards Database Committee of the National Center for Film and Video Preservation at the American Film Institute and published by the Library of Congress. Its stated purpose was "to standardize terms used to designate genres and forms of moving image materials."[2] The development committee included representatives from institutions including the Museum of Broadcasting (New York), the UCLA Film and Television Archive, and the Motion Picture, Broadcasting and Recorded Sound Division at LC. *MIM* therefore had the imprimatur provided by a body of recognized experts. It was not, however, designed for seamless integration with other controlled vocabularies. At the time of its publication in 1988, this may not have been considered to be a particular drawback. The successful integration of multiple thesauri in one electronic file was so far in the future that provision of separate indexes for separate controlled vocabularies was the default condition, whether or not this was actually considered optimal.

My essay in the first edition of this book examined "levels of compatibility" between *MIM* and *LCSH* terms when used in the same index.[3] The essay was occasioned by the practical need to reconcile these two vocabularies, as I had begun to use *MIM* in film and video cataloging for my college library, and in the consortium catalog in which I worked, these could only be included in a traditional "subject" index.

The analysis focused on the extent to which the terms in *MIM* were compatible as character strings with equivalent headings in *LCSH*. This narrow starting point for analysis was justified by noting that, at the time, "in most automated systems specific cross-reference conflicts will not arise unless one specific character string is matched with another."[4] The minimal condition for compatibility was considered to be the lack of explicit conflict between an established heading in one vocabulary and a reference heading in another. At the same time, semantic issues were considered, including instances of headings that matched as character strings but pointed to different conceptual matter.

The majority of *MIM* headings did not conflict with *LCSH* to any significant extent either as character strings or conceptually. Three groups of *MIM* headings, while differing from *LCSH* as character strings, still presented potential problems of overlap and synonymy. I described the first group as "pseudo-synonyms," e.g., **Debates** in *MIM* and **Debates and debating** in *LCSH*. The second group comprised pairs of terms with similar though not identical wording, with implications for differences in scope, e.g., **Horror films and programs** in *MIM* and **Horror films** in *LCSH*. The third group included headings that presented no conflicts because they were identical in both vocabularies, such as **Film noir** and **Vaudeville**. Ironically, however, "with this set of terms, the difficulty of distinguishing subject from form/genre . . . becomes most acute."[5] Further points of analysis included a set of *MIM* headings which directly conflicted with *see* references in *LCSH*, a small set of homographic problems, a group of *MIM* headings which could not be simply resolved either as compatible or conflicting with *LCSH*, and a final group of "pseudo-see references."

The finer points of this analysis may be of historical interest today, and the inquiring reader is heartily invited to refer to the first edition. Still, the essay attempted to explicate some of the larger issues involved in access to forms and genres in a still recently automated, pre–World Wide Web environment. These included "the proper place of form and genre terms in a controlled subject vocabulary, and to what degree our reliance on title/author/subject, as the trinity of access modes, will continue to serve our needs. . . . As online catalogs evolve from electronic reproductions of card catalogs toward access tools in their own right, (these are problems) that will have to be solved."[6]

Although *MIM* was, at the time, the sole vocabulary available for assignment of form and genre terms to moving image materials, a mini-explosion of genre/form thesauri in the cataloging community at large was already underway.[7] The movement originated in the rare books and materials community, beginning with the publication in 1983 of *Genre Terms: A Thesaurus for Use in Rare Book and Special Collections Cataloguing*.[8] By the end of the decade, additional vocabularies for use with graphic materials, archives and manuscripts had appeared, and the *Art & Architecture Thesaurus* was in development.[9] The *Guidelines on Subject Access to Individual Works of Fiction, Drama, Etc. (GSAFD)*, produced by the Subject Analysis Committee of the American Library Association's Resources and Technical Services Division (the division is now known as the Association for Library Collections & Technical Services) was published in 1990.[10] Two-thirds of *GSAFD* consisted of a list of genre and form headings, some of which could be applied to moving image materials, although the latter were not the primary materials of interest. (A second edition of *GSAFD* was published in 2000; there are no plans for a third edition.[11]) A chapter by Jackie M. Dooley and Helena Zinkham provides an excellent summary of the state of the art as of 1990, excluding *GSAFD*, which was most likely not available at the time of writing.[12] Dooley and Zinkham also discuss the difficulties surrounding indexing and display, at a time when genre/form headings could rarely be searched separately from cognate subject headings.

The next stage in genre and form access to the materials considered here occurred in 1998, with the appearance of *The Moving Image Genre-Form Guide* (MIGFG). MIGFG was developed by a committee within the Motion Picture/Broadcasting/Recorded Sound Division (MBRS) of the Library of Congress, chaired by Brian Taves.[13] It was notable for taking an explicitly faceted approach, providing different lists of terms to indicate genre and form. The concept of genre, which received greater emphasis, was discussed as follows:

> Genres are recognizable primarily by content, and to a lesser degree by style. Genres contain conventions of narrational strategy and organizational structure, using similar themes, motifs, settings, situations, and characterizations. In this way, the makers of moving image works use recognizable patterns of storytelling that are readily understood by audiences. Typical formulas range from the varieties of Hollywood feature films to modes of nonfictional discourse.[14]

More than 130 genre terms were included, including a list for subgenres of **Experimental film**. Definitions were given for each term, which ranged from the familiar, such as **Western** and **Mystery**, to the less expected, such as **Ancient world**, **Trigger**, and **Yukon**.

Forms were defined as "the basic categories indicating a moving image work's original exhibition and release parameters (such as length and medium), and which are separate from its actual content, not necessarily implying a particular narrative construction. Form terms include **Feature**, **Short**, **Serial**, **Animation**, and **Television**, and can be associated as needed with any genre, in a manner similar to free-floating subdivisions."[15] Nearly 40 form terms were given: these include, however, two lists of subtypes for **Animation** and **Advertising**, so the basic list of forms totaled fewer than half that number. The introductory text distinguished the concept of form from that of physical format (e.g., **Videodisc**), but did not provide a separate term list for the latter.

Given that genre, form, and format concepts were provided as facets, *MIGFG* headings as coded in the MARC21 655 field would appear as (for example):

655 _7 $a Adventure $v Feature. $2 migfg
655 _7 $a Western $v #Television series $v DVD. $2 migfg
655 _7 $a Science fiction $v Anthology $v Television series. $2 migfg

In 2001, Yee published a comparison of *MIGFG* and *LCSH* as sources for moving image genre and form terms.[16] Her analysis was based on these questions:

- Are some of the headings in each of the two lists actually topical subject headings in disguise?
- Do some of the headings in the two lists express concepts other than form or genre, such as audience, time slot, fictitious characters or type of broadcast or distribution?
- Are the headings in the two lists under consideration as specific and direct as they could be?
- Are the headings consistent in their facet analysis and citation order?
- Do the headings obey literary warrant?
- Do the number and grammatical part of speech of each heading in each list follow standard usage and are they consistent?
- Are the syndetic structures adequate and consistent in both lists?
- Do both lists include all useful genre and form terms for moving image materials commonly found in moving image and broadcast material collections and commonly studied by scholars?
- Can the headings in each list be integrated easily into heading displays that draw headings from a number of different sources of headings?
- (Does) either list (contain) headings that create categories into which so many moving image titles fall that they become virtually unusable for direct searching(?)[17]

Yee concluded that "any library, media collection or archive that uses *LCSH* for the provision of topical subject access to moving image and broadcast materials (should) strongly consider *LCSH* for genre and form access to moving images and broadcast materials as well,"[18] and provided 15 suggestions to improve *LCSH* for this purpose. Nevertheless, this analysis and set of suggestions were set in the context of a controlled vocabulary maintained and developed for subject access proper, notwithstanding the existence of individual LC headings intended to designate genres and forms. The development of an *LCSH*-based genre/form vocabulary, with a complementary authority structure, was still in the future.[19]

The first steps toward development of a MARC-based authority file for specific support of genre/form vocabularies were taken in 1995, with a proposal from the Stockton-San Joaquin County Public Library to the USMARC Advisory Group.[20] In June of that year, a discussion at the Machine-Readable Bibliographic Information (MARBI) committee meeting during the American Library Association (ALA) Annual Conference resulted in agreement to establish X55 authority fields in the USMARC Authority Format (now MARC 21) in order to control headings entered in the Bibliographic 655 field.

In 1998, the same year as the publication of *MIGFG*, the Library of Congress Cataloging Policy and Support Office (CPSO, now known as the Policy and Standards Division) announced its intention to create "authority records for form/genre headings in 155 fields" and implement "more widespread assignment of form/genre terms in 655 fields of bibliographic records," but noted that it was not able to announce a specific timeline.[21] In 2001, the movement toward establishing genre/form terms for moving image materials began, as a first experiment in pursuit of comprehensive development of such terms in *LCSH*. The Motion Picture/Broadcasting/Recorded Sound Division (MBRS) began discussions with CPSO, "to inquire whether [*MIGFG*] could be integrated into *LCSH*. The request was made in part because *MIGFG* needed to be updated, but there was no mechanism to do so, and no staff to do it. *LCSH* already had both a staff and a mechanism."[22]

At the ALA Midwinter Meeting in January 2006, Lynn El-Hoshy reported that CPSO and MBRS had done the following:

> begun a project to analyze the genre/form terms from *Moving Image Genre-Form Guide (MIGFG)* and reconcile the terminology with LCSH. The terminology from *Moving Image Materials: Genre Terms (MIM)* will also be consulted as part of this project. The goal will be to move as much of MIGFG as possible to LCSH, and to unambiguously indicate in LCSH whether the terms are to be used as topics (i.e., subject authority records tagged as 150) or genre/form headings (i.e., subject authority records tagged as 155). The resulting subject authority records will be the first issued as part of LCSH with the 155 tag and will be supplemented with instructions for applying such headings in bibliographic records in the *Subject Cataloging Manual: Subject Headings*. Once LC has developed a draft list of headings to be established in LCSH as genre/form headings, along with scope notes where necessary and a list of principles used to establish such headings, the proposal will be shared with the larger moving image community for input and comment before the genre/form headings are established and distributed as part of LCSH.[23]

CPSO's first release of genre/form authority records for moving-image materials took place in September 2007.[24] With this release, the essential components for providing genre/form access, based in *LCSH* and MARC 21, were put in place. Individual libraries had already begun to adapt *LCSH* subject authority records for use in genre-form indexes, following the establishment of Bibliographic Format X55 fields in the mid-1990s. However, those local efforts were not necessarily emulated by libraries who had to have mainstream support systems. MBRS began using LC genre/form headings in its own cataloging on January 1, 2009.[25]

Library of Congress Policy

The following discussion of LC policy for assignment of genre/form terms to moving-image materials is drawn primarily from two documents: section H1913, "Moving Image Genre/Form Terms," of the *Subject Headings Manual*,[26] and "Frequently Asked Questions About LC Genre/Form Headings."[27] Both documents are available online, and are referred to in this discussion as H1913 and FAQ respectively.

LC policy in this area is still under development, although its fundamental elements are in place. This summary expresses conditions as of early 2010, but it is always advisable to examine the latest versions of the abovementioned documents.

LC defines moving-image works as "those created by recording moving visual images, with or without sound" (H1913 Background). "Form" is defined as "a characteristic of works with a particular format and/or purpose," such as short films or animations, while "genre" denotes "categories of works that are characterized by similar plots, themes, settings, situations, and characters," such as westerns or thrillers (FAQ 1). The two primary categories of moving images are films, defined as "works that are originally recorded and released on motion picture film, on video, or digitally," and television programs, defined as "those works that are originally telecast" (H1913 Background). These definitions, then, refer to the *original* release or broadcast medium, not necessarily a medium of subsequent distribution. To take a typical example, DVD manifestations of feature films will be assigned genre headings such as **Biographical films**, not **Biographical videos**. To put it in *Functional Requirements for Bibliographic Records* terms, genre/form headings are assigned for *expressions*, not *manifestations* (FAQ 2).[28] A few exceptions to this principle will be described below.

Genre/form headings are established by first determining if topical subject headings already exist in *LCSH* that are appropriate for this added use, rather than attempting to develop an altogether new vocabulary. If appropriate topical terms do not already exist, the *Subject Headings Manual* requires that new headings use "the formulas [. . .] **films** and [. . .] **television programs**, or **Film** [. . .] or **Television** [. . .]" (H1913 ¶ 2b(2)). Usage or literary warrant may sometimes require the qualifiers **(Motion pictures)** or **(Television programs)**. Headings constructed in these forms include examples such as **Documentary television programs**, **Film adaptations**, and **Variety shows (Television programs)**. Other forms may be required in specific cases, with **Televised sports events** given as an example.

As noted, LC has established a few genre/form headings that are exceptional in terminology, and/or in referring to manifestations rather than expressions. **Video recordings for the hearing impaired** and **Video recordings for people with visual disabilities** are form headings which typically refer to manifestations, but provide information of importance in many libraries. Three headings, **Rock videos**, **Music videos**, and **Interactive videos**, have been established with the "videos" terminology due to preponderant common usage. Three additional headings, **Podcasts**, **Internet videos**, and **Webisodes** present the interesting case of new forms of manifestations that, nevertheless, have the potential to develop as true forms and/or genres in themselves. "As these 'new media' evolve they are developing their own stylistic and/or release and exhibition parameters, which are aspects of genre and form" (FAQ 2). At the same time, LC states that the establishment of these three headings "should not be construed as a desire to create subgenres of podcasts and Internet videos (e.g., **Comedy podcasts**, **Animated Internet videos**, **Legal webisodes**)".[29] Catalogers who wish to provide access to such characteristics should assign additional film or television headings as appropriate.

The *Subject Headings Manual* places no limit on the number of headings that may be assigned in a record, calling for "as many as necessary" to bring out all important genres and forms represented by a work. The example given lists six headings for

The Wizard of Oz (H1913 ¶ 1d). Interestingly, the guidelines allow assigning headings from different levels of the same hierarchy if it is judged advisable. This appears to be interpreted more liberally than the general instructions in *SHM* H180, "Assigning and Constructing Subject Headings," where specificity, or co-extensiveness of headings with the subjects of a work, is the norm, and deliberate assignment of broader headings is allowed only in special situations.[30]

A few form headings are deemed important enough to be assigned in a broad range of instances. For people with disabilities, **Films** (or **Television programs**) **for the hearing impaired**, and/or **Films** (or **Television programs**) **for people with visual disabilities** are mandated whenever applicable, although the **Video recordings** forms noted above may also be assigned (H1913 ¶ 1e). For motion pictures only, either **Short films** or **Feature films** should be assigned in all cases, the division between the two given as a running time of 40 minutes (H1913 ¶ 1c). One of four other headings should be assigned in all cases. These are **Fiction films**, **Nonfiction films**, **Fiction television programs**, and **Nonfiction television programs** (H1913 ¶ 1b). It is assumed these headings are not useful for direct end-user searching, but are good for limiting searches, and will also provide useful information where the fiction/nonfiction nature of a work is not otherwise evident.

LC has also established the "top term" headings **Motion pictures**, **Television programs**, and **Video recordings**. These are not to be assigned to individual works, if a cataloging agency wishes to follow LC policy. They exist "mostly for hierarchical purposes, in order to give catalog users a useful collocation point for all of the form/genre headings in a given discipline" (FAQ 11). If an individual library wishes to assign one of these headings to an individual work and is cataloging in one of the MARC formats, it should code the heading as local. An example of such coding is given below.

This text will not provide a complete list of genre/form headings for moving image materials, as they can be found in several different ways. A good source for the general public is the compiled list provided by the Online Audiovisual Catalogers, Inc. (OLAC). This frequently updated list is available from the OLAC Web site.[31] Libraries subscribing to LC's *Classification Web* product can search genre/form headings from an option on the opening menu, and those using OCLC's Connexion can search the authority file for genre/form headings. These sources are the most up-to-date as well as interactive, compared to OLAC's pdf-format document, but they are available only to subscribers.

LC provides genre/form authority records free through the *Library of Congress Authorities* site[32] and the newer *Authorities & Vocabularies* page.[33] At the former site, genre/form authorities are interfiled with subject authority records, rather than in a separate file as in *Classification Web* and Connexion. Still, it is possible to start with a top term heading like **Motion pictures**, and with persistence arrive at an exportable MARC 21 authority record for the heading sought. Records may also be printed or sent via email. It is also possible to search the subject index for a specific genre/form heading, such as **Zombie films**, directly. The *Authorities & Vocabularies* site was developed to allow both human beings and machines to access authority data via URIs. Individual records and the *LCSH* dataset as a whole may be downloaded in formats designed for use in the Semantic Web, but not in MARC 21 format.[34] Those who do not yet require this level of technical support will still be able to search for established genre/form headings and discover related headings, scope notes, etc. Libraries without access to *Classification Web* or Connexion should consider either of these useful sources.

Finally, libraries that receive *LCSH* in printed form will find genre/form headings in the *Supplemental Vocabularies* volume, an addition to the "Big Red Books" as of 2009 (FAQ 3).

The Debate Over Geographic Subdivision

LC's Policy and Standards Division (PSD, formerly known as CPSO) has regularly engaged the cataloging community in discussions about its developing genre/form policies. While there has been reasonably broad community consensus on most aspects of its policies, controversy has arisen on the subject of allowing subdivisions with genre/form headings. At present, catalogers following LC policy should not use subdivisions of any kind—topical, chronological, geographical, or form (FAQ 9–10). If subdivision information is regarded as important in a local situation (as it frequently is in the author's library), the heading may be coded as local. In MARC 21 Bibliographic format, this would appear as, for example:

655 _7 Short films $y 21st century. $2 local[35]

Many catalogers have expressed the wish that geographic subdivision, in particular, be allowed as part of LC policy. They point out that different types of patrons, frequently but not exclusively in public libraries, wish to focus on films or television programs produced in a particular country, or perhaps (by extension) in a given language. Reference librarians find this information of great value as well. It is possible in MARC 21 Bibliographic Format to indicate "country of publication, production, or execution" by entering codes in bytes 15–17 of field 008, Fixed-length data elements.[36] This is of limited value, however, for materials produced by multinational companies, as only one country can be coded using this element. Field 043, Geographic Area Code, may contain multiple codes for geographic areas "associated with an item," but the understanding of what this means will certainly vary from one person (patron or librarian) to another.[37] In addition, libraries that have independently implemented genre/form access to moving-image materials, some for well over a decade, have consistently provided geographic subdivision and wish to continue doing so.

In reply, LC points to the ambiguity of geographic subdivision. "Within the context of moving images, geographic subdivision could have many different meanings: the country of filming, the country of production, the country of distribution, the nationality of the director, and the setting of the film are several possibilities" (FAQ 10). Although it is plausible that a majority of catalogers have country of production in mind, there is no unanimity on this point, and it is likely that many library users would think of the location of the setting or a director's nationality.

As of early 2010, the PSD has indicated that it "would like to hear from more interested parties, particularly those who have empirical data on user behavior with regard to geographic subdivisions in genre/form searches, before making a final decision" (FAQ 10). In other words, if LC is to change its policy regarding subdivision of genre/form headings, it is likely be on the basis of research-based evidence rather than informal discussion or anecdotal evidence.

There are likely to be further developments in the matter of associating geographic and related attributes with moving image materials, and the best solutions to this dilemma may lie elsewhere than with geographic subdivisions. In June 2009, OLAC's Cataloging Policy Committee made a proposal to change MARC 21 Bibliographic Format field 257, formerly named Country of Producing Entity for Archival Films, so that it would no longer be restricted to archival materials, and could be used to represent multiple countries of production. The MARC 21 Advisory Committee accepted the proposal at the American Library Association Annual conference that summer.[38] Although this will require further advances in indexing and retrospective application to existing records in order to be broadly useful, it is an example of the work being done. A subcommittee of the ALA ALCTS Subject Analysis Committee also has begun to investigate "the possible and the preferred methods of relating geographical, ethnicity, and language limiters to genre-form headings," broadening this question beyond moving image materials alone.[39]

Readers should take care not to become too distracted by the details of current, and no doubt future, discussions and controversies. When it comes to provision of genre-form access for moving image materials, the field has traveled a great distance between 1992 and 2010. What once was *terra incognita* is now reasonably well-charted territory; and, even the very debates taking place at this writing are evidence of it. There are still unsettled questions, but for those who work with *LCSH* and its supplemental vocabularies, "There Be Monsters" no longer.

Notes

1. Martha M. Yee, comp. *Moving Image Materials: Genre Terms* (Washington, D.C.: Library of Congress Cataloging Distribution Service, 1988).

2. Yee, *Moving Image Materials*, 11.

3. David P. Miller, "Levels of Compatibility Between *Moving Image Materials: Genre Terms* and *Library of Congress Subject Headings* in a General Library Catalog." In Sheila S. Intner and William E. Studwell, *Subject Access to Films and Videos* (Lake Crystal, Minn.: Soldier Creek Press, 1992), 17–30.

4. Miller, 19.

5. Miller, 23.

6. Miller, 17, 29.

7. It should be noted that this essay assumes an Anglo-American environment and mainstream standards, in particular the *Library of Congress Subject Headings* and MARC 21.

8. Rare Books and Manuscripts Section Standards Committee Association of College and Research Libraries, *Genre Terms: A Thesaurus for Use in Rare Book and Special Collections Cataloguing* (Chicago: Association of College and Research Libraries, 1983).

9. Toni Peterson, director, *Art & Architecture Thesaurus* (New York: Oxford University Press, 1990). Online version: http://www.getty.edu/research/conducting_research/vocabularies/aat/(accessed January 23, 2010).

10. Subcommittee on Subject Access to Individual Works of Fiction, Drama, etc., Subject Analysis Committee, Resources and Technical Services Division, American Library Association, *Guidelines on Subject Access to Individual Works of Fiction, Drama, Etc.* (Chicago: American Library Association, 1990).

11. Subcommittee on the Revision of the Guidelines on Subject Access to Individual Works of Fiction, Subject Analysis Committee, Association for Library Collections & Technical

Services, American Library Association, *Guidelines on Subject Access to Individual Works of Fiction, Drama, Etc.* (Chicago: American Library Association, 2000).

12. Jackie M. Dooley and Helena Zinkham, "The Object as 'Subject': Providing Access to Genres, Forms of Material, and Physical Characteristics." In Toni Petersen and Pat Moholt, eds., *Beyond the Book: Extending MARC for Subject Access* (Boston: G. K. Hall, 1990).

13. Brian Taves, Judi Hoffman, Karen Lund, comps., *The Moving Image Genre-Form Guide* (Washington, D.C.: Motion Picture, Broadcasting, and Recorded Sound Division, Library of Congress, 1998), http://www.loc.gov/rr/mopic/migintro.html (accessed January 23, 2010).

14. Ibid.

15. Ibid.

16. Martha M. Yee, "Two Genre and Form Lists for Moving Image and Broadcast Materials: A Comparison." *Cataloging and Classification Quarterly* 31 no. 3–4 (2001): 237–295.

17. Yee, "Two Genre and Form Lists," 242–256.

18. Yee, "Two Genre and Form Lists," 261

19. Jay Weitz has kindly provided the information that, as of December 2007, there were 327,043 instances of *MIM* headings and 59,172 instances of *MIGFG* headings in OCLC's WorldCat database (personal communication, November 16, 2009).

20. Stockton-San Joaquin County Public Library, "Definition of X55 Fields for Genre/Form Terms in the USMARC Authority Format," http://www.loc.gov/marc/marbi/1995/95-11.html (accessed January 23, 2010).

21. Thompson Yee, Cataloging Policy and Support Office, Library of Congress, "Subject Authority Data Elements and Form/Genre Implementation," http://www.loc.gov/catdir/cpso/formgenr.html (accessed January 23, 2010).

22. Cataloging Policy and Support Office, Library of Congress, "Report on the Moving Image Genre/Form Project," http://www.loc.gov/catdir/cpso/movimgenre.pdf (accessed January 23, 2010).

23. "ALCTS CCS Subject Analysis Committee, ALA Midwinter Meeting 2006, San Antonio, TX" ([meeting minutes, 22–23]), http://www.ala.org/ala/mgrps/divs/alcts/mgrps/ccs/cmtes/sac/ccs_SAC_MW06min.doc (accessed January 23, 2010).

24. Acquisitions and Bibliographic Access Directorate, Library of Congress, "Genre/Form Authority Records," http://www.loc.gov/catdir/cpso/genre.html (accessed January 23, 2010).

25. Acquisitions and Bibliographic Access Directorate, Library of Congress, "Frequently Asked Questions about LC Genre/Form Headings," http://www.loc.gov/catdir/cpso/genre_form_faq.pdf (accessed January 23, 2010), 6.

26. Accessed via Cataloger's Desktop, http://desktop.loc.gov (January 21, 2010).

27. Acquisitions and Bibliographic Access Directorate, Library of Congress, "Frequently Asked Questions about LC Genre/Form Headings."

28. International Federation of Library Associations and Institution's Study Group on the Functional Requirements for Bibliographic Records, *Functional Requirements for Bibliographic Records: Final Report* (München K. G. Saur, 1998). Online version: http://www.ifla.org/en/publications/functional-requirements-for-bibliographic-records (accessed January 23, 2010).

29. Acquisitions and Bibliographic Access Directorate, Library of Congress, "Decision regarding the final disposition of LCSH headings for video recordings," http://www.loc.gov/catdir/cpso/videorecheadings2.pdf (accessed January 23, 2010), [(2)].

30. Accessed via Cataloger's Desktop, http://desktop.loc.gov (January 21, 2010).

31. Scott M. Dutkiewicz, comp., *List of LCSH Moving Image Genre-Form Headings*, http://www.olacinc.org/drupal/capc_files/GenreFormHeadingsList.pdf (accessed January 23, 2010).

32. http://authorities.loc.gov/(accessed January 23, 2010).

33. http://id.loc.gov/(accessed January 23, 2010).

34. "LCSH in this service includes all Library of Congress Subject Headings, free-floating subdivisions (topical and form), Genre/Form headings, Children's (AC) headings, and validation strings for which authority records have been created." http://id.loc.gov/authorities/about.html#lcsh (accessed January 23, 2010).

35. Note that this "local" coding also applies to other types of LC headings sometimes used with the intention of providing form/genre access in local catalogs, e.g., Motion pictures, German; DVDs; Love in motion pictures.

36. http://www.loc.gov/marc/bibliographic/bd008.html (accessed January 23, 2010).

37. http://www.loc.gov/marc/bibliographic/bd043.html (accessed January 23, 2010).

38. Online Audiovisual Catalogers, Cataloging Policy Committee, "Changes to field 257 (Country of Producing Entity) for use with non-archival materials in the MARC 21 Bibliographic Format," http://www.loc.gov/marc/marbi/2009/2009-08.html (accessed January 23, 2010).

39. "Report from the Subcommittee on Genre-Form Implementation," submitted by Patricia Dragon to the ALCTS Cataloging and Classification Section Subject Analysis Committee, ALA Annual Conference, July 2009.

3

Metadata for Subject Access

Andrea Leigh

There is no question that library catalog data is metadata. However, library catalog data tends to take a narrow perspective. As Karen Coyle (2009) observes, "libraries have operated for over 150 years with a very singular view of bibliographic metadata: the catalog record. In a new world of interactive, networked information, the catalog record can no longer stand apart if it is to serve information users. The focus must move from the record to the data itself, and to the many contexts where bibliographic data elements must be designed to interact with the online information universe."[1] In essence, library catalogs present whole records to users on the Web, rather than allowing the individual data elements contained within each record to be exploited for re-use and re-purposing.

The stalwart catalog record that libraries and archives create for each completed moving image work continues to be the *status quo*. Yet, increasingly, in this age of bonus materials and extras, libraries and archives are challenged to manage, sustain, and provide access to the multiple stages that a work goes through in the pre-production and post-production process. This is not a new challenge, as moving image archives in particular have always had to manage both pre-print and print elements. The difference is that in a digital environment, sustaining that material and making it accessible for future generations requires a broader conceptual model that goes beyond traditional library catalog data.

Unlike traditional library catalog data, metadata is more encompassing in that it is made up of a range of types that carry specific functions that facilitate the understanding, usage, and management of a digital object, both by humans *and* computers. A robust metadata strategy will enable the discovery, transport, and re-use of digital objects across disparate repository and media management systems, which suggests that metadata must be actionable and designed for use on a computer that is part of a network. Actionable refers to the data interacting with other data so that it is not static. Sir Ian McKellan in *Acting Shakespeare* on PBS is a representation of the stage play where McKellan performs monologues from Shakespeare and discusses some of his plays, but a viewer must watch passively. A conversational interactive online video with McKellan about William Shakespeare's *Richard III* is actionable as it allows the viewer to engage directly, or, as McKellan beckons as you stare at him on screen: "Come on, don't just sit there, this isn't TV. Choose a question, please."[2]

Besides describing the intellectual content of a resource so users can understand what the entity is, metadata can describe the data syntactically. The two types of descriptions facilitate decisions about how the metadata is managed. Metadata is comprised of structured fields populated by unique information according to rules intended to serve a particular audience. Descriptive metadata identifies a resource and describes its intellectual content and is typified by a set of rules or content standards that are used to populate a hierarchical arrangement or schema augmented by a set of value standards or authorities. Cataloging traditionally carried out in libraries using a combination of MARC 21, *Anglo-American Cataloguing Rules*, and Library of Congress Authorities constitute a form of descriptive metadata.

Technical metadata focuses on how a digital object was created, its format, and format-specific technical characteristics. Preservation metadata stores technical details on the format, structure, and use of the digital content, the history of all actions performed on the resource including changes and decisions, and authenticity information such as custodial history. Rights management metadata details how the resource can be used and by whom. Source metadata documents information about the analog original, while structural metadata defines a hierarchical structure that can be presented to users to allow them to navigate a digital object, such as allowing users to move forward to a particular scene or chapter of a film made available on DVD or Blu-ray. A good repository design concatenates—or links together in a chain—all types of metadata to support both preservation and access.

A critical component of descriptive metadata for the discovery and identification of moving images is the assignment of topics, genres, and forms. When topics, genres, and forms are assigned to a film or television program, an attempt is made to apply specific relevant terms that will facilitate discovery by not only naming the work to distinguish it from other works, but by grouping it among an array of similar entities. A short film in the collections of the Library of Congress showing President Theodore Roosevelt taking the oath of office on March 4, 1905, is provided with a cataloger-supplied descriptive title and assigned the following LCSH headings, as shown in Figure 3.1.

The same footage uploaded on YouTube is assigned a variant of the title and a set of non-standard descriptors or tags. The summary of the film was taken directly from the Library of Congress (LC) catalog entry, as shown in Figure 3.2.

The primary advantage of the descriptive metadata describing the footage in the LC catalog is in the assignment of access points using controlled vocabularies. Topic, genre, and form headings are assigned from *Library of Congress Subject Headings* (LCSH) allowing resources containing the identical subject matter to be brought together in the catalog. So, if a researcher is interested in any resource *about* Theodore Roosevelt, in addition to the film, that researcher is able to gather together any books, photographs, manuscripts, or other material just by entering the topical search term "Roosevelt Theodore." When the initial search is completed, the browse display will

```
Main Title:
[TR's inaugural ceremony, 1905] / [production company unknown].

Summary:
On Mar. 4, 1905, TR is inaugurated in Washington, D.C. with much celebration and
fanfare. TR rides in an open landau on Fifteenth St., NW, escorted by mounted
Rough Riders; Secret Service men and detectives walk on either side of the
carriage; TR tips his hat to the crowd. Sitting beside him is Sen. John C. Spooner
of Wis., Chairman of the joint Congressional Committee on Inaugural Ceremonies.
Opposite, but not clearly visible, are Sen. Henry Cabot Lodge of Mass. and Rep.
John Dalzell of Penn., members of the committee. Second sequence consists of
long shots of TR taking the oath of office on a platform erected on the east front
of the Capitol; Chief Justice Melville Weston Fuller (1888-1910) administers
the Presidential oath of office as Chief Clerk of the Supreme Court James H.
McKenney holds the Bible. The platform is decorated with plants and garlands and
a large banner with the American eagle on it hangs from the center of the railing.
West Point cadets and Annapolis midshipmen are assembled below the platform.

Subjects:
Roosevelt, Theodore, 1858-1919 —Inauguration, 1905. United States. Army.
Cavalry, 1st.
United States Military Academy.
United States Naval Academy.
United States Capitol (Washington, D.C.)
Oaths.
Inauguration Day.
Processions.
Midshipmen.
Pennsylvania Avenue (Washington, D.C.)
Fifteenth Street (Washington, D.C.)

Form/Genre:
Nonfiction films.
Short films.
```

Figure 3.1.   Library of Congress title, summary, and LCSH headings

---

Teddy Roosevelt Oath of Office 1905

On Mar. 4, 1905, TR is inaugurated in Washington, D.C. with much celebration and fanfare. TR rides in an open landau on Fifteenth St., NW, escorted by mounted Rough Riders; Secret Service men and detectives walk on either side of the carriage; TR tips his hat to the crowd. Sitting beside him is Sen. John C. Spooner of Wis., Chairman of the joint Congressional Ceremonies. Opposite, but not clearly visible, are Sen. Henry Cabot Lodge of Mass. and Rep. John Dalzell of Penn., members of the committee. Second sequence consists of long shots of TR taking the oath of office on a platform erected on the east front of the Capitol; Chief Justice Melville Weston Fuller (1888–1910) administers the Presidential oath of office as Chief Clerk of the Supreme Court James H. McKenney holds the Bible. The platform is decorated with plants and garlands and a large banner with the American eagle on it hangs from the center of the railing. West Point cadets and Annapolis midshipmen are assembled below the platform.

Category: People & Blogs

Tags:
Roosevelt Theodore Spooner John Coit Lodge Henry Cabot Cavalry D.C. Washington Inauguration Rough Rider Riders 15th St

Figure 3.2.   YouTube title, summary, and tags

categorize a large result set by subtopic so that a researcher can then choose with more specificity:

Roosevelt, Theodore, 1858–1919
Roosevelt, Theodore, 1858–1919—Anecdotes
Roosevelt, Theodore, 1858–1919—Archives
Roosevelt, Theodore, 1858–1919—Awards
Roosevelt, Theodore, 1858–1919—Birthplace
Roosevelt, Theodore, 1858–1919—Childhood and youth
Roosevelt, Theodore, 1858–1919—Correspondence
Roosevelt, Theodore, 1858–1919—Family
Roosevelt, Theodore, 1858–1919—Fiction
Roosevelt, Theodore, 1858–1919—Homes and haunts
Roosevelt, Theodore, 1858–1919—Inauguration, 1893
Roosevelt, Theodore, 1858–1919—Inauguration, 1901
Roosevelt, Theodore, 1858–1919—Inauguration, 1905
Roosevelt, Theodore, 1858–1919—Journeys—Arizona—Grand Canyon
Roosevelt, Theodore, 1858–1919—Journeys—California—Yosemite Valley
Roosevelt, Theodore, 1858–1919—Journeys—Yellowstone National Park
Roosevelt, Theodore, 1858–1919—Military service
Roosevelt, Theodore, 1858–1919—Political and social views
Roosevelt, Theodore, 1858–1919—Public appearances
Roosevelt, Theodore, 1858–1919—Travel

The heading containing the subdivision—**Inauguration, 1905** represents 20 catalog entries, including the footage of TR's inaugural ceremony. As Thomas Mann (2009) points out, "such 'road map' arrays . . . enable scholars who are entering a new subject area to recognize what they cannot specify in advance. They enable scholars to see 'the shape of the elephant' . . . on their topic *early* in their research."[3] Mann goes on to argue that traditional subject cataloging extends the scope of scholars' inquiries by exposing them to a "full range of what is available than they know how to ask for before they are exposed to it."[4] The display enables the scholar to choose a topic of interest without having to re-do the search over, as all the titles brought together by the pre-coordinated LCSH string **Roosevelt, Theodore, 1858–1919—Inauguration, 1905** contain no irrelevant resources:

1. Inaugural Ball-room—from President Roosevelt's box—Pension Building, Washin[g]ton, D.C. [graphic]
2. Inaugural souvenir 1905
3. [Inauguration of President Theodore Roosevelt, March 4, 1905] [graphic]
4. Inauguration of the President, Washington, D.C. [graphic]
5. Indian chiefs headed by Geronimo, passing in review before President T. Roosevelt, inauguration, March 4, 1905, Washington, D.C., U.S.A. [graphic]
6. President Roosevelt delivering his inaugural address, Washington [graphic]
7. President Roosevelt, 1901–1909
8. President Roosevelt after inauguration leaving the Capitol to head the parade—Washington [graphic]

9. President Roosevelt passing 10th Street and Pennsylvania Avenue inauguration parade on way to the Capitol [graphic]
10. President Roosevelt reviewing troops in the inaugural parade, March 4, 1905 [graphic]
11. President Roosevelt delivering his inaugural address in front of the Capitol, Washington, D.C. [graphic]
12. President Roosevelt taking the oath of office, March 4, 1905 [graphic]
13. President Theodore Roosevelt delivering his inaugural address, Washington, D.C. [graphic]
14. [Theodore Roosevelt and two other men in horse-drawn carriage, men walking along side, during inauguration day] [graphic]
15. [Theodore Roosevelt in carriage on Pennsylvania Avenue on way to Capitol, March 4, 1905] [graphic]
16. [Theodore Roosevelt sitting in an open carriage enroute to the U.S. Capitol on his inauguration day tips his hat to spectators] [graphic]
17. [TR's inaugural ceremony, 1905]/[production company unknown]
18. TR's inauguration, 1905 [1]/[production company unknown]
19. TR's inauguration, 1905 [2]/[production company unknown]
20. TR speaking at Sagamore Hill [1916–1918 and scenes of his early career]

In addition, controlled vocabularies such as LCSH attempt to solve the semantic relations between words and their referents. For example, a fan may relate to a person or a thing, a television may be called a television or TV, or Theodore Roosevelt may be referred to as simply "TR."

If a library or archive has chosen to use either Dublin Core or PBCore as its metadata standard to describe digital moving image objects as part of its repository, topics, genres, and forms will not be entered as strings and subdivided by place as they are when assigning LCSH terms in MARC21. Instead, each subject term will be entered individually and qualified by the controlled vocabulary used. To describe the spatial or temporal topic of the resource, use of the element **coverage** is recommended. In PBCore, the element **genre** is added to distinguish what the intellectual content of the resource is, rather than what it is about. PBCore is an emerging metadata standard developed for public broadcasting and its associated communities intended for describing video, audio, text, images, and interactive learning objects for television, radio, and Web activities.[5] The standard is built on the foundation of Dublin Core that is more commonly used in libraries.[6]

In providing subject access to the video of Theodore Roosevelt's inauguration, the same topics, genres, and forms used in the LC catalog entry can be mapped to Dublin Core or PBCore, as shown in Figure 3.3.

As in the Library of Congress catalog, the subjects can be categorized in browse displays of predictable terms, limiting results to those terms assigned from a controlled vocabulary, rather than dependent on full text keyword searching. When mapping elements from one metadata standard to another, some granularity will be lost, such as in the case of Dublin Core, where there is not an element available for genre. As such, topics will not be distinguished from genre/forms as they are in both MARC21 and PBCore.

MARC21	Dublin Core	PBCore
Topic (600, 610, 611, 650, 650 $x)	<subject>	<subject>
Genre/Form (655, 650 $v)	<subject>	<subject>
Time (650 $y)	<coverage.temporal>	<coverage.temporal>
Place (651, 650 $z)	<coverage.spatial>	<coverage.spatial>

MARC 21 coding of LCSH topics, genres and forms.

```
600 10 $a Roosevelt, Theodore, $d 1858-1919 $x Inauguration, 1905.
610 10 $a United States. $b Army. $b Cavalry, 1st.
610 20 $a United States Military Academy.
610 20 $a United States Naval Academy.
610 20 $a United States Capitol (Washington, D.C.)
650 #0 $a Oaths.
650 #0 $a Inauguration Day.
650 #0 $a Processions.
650 #0 $a Midshipmen.
651 #0 $a Pennsylvania Avenue (Washington, D.C.)
651 #0 $a Fifteenth Street (Washington, D.C.)
655 #0 $a Nonfiction films.
655 #0 $a Short films.
```

Figure 3.3.   Mapping MARC 21 subjects, genres, and forms to Dublin Core and PBCore

Another common result of mapping from MARC21 to another metadata standard is the loss of the concept of names as subjects. There is a tendency to map names as creators or contributors and not as subjects for moving image resources. This is attributed to the fact that a moving image can *depict* as well as can be *about* a person, object, or place. The general guideline that should be applied is to put a name in a subject element when the work is about or depicts the person or corporate body. Put a name into a creator or contributor element when the person or corporate body has contributed to the intellectual and artistic work conveyed by a particular moving image work, including contribution by means of performance. This does mean that there are times when double-indexing of names will occur.

When searching for material about Theodore Roosevelt on YouTube where uncontrolled user-generated tags are assigned for discovery, a different scenario is presented to the user. Instead of receiving a display with a choice of categorized headings, the result is a display sorted by relevance of about 1,440 videos.

TR's 1905 inaugural ceremony footage is among the first five resources displayed in the YouTube search. However, it will take some sleuthing to discover the film's provenance and authenticity without knowing beforehand the context provided by the descriptive metadata in the Library of Congress catalog. Also, by not providing the option of gathering together all the resources available about Roosevelt's 1905 inaugural ceremony, one does not know if other material exists without either browsing all the videos available screen by screen or by conducting a second search adding the keyword "inaugural." Even if that search is successful in bringing together relevant resources, lacking the systematic approach of a controlled vocabulary means that it is left to the user to think up all possible search terms and hope for the best.

The sparse YouTube descriptive metadata does have an advantage over the library catalog metadata in that it can easily be shared in other applications. For instance, it can be shared via Facebook, Twitter, or other social networking sites. By getting the content out to where users live may incite renewed interest in the subject matter and could lead to outside experts or interested novices suggesting richer context. In other words, a non-commercial micro-community can develop that otherwise would not have existed, providing new insight and awareness.

The challenge is in harnessing that outside data, as it is likely to fray the edges of the classical practice of cataloging. As Margaret Mann (1930) informs, "the cataloger must envisage the needs of the reader, endeavoring in every way to make it a simple process for him to find books. He should, like the librarian adopt a neutral stand between the reader and his books, giving emphasis to what the author intended to describe rather than to his own views."[7] This stance is in support of scholarship. If access to a library or archives' collections becomes dependent on user created content or keyword access provided by Google, Amazon, or other Internet search mechanisms, it is argued that the information needs of scholars would be seriously compromised. Users tend to be interested in providing tags that have meaning that reaches beyond authorial intent and Internet search mechanisms function to gain quick and easy access to the most popular resources to generate short-term profit. Both methods appear contrary to the mission of libraries and archives that aim to preserve and provide access to resources for the primary purpose of seeking knowledge. Yet there are scholars who insist that tagging has the potential to render all knowledge into a single, universal framework that was not possible prior to the advent of networked computing environments. The basis of this claim is rooted in a grassroots effort to circumvent taxonomy experts to better reflect the needs and thinking of a particular community. As Adam Mathes (2004) suggests, "transforming the creation of explicit metadata for resources from an isolated, professional activity into a shared, communicative activity by users is an important development that should be explored and considered for future systems development," as systems employing social tagging are "supremely responsive to user needs and vocabularies."[8]

To add to the dilemma, providing adequate topical, genre, and form access to films and television programs for the purpose of advancing scholarship has traditionally been a conundrum. The puzzling aspects are deciding what the film or program is about without being subjective, a general lack of consensus over the scope of moving image genres and forms, and the fact that LCSH, the major controlled vocabulary used by libraries and archives, was designed for books and not specifically designed for moving image materials. Therefore, distinctions are not made consistently about what is depicted as opposed to what the film or program is about. LCSH also leans heavily towards a bias on nonfiction textual material. These shortfalls become especially apparent for resources identified in a digital environment where the moving images are more commonly segregated from other material types. Applying literary terminology as concepts to gain access to visual materials is not always intuitive.

Another major challenge in applying LCSH to digital moving images is that the resources made available are rarely films and programs that are well known stand-alone works cited in reference sources. It is not hard to locate resources within the context of CNN, NBC, PBS, or another large network, but it is difficult to locate works that do not benefit from an association with a major content provider. Library catalogs are oriented to seeking out films and programs by title. Yet newsreel footage, educational films, home movies, and other orphan or ephemeral moving image works are the most likely candidates to be made available digitally by libraries and archives. Users seeking ephemeral moving image works are more often interested in seeking out the subject of the film or program and its genre. *I want a film showing contralto Marian Anderson singing on the steps of the Lincoln Memorial. I am looking for some footage on the opening of Disneyland. Isn't there an educational film available teaching kids how to duck and cover?* It is these ephemeral moving images that are best served by applying concepts as access points.

For instance, if a researcher is seeking out a film showing kids how to "duck and cover," the film is easily made available by entering those keyword search terms in a Google search box. The cold war social guidance film *Duck and Cover* (1951) is the first resource displayed. If the same keyword search is made at the Internet Archive, again the film *Duck and Cover* (1951) is displayed as the first four available resources, not necessarily because these are different versions of the same film, but because each individual record is made available from four moving image collections. They were brought together in the same search by title. If a researcher were to seek out the film in a library catalog by concept, the film would be more difficult to locate since "duck and cover" is not an LCSH heading. The closest subject term would be less intuitive: **Atomic bomb—Safety measures**. Applying genre/form terms is also problematic since the film is now more commonly considered a propaganda film, as the instructions provided would not save a child from nuclear attack. If Mann's directive is followed in that the cataloger's job is to characterize authorial intent, rather than others' interpretations, the genre of the film assigned in a library catalog will likely be "educational films." An end user is not likely to know current library descriptive practices and may not think to look for what is now considered a cold war propaganda film as an educational film.

Highly structured controlled vocabularies such as LCSH are hierarchical and exclusive. In such a system, each concept is in one unambiguous category, such as *figure skating*, which is then inside a more general concept, such as *sports*. In contrast, tagging is non-hierarchical and inclusive. Del.icio.us (http://delicious.com), a bookmarking Web site, emerged as one of the earliest adopters of user-generated tagging. Del.icio.us permits users to organize their own bookmarked sites under any category descriptor they desire, as opposed to imposing a pre-determined vocabulary. The scholarly community took notice, discussing the merits, pitfalls, and implications of tagging. By 2004, the practice of tagging was given a name by Thomas Vander Wal, who combined "folk" and "taxonomy" to a single term, "folksonomy."[9] Folksonomy or collaborative tagging has since emerged as an alternative to traditional hierarchical subject cataloging.[10]

At the Internet Archive, moving images are brought together based on broad genre/form categories such as Animation & Cartoons, Cultural & Academic Films,

Ephemeral Films, Home Movies, News & Public Affairs, Open Source Movies, etc. The most interesting category is Prelinger Archives, a category not based on the type of film, but by provenance. The categorizations or "sub-collections" assigned by the Internet Archive are then given contextual information about what the user can expect to find under each of the categories. For example, it is explained that the Prelinger Archives has made available over 2000 "ephemeral films"—advertising, educational, industrial, and amateur films.

Users have the option to browse the Prelinger Archives by sorting results by relevance, user rating, download count, date or date added, and can group results either by relevance, media type, or collection. The next search option provided is browsing by subject keywords. A listing of the assigned subject keywords is made available so users can get a good idea before searching further what the content may contain. Many of the subject keywords are categorized by broad type first, then more specific, such as the largest broad category, Occupations, which is then subdivided more specifically by occupation type, e.g., Occupations: Housework; Occupations: Insurance; Occupations: Ironworks; Occupations: Janitorial; Occupations: Laundry; Occupations: Librarians, etc. A tag cloud, or visual depiction of user-generated tags, is made available so that users can delineate among the most commonly searched terms based on font type and size.

The Internet Archive provides a context to manage content within a category or by provenance that is conducive to social tagging. Users comment or provide tags to aid in the discovery of an online resource. Tags identify who or what the content is about, what it is (a home movie, amateur film, etc.), use adjectives according to the tagger's opinion of the content, identify content in terms of its relation to the tagger (mycomments, mystuff), and provide terms to organize the content to perform a task, such as whether the content is needed for a book, article, or presentation.[11] In the process, users create tagstreams that can be re-used and re-purposed for other content by other users. Wichowski (2009) compares the evolution of folksonomies to the aggregated concept of the "long tail," referencing "the statistical distribution describing how small, specialized consumer markets, when added together, can rival the economic power of the mainstream."[12] When users aggregate content collaboratively, they are collectively making decisions about the relevance of that content in relation to their needs. Content that was not considered high use may suddenly become so and be utilized in ways that had not been imagined previously.

It is still too early to adequately analyze the value and merit of social tagging as a legitimate indexing system. As Trant (2008) comments, "studies of tagging and social folksonomy need to come together with studies of searching in holistic analyses of information discovery and use . . . that are sensitive to the complex personal information-seeking context" of re-use and re-discovery.[13] According to a report on online video, statistics show that a third of all Internet users 18–29 years of age watch or download a video online every day, suggesting that viewing habits are dramatically shifting away from film exhibition and television.[14] In a culture that increasingly expects that all forms of media are available online and at a moment's notice, established library descriptive practices will continue to be challenged and tested against emerging systems that are modular, less prescriptive, and more fluid in an effort to satisfy end user expectations.

Notes

1. Karen Coyle, "Metadata is a Plural Noun," presentation given at New England Technical Services Librarians (NETSL) annual spring conference, Hogan Campus Center, College of the Holy Cross, Worcester, Mass. (April 17, 2009).

2. *A Conversation with Sir Ian McKellan* at http://www.stagework.org.uk/mckellen/index.htm, retrieved from Stagework—from the National Theatre and its regional partners Web site (accessed February 12, 2010).

3. Thomas Mann, "What is Distinctive about the Library of Congress in Both Its Collections and Its Means of Access to Them, and the Reasons LC Needs to Maintain Classified Shelving of Books Onsite, and a Way to Deal Effectively with the Problem of 'Books on the Floor.' " Paper prepared for AFSCME 2910, The Library of Congress Professional Guild representing over 1,600 professional employees (November 6, 2009): 12.

4. Ibid.

5. PBCore Metadata Dictionary, available online at: http://www.pbcore.org/ (accessed February 12, 2010).

6. Dublin Core Metadata Initiative, available online at: http://www.dublincore.org/ (accessed February 12, 2010).

7. Margaret Mann, *Introduction to Cataloging and Classification of Books* (Chicago: American Library Association, 1930): 3.

8. Adam Mathes, "Folksonomies—Cooperative Classification and Communication Through Shared Metadata" (December 2004), at: http://www.adammathes.com/academic/computer-mediated-communication/folksonomies.html (accessed January 16, 2010).

9. Thomas Vander Wal, "Folksonomy Coinage and Definition," *Vanderwal.net* (2007), at http://www.vanderwal.net/folksonomy.html (accessed December 4, 2009).

10. Elaine Peterson, "Parallel Systems: The Coexistence of Subject Cataloging and Folksonomy," *Library Philosophy and Practice* (April 2008): 1.

11. Scott A. Golder and Bernardo A. Huberman, "Usage Patterns of Collaborative Tagging Systems," *Journal of Information Science*, vol. 32, no. 2 (2006): 203.

12. Alexis Wichowski, "Survival of the Fittest Tag: Folksonomies, Findability, and the Evolution of Information Organization,"*First Monday*, vol. 14, no. 5 (May 4, 2009), at http://www.uic.edu/htbin/cgiwrap/bin/ojs/index.php/fm/article/view/2447/2175 (accessed January 16, 2010).

13. J. Trant, "Studying Social Tagging and Folksonomy: a Review and Framework," *Journal of Digital Information: Special Issue on Digital Libraries and User Generated Content* (2008): 23.

14. Mary Madden, *Online Video* (July 25, 2007), at http://www.pewinternet.org/Reports/2007/Online-Video, retrieved from PEW Internet & American Life Project Web site (accessed January 16, 2010).

4

Developing Film and Video Collections

Sheila S. Intner

A Bit of History

Libraries in schools, colleges, universities, and communities have been collecting moving image materials for a long time, although the pace of such collecting intensified in the years following World War II. In part, this was due to the passage of federal legislation that funded efforts to collect audiovisual media. In part, it was due to the increasing number of topics being described, explained, and portrayed in the media, making a greater proportion of the larger number of titles being released attractive to library collectors. And, in part, it was due to advances in technology that accomplished several things: first, newer camera and film technologies made the creation of moving image products simpler and less costly; second, the newer storage media were easier to distribute; and, third, they could be marketed not only to a small number of theaters, but also to huge numbers of individuals.

In the mid-twentieth century, the typical moving image carrier was a length of film wound on a reel, which was projected onto a screen in a theater, an auditorium, or a classroom, for audiences of up to several hundred people at a time. Libraries collected these motion pictures and showed them to audiences in film series, classrooms, and school auditoriums. Home movies made with small-scale movie cameras were being made and shown in private homes, but the technology was expensive and not widespread.

When the newer technology of television emerged in the years after mid-century, it quickly rivaled its predecessor. Television production used magnetic tape in place of film, but began by emulating film—winding lengths of tape around reels. Before long, however, newer storage systems were devised. Videotape was mounted onto cassettes or cartridges. The new carriers were more durable and protected their contents better than reels. They were more easily mounted and played. They were made of plastic and, thus, were lighter than movie reels in cans. The projectors needed to play them were smaller, less fragile, more easily used and maintained, and less costly than motion picture projectors. But these were only the external virtues of videotape over film. Other, more far-reaching changes in the delivery of moving image products were developing.

Movies were shown in theaters to large audiences. Emulating live stage performances, people *went to the movies*, sometimes traveling distances to see a desired film. In contrast, television shows began by being broadcast, like radio shows, directly into people's homes. If a family bought a television set (and every one that could, did), they could watch hours of moving images, both live and *canned*, in the privacy of their homes. Television brought the product to the audience instead of *vice versa*. Experts who studied such things determined that motion pictures were *hot* media and television shows were *cool* media.

Before long, television programs of all kinds were being packaged and sold to individuals. The buyers already had television sets. If they added another relatively reasonable piece of equipment to it—the videotape recorder—they could record broadcasts and see them whenever they wished or they could buy or rent prerecorded tapes for showing at their convenience. Libraries, which had always catered to what people were reading, began to delve into the world of what they were viewing.

It was only a small step beyond recording new television programs on cassettes (which, overtook cartridges as the carrier of choice) to re-recording older films on videotape and packaging them on cassettes for sale to individuals. A variety of video products began to be marketed to the public, including libraries, that found them an immediate hit with borrowers. Whereas books might circulate for two to four weeks, videos were circulated for two or three days and, sometimes, less—just 24 hours. In academic libraries, use policies varied. Videos might circulate only to instructors, or they might be shown on closed circuit television that had to be reserved in advance, or they might be available to any members of the academic community who wanted to borrow them. In this volatile environment, librarians soon felt a need to formalize the way videos were selected and purchased, and the same guidelines that governed book collecting began to be applied to videos.

In the first edition of *Subject Access To Films And Videos* (SAFV1), this author wrote a chapter titled "From Teenage Turtles to 'Cosmos': Ten Steps in Developing Video Collections." The chapter aimed to provide a framework within which video collecting could be systematized. Its steps were as follows:

1. Feeling the need
2. Profiling the audiences
3. Targeting the library's market
4. Rating the competition
5. Plumbing the marketplace
6. Selecting genres
7. Selecting titles
8. Working with vendors
9. Working with staff
10. Building a quality collection

The chapter concluded with a checklist of video genres, including: Preschooler's stories; Educational subjects for K through 12; How-to's; Health and exercise; Nostalgia; Science; Music and art; Fiction, etc.; Games; Folk tales; Sports; Lectures; Comedy; History; Religion; and Other. A selected bibliography of sources for title listings and reviews completed the chapter.

Much of what was said in that chapter is still valid. Good collection development librarians still do have to know for whom they are buying materials, what their audiences need and want, what is available for purchase (or lease), what is appropriate to acquire given the library's goals, objectives, and priorities, how to plan what to buy, how to deal with key players, and to aim for quality results. Since that time, the video marketplace has broadened in its range of offerings and their technical, educational, intellectual, and artistic variety. At the same time, costs for videos have fallen dramatically, to the point that a mainstream trade video costs approximately the same as many books, although some titles continue to be priced higher than the norm. Library collecting plans, too, have broadened, increasing both in sophistication and precision. The next section covers another collecting framework developed by the author several years after *SAFV1* appeared, based on additional experience as a collection development consultant and coach as well as on continuing observation of this area of the field.

"Ten Steps" in the Twenty-First Century

In 2002, this author presented a slightly different framework for collection development in general,[1] consisting of 10 simple-sounding steps. The steps may sound simple, but their conduct is not. A great deal of time, effort, and learning experience goes into the execution of each step. Without those inputs on the part of the people using it, the framework does not work. Each of the rules is given here, with an up-to-date interpretation focused on video collecting in the 2010s. Readers need to keep in mind that the steps are a process and, like other 10 step systems intended to help adherents change their habits, the process is, perhaps, more important than the actual product.

1. Know Your Public!

The most basic rule of gathering useful collections is to be knowledgeable about the tastes, activities, and interests the people for whom it is being assembled. A newly hired collection development librarian who comes from a distant location or a different institution—for example, from a small liberal arts college to a large research university—may find it difficult to step into the job and do great work at the start. This is no less an issue for video collecting than for other materials.

If the video librarian is initiating an entirely new collection for the library, a great deal can be accomplished even before spending time getting to know the public, but acting slowly may still be a good strategy. Once the librarian feels confident about analyzing the groups that make up the potential audience for the collection, compiling statistics to document the demographics is important to confirm the relative size and activity of different user groups within the whole, along with what can be anticipated about their uses of video materials.

Academic institutions usually track the demographics of incoming classes. Obtaining this data from admission offices can save time. In addition, statistics usually are available on the registration for classes, numbers of students participating in campus activities, numbers of majors in each department, etc. Librarians also need to keep up with information on faculty research projects and departmental plans. The results of compiling available data, adding the anticipated needs for each group of users, and analyzing the resulting array of wanted materials, is a needs analysis that becomes the foundation underlying collecting plans.

The initial compilation of demographics provides a baseline against which changes can be measured periodically, generally once a year or, at most, once every two years. Small changes might not dictate immediate changes in collecting, but the statistics are helpful in discovering trends before they are obvious. Staying ahead of the curve helps keep collecting plans fresh and relevant.

2. Understand It Takes a Village to Build Great Collections

The job of a good collection development librarian is not to sit in his or her office day after day, thinking up plans, but to be an active participant in the community and the world beyond the library. Four kinds of interactions help in developing the collection: interactions with collection users; interactions with members of the library staff; interactions with collection providers; and interactions with peers outside the local library.

Tuning in to and having direct connections with members of the public using the library helps the video collector focus on the potential emphases for the collection. Working with people on community projects, encountering them at social events, or sharing leisure activities brings the video librarian closer to the community the collection is intended to serve. Interacting with other members of the library staff—librarians and other staff who might serve as part-time selectors, have personal interests in film, or who are, themselves, integral members of community groups—can contribute to the video librarian's knowledge and aid in outreach initiatives.

Finding ways to work with and get to know others interested in film and video, such as the wholesalers from whom the library buys its materials, local video store managers, and peers at other libraries, provide opportunities to broaden the video collector's understanding of the industry and its products. Public library boards sometimes think their video collections are competing with local businesses in providing the same free (or nearly free) videos to the same people and are wary of starting or expanding library video collections. They do not see the similarity to the relationship of library books and bookstore offerings. Yet, bookstores and libraries have coexisted for years without seeming to impact one another negatively. Libraries are, sometimes, good customers of commercial video stores, buying materials from them on a regular basis and supplementing the collections offered by commercial video stores.

3. Put Everything in Writing

The old business adage, *get it in writing*, holds true in collection development for a number of reasons. First, it forces lofty statements about what the library wants to accomplish to be translated into down-to-earth, detailed goals and objectives that can prompt specific actions. It is one thing to say the library wants to "develop" its educational video collection and quite another to say that 50 new videos are to be purchased, 10 each in five subject areas such as health and exercise, home maintenance, plant science, weather and meteorology, and cooking.

A second reason for putting collecting plans in writing is that written records ensure continuity when changes in directors, librarians, staff members, vendors, and other partners in the collection development enterprise give rise to conflicting ideas. While it is true that new ideas are welcome, failing to complete one plan before adopting another is counterproductive. Shifting goals in midstream often results in little being accomplished that serves any goals—old or new ones—and ends up wasting the library's money.

A third reason for writing everything down is that, sometimes, when one sees the data together in a coherent document—needs assessment, goals and objectives, budget plans, etc.—the feasibility of a particular plan becomes clear. It is easier to see the relationship of goals and objectives to the needs of the people who use the collection, and the sufficiency of the budget to support the plan. It is also possible to see the discrepancies between the parts of the plan when they are there, because they are spelled out on the pages of the document in black and white rather than existing solely as ideas in the minds of the planners.

While having a written plan is no guarantee of success, not having one leaves too much to chance, to memory, to possible misinterpretation or bias, and to promises about funding. When a plan is committed to paper and approved by funding authorities, it has a much better chance of happening as written.

4. Distinguish Between Policy and Practice, and Mind Them Both

Policy represents the results of decision making, whereas *practice* describes activities that implement the decisions. Allowing policy and practice to become confused can result in loss of direction and focus. The decisions about how to shape video collections define the overall goals the library aims to reach and are the policy part of a *policy and procedure* manual. The activities being undertaken to achieve the goals are the *procedure* part, and may include purchasing, soliciting gifts, or, even, undertaking local video productions. Outcomes are evaluated later, at the close of a designated period of time, by comparing them with the stated goals. Believing that satisfying results can be obtained if librarians work backward from the results to the goals is a mistake often made, allowing whatever purchases are made to determine the shape of the collection. That kind of growth is unsystematic and unfocused. When that is how a library operates, satisfying results happen purely by chance.

When collecting is intended to be exhaustive—everything issued on video about Africa or every video title issued by MGM Home Entertainment—setting goals is not so important. It is easy to see when purchases match the goals. Either everything that could be purchased is purchased or the goal is not met. But, when there are many areas to cover and more possible purchases than a library's budget can support, selecting the right titles to buy is not easy. Selectors have to be guided by a set of goals that defines the most important titles, or its budget will be frittered away on less useful or irrelevant titles. Selectors cannot even rely on buying only the good quality titles. Many more titles are likely to meet technical quality standards and/or get good reviews than local libraries can afford, so selectors must look beyond those general factors to zero in on available titles in the library's high priority subject, genre, and interest areas.

Once decisions are made and recorded about which subjects, genres, and interest areas to initiate, maintain, increase, or decrease, it is easier to select titles to buy. Unless video industry releases in those areas fail to consume the budget for the time period, once it spends the whole video materials budget, the local library must find new funding before buying more.

Following a set of subject, genre, and interest area goals for purchasing—a collecting plan—helps librarians avoid giving too large a share of the budget to a few departments or user groups and too little to others. The plan can also suggest minimum quality standards and maximum cost limits so that one user group does not end up with one hugely expensive title while another user group is saturated with numerous cheap, low quality titles. Having a collecting plan can also ensure that selectors do not have to spend time and energy getting their choices approved, one by one, by administrators, if it allows titles that fit within the plan's *buy* areas to be purchased immediately as long as uncommitted funds remain. Approvals might continue to be needed for titles falling outside the *buy* areas, or that fail to meet quality standards, or whose prices exceed cost limits, but in the long run, those categories should comprise a small slice of the pie.

5. Count Everything and Use the Data Well

Data that has been collected carefully and analyzed properly is the foundation for deciding who is to be served and what materials are best suited to the task. Collecting information about library users helps to determine who they are. Who is using the collection? Who can be expected to use it? If only a small segment of the potential market for videos uses the existing collection, it raises more questions. Why is the segment so small? Why is the rest of the viewing public not interested? What would attract them? If the collection is geared to subjects within an academic institution, the issue may be that the curriculum has changed and existing materials reflect a former curriculum no longer being taught. If the collection is geared to public library users, the reasons may be more varied and warrant study. Do current users of the collection exhibit different demographics than those who used it in former years? Are there just as many people using the collection but fewer heavy users? Are the total numbers of users falling? Is it possible to attract new groups of users to the collection? What kinds of materials might accomplish this? Careful monitoring of borrower/user demographics combined with comparisons with community trends can help to answer the questions.

Analyzing the use of materials is equally important. What materials are and are not being used? If the materials now languishing on the shelves were once popular, what explains the change? Are the topics or genres out-of-date? Is the technical quality unappealing or has it been superseded? Are video producers taking a different approach to content? Are events and trends in the larger worlds of art, literature, music, science, history, or business helping to generate new and different expressions on our video screens? How can the collector take advantage of this knowledge to create a collecting plan with appeal to a larger share of the audience? Input from library users obtained through objective interactions such as interviews, focus groups, and surveys limited to a few salient points can suggest answers to these questions. Reference librarians may be able to augment the controlled data with observations from their work with library users, but this kind of data is anecdotal and is not a substitute for carefully controlled data. Putting together what can be learned from circulation statistics, collection condition statistics, market analysis, etc., and asking how the results match with interview data and other available user input helps to clarify the way that the collection should go to remain fresh, relevant, and desirable to its users.

6. Make Money Work for You

Money may not be everything, but having enough of it goes a long way toward ensuring video collections that can change with the changing dynamics of curriculum and teaching methods, community trends, and industry developments. Video has proved to be a popular medium for libraries and good collections need constant development. Newly established collections need to be large enough that potential users are not frustrated by being unable to obtain what they want and, over time, that the flow of new titles and genres into established collections meets the needs of the public. Although the cost of videos has dropped considerably and they can no longer be faulted for being expensive and fragile, it is a rare library that buys enough titles and enough copies of titles to accommodate everyone. Striking a good balance between classics and new titles, among genres of interest to the public, and among materials geared to particular age groups and/or subject areas is a collector's challenge—one made considerably easier when materials budgets are adequate, or, perhaps, even generous.

The change from one technology to another is costly, both in terms of having to buy new hardware and software, and in terms of educating staff members so they can work comfortably with the new materials. When the shift from VHS to DVD occurred, catalogers had to learn to deal with the new format, processing had to change, and storage units had to accommodate a very different type of material. While collectors are concerned mainly with the materials themselves, it is wise to think beyond what titles should be purchased to make certain everyone concerned is ready to incorporate them into the library.

Obtaining an adequate materials budget is not the end of the budget process. The next step is demonstrating the value of what that budget has funded to the library administration. Some video librarians believe that an active collection speaks for itself, but that view is mistaken. Hard data on how well the materials budget has been spent and what specific benefits the dollars have brought to the public goes a long way toward ensuring that the next budget is equal to or better than the current budget. When funds are limited, which has been true for libraries in good times and bad, do video librarians demonstrate clearly that video is a core offering for a large segment of users? If they do not make sure that video is not considered merely an add-on to books and databases, video librarians may find themselves with flat or declining budgets despite years of success.

7. Learn Your (Video) Databases—They Belong to the Collection

A great deal of information is available on the Internet, from filmographies, videographies, and reviews to film- and video-related Web sites covering all sorts of topics: film stars, production, directors, music, history, technology, and more. Discovering those that are helpful to collectors and monitoring them on an ongoing basis should be part of a video librarian's day-to-day tasks. Certainly, some useful databases may grow stale or disappear altogether, but others will be kept current and new ones will appear. Maintaining good film and video reference sources and making them available for users as well as librarians is a beneficial addition to the materials in the collection.

Databases of local materials, historical materials, classes, conferences, and other film- and video-related content (and general content captured on film and video) are useful for research as well as for documenting library activities. Just as books are digitized, videos are incorporated into digital libraries for future use. Librarians think of building databases of digitized books. Why not build databases of digitized films? Care needs to be taken that copyrighted material is not digitized without permission, but libraries and other institutions with which libraries are affiliated often create content that can be captured as part of the historical record or as part of a learning module, an aesthetic program, and the like.

8. Love the Internet—It's Yours, Too

The Internet has created new issues for library and commercial video stores, just as e-books have created them for libraries, bookstores, and publishers. The more that people use their computer screens to view all sorts of informational, educational, and esthetic offerings, including videos, the less they may want to utilize library video collection on analog media—discs or cassettes. While libraries accept that they are merely a conduit between end users and the materials in their collections, it might be a tad harder to get them to admit they are practically invisible when the Internet is involved. But just as libraries buy access to e-books and allow people to borrow them, they can buy access to e-videos as well, perhaps becoming a desirable provider if search services go hand-in-hand with that access.

No one whose computer is linked to the Internet is going to put up with traditional-style library circulation services that gave users video loans for 24 or 48 hours, charged high fines for late returns (sometimes penalizing people by the minute!), and were almost begrudging about lending videos at all, as if they were doing people a huge favor. Now, with the advent of computer video services, librarians will be challenged to add value to the transaction or people will not need the library at all. One feature in making library books and other analog materials attractive is the fact that users do not have to go out to buy them and do not have to store them somewhere after they have been used. In return for having to wait, sometimes, to get the book, record, or DVD they want, users do not have to pay for the materials or, if charges are levied, they are minimal and can be excused as being an unselfish contribution that benefits the whole community of users. Digital materials, on the other hand, may be so easily obtained on the Internet—sometimes free or, at most, for minimal charges—that an intermediary like the library is unnecessary. In this scenario, if the library does not do something more for the user, why should he or she bother with it? Libraries must either provide different materials or better ancillary services. Creativity is called for in dealing with e-videos and the Internet, but deal with them we must.

9. Own Up to Gaps and Mistakes—Then, Move On

This author has observed over the years that many librarians are so self-effacing that they rarely take credit for all the good things they accomplish, but they also suffer from an inordinate unwillingness to accept any blame when things go wrong. Class upon class of library school students taking my collection development class submitted evaluations of local library collections they studied during the semester, saying that the collecting gaps they discovered were really not as bad as the evidence showed, although they had painstakingly gathered and carefully analyzed the data. They said that the gaps could be excused because library users were accustomed to them, or because librarians did not want to compete with video rental stores, or that the budget was tight, and so on. The excuses were legion and it was a rare student who had the gumption to conclude that the library's collection was weak, old, full of holes, or otherwise not *good*. (In my collection development classes, we never used the term *bad*.) The bottom line was and still is that conclusions like that are bunk, and unworthy of their authors. Excusing weaknesses in collections perpetuates them by making it appear that action is not needed to address them.

Collection problems result from human errors of one kind or another, such as failing to allocate funds where they are needed, failing to recognize needs of particular groups or genres, or failing to buy the right materials. Human beings make mistakes. How individuals handle them separates those whose mistakes limit their progress and those who learn from them and use them as a springboard to improvement. Like 12-step programs that require participants to admit their problems before they can go on, collection development librarians must accept and admit that they made mistakes before moving beyond them. Sometimes, mistakes can be rectified. When that's possible, it should be done speedily. Sometimes, mistakes cannot be erased, but they can teach lessons that good collection development librarians heed and never repeat.

Generally, mistakes occur in two areas: evaluating an existing collection badly and doing poor planning for a future collecting cycle. Evaluating video collections should be done as objectively as possible, with data that either confirms or denies the achievement of pre-set, pre-recorded collecting goals. Fudging the data or stretching the interpretation of the data to make the outcome look brighter only perpetuates the problems. Taking a common sense approach to recognizing and addressing collection problems in order to provide library users with a better, more relevant and appealing collection is a much better strategy.

10. Never Be Satisfied

When things are going well, it is natural to sit back and enjoy the success. Doing that, however, is dangerous. If a collection is really awful, almost anything one does to it is likely to make it better, but, probably, not so much better that more work no longer needs to be done. Initial successes should not put a damper on the need to continue improving the collection. By the same token, when a collection is really good, there are many things that can spoil it, or skew it, or otherwise interfere with its ability to satisfy its audience. The video industry is far from static, prompting the need for library collecting plans to be dynamic as well.

Good collections depend on continuous assessment of the video audience as well as continuous monitoring of the video marketplace. As new genres emerge and new types of offerings are made available, collecting plans should include them and, possibly, rethink purchases in some of the tried and true genres or types of offerings. Libraries usually are quick to recognize when new materials are desirable, but less flexible about giving up the older ones. And, they are rarely happy to weed as an ongoing activity to keep collections fresh. Both activities—buying new materials to keep up with new trends and weeding out the materials that have outlived their usefulness—are ongoing and never end, and both contribute to the relevance and effectiveness of the collections.

Conclusion

One benefit of step 10 is that video collecting never runs out of interesting challenges that keep librarians on their toes. Something new is always on the horizon and successful collecting requires constant vigilance to bring it to the local collection when library users are ready for it. A very important point to remember is that the collection should not get too far ahead of its audience, or its usefulness will suffer just as much as if it lagged too far behind them. Timing is not only a critical feature of good comedy, great drama, and heartfelt tragedy, but of good library collecting.

Selected Sources for Film and Video Collectors

The compiler viewed the seven sources listed below on March 22–23, 2010. The list provides examples of the kinds of review and news sources focusing on films and videos available via the Internet, especially educational offerings as well as reviews of popular, mainstream materials. For example, one listing—for exercise films/videos—is an example of genre-specific databases, but others are available for video games, TV series, interest area networks (FoodTV, ESPN, etc.), specific programs, etc., as well as for public television, major studios, and many more subject-oriented materials. Specialized sources advertising themselves as *family friendly*, which is often used to identify political orientation, or religiously affiliated, are not included here, but, if desired, are available using simple search requests via Google Search.

Educational Media Reviews Online (EMRO). Available at http://libweb.lib.buffalo.edu/emro.

A growing database of nearly 4,000 reviews at this writing of educational materials on film and video likely to be of use to academic librarians. The database is searchable by keywords, reviewers, and subjects. Signed reviews are lengthy, averaging 500 words or more. Reviewers describe and evaluate titles' scope and coverage, technical quality, and usefulness for specific educational purposes and settings and with particular audiences.

Film Studies: UC Berkeley Library. Film Reviews and Film Criticism Resources. Available at http://www.lib.berkeley.edu/MRC/filmstudies/reviewslist.html.

Lists online indexes to film literature, general interest periodicals, newspapers, and humanities/ arts/social science journals, including the International Index to Film/TV Periodicals *of the FIAF. Many of the listings can be accessed through the Web site solely by UCB users, but are available to others if they access them directly. Movie review databases include* Cinefiles *(Pacific Film Archives),* Critics.com, FilmCritic.com, Metacritic, Movie Review Query Engine, Mr. Cranky, New York Times Movie Reviews, SAWNET *(South Asian Women's Network),* Video Librarian *(only accessible to UCB users),* QuickCheck, Variety, *and* Women's Studies Database Film Reviews.

The Internet Movie Database (IMDb). Available at http://www.imdb.com.

An Amazon.com company, the IMDb provides news, reviews, and other information about movies, TV, and videos in the mainstream marketplace. It is a good place to find information about current and forthcoming films, series, and individual TV programs.

Exercise Video Reviews. Available at http://www.exercisevideosreviews.com.

Reviews and previews of numerous exercise videotapes and DVDs for people seeking home workout materials. Includes an exercise video "store" as well as searchable sections that deal with Pilates, Cardio, strength training, Yoga, and more.

Rogerebert.com. Available at http://rogerebert.suntimes.com.

The database of reviews from the Chicago Sun-Times *written by the famous U.S. film critic Roger Ebert. Covers most mainstream feature films from U.S. studios, indies, and selected documentaries as well as films from around the world. Ebert gives his well-known "thumbs up" or "thumbs down" evaluations along with the reviews.*

Video Librarian. Available at http://www.videolibrarian.com.

Aimed specifically at librarians in all types of libraries, Video Librarian *is a review journal. Each issue includes about 225 critical reviews as well as alerts to forthcoming titles and purchasing advice.*

The Washington Post. (Media reviews) Available at http://projects.washingtonpost.com.

Like the New York Times, *the* Boston Globe, *the* Manchester Guardian, *and other major newspapers, this database is a subset of media reviews from the* Washington Post. *It is listed here primarily as an example of major newspaper review sources, but local and regional newspapers should be of greater interest to collection development librarians, because they reflect the attitudes and interests of the libraries local area and its residents.*

Note

1. Sheila S. Intner, "Ten Steps to Great Collections," *Technicalities* 22, no. 4 (July/ August 2002): 1, 5–7, 24.

Film and Video Subject Heading List

Bobby Ferguson, Compiler

007 (Fictitious character)
   USE Bond, James (Fictitious character)
1-sheet posters
   USE One-sheet posters
1080 Degree Snowboarding (Game)
    [GV1469.35.A16]
    UF 1080° Snowboarding (Game)
        One Thousand Eighty Degree Snowboarding
          (Game)
        Ten Eighty Snowboarding (Game)
    BT Video games
16SR (Motion picture camera)
   USE Arriflex 16SR motion picture
        camera
24-sheet posters
   USE Twenty-four-sheet posters
3-D films *[LCSH Genre]*
3D game-based animated films
   USE Machinima films
3D game-based films
   USE Machinima films
3-sheet posters
   USE Three-sheet posters
3 Stooges (Comedy Team)
   USE Three Stooges (Comedy Team)
35 mm cameras
   USE 35 mm cameras
35mm cameras *(May Subd Geog)*
    [TR262]

   UF 35 mm cameras
       Thirty-five millimeter cameras
   BT Cameras
   RT Miniature cameras
   NT Autofocus cameras
   SA *individual makes of cameras, e.g.,* Ciroflex
       camera; Nikon camera
6-sheet posters
   USE Six-sheet posters
A-train (Game)
    [GV1469.35.A18]
   BT Video games
Ability[†]
—Testing[†]
      BT Motion pictures in ability
          testing
Abjection in motion pictures
  (Not Subd Geog)
   BT Motion pictures
Aboriginal Australians and mass media
  (May Subd Geog)
    UF Mass media and Aboriginal Australians
    BT Mass media

[†]**Subject headings noted with a dagger contain additional access points and subheadings that are not pertinent to this text and are not included here.**

Aboriginal Australians in mass media
(Not Subd Geog)
[P94.5.A85]
UF Australian aborigines in mass media
BT Mass media
Aboriginal Australians in motion pictures
(Not Subd Geog)
[PN1995.9.A835]
UF Australian aborigines in motion pictures
BT Motion pictures
Aboriginal Australians in television broadcasting
(May Subd Geog)
UF Aboriginal Australians in the television
    industry
    Australian aborigines in television
    broadcasting
BT Television broadcasting—Australia
Aboriginal Australians in the television industry
USE Aboriginal Australians in television
    broadcasting
Abortion in motion pictures
(Not Subd Geog)
BT Motion pictures
Abstract animation films
USE Abstract films
Abstract cinematography
USE Cinematography, Abstract
Abstract films *(May Subd Geog)*
UF Abstract animation films
    Abstract live action films
    Concrete films
    Nonobjective films
    Nonrepresentational films
    Experimental films
RT Animated films
Abstract films *[LCSH Genre]* Abstract
live-action films
USE Abstract films
Academy Awards (Motion pictures)
UF Oscars (Motion pictures)
BT Motion pictures—Awards—United States
Access to cable television
USE Cable television—Access
Accountants in motion pictures
(Not Subd Geog)
BT Motion pictures
Accounting in motion pictures
(Not Subd Geog)
BT Motion pictures
Ace Combat (Game)
[GV1469.A33]
UF AceCombat (Game)
BT Video games

AceCombat (Game)
USE Ace Combat (Game)
Acetate film
USE Safety film
Acquisition of audio-visual materials
(May Subd Geog)
BT Audio-visual materials
Acquisition of non-book materials
USE Acquisition of nonbook materials
Acquisition of nonbook materials
(May Subd Geog)
UF Acquisition of non-book
    materials
BT Nonbook materials
Acquisition of video recordings
(May Subd Geog)
BT Video recordings
Acquisitions (Film archives)
USE Film archives—Acquisitions
Acquisitions (Libraries)†
NT Instructional materials centers— Acquisitions
SA *headings beginning with the word* Acquisition
Acting
UF Histrionics
    Stage
BT Elocution
RT Actors
    Actresses
    Amateur theater
    Drama
    Expression
    Theater
    Acting in a foreign language
    Elocution
NT Acting in a foreign language
    Elocution
    Gesture
    Improvisation
    Improvisation (Acting)
    Motion picture acting
    Movement (Acting)
    Multiple roles (Acting)
    Television acting
—**Auditions** *(May Subd Geog)*
    UF Acting auditions
    BT Auditions
    NT Screen tests
—**Breathing exercises**
    BT Breathing exercises

†**Subject headings noted with a dagger contain
additional access points and subheadings that
are not pertinent to this text and are not
included here.**

—Makeup
    USE   Theatrical makeup
—Study and teaching
    UF   Dramatic education
—Therapeutic use
    USE   Drama—Therapeutic use
—Vocational guidance
    (May Subd Geog)
    UF   Acting as a profession
Acting as a profession
    USE   Acting—Vocational guidance
Acting auditions
    USE   Acting—Auditions
Acting for television
    USE   Television acting
Acting for video
    USE   Television acting
Acting in a foreign language
    (May Subd Geog)
    BT   Acting
Action-adventure films
    USE   Action and adventure films
Action and adventure films *(May Subd Geog)*
    UF   Action-adventure films
        Action cinema
        Action films
        Action movies
        Adventure and action films
        Adventure films
        Adventure movies
    BT   Motion pictures
    NT   Flash Gordon films
        Indiana Jones films
        James Bond films
        Jungle films
        Martial arts films
    RT   Swashbuckler films
Action and adventure films
    [LCSH Genre]
Action and adventure television programs
    (May Subd Geog)
    [PN1992.8.A317]
    UF   Action television programs
        Adventure television programs
    BT   Television programs
Action and adventure television programs
    [LCSH Genre]
Action cinema
    USE   Action and adventure films
Action films
    USE   Action and adventure films
Action films, Black
    USE   Blaxploitation films

Action movies
    USE   Action and adventure films
Action television programs
    USE   Action and adventure television programs
Actors *(May Subd Geog)*
    [PN2205–PN2217]
    Here are entered general works on both men and women actors collectively, works on both men and women stage actors collectively and works on individual men and women stage actors. Works on men actors collectively are entered under Male actors. Works on women actors collectively are entered under Actresses. Works on actors, collectively or individually, specializing in particular media are entered under the appropriate specific heading, e.g., Television actors and actresses, with an additional heading for Male actors or Actresses, if necessary.
    BT   Artists
        Entertainers
        Female impersonators
        Motion picture actors and actresses
        Theaters—Employees
    RT   Acting
        Theater
    NT   Actors with disabilities
        Actresses
        Blacklisting of entertainers
        Character actors and actresses
        Child actors
        Extras (Actors)
        Gay actors
        Jewish actors
        Male actors
        Mimes
        Sailors as actors
        Screenwriters as actors
        Shakespearean actors and actresses
        Soldiers as actors
        Stunt performers
        Teenage actors
        Voice actors and actresses
        Young actors
—Collective labor agreements
    USE   Collective labor agreements—Actors
—Credits
    UF   Credits for actors
—Labor unions *(May Subd Geog)*

†**Subject headings noted with a dagger contain additional access points and subheadings that are not pertinent to this text and are not included here.**

—Professional ethics *(May Subd Geog)*
    [PN 2056]
      UF Actors, Professional ethics for
—Social status
      USE Theater and society
—United States
      NT African American actors
          Asian American actors
          Hispanic American actors
          Mexican American actors
Actors, African-American
    USE African-American actors
Actors, Arab *(May Subd Geog)*
    UF Arab actors
Actors, Asian American
    USE Asian American actors
Actors, Black *(May Subd Geog)*
    UF Black actors
    BT Black theater
Actors, Hispanic American
    USE Hispanic American actors
Actors, Jewish
    USE Jewish actors
Actors, Men
    USE Male actors
Actors, Mexican American
    USE Mexican American actors
Actors, Professional ethics for
    USE Actors—Professional ethics
Actors as artists *(May Subd Geog)*
    BT Artists
Actors as sailors *(May Subd Geog)*
    BT Sailors
Actors as soldiers *(May Subd Geog)*
    BT Soldiers
Actors in art
Actors in literature
    SA *subdivision* Characters—
        Actors *under names of*
        individual literature authors,
        e.g., Shakespeare, William, 1564–1616—
        Characters—Actors
Actors in the advertising industry
    BT Advertising
Actors' spouses *(May Subd Geog)*
    UF Actresses' husbands
        Male actors' wives
    BT Spouses
Actors with disabilities *(May Subd Geog)*
    UF Physically handicapped actors
    NT Blind actors
    BT Actors
        People with disabilities

Actresses *(May Subd Geog)*
    [PN2205–PN2217]
    Here are entered works on women actors collectively. Works on men actors collectively are entered under Male actors. General works on both men and women actors collectively, works on both men and women state actors collectively and works on individual men and women state actors are entered under Actors. Works on actors, collectively or individually, specializing in particular media are entered under the appropriate specific heading, e.g., Television actors and actresses, with an additional heading for Male actors or Actresses, if necessary.
    UF Female actors
    BT Actors
        Women actors
        Women in the theater
    RT Acting
        Male impersonators
    NT Character actors and actresses
        Leading ladies (Actresses)
        Lesbian actresses
        Motion picture actors and actresses
        Shakespearean actors and actresses
        Television actors and actresses
        Voice actors and actresses
        Women stunt performers
—United States
      NT African American actresses Asian
          American actresses
Actresses, Afro-American
    USE African American actresses
Actresses, Asian American
    USE Asian American actresses
Actresses, Black
    UF Black actresses
Actresses' husbands
    USE Actor's spouses
Actresses in art
Actresses in literature
Actualités (Motion pictures)
    USE Actualities (Motion pictures
Actualities (Motion pictures)
(May Subd Geog)
    This heading is used as a topical heading for works about short, unedited, silent films, primarily from the period of early cinema, that portray daily life or specific events or occurrences as filmed by a camera in a fixed location without commentary.

[†]**Subject headings noted with a dagger contain additional access points and subheadings that are not pertinent to this text and are not included here.**

When used as a topical heading it is subdivided by the appropriate geographical, topical, and/or form subdivisions.

    UF Actualités (Motion pictures)
         Actuality films
    BT Nonfiction films
         Short films
         Silent films
    RT Documentary films
         Newsreels

Actualities (Motion pictures)
    [LCSH Genre]
Actuality films
    USE Actualities (Motion pictures)
Ada Theatre (Boise, Idaho)
    USE Egyptian Theatre (Boise, Idaho)
Adaptations, Film
    USE Film adaptations
Adaptations, Television
    USE Television adaptations
Addiction to television
    USE Television addiction
Addiction to video games
    USE Video game addiction
Addictive use of television
    USE Television addiction
Addictive use of video games
    USE Video game addiction

Adolf-Grimme-Preis
    UF Adolf Grimme prize
         Grimme-Preis
    BT Television in adult education—Awards
Adolf Grimme prize
    USE Adolf-Grimme-Preis

Adult education[†]
    NT Television in adult education
  —Audio-visual aids
Adult films (Erotic films)
    USE Erotic films
Adult films (Pornographic films)
    USE Pornographic films

Adult movie theaters *(May Subd Geog)*
    UF X-rated movie theaters
    BT Motion picture theaters
         Sex-oriented businesses
    NT All-male adult movie theaters
Adventure and action films
    USE Action and adventure films

Adventure and adventurers[†]
    NT Daredevils
  —Computer games
       USE Computer adventure games
Adventure films

    USE Action and adventure films

Adventure games *(May Subd Geog)*
    UF Games, Adventure
    BT Games
    NT Computer adventure games
Adventure games, Computer
    USE Computer adventure games
Adventure movies
    USE Action and adventure films
Adventure of Link (Game)
    UF Legend of Zelda (Game)

Advertising[†]
    Also subdivided by topic, as authorized
    below, with further geographic subdivision,
    e.g., Advertising—Agriculture
    (May Subd Geog).
    NT Actors in advertising industry
         Broadcast advertising
         Motion pictures in advertising
         Product placement in mass media
         Promotional films
         Television advertising
         Video tape advertising
  —Audio-visual equipment
      UF Audio-visual equipment
  —Audio-visual materials
      UF Audio-visual materials—Advertising
  —Motion pictures *(May Subd Geog)*
      UF Motion pictures—Advertising
      NT Film trailers
         Half-sheet posters
         Insert posters
         Lobby cards
         One-sheet posters
         Pressbooks
         Six-sheet posters
         Three-sheet posters
         Twenty-four-sheet posters
  —Television programs *(May Subd Geog)*
      UF Television programs—Advertising
  — —Law and legislation
      (May Subd Geog)
        BT Advertising laws
Advertising, Cable television
    USE Cable television advertising
Advertising, Motion pictures in
    USE Motion pictures in advertising

[†]**Subject headings noted with a dagger contain additional access points and subheadings that are not pertinent to this text and are not included here.**

Advertising, Television
  USE Television advertising
Advertising, Video tape
  USE Video tape advertising
Advertising films
  USE Promotional films
Advertising films, Television
  USE Television commercial films
Advertising in motion pictures
  (Not Subd Geog)
    Here are entered works on the use of advertising in motion pictures. Works about films that promote or advertise a product, industry, service, organization, etc., are entered under Promotional films, subdivided by appropriate geographic, topical, and/or form subdivisions.
    BT Motion pictures
Advertising in video tapes
  USE Video tape advertising
Advertising laws[†]
    NT Product placement in mass media—Law and legislation
Television advertising—Law and legislation
Advertising media, Choice of
  USE Advertising media planning
Advertising media planning *(May Subd Geog)*
    UF Advertising media, Choice of
        Advertising media selection Media planning in advertising
Advertising media selection
  USE Advertising media planning
Aerial cinematography *(May Subd Geog)*
    UF Airborne cinematography
    BT Aerial photography
        Cinematography
    SA *subdivision* Aerial film and video footage *under names of countries, cities, etc.*
Aerial photography[†]
    Here are entered works on creating aerial photographs. Works on interpreting aerial photographs are entered under Photographic interpretation. Works on handling, maintaining, and indexing aerial photographs in unbound collections are entered under Aerial photographs.
    UF Aerophotography
        Air photography
        Airborne photography
        Balloon photography
        Photography, Aerial
    NT Aerial cinematography
    BT Photography
        Remote sensing
Aerial video recording

  USE Aerial videography
Aerial videorecording
  USE Aerial videography
Aerial videography *(May Sub)*
    UF Aerial video recording
        Aerial videorecording
        Airborne video recording
        Airborne videography
    BT Video recording
Aeronautics[†]
    NT Motion pictures in aeronautics
Aeronautics in motion pictures
  USE Flight in motion pictures
Aerophotography
  USE Aerial photography
Aesthetics[†]
    NT Mass media—Aesthetics
        Motion pictures—Aesthetics
        Television—Aesthetics
AF cameras
  USE Autofocus cameras
African American actors
  (May Subd Geog)
    [PN2286]
    UF Actors, African American
    BT Actors—United States
        African American entertainers
    NT African American gay actors
African American actresses
  (May Subd Geog)
    UF Actresses, African American
    BT Actresses—United States
African American entertainers
  (May Subd Geog)
    UF Entertainers, African American
    BT African Americans in the performing arts
        Entertainers—United States
African American film critics
  (May Subd Geog)
    UF Film critics, African American
    BT Film critics—United States
African American gay actors
  (May Subd Geog)
    UF Gay actors, African American
    BT Gay actors—United States
African American mass media
  (May Subd Geog)
    [P94.5.A37]

[†]**Subject headings noted with a dagger contain additional access points and subheadings that are not pertinent to this text and are not included here.**

UF Mass media, African American
BT Ethnic mass media—United States
       Mass media—United States

African American men in motion pictures
(Not Subd Geog)
BT Motion pictures

African American motion picture actors and actresses
(May Subd Geog)
UF Motion picture actors and actresses, African American
BT Motion picture actors and actresses—United States

African American motion picture producers and directors
(May Subd Geog)
UF Motion picture producers and directors, African American
BT Motion picture producers and directors—United States

African American screenwriters
(May Subd Geog)
UF Screenwriters, African American
BT Screenwriters—United States

African American television journalists
(May Subd Geog)
NT Television journalists, African American
BT African Americans in television broadcasting
       Television journalists—United States

African American television personalities
(May Subd Geog)
UF Television personalities, African American
BT Television personalities—United States

African American television producers and directors *(May Subd Geog)*
UF Television producers and directors, African American
BT African Americans in television broadcasting
       Television producers and directors—United States

African American women entertainers
(May Subd Geog)
NT Women entertainers, African American
BT Women entertainers—United States

African American women heroes in motion pictures *(Not Subd Geog)*
BT Motion pictures

African American women in motion pictures
(Not Subd Geog)
BT Motion pictures

African American women motion picture producers and directors *(May Subd Geog)*

UF Women motion picture producers and directors, African American
BT Women motion picture producers and directors—United States

African American women on television
(Not Subd Geog)
BT Television

African American women screenwriters
(May Subd Geog)
UF Women screenwriters, African American
BT Women screenwriters—United States

African American yuppies in motion pictures
(Not Subd Geog)
BT Motion pictures

African Americans and mass media
(May Subd Geog)
[P94.5.A37–P94.5.A372]
   Here are entered works on all aspects of the involvement of African Americans in the mass media. Works on the portrayal of African Americans in the mass media are entered under African Americans in mass media. Works on the employment of African Americans in the mass media are entered under African Americans in the mass media industry.
UT Mass media and African Americans
BT Mass media

African Americans in mass media
(Not Subd Geog)
[P94.5.A37–P94.5.A372]
   Here are entered works on the portrayal of African Americans in the mass media. Works on the employment of African Americans in the mass media are entered under African Americans in the mass media industry. Works on all aspects of the involvement of African Americans in the mass media are entered under African Americans and mass media.
BT Mass media

African Americans in motion pictures
(Not Subd Geog)
   Here are entered works on the portrayal of African Americans in motion pictures. Works on all aspects of African American involvement in motion pictures are entered under African Americans in the motion picture industry. Works on specific aspects of African American involvement are entered under

---

†Subject headings noted with a dagger contain additional access points and subheadings that are not pertinent to this text and are not included here.

the particular subject, e.g., African American motion picture actors and actresses.
> BT Motion pictures
> RT Race films

African Americans in television broadcasting
> *(May Subd Geog)*
> *[PN1992.8.A34]*
> Here are entered works on the employment of African Americans in television. Works on the portrayal of African Americans on television are entered under African Americans on television.
> UF Television broadcasting—United States
> BT Television industry—United States
> NT African American television journalists
>   African American television producers and directors

African Americans in the mass media industry
> *(May Subd Geog)*
> BT Mass media

African Americans in the motion picture industry
> *(May Subd Geog)*
> *[PN1995.9.N4]*
> Here are entered works on all aspects of African American involvement in motion pictures. Works on the portrayal of African Americans in motion pictures are entered under African Americans in motion pictures. Works on specific aspects of African American involvement are entered under the particular subject, e.g., African American motion picture actors and actresses.
> BT Motion picture industry—United States
> RT Race films

African Americans in the performing arts[†]
> NT African American actors
>   African American entertainers

African Americans on television
> *(Not Subd Geog)*
> *[PN1992.8.A34]*
> Here are entered works on the portrayal of African Americans on television. Works on the employment of African Americans in television are entered under African Americans in television broadcasting.
> BT Television

African film posters
> USE Film posters, African

African motion pictures
> USE Motion pictures, African

Afro-American . . .
> USE *subject headings beginning with the words* African American . . .

Afro-Americans in . . .
> USE *subject headings beginning with the words* African Americans in . . .

Afro mass media
> USE Black mass media

Aged in mass media
> USE Older people in mass media

Aged in television
> USE Older people on television

Aged on television
> USE Older people on television

Agfa camera *(Not Subd Geog)*
> BT Cameras

Aggressiveness on television
> *(Not Subd Geog)*
> UF Aggressiveness (Psychology) in television
>   Aggressiveness (Psychology) on television
> BT Television

Aggressiveness (Psychology) in television
> USE Aggressiveness on television

Aggressiveness (Psychology) on television
> USE Aggressiveness on television

Aging in motion pictures *(Not Subd Geog)*
> BT Motion pictures

Agreements, Collective labor
> USE Collective labor agreements

Agricultural extension work[†]
> NT Mass media in agricultural extension work
>   Television in agriculture

Agriculture[†]
> NT Motion pictures in agriculture
> **—Study and teaching**[†]
> **— —Audio-visual aids**
>   NT Television in agriculture

AIDS (Disease) and mass media
> *(May Subd Geog)*
> *[P96.A39]*
> UF Mass media and AIDS (Disease)
> BT Mass media

AIDS (Disease) in mass media
> *(Not Subd Geog)*
> *[P96.A39]*
> BT Mass media

AIDS (Disease) in motion pictures
> *(Not Subd Geog)*
> *[PN1995.9.A435]*
> BT Motion pictures

Air photography
> USE Aerial photography

[†]**Subject headings noted with a dagger contain additional access points and subheadings that are not pertinent to this text and are not included here.**

Air power in mass media
   (Not Subd Geog)
   BT   Mass media
Air warfare in mass media
   (Not Subd Geog)
   BT   Mass media
Airborne cinematography
   USE   Aerial cinematography
Airborne photography
   USE   Aerial photography
Airborne video recording
   USE   Aerial videography
Airborne videorecording
   USE   Aerial videography
Aires camera *(Not Subd Geog)*
   BT   Cameras
Akan drama[†]
   NT   Television plays, Akan
Akan television plays
   USE   Television plays, Akan
Akeley motion picture camera *(Not Subd Geog)*
   BT   Motion picture cameras
Akron Civic Theatre (Akron, Ohio)
   UF   Akron Loew's Theatre (Akron Ohio)
        Cinema, The (Akron, Ohio)
        Civic Theatre (Akron, Ohio)
        Loew's Theatre (Akron, Ohio)
   BT   Motion picture theaters—Ohio
        Theaters—Ohio
Akron Loew's Theatre (Akron, Ohio)
   USE   Akron Civic Theatre (Akron, Ohio)
Alameda, Teatro (Querétaro, Mexico)
   USE   Teatro Alameda (Querétaro, Mexico)
Albert Odyssey (Game)
   [GV1469.35.A43]
   BT   Video games
Alcoholism in mass media
   (Not Subd Geog)
   [P96.A42]
   BT   Mass media
Alcoholism in motion pictures
   (Not Subd Geog)
   [PN1995.9.A45]
   BT   Motion pictures
Alekon-Gerard process
   USE   Front-screen projection
Alien films
   This heading is used as a topical heading for works that collectively discuss films featuring the character Ellen Ripley, including Alien, Aliens, Alien 3, and Alien Resurrection. When used as a topical heading it is subdivided by the appropriate geographical, topical, and/or form subdivisions.

   BT   Science fiction films
Alien films *[LCSH Genre]*
Alien labor
   USE   Foreign workers
Alien labor and mass media
   USE   Mass media and foreign
         workers
Alien labor in motion pictures
   USE   Foreign workers in motion pictures
Alienation (Social psychology) in motion pictures
   (Not Subd Geog)
   [PN1995.9.A47]
   BT   Motion pictures
Aliens in motion pictures *(Not Subd Geog)*
   [PN1995.9.A48]
   Here are entered works on the portrayal of aliens in motion pictures.
   BT   Motion pictures
All-male adult movie theaters *(May Subd Geog)*
   BT   Adult movie theaters
Alternative mass media *(May Subd Geog)*
   [P96.A44]
   UF   Alternative media
        Countercultural mass media
        Underground mass media
   BT   Mass media
Alternative media
   USE   Alternative mass media
Altix camera *(Not Subd Geog)*
   BT   Cameras
Alundra (Game)
   [GV1469.35.A848]
   BT   Video games
Amateur films *(May Subd Geog)*
   UF   Home movies
        Personal films
   BT   Motion pictures
   NT   Fan films
   —Direction
        USE   Amateur films—Production and
              direction
   —Production and direction
        (May Subd Geog)
        UF   Amateur films—Direction
Amateur films *[LCSH Genre]*
Amateur television stations *(May Subd Geog)*
   [TK9960]
   UF   Ham television
   BT   Television stations

[†]**Subject headings noted with a dagger contain additional access points and subheadings that are not pertinent to this text and are not included here.**

NT Student television stations

Amateur theater[†]

RT Acting

NT Improvisation (Acting)

Ambiguity in motion pictures

(Not Subd Geog)

BT Motion pictures

American drama[†]

NT Motion picture plays, American

Television plays, American

American dream on television

(Not Subd Geog)

BT Television

American fiction[†]

—Film and video adaptations

American film posters

USE Film posters, American

American motion picture plays

USE Motion picture plays, American

American motion pictures

USE Motion pictures, American

American national characteristics in motion pictures

USE National characteristics, American,

in motion pictures

American Television and Radio

Commercials Awards

USE Clio Awards

American television plays

USE Television plays, American

Amish[†]

NT Mass media and the Amish

Amish and mass media

USE Mass media and the Amish

Amusement arcades (Video arcades)

USE Video arcades

Amusement ride films

(May Subd Geog)

UF Ride films

Ride movies

Thrill ride films

BT Motion pictures

Amusement ride films *[LCSH Genre]*

Anarchism in motion pictures *(Not Subd Geog)*

[PN1995.9.A487]

BT Motion pictures

Anchor men

USE Television news anchors

Anchor persons

USE Television news anchors

Anchormen

USE Television news anchors

Anchorpersons

USE Television news anchors

Anchors (Television journalism)

USE Television news anchors

Andy Hardy films

Angélique films

[PN1995.9.A49]

BT Motion pictures

Angélique films *[LCSH Genre]*

Angels in motion pictures *(Not Subd Geog)*

BT Motion pictures

Angiography

NT Cineangiography

Animal films *(May Subd Geog)*

BT Motion pictures

Animal films *[LCSH Genre]*

Animals, Fossil, in motion pictures

USE Prehistoric animals in motion pictures

Animals, Prehistoric, in motion pictures

USE Prehistoric animals in motion pictures

Animals in mass media *(Not Subd Geog)*

[P96.A53]

BT Mass media

Animals in motion pictures

(Not Subd Geog)

[PN1995.9.A5]

BT Motion pictures

NT Dogs in motion pictures

Animals in television

USE Animals on television

Animals on television *(Not Subd Geog)*

[PN1992.8.A58]

UF Animals in television

BT Television

Working animals

NT Dogs on television

Animated cartoons (Motion pictures)

USE Animated films

Animated film music *(May Subd Geog)*

UF Animated films—Musical accompaniments

Music for animated films

BT Motion picture music

Animated films *(May Subd Geog)*

[NC1765–NC1766 (Drawing)]

[PN1997.5 (Scenarios)]

This heading is used as a topical heading for works about films that create the illusion of movement in drawings, clay, inanimate objects, or the like, through an animation technique. Works on the technical aspects of making animated films,

---

[†]**Subject headings noted with a dagger contain additional access points and subheadings that are not pertinent to this text and are not included here.**

television programs, or videos are entered under
Animation—Cinematography.
> UF Animated cartoons
> > (Motion pictures
> > Animated videos
> > Cartoons, Animated (Motion pictures)
> > Motion picture cartoons
> BT Caricatures and cartoons
> > Motion pictures
> RT Abstract films
> > Animation (Cinematography)
> > Animation cels
> NT Clay animation films
> > Machinima films
> > Private Snafu films
> > Television broadcasting of animated films
> > Tom and Jerry films

—Musical accompaniments
> USE Animated film music

—Sound effects
> UF Cartoon sound effects

Animated films and children
(May Subd Geog)
> UF Children and animated films
> BT Children

Animated television music
(May Subd Geog)
> UF Animated television programs—Musical
> > accompaniments
> > Music for animated television programs
> BT Television music

Animated television programs *(May Subd Geog)*
> This heading is used as a topical heading for
> works about television programs that create the
> illusion of movement in drawings, clay, inanimate
> objects, or the like, through an animation technique.
> Works on the technical aspects of making animated
> films, television programs, or videos are entered
> under Animation—Cinematography).
> > UF Cartoons (Television programs)
> > > Television cartoon shows
> > RT Animation (Cinematography)
> > BT Television programs
> > NT Pink Panther television programs
> > > Scooby-Doo television programs

—Musical accompaniments
> USE Animated television music

Animated videos
> USE Animated films

Animation (Cinematography)
(May Subd Geog)
> Here are entered works on the technical aspects
> of making animated films, television programs, or

videos. Works on motion pictures, television
programs, or videos that create the illusion of
movement in drawings, clay, inanimate objects, or
the like, through an animation technique, are
entered under Animated films, Animated television
programs, or Animated videos with appropriate
geographic, topical, and/or form subdivisions.
> BT Cinematography
> RT Animated films
> > Animated television programs
> NT Animators
> > Computer animation

Animation, Computer
> USE Computer animation

Animation cells
> USE Animation cels

Animation cels *(May Subd Geog)*
> UF Animation cells
> > Cells, Animation
> > Cels, Animation
> NT Animated films

Animators *(May Subd Geog)*
> UF Cartoon makers
> BT Animation cinematography
> NT Women animators

Anime *(Not Subd Geog)*
> USE subject *headings for specific types of*
> > *animated media subdivided by Japan,*
> > *e.g.,* Animated films—Japan

Announcing for television
> USE Television announcing

Antennas (Electronics)[†]
> NT Television—Antennas

Anteo Spazio Cinema (Milan, Italy)
> BT Motion picture theaters—Italy

Anthology films *(May Subd Geog)*
> This heading is used as a topical heading for
> works about feature-length films made up of differ-
> ent episodes or stories which are usually connected
> by a theme, event, location, or original author, often
> having a wrap-around tale. When used as a topical
> heading it is subdivided by the appropriate
> geographical, topical, and/or form
> subdivisions.
> > UF Composite films
> > > Episode films
> > > Episodic films
> > > Multiple story films
> > > Omnibus films

[†]**Subject headings noted with a dagger contain
additional access points and subheadings that
are not pertinent to this text and are not
included here.**

Portmanteau films
Sketch films
BT Motion pictures
Anthology films *[LCSH Genre]*
Anthology television programs
[LCSH Genre]
Anthropological films
USE Ethnographic films
Anthropological television programs
USE Ethnographic television programs
Anthropological videos
USE Ethnographic videos
Anthropology[†]
NT Mass media and anthropology
Anthropology and mass media
USE Mass media and anthropology
**Anti-fascist movements in motion
pictures** *(Not Subd Geog)*
Anti-Jewish motion pictures
This heading is not used for individual films,
which are entered under headings appropriate to
the content, genre, and/or form of the film.
UF Antisemitic motion pictures
BT Antisemitism
Motion pictures
Anti-militarism films
USE Anti-war films
Anti-militarism television programs
USE Anti-war television programs
Anti-Nazi movement in motion pictures
(Not Subd Geog)
BT Motion pictures
Anti-war films *(May Subd Geog)*
When subdivided by the appropriate
geographic, topical and/or form subdivisions,
this heading is used for works about
anti-war films.
UF Anti-militarism films
Antimilitarism films
Antiwar films
Pacifist films
BT Motion pictures
RT War films
SA *subdivisions* Motion pictures and the war;
Motion pictures and the revolution;
etc., under individual wars, e.g., World
War, 1939–1945—Motion pictures and
the war.
Anti-war films *[LCSH Genre]*
Anti-war television programs
(May Subd Geog)
UF Anti-militarism television programs
Antimilitarism television programs

Antiwar television programs
Pacifist television programs
BT Television programs
RT War television programs
SA *subdivisions* Television and the war;
Television and the revolution, *etc., under
individual wars, e.g.,* World War, 1939–
1945—Television and the war
Anti-war television programs
[LCSH Genre]
Antichrist in motion pictures
(Not Subd Geog)
BT Motion pictures
Antiheroes in motion pictures
(Not Subd Geog)
BT Motion pictures
Antimilitarism films
USE Anti-war films
Antimilitarism television programs
USE Anti-war television programs
Antipsychiatry in motion pictures
(Not Subd Geog)
BT Motion pictures
Antisemitic motion pictures
USE Anti-Jewish motion pictures
Antisemitism[†]
NT Anti-Jewish motion pictures
Antisemitism in motion pictures
(Not Subd Geog)
[PN1995.9.A55]
BT Motion pictures
Antiwar films
USE Anti-war films
Antiwar television programs
USE Anti-war television programs
Apartheid in mass media *(Not Subd Geog)*
BT Mass media
Apartments in motion pictures
(Not Subd Geog)
BT Motion pictures
Apes in motion pictures *(Not Subd Geog)*
BT Motion pictures
Apocalypse in mass media *(Not Subd Geog)*
[P96.A66–P96.A662]
BT Mass media
Apocalypse in motion pictures
(Not Subd Geog)
BT Motion pictures

[†]**Subject headings noted with a dagger contain
additional access points and subheadings that
are not pertinent to this text and are not
included here.**

Appalachians (People) in motion pictures
(Not Subd Geog)
[PN 1995.9.M67]
UF Mountain whites (Southern States)
in motion pictures
BT Motion pictures
Apple Quick Take camera
USE Apple QuickTake camera
Apple QuickTake camera
(Not Subd Geog)
UF Apple Quick Take camera
QuickTake camera
BT Digital cameras
Apple TV (Digital media receiver)
(Not Subd Geog)
BT Digital television
Application software
NT Computer games
Appreciation of motion pictures
USE Motion pictures—Appreciation
Appreciation of television broadcasting
USE Television broadcasting—Appreciation
Arab actors
USE Actors, Arab
Arab motion pictures
USE Motion pictures, Arab
Arab-Israeli conflict[†]
—Mass media and the conflict
UF Arab-Israeli conflict in mass media
Arab-Israeli conflict in mass media
USE Arab-Israeli conflict—Mass media
and the conflict
Arabic drama[†]
NT Television plays, Arabic
Arabic television plays
USE Television plays, Arabic
Arabs in mass media *(Not Subd Geog)*
BT Mass media
Arabs in motion pictures *(Not Subd Geog)*
[PN1995.9.A]
BT Motion pictures
Arabs in television
USE Arabs on television
Arabs on television *(Not Subd Geog)*
[PN1992.8.A7]
UF Arabs in television
BT Television
Arcades, Video
USE Video arcades
Archaeology in motion pictures
(Not Subd Geog)
[PN1995.9.A69]
BT Motion pictures

Archetype (Psychology) in motion pictures
(Not Subd Geog)
BT Motion pictures
Archetype (Psychology) on television
(Not Subd Geog)
BT Television
Architects in motion pictures *(Not
Subd Geog)*
[PN1995.9.A695]
BT Motion pictures
Architecture[†]
NT Mass media and architecture
Architecture in motion pictures
(Not Subd Geog)
BT Motion pictures
Archives[†]
NT Audio-visual archives
Film archives
—Classification
UF Classification—Archives
Archives, Audio-visual
USE Audio-visual archives
Archives, Motion picture
USE Film archives
Argentine drama[†]
NT Motion picture plays,
Argentine
Argentine film posters
USE Film posters, Argentine
Argentine motion picture plays
USE Motion picture plays, Argentine
Argus camera *(Not Sub Geog)*
BT Cameras
Armed Forces and mass media
(May Subd Geog)
[P96.A75]
BT Mass media
Armed Forces in motion pictures
(Not Subd Geog)
[PN1995.9.A72]
BT Motion pictures
Armenian film posters
USE Film posters, Armenian
**Armenian massacres, 1915–1923, in motion
pictures** *(Not Subd Geog)*
Armor in motion pictures *(Not Subd Geog)*
BT Motion pictures
Army Men World War (Game)
[GV1469.35.A75]

[†]**Subject headings noted with a dagger contain
additional access points and subheadings that
are not pertinent to this text and are not
included here.**

BT Video games
Arriflex 16SR motion picture camera
(Not Subd Geog)
[TR883.A]
BT Motion picture cameras
Arriflex 35 motion picture cameras
(Not Subd Geog)
[TR883.A68]
BF Motion picture cameras
Art†
NT Mass media and art
Television and art
Video art
Art, Modern†
—20th century
NT Video art
Art and mass media
USE Mass media and art
Art and motion pictures *(May Subd Geog)*
[N72.M6]
UF Motion pictures and art
BT Motion pictures
Art and television
USE Television and art
Art direction†
NT Motion pictures—Art direction
Television—Art direction
Art directors, Motion picture
USE Motion picture art directors
Art in motion pictures *(Not Subd Geog)*
BT Motion pictures
Art in television
USE Art on television
Art on television *(Not Subd Geog)*
[PPN1992.8.A75]
UF Art in television
BT Television
Arthurian romances in motion pictures
(Not Subd Geog)
[PN1995.9.A75]
BT Motion pictures
Arthurian romances on television
(Not Subd Geog)
BT Television
Artificial satellites in telecommunication†
NT Television
Artists†
NT Actors
Actors as artists
Artists in motion pictures *(Not Subd Geog)*
BT Motion pictures
Arts†
NT Documentary mass media and the arts

Mass media and the arts
Motion pictures and the arts
Television and the arts
Arts and documentary mass media
USE Documentary mass media and the arts
Arts and mass media
USE Mass media and the arts
Arts and motion pictures
USE Motion pictures and the arts
Arts and television
USE Television and the arts
Arts television programs
USE Cultural television programs
Asahiflex camera *(Not Subd Geog)*
BT Cameras
Asian American actors *(May Subd Geog)*
[PN2286.2]
UF Actors, Asian American
BT Actors—United States
Asian American actresses *(May
Subd Geog)*
UF Actresses, Asian American
BT Actresses—United States
Asian American mass media *(May
Subd Geog)*
UF Mass media, Asian American
BT Ethnic mass media—United States
Asian American men in motion pictures
(Not Subd Geog)
BT Motion pictures
**Asian American motion picture producers and
directors** *(May Subd Geog)*
UF Motion picture producers and directors,
Asian Americans
BT Motion picture producers and directors—
United States
Asian American women in motion pictures
(May Subd Geog)
BT Motion pictures
Asian Americans and mass media
(May Subd Geog)
UF Mass media and Asian Americans
BT Mass media
Asian Americans in motion pictures
(Not Subd Geog)
Here are entered works on the portrayal of Asian
Americans in motion pictures. Works on all aspects

†**Subject headings noted with a dagger contain
additional access points and subheadings that
are not pertinent to this text and are not
included here.**

of Asian American involvement in motion pictures are entered under Asian Americans in the motion picture industry. Works on specific aspects of Asian American involvement are entered under the particular subject, e.g., Asian American motion picture producers and directors.

    BT Motion pictures

Asian Americans in television
    USE Asian Americans on television

Asian Americans in television broadcasting
(May Subd Geog)

    Here are entered works on the employment of Asian Americans in television. Works on the portrayal of Asian Americans on television are entered under Asian Americans on television.

    BT Television broadcasting—United States

Asian Americans in the motion picture industry
(May Subd Geog)
    [PN1995.9.A77]

    BT Motion picture industry—United States

Asian Americans on television

(Not Subd Geog)
    [PN1992.8.A78]

    Here are entered works on the portrayal of Asian Americans on television. Works on the employment of Asian Americans in television are entered under Asian Americans in television broadcasting.

    UF Asian Americans in television
    BT Television

Asians in mass media *(Not Subd Geog)*
    BT Mass media

Asians in motion pictures *(Not Subd Geog)*
    [PN1995.9.A78]
    BT Motion pictures

Astronautics[†]
  —Communication systems[†]
    NT Television in astronautics

Astronautics in mass media *(Not Subd Geog)*
    [P96.A79]
    BT Mass media

Astronomical photography[†]
    NT Video astronomy

Astronomy[†]
    NT Television in astronomy

Astronomy in mass media *(Not Subd Geog)*
    [P96.A82]
    BT Mass media

Astoria (Brixton, London, England)
    USE Carling Academy Brixton (London, England)

Atari computer[†]
    NT Pac-Man (Game)

Athletes in mass media *(Not Subd Geog)*
    BT Mass media

Atomic bomb victims in motion pictures
(Not Subd Geog)
    BT Motion pictures

Atomic warfare in motion pictures
    USE Nuclear warfare in motion pictures

Audience participation television programs
    [LCSH Genre]

Audiences[†]
    NT Mass media—Audiences

Audiences, Mass media
    USE Mass media—Audiences

Audiences, Television
    USE Television viewers

Audio-description
    USE Audiodescription

Audio-visual aids
    USE Audio-visual materials

Audio-visual archives *(May Subd Geog)*
    [CD973.2]
    UF Archives, Audio-visual
    BT Archives

Audio-visual education *(May Subd Geog)*

    Here are entered works about the use of motion pictures in education. Works about films that are intended to impart knowledge and information, including those for classroom viewing, are entered under Educational films with appropriate geographic, topical, and/or form subdivisions.

    BT Educational technology
       Teaching
    RT Instructional materials personnel
       Visual education
    NT Audio-visual materials
       Motion pictures in education
       Television in education
       Video tapes in education
       Videodiscs in education
    SA *subdivision* Audio-visual aids *under educational headings, e.g.,* Adult education—Audio-visual aids; *and subdivision* Study and teaching—Audio-visual aids *under subjects*
  —Equipment and supplies
    NT Audio-visual equipment
  —Law and legislation *(May Subd Geog)*
    BT Educational law and legislation

Audio-visual education and copyright
    USE Copyright and audio-visual education

[†]**Subject headings noted with a dagger contain additional access points and subheadings that are not pertinent to this text and are not included here.**

Audio-visual equipment (*May Subd Geog*)
    [LB1043.5 (Education)]
    [TS2301.A7 (Manufacture)]
    Here are entered general works on projectors, screens, sound equipment, pointers, tables, exhibit boards, etc.
    NT Audio-visual education—
         Equipment and supplies
  —Advertising
    USE Advertising—Audio-visual materials
Audio-visual equipment in interior decoration
    BT Interior decoration
Audio-visual equipment industry
    BT Electronic industries
Audio-visual library service (*May Subd Geog*)
    [Z716.65–Z716.8]
    BT Instructional materials centers
    NT Libraries and television
Audio-visual materials (*May Subd Geog*)
    [LB1042.5–LB1044.868]
    UF Audio-visual aids
        Audio-visuals
        Audiovisual materials
        Audiovisuals
        AV materials
    BT Audio-visual education
        Nonbook materials
    NT Acquisition of audio-visual
        materials
        Instructional materials industry
        Motion pictures
    SA *subdivision* Audio-visual aids *under subjects; and subdivision* Study and teaching—Audio-visual aids *under subjects for the use of audio-visual aids in the learning and teaching of those subjects, e.g.,* Geography—Study and teaching—Audio-visual aids
  —Advertising
    USE Advertising—Audio-visual materials
  —Circulation
    UF Audio-visual materials circulation
        Circulation of audio-visual materials
  —Copyright
    USE Copyright—Audio-visual materials
  —Tariff
    USE Tariff on audio-visual materials
Audio-visual materials centers
  USE Instructional materials centers
Audio-visual materials circulation
  USE Audio-visual materials– Circulation
Audio-visual materials industry
  USE Instructional materials industry

Audiodescription (*May Subd Geog*)
    Here are entered works on the technique in which, during lapses in the audio or scripted dialogue of plays, films, and television programs, trained narrators describe the visual and nonverbal cues and information that may be essential for people with visual disabilities to understand and appreciate these cultural and informational media.
    UF Audio-description
    BT People with visual disabilities—
        Services for
    NT Video description
Audiovisual . . .
  USE *subject headings beginning with the word* Audio-visual . . .
Audiovisual materials
  USE Audio-visual materials
Audiovisuals
  USE Audio-visual materials
Auditions†
    NT Acting—Auditions
        Television broadcasting—Auditions
Australian aborigines in mass media
  USE Aboriginal Australians in mass media
Australian aborigines in motion pictures
  USE Aboriginal Australians in motion pictures
Australian aborigines in television broadcasting
  USE Aboriginal Australians in television broadcasting
Australian drama†
    NT Motion picture plays, Australian
        Television plays, Australian
Australian film posters
  USE Film posters, Australian
Australian motion picture plays
  USE Motion picture plays, Australian
Australian motion pictures
  USE Motion pictures, Australian
Australian television plays
  USE Television plays, Australian
Austrian American motion picture actors and actresses (*May Subd Geog*)
    NT Motion picture actors and actresses, Austrian
    BT Motion picture actors and actresses—United States

†**Subject headings noted with a dagger contain additional access points and subheadings that are not pertinent to this text and are not included here.**

Austrian drama†
   NT Motion picture plays, Austrian
Austrian motion picture plays
   USE Motion picture plays, Austrian
Auteur theory (Motion pictures)
   [PN1995.9.A837]
   Here are entered works on the theory that
the director is the primary creator of a motion
picture.
   UF Politique des auteurs (Motion pictures)
   BT Motion pictures
Authoring programs for video CDs
   USE Video CDs—Authoring programs
Authority in motion pictures *(Not Subd Geog)*
   BT Motion pictures
Authors†
   NT Blacklisting of authors
      Dramatists
      Television writers
Authors in motion pictures
   (Not Subd Geog)
   [PN1995.9.A84]
   BT Motion pictures
Authorship†
   NT Motion picture authorship
      Television authorship
      Video authorship
Autobiographical films *[LCSH Genre]*
Autobiographical television programs
   [LCSH Genre]
Autofocus cameras *(May Subd Geog)*
   [TR260.7]
   UF AF cameras
      Automatic focusing cameras
   BT 35 mm cameras
Automatic focusing cameras
   USE Autofocus cameras
Automatic cameras
   USE Electric eye cameras
Automatic picture transmission†
   BT Data transmission system
      Image transmission
   NT Video telephone
Automobiles in mass media
   (Not Subd Geog)
   BT Mass media
Automobiles in motion pictures
   (Not Subd Geog)
   [PN1995.9.A85]
   BT Motion pictures
Autonomy (Psychology) in motion pictures
   (Not Subd Geog)
   BT Motion pictures

AV materials
   USE Audio-visual materials
Avant-garde films
   USE Experimental films
Aviation films *[LCSH Genre]*
Aviation television programs
   [LCSH Genre]
Award presentations (Motion pictures)
   [LCSH Genre]
Award presentations (Television programs)
   [LCSH Genre]

B. F. Keith's (Portland, Me.)
   USE Civic Theatre (Portland, Me.)
B films *(May Subd Geog)*
   This heading is used as a topical heading for
works about low budget feature films that were
usually shown in a double feature program along
with the major production, the A film. When used
as a topical heading it is subdivided by the
appropriate geographical, topical, and/or form
subdivisions.
   UF B movies
      B pictures
   RT Low budget films
B films *[LCSH Genre]*
B movies
   USE B films
B pictures
   USE B films
Background artists (Actors)
   USE Extras (Actors)
Background music for motion pictures
   USE Motion picture music
      Background music for television
   USE Television music
Bagdad Theater (Portland, Ore.)
   BT Motion picture theaters—Oregon
Balaban & Katz Oriental Theatre
   (Chicago, Ill.)
   USE Oriental Theatre (Chicago, Ill.)
Balboa, Rocky (Fictitious character)
   (Not Subd Geog)
   UF Rocky Balboa (Fictitious character)
Ballet films *[LCSH Genre]*
Ballet in motion pictures, television, etc.
   [GV1779]
   UF Ballet in television

†Subject headings noted with a dagger contain
additional access points and subheadings that
are not pertinent to this text and are not
included here.

BT Motion pictures
      Television
Ballet in television
    USE Ballet in motion pictures, television, etc.
Ballet on television
    USE Ballet in motion pictures, television, etc.
Ballet television programs *[LCSH Genre]*
Balloon photography
    USE Aerial photography
Bandit gangster films
    USE Gangster films
Banjo-Kazooie (Game)
      [GV1469.35.B33]
      BT Video games
Baseball[†]
      NT Baseball films
          Television and baseball
Baseball and television
    USE Television and baseball
Baseball films *(May Subd Geog)*
      [PN1995.9.B28]
      BT Baseball
          Sports films
Baseball films *[LCSH Genre]*
Baseball television programs
      [LCSH Genre]
Basketball films *(May Subd Geog)*
      UF Cage films (Basketball films)
      BT Sports films
Basketball films *[LCSH Genre]*
Basketball television programs
      [LCSH Genre]
Basques in motion pictures
    (Not Subd Geog)
      [PN1995.9.B29]
      BT Motion pictures
Baths in motion pictures *(May Subd Geog)*
      [PN1995.9.B3]
      BT Motion pictures
Batman (Fictitious character)
    (Not Subd Geog)
      UF Bruce Wayne (Fictitious character)
          Wayne, Bruce (Fictitious character)
Batman (Fictitious character) in mass media
    (Not Subd Geog)
      [P96.B37]
      BT Mass media
Batman & Robin (Game)
      [GV1469.35.B34]
      UF Batman and Robin (Game)
      BT Video games
Batman and Robin films
  USE Batman films

Batman and Robin (Game)
    USE Batman & Robin (Game)
Batman and Robin films
    USE Batman films
Batman films *(May Subd Geog)*
      UF Batman and Robin films
      BT Superhero films
Batman films *[LCSH Genre]*
Battle Arena Toshinden (Game)
      [GV1469.35.B35]
      BT Video games
Battle Tanx Global Assault (Game)
      [GV1469.35.B36]
      BT Video games
Battletoads (Game)
      [GV1469.35.B]
      BT Video games
Bayerischer Filmpreis
      BT Motion pictures—Awards—Germany
Bayerischer Fernsehpreis
      BT Television broadcasting—Awards—Germany
BDA Awards
    USE BDA International Design Awards
BDA International Design Awards
      UF BDA Awards
          Broadcast Designers' Association
            International Design Awards
      BT Design—Awards
          Television broadcasting—Awards
          Television graphics—Awards
Beach-blanket films
  USE Beach party films
Beach-bunny films
  USE Beach party films
Beach party films *(May Subd Geog)*
      This heading is used as topical heading for works
    about films that feature groups of teens who gather
    on the beach to party, surf, etc., When used as a
    topical heading it is subdivided by the appropriate
    geographical, topical, and/or form subdivisions.
      UF Beach-blanket films
          Beach-bunny films
          Sand-and-surf films
          Sun-and-sand films
      BT Teen films
Beach party films *[LCSH Genre]*
Beauty, Personal, in motion pictures
    (Not Subd Geog)
      UF Personal beauty in motion pictures

**[†]Subject headings noted with a dagger contain
additional access points and subheadings that
are not pertinent to this text and are not
included here.**

BT Motion pictures
Beauty contest films *[LCSH Genre]*
Beauty contest television programs
    [LCSH Genre]
Beheading in motion pictures *(Not Subd Geog)*
    BT Motion pictures
Belgian film posters
    USE Film posters, Belgian
Bell and Howell motion picture camera
    (Not Subd Geog)
    BT Motion picture cameras
Beltica camera *(Not Subd Geog)*
    BT Cameras
Bengali motion picture plays
    USE Motion picture plays, Bengali
Bengali drama[†]
    NT Motion picture plays, Bengali
Bergfilme
    USE Mountain films
Beseler Topcon camera *(Not Subd Geog.)*
    BT Cameras
Beyond the Beyond (Game)
    [GV1469.35.B48]
    BT Video games
Bias in documentary television programs
    USE Documentary television
           programs—Objectivity
Bias in mass media
    USE Mass media—Objectivity
Bible[†]
  —In motion pictures
      Here are entered works on Biblical themes in
    motion pictures that are not themselves Bible
    films. Works on film versions of Biblical stories
    are entered under Bible films subdivided by the
    appropriate geographic, topical, and/or form
    subdivisions.
      UF Biblical themes in motion pictures
Bible films *(May Subd Geog)*
    [PN1995.9.B53]
    This heading is used as a topical heading for
  works about film versions of Biblical stories. When
  used as a topical heading it is subdivided by the
  appropriate geographic, topical, and/or form
  subdivisions. Works on Biblical themes in motion
  pictures that are not themselves Bible films are
  entered under Bible—In motion pictures.
    UF Biblical films
    BT Religious films
Bible films *[LCSH Genre]*
Bible television programs *[LCSH Genre]*
Biblical films
    USE Bible films

Biblical themes in motion pictures
    USE Bible—In motion pictures
Big bands in motion pictures *(Not Subd Geog)*
    BT Motion pictures
Big Brother television programs
    [PN1992.8.B54]
    Here are entered works on Big Brother television
  programs discussed collectively. Works on
  individual Big Brother television programs or series
  are entered under the specific title.
    BT Reality television programs
Big Brother television programs
    [LCSH Genre]
Big-caper films
    USE Caper films
Biker films
    USE Motorcycle films
Bildungsfilms
    USE Coming-of-age films
Bill Graham's Fillmore East
  (New York, N.Y.)
    USE Fillmore East
        (New York, N.Y.)
Billboards[†]
    NT Motion picture billboards
Bio-pics
    USE Biographical films
Bioethics in motion pictures
  (Not Subd Geog)
    BT Motion pictures
Biographical films *(May Subd Geog)*
    UF Bio-pics
        Biopics
        Film biographies
        Screen biographies
    BT Biography
        Motion pictures
Biographical films *[LCSH Genre]*
Biographical television programs
  (May Subd Geog)
    UF Portraits (Biographical television programs)
        Profiles (Biographical television)
    BT Biography
        Television programs
Biographical television programs
    [LCSH Genre]
Biographical videos *(May Subd Geog)*
    BT Biography
        Video recordings

[†]**Subject headings noted with a dagger contain
additional access points and subheadings that
are not pertinent to this text and are not
included here.**

Biography[†]
  NT Biographical films
Biographical television programs
    Biographical television programs
    Broadcasting—Biography
    Cinematography—Biography
    Motion pictures—Biography
    Motion pictures—Production and direction
—Television
        USE Television—Biography
Biology[†]
—Study and teaching[†]
        NT Television in biology education
Biology in motion pictures (*Not Subd Geog*)
    BT Motion pictures
Biology in television
  USE Biology on television
Biology on television (*Not Subd Geog*)
    UF Biology in television
    BT Television
Biopics
  USE Biographical films
Bioscope
  USE Motion picture projection
Bioterrorism and mass media
  (*May Subd Geog*)
    UF Mass media and bioterrorism
    BT Mass media
Birth control[†]
    NT Mass media in family planning
        Television in birth control
Bisexuality in motion pictures (*Not Subd Geog*)
    [PN1995.9.B57]
    BT Motion pictures
Bisexuality on television (*Not Subd Geog*)
    UF Bisexuals on television
    BT Television
Bisexuals on television
  USE Bisexuality on television
Black action films
  USE Blaxploitation films
Black actors
  USE Actors, Black
Black actresses
  USE Actresses, Black
Black English in mass media
  (*Not Subd Geog*)
    BT Mass media
Black exploitation films
  USE Blaxploitation films
Black-face entertainers
  USE Blackface entertainers
Black Film Collection, Tyler, Texas

  USE Tyler, Texas, Black Film Collection
Black mass media (*May Subd Geog*)
    [P94.5.B55]
    Here are entered works on mass media owned or
produced by blacks. Works on the portrayal of
blacks in mass media are entered under Blacks in
mass media. Works on all aspects of black
involvement with the mass media are entered under
Blacks and mass media.
    UF Afro mass media
    BT Mass media
Black men in motion pictures (*Not Subd Geog*)
    BT Motion pictures
Black theater
    NT Actors, Black
Blackface entertainers (*May Subd Geog*)
    [PN2071.B58]
    UF Black-face entertainers
        Entertainers, Blackface
    BT Entertainers
    RT Minstrel shows
Blackfaced minstrel shows
  USE Minstrel shows
Blacklisting of authors (*May Subd Geog*)
    UF Authors—Blacklisting
    BT Authors
        Mass media—Censorship
Blacklisting of entertainers
  (*May Subd Geog*)
    UF Entertainers—Blacklisting
    BT Actors
        Entertainers
Blacks and mass media (*May Subd Geog*)
    [P94.5.B55]
    Here are entered works on all aspects of black
involvement with the mass media. Works on the
portrayal of blacks in mass media are entered under
Blacks in mass media. Works on mass media owned
or produced by blacks are entered under Black mass
media.
    UF Mass media and Blacks
    BT Mass media
Blacks in mass media (*Not Subd Geog*)
    [P94.5.B55]
    Here are entered works on the portrayal of blacks
in mass media. Works on mass media owned or
produced by blacks are entered under Black mass
media. Works on all aspects of black involvement

[†]**Subject headings noted with a dagger contain
additional access points and subheadings that
are not pertinent to this text and are not
included here.**

with the mass media are entered under Blacks and
mass media.

    BT Mass media

Blacks in motion pictures *(Not Subd Geog)*

    [PN1995.9.N4]

    Here are entered works on the portrayal of blacks
in motion pictures. Works on all aspects of
black involvement in motion pictures are entered
under Blacks in the motion picture industry.
Works on specific aspects of black involvement
are entered under the particular subject, e.g.,
Actors, Black.

    BT Motion pictures

Blacks in television

    USE Blacks on television

Blacks in television broadcasting *(May Subd Geog)*

    UF Blacks in the television industry

    BT Television broadcasting

Blacks in the motion picture industry

    (May Subd Geog)

    [PN1995.9.N4]

    Here are entered works on all aspects of black
involvement in motion pictures. Works on the
portrayal of blacks in motion pictures are entered
under Blacks in motion pictures. Works on specific
aspects of black involvement are entered under the
particular subject, e.g., Actors, Black.

    BT Motion picture industry

Blacks in the television industry

    USE Blacks in television broadcasting

Blacks on television *(Not Subd Geog)*

    [PN1992.8.A34]

    UF Blacks in television

    BT Television

Blacksploitation films

    USE Blaxploitation films

Blast Corps (Game)

    [GV1469.35.B54]

    BT Nintendo video games

Blaxploitation films *(May Subd Geog)*

    UF Action films, Black

        Black action films

        Black exploitation films

        Blacksploitation films

        Exploitation films, Black

    BT Motion pictures

Blaxploitation films *[LCSH Genre]*

Blind[†]

    NT Blind actors

        Television and the blind

Blind actors *(May Subd Geog)*

    BT Actors with disabilities

        Blind

Blind and television

    USE Television and the blind

Blind in motion pictures *(Not Subd Geog)*

    BT Motion pictures

Blitz: the League (Game)

    BT Video games

Block booking

    BT Motion pictures—Distribution

Blockbusters (Motion pictures)

    (May Subd Geog)

    [PN1995.9.B598]

    Here are entered works on films that sustain
extremely high attendance and enormous gross sales
at the box office. This heading is not used for
individual blockbusters. Individual blockbusters are
entered under headings appropriate to the content,
genre, and/or form of the film.

    BT Motion pictures

Blocking (Motion pictures) *(May Subd Geog)*

    UF Blocking of motion picture plays

    BT Motion pictures—Production and direction

Blocking of motion plays

    USE Blocking (Motion pictures)

Blondes in motion pictures *(Not Subd Geog)*

    BT Motion pictures

Blood in motion pictures *(Not Subd Geog)*

    [PN1995.9.B6]

    BT Motion pictures

Blood Omen (Game)

    [GV1489.35.B56]

    BT Video games

Blue Dragon (Game)

    BT Video games

Blue movies

    USE Pornographic films

Blue Stinger (Game)

    [GV1469.35.B57]

    BT Video games

Blues (Music) in motion pictures *(Not Subd Geog)*

    BT Motion pictures

Boating in motion pictures

    USE Boats and boating in motion pictures

Boats and boating in motion pictures

    (Not Subd Geog)

    UF Boating in motion pictures

        Boats in motion pictures

    BT Motion pictures

Boats in motion pictures

    USE Boats and boating in motion pictures

[†]**Subject headings noted with a dagger contain
additional access points and subheadings that
are not pertinent to this text and are not
included here.**

Body, Human, in mass media
　　USE Human body in mass media
Body, Human, in motion pictures
　　USE Human body in motion pictures
Body, Human, on television
　　USE Human body on television
Body Harvest (Game)
　　[GV1469.35.B59]
　　BT Video games
Body-worn video cameras
　　USE Wearable video devices
Body-worn video devices
　　USE Wearable video devices
Bodycount films
　　USE Slasher films
Bolex H16 motion picture camera
　　(Not Subd Geog)
　　　　UF H16 motion picture camera
　　　　BT Bolex motion picture cameras
Bolex motion picture cameras
　　(May Subd Geog)
　　　　UF Paillard motion picture cameras
　　　　BT Motion picture cameras
　　　　NT Bolex H16 motion picture camera
Bolex motion picture projectors
　　(Not Subd Geog)
　　　　UF Paillard motion picture projectors
　　　　BT Motion picture projectors
Bollywood
　　USE Motion picture industry—
　　　　　　India—Bombay
Bolsey camera *(Not Subd Geog)*
　　BT Miniature cameras
Bomberman 64 (Game)
　　BT Nintendo video games
Bomberman World (Game)
　　BT Video games
Bond films
　　USE James Bond films
Bond, James (Fictitious character)
　　(Not Subd Geog)
　　　　UF 007 (Fictitious character)
　　　　　　James Bond (Fictitious character)
　　　　RT James Bond films
Bondage (Sexual behavior) in motion pictures
　　(Not Subd Geog)
　　　　[PN1995.9.B64]
　　　　BT Motion pictures
Bondage (Sexual behavior) in television
　　USE Bondage (Sexual behavior) on television
Bondage (Sexual behavior) on television
　　　　UF Bondage (Sexual behavior) in television
　　　　BT Television

Boogerman (Game)
　　[GV1469.35.B65]
　　BT Video games
Book review programs, Television
　　USE Book review television programs
Book review television programs
　　(May Subd Geog)
　　　　UF Book review programs, Television
　　　　　　Television book review programs
　　　　BT Nonfiction television programs
Book review television programs
　　[LCSH Genre]
Book selection†
　　　　NT Instructional materials centers—Book
　　　　　　selection
Books, Filmed
　　USE Film adaptations
Books, Press (Motion picture advertising)
　　USE Pressbooks
Books and reading†
　　　　NT Television and reading
Bookstores in motion pictures
　　(Not Subd Geog)
　　　　BT Motion pictures
Bootleg video recordings
　　USE Video recordings—Pirated editions
Botchergate Picture House (Carlisle, England)
　　　　BT Motion picture theaters—England
Boundaries in motion pictures
　　(Not Subd Geog)
　　　　BT Motion pictures
Bovill Opera House (Bovill, Idaho)
　　　　BT Motion picture theaters—Idaho
Bowery Boys films
　　[PN1995.9.B68]
　　　　UF Dead End Kids films
　　　　　　Eastside Kids films
　　　　BT Motion pictures
Bowery Boys films *[LCSH Genre]*
Boxing films *(May Subd Geog)*
　　　　UF Fight films
　　　　　　Prize-fight films
　　　　　　Prize-fighting films
　　　　　　Prizefight films
　　　　　　Prizefighting films
　　　　BT Sports films
—History and criticism
　　　　UF Boxing in motion pictures
Boxing films *[LCSH Genre]*

†**Subject headings noted with a dagger contain
additional access points and subheadings that
are not pertinent to this text and are not
included here.**

Boxing in motion pictures
    USE Boxing films—History and criticism
Boys in motion pictures *(Not Subd Geog)*
    BT Motion pictures
Brainwashing in motion pictures
    (Not Subd Geog)
    BT Motion pictures
Brave Fencer Musashi (Game)
    BT Video games
Brazilian drama[†]
    NT Motion picture plays, Brazilian
         Television plays, Brazilian
Brazilian film posters
    USE Film posters, Brazilian
Brazilian motion picture plays
    USE Motion picture plays, Brazilian
Brazilian motion pictures
    USE Motion pictures, Brazilian
Brazilian television plays
    USE Television plays, Brazilian
Breakfast television
    USE Morning news talk shows
Breastfeeding promotion[†]
    NT Mass media in breastfeeding promotion
Breath of Fire (Game)
    BT Video games
Breathing exercises[†]
    NT Acting—Breathing exercises
Brigandine (Game)
    BT Video games
British motion pictures
    USE Motion pictures, British
Brixton Academy (London, England)
    USE Carling Academy Briton (London, England)
Brixton Astoria (London, England)
    USE Carling Academy Brixton (London, England)
Broadcast advertising *(May Subd Geog)*
    [PN4784.B74]
    RT Home shopping television programs
         Infomercials
    NT Television advertising
Broadcast Designers' Association International
  Design Awards
    USE BDA International Design Awards
Broadcast journalism *(May Subd Geog)*
    [PN4784.B75]
    UF Broadcast news
         News broadcasting
    BT Broadcasting
         Journalism
         Press
    NT Television broadcasting of news
Broadcast journalists

    USE Television journalists
Broadcast news
    USE Broadcast journalism
Broadcasting *(May Subd Geog)*
    UF Broadcasting industry
    BT Communication and traffic
         Cultural industries
         telecommunication
    NT Broadcast journalism
         Ethnic broadcasting
         Minorities in broadcasting
         Public broadcasting
         Religious broadcasting
         Television broadcasting
         Weather broadcasting
         Women in television broadcasting
         Women in the broadcasting industry
  —Government policy
    USE Broadcasting policy
  —Law and legislation *(May Subd Geog)*
    RT Equal time rule (Broadcasting)
         Fairness doctrine (Broadcasting)
  —Public relations *(May Subd Geog)*
    UF Public relations—Broadcasting
Broadcasting, Educational
    USE Educational broadcasting
Broadcasting, Religious
    USE Religious broadcasting
Broadcasting and state
    USE Broadcasting policy
Broadcasting archives[†]
    NT Television archives
Broadcasting industry
    USE Broadcasting
Broadcasting libraries *(May Subd Geog)*
    BT Special libraries
Broadcasting policy[†]
    UF Broadcasting—Government policy
         Broadcasting and state
    BT Mass media policy
    RT Equal time rule (Broadcasting)
         Fairness doctrine (Broadcasting)
    NT Television broadcasting policy
Broksonic televisions *(Not Subd Geog)*
    BT Television—Receivers and reception
Bronica cameras *(Not Subd Geog)*
    UF Zenza Bronica cameras
    BT Cameras
Brownie camera *(Not Subd Geog)*

[†]**Subject headings noted with a dagger contain
additional access points and subheadings that
are not pertinent to this text and are not
included here.**

BT Kodak camera
Bubsy Bobcat (Game)
 [GV1469.35.B]
 BT Video games
Bruce Wayne (Fictitious character)
 USE Batman (Fictitious character)
Buck Bumble (Game)
 [GV1469.35.B85]
 BT Video games
Buddy films *[LCSH Genre]*
Buddy television programs *[LCSH Genre]*
Bugs Bunny (Fictitious character)
 UF Bunny, Bugs (Fictitious character)
Bugs Bunny, Lost in Time (Game)
 [GV1469.35.B86]
 BT Video games
Bulgarian drama[†]
 BT Television plays, Bulgarian
Bulgarian television plays
 USE Television plays, Bulgarian
Bull-fights in moving pictures
 USE Bullfights in motion pictures
Bullfights in motion pictures
 (Not Subd Geog)
 [PN1995.9.B8]
 UF Bull-fights in moving pictures
 BT Motion pictures
Bunny, Bugs (Fictitious character)
 USE Bugs Bunny (Fictitious character)
Bureaucracy in motion pictures
 (Not Subd Geog)
 [PN1995.9.B85]
 BT Motion pictures
Burmese drama[†]
 NT Motion picture plays, Burmese
Burmese motion picture plays
 USE Motion picture plays, Burmese
Bushido Blade 2 (Game)
 [GV1469.35.B88]
 UF Bushidō burēdo ni (Game)
 BT Video games
Business[†]
 NT Mass media and business
  Industrial films
Business enterprises[†]
 NT Motion picture studios
Business ethics in motion pictures
 (Not Subd Geog)
 BT Motion pictures
Business films
 USE Industrial films
Business in motion pictures *(Not Subd Geog)*
 [PN1995.9.B87]

 BT Motion pictures
Business television
 USE Industrial television
  Television in management
Businessmen in television
 USE Businessmen on television
Businessmen on television
 (Not Subd Geog)
 [PN1992.8.B87]
 UF Businessmen in television
 BT Television
Businesspeople[†]
 NT Video gamers as businesspeople
BWVs (Video recording)
 USE Wearable video devices

Cable television *(May Subd Geog)*
 [He8700.7–HE8700.72 (Economics)]
 [TK6675 (Engineering)]
 UF CATV
  Cable TV
  Community antenna television
  Television, Cable
 BT Subscription television
  Television broadcasting
  Television relay systems
 RT Public-access television
 NT Satellite master antenna television
—Access *(May Subd Geog)*
 UF Access to cable television
—Scrambling systems
  BT Scrambling systems
   (Telecommunication)
Cable television advertising
 (May Subd Geog)
 [HF6146.T42]
 UF Advertising, Cable television
 BT Telemarketing
  Television advertising
Cable television in . . .
 USE *subject headings beginning with the words*
   Television in . . .
Cable TV
 USE Cable television
Cage films (Basketball films)
 USE Basketball films
Cairo Theater (Rosario, Santa Fe, Argentina)
 USE Cine El Cairo (Rosario, Santa Fe, Argentina)
Call letters (Television stations)

[†]**Subject headings noted with a dagger contain
additional access points and subheadings that
are not pertinent to this text and are not
included here.**

USE Television stations—Call signs
Call signs (Television stations)
   USE Television stations—Call signs
Camcorders *(May Subd Geog)*
   [TR882.3]
   UF Video cameras/recorders
   BT Home video systems
Camera industry *(May Subd Geog)*
   [HD9708.5.C35–HD9708.5.C354]
   BT Photographic industry
Camera operators *(May Subd Geog)*
   Here are entered works on the members of a film, television, or video production crew who are responsible for the focus and movement of the camera and for composing the picture. Works on the directors of photography who are in charge of all aspects of photography, including the lighting, for a film, television, or video production are entered under Cinematographers.
   UF Cameramen
      Cinematographers (Camera operators)
      Operating cameramen
      Operators, Camera
   RT Photographers
   NT Television camera operators
Camera shutters *(May Subd Geog)*
   [TR272]
   UF Shutters, Camera
   BT Cameras
Cameraless animation films *[LCSH Genre]*
Cameramen
   USE Camera operators
      Cinematographers
Cameras *(May Subd Geog)*
   [TR250–TR265]
   BT Photography—Equipment and supplies
   NT 35 mm cameras
      Agfa camera
      Aires camera
      Altix camera
      Argus camera
      Asahiflex camera
      Beltica camera
      Beseler Topcon camera
      Bronica cameras
      Camera shutters
      Canon camera
      CCD cameras
      Ciro-flex camera
      Contaflex camera
      Digital cameras
      Disposable cameras
      Edixa camera
      Electric eye cameras
      Ernemann cameras
      Exa camera
      Exakta camera
      Foca camera
      Graflex camera
      Hasselblad camera
      Icarex camera
      Ikoflex camera
      Ikonta camera
      Instamatic camera
      Karat camera
      Kardon camera
      Kiev camera
      Kodak camera
      Kodak instant camera
      Konica camera
      Korelle camera
      Leica camera
      Leicaflex camera
      Linhof cameras
      Lomo Kompakt Automat camera
      Medium format cameras
      Miniature cameras
      Minolta camera
      Minox camera
      Motion picture cameras
      Nagel camera
      Nikkormat camera
      Nikon camera
      Nikonos camera
      Nizo camera
      Olympus camera
      Optima camera
      Pentax cameras
      Penti camera
      Petri camera
      Photographic lenses
      Polaroid Land camera
      Praktina camera
      Premo camera
      Retinette camera
      Ricoh camera
      Robot camera
      Rollei camera
      Rolleicord camera
      Rolleiflex camera
      Scintillation cameras
      Scouting cameras

†**Subject headings noted with a dagger contain additional access points and subheadings that are not pertinent to this text and are not included here.**

Selfix camera
Silette camera
Single-lens reflex cameras
Sony cameras
Stereoscopic cameras
Streak cameras
Twin-lens cameras
Underwater cameras
View cameras
Vitessa camera
Vitomatic camera
Voigtlander camera
Yashica camera
Zeiss camera
Zenith cameras
Campaign books (Motion picture advertising)
 USE Pressbooks
Canadian drama[†]
 NT Motion picture plays, Canadian
   Television plays, Canadian
Canadian film awards
 USE Genie Awards
Canadian motion picture plays
 USE Motion picture plays, Canadian
Canadian motion pictures
 USE Motion pictures, Canadian
Canadian television plays
 USE Television plays, Canadian
Cannibalism in motion pictures
 (Not Subd Geog)
 BT Motion pictures
Canon camera *(Not Subd Geog)*
 BT Cameras
 NT Canon digital cameras
Canon digital cameras *(Not Subd Geog)*
 BT Canon camera
   Digital cameras
Cantors (Judaism) in motion pictures
 (Not Subd Geog)
 BT Motion pictures
Caper films *(May Subd Geog)*
 This heading is used as a
topical heading for works about films that feature
the execution of a particularly difficult undertaking,
often questionable or illegal, the success of which
depends on skill and careful planning. When used as
a topical heading it is subdivided by the appropriate
geographical, topical, and/or form subdivisions.
 UF Big-caper films
   Heist films
 BT Motion pictures
 RT Crime films
Caper films *[LCSH Genre]*

Caper television programs *[LCSH Genre]*
Capitalism and mass media *(May Subd Geog)*
 UF Mass media and capitalism
 BT Mass media
Capitole (Lausanne, Switzerland)
 UF Cinéma Capitole Lausanne (Lausanne,
   Switzerland)
 BT Motion picture theaters—Switzerland
Captioned media in reading *(May Subd Geog)*
 [LB1050.375]
 BT Reading—Aids and devices
Captioning, Closed
 USE Closed captioning
Captivity in motion pictures *(Not Subd Geog)*
 BT Motion pictures
Car-chase films *(May Subd Geog)*
 UF Car-crash films
   Crash-and-wreck films
 BT Motion pictures
Car-chase films *[LCSH Genre]*
Car-crash films
 USE Car-chase films
Cards, Insert (Film posters)
 USE Insert posters
Cards, Lobby
 USE Lobby cards
Caricatures and cartoons[†]
 NT Animated films
Carling Academy Brixton (London, England)
 UF Astoria (Brixton, London, England)
   Brixton Academy (London, England)
   Brixton Astoria (London, England)
   Fair Deal (London, England)
   Odeon-Astoria, Brixton (London, England)
   Sundown Centre (London, England)
 BT Motion picture theaters—England
   Music-halls—England
Carmen films
 [PN1995.9.C334]
 BT Motion pictures
Carmen films *[LCSH Genre]*
Carnival in motion pictures
 (Not Subd Geog)
 [PN1995.9.C3343]
 BT Motion pictures
Carrier (Game)
 [GV1469.35.C36]
 BT Video games

[†]**Subject headings noted with a dagger contain
additional access points and subheadings that
are not pertinent to this text and are not
included here.**

Carry On films
  BT Comedy films
Carry On films *[LCSH Genre]*
CART (Real-time closed captioning)
  USE Real-time closed captioning
Cartoon makers
  USE Animators
Cartoon sound effects
  USE Animated films—Sound effects
Cartoons, Animated (Motion pictures)
  USE Animated films
Cartoons, Television programs
  USE Animated television programs
Cassidy, Hopalong (Fictitious character)
  (Not Subd Geog)
    UF Hopalong Cassidy
        (Fictitious character)
Casting (Performing arts)†
    NT Motion pictures—Casting
        Television programs—Casting
Casting directors *(May Subd Geog)*
    BT Motion picture producers and
        directors
        Theatrical producers and directors
Castlevania (Game)
    [GV1469.35.C37]
    BT Nintendo video games
Cataloging of DVDs *(May Subd Geog)*
    [Z695.255]
    BT DVDs
Cataloging of educational media
    UF Cataloging of teaching aids and devices
    BT Educational media, Cataloging of Teaching—
        Aids and devices
Cataloging of interactive multimedia
    (May Subd Geog]
    [Z695.37]
    RT Interactive multimedia
Cataloging of motion picture literature
    (May Subd Geog)
    BT Motion picture literature
Cataloging of non-book materials
  USE Cataloging of nonbook materials
Cataloging of nonbook materials
    (May Subd Geog)
    [Z695.66]
    UF Cataloging of non-book
        materials
    BT Nonbook materials
—Data processing
Cataloging of teaching aids and devices
  USE Cataloging of educational
        media

Cataloging of video recordings
    (May Subd Geog)
    [Z695.64]
    BT Video recordings
Catalogs, Film
  USE Motion pictures—Catalogs
Catastrophe films
  USE Disaster films
Catastrophical, The, in motion pictures
    (Not Subd Geog)
    [PN1995.9.C345]
    BT Motion pictures
Catholic Church and motion pictures
  USE Motion pictures—Religious aspects—
        Catholic Church
Catholic Church†
  —In motion pictures
        UF Catholic Church in motion pictures
Catholic Church in motion pictures
  USE Catholic Church—In motion pictures
Catholic television personalities *(May Subd Geog)*
    BT Television personalities
Catholics in motion pictures *(Not Subd Geog)*
    [PN1995.9.C35]
    BT Motion pictures
Cats in motion pictures *(Not Subd Geog)*
    BT Motion pictures
CATV
  USE Cable television
CCD cameras *(May Subd Geog)*
    UF Charge coupled device cameras
    BT Cameras
        Charge coupled devices
CCTV (Closed-circuit television)
  USE Closed-circuit television
Celebrities†
    NT Television personalities
Celebrities in mass media *(Not Subd Geog)*
    [P96.C35]
    BT Mass media
Cells, Animation
  USE Animation cels
Cels, Animation
  USE Animation cels
Centipede (Game)
    [GV1469.35.C45]
    BT Video games
Central Asian motion pictures
  USE Motion pictures, Central Asian

†**Subject headings noted with a dagger contain
additional access points and subheadings that
are not pertinent to this text and are not
included here.**

Chan, Charlie (Fictitious character)
  (Not Subd Geog)
    UF Charlie Chan (Fictitious character)
       Inspector Charlie Chan
          (Fictitious character)
Chance in motion pictures
  (Not Subd Geog)
    BT Motion pictures
Channel selectors for television
    USE Television—Channel selectors
Channel surfing (Television)
    USE Grazing (Television)
Channel switching (Television)
    USE Grazing (Television)
Chapterplay films
    USE Film serials
Character actors and actresses
  (May Subd Geog)
    BT Actors
       Actresses
Characters and characters[†]
    NT Video game characters
Characters and characteristics in mass media
  (Not Subd Geog)
    [P96.C43]
    BT Mass media
    SA *headings for individual characters and*
       classes of persons in mass media, e.g., Tarzan
       (Fictitious character) in mass media;
       Detectives in mass media.
Characters and characteristics in motion pictures
  (Not Subd Geog)
    [PN1995.9.C36]
    UF Motion picture characters
    BT Motion pictures
    SA *headings for individual character-*
       istics and classes of persons in motion
       pictures, and headings for films based on
       the name of the central character or
       characters, e.g., Cruelty in motion pictures;
       Heroes in motion pictures; Charlie Chan
       films; Bowery Boys films.
Characters and characteristics in television programs
    USE Characters and characteristics on television
Characters and characteristics on television
  (Not Subd Geog)
    UF Characters and characteristics in television
          programs
       Television characters
       Television program characters
       Television programs—Characters
       TV characters
    BT Television

    SA *headings for individual characteristics and*
       classes of persons on television; also
       headings for television programs based on
       the name of the central character or
       characters or the type of character; an
       headings for individual television program
       characters, e.g., Racism on television;
       Heroes on television; Sherlock Holmes
       television programs; Superhero television
       programs; Simpsons (Fictitious characters)
Charged coupled device cameras
    USE CCD cameras
Charge coupled devices[†]
    NT CCD Cameras
Charisma (Personality trait) in mass media
  (Not Subd Geog)
    [P96.C442]
    BT Mass media
Charlie Chan (Fictitious character)
    USE Chan, Charlie (Fictitious character)
Charlie Chan films
    BT Detective and mystery films
Charlie Chan films *[LCSH Genre]*
Chase films *[LCSH Genre]*
Cheating at video games *(May Subd Geog)*
    UF Cheating in video games
    BT Video games
Cheating in video games
    USE Cheating at video games
Cheherazade (Legendary character)
    USE Scheherazade (Legendary character)
Chemical engineering[†]
    NT Motion pictures in chemical engineering
Chick flicks
    USE Romance films
Child actors *(May Subd Geog)*
    [PN3157–PN3159]
    UF Children as actors
    BT Actors
Child psychology[†]
    NT Motion pictures in child psychology
Child sexual abuse in mass media
  (Not Subd Geog)
    BT Mass media
Child sexual abuse in motion pictures
  (Not Subd Geog)
    [PN1995.9.C39]
    BT Motion pictures
Childhood in motion pictures

[†]**Subject headings noted with a dagger contain
additional access points and subheadings that
are not pertinent to this text and are not
included here.**

USE Children in motion pictures

Children[†]
    NT Animated films and children
        Films for children
        Mass media and children
        Motion pictures and children
        Motion pictures for children
        Television advertising and children
        Television and children
        Television programs for children
        Video games and children

Children and animated films
    USE Animated films and children

Children and mass media
    USE Mass media and children

Children and motion pictures
    USE Motion pictures and children

Children and television
    USE Television and children

Children and video games
    USE Video games and children

Children as actors
    USE Child actors

Children in motion pictures *(Not Subd Geog)*
    [PN1995.9.C45]
    BT Motion pictures

Children of entertainers *(May Subd Geog)*
    UF Entertainers' children
    BT Entertainers

Children of motion picture actors and actresses
(May Subd Geog)
    BT Motion picture actors and actresses

Children's films *(May Subd Geog)*
    This heading is used as a topical heading for works about films produced especially for children. When used as a topical heading it is subdivided by the appropriate geographical, topical, and/or form subdivisions.
    UF Juvenile films
        Motion pictures for children
    BT Motion pictures
    SA *subdivision* Juvenile films *under subjects*

Children's films *[LCSH Genre]*

Children's literature[†]
    —Film and video adaptations
        UF Children's literature—Film adaptations
    —Film adaptations
        USE Children's literature—Film and video adaptations

Children's mass media *(May Subd Geog)*
    UF Children's media
        Mass media for children
    BT Mass media

    NT Television programs for children
        Videocassettes for children

Children's media
    USE Children's mass media

Children's nonbook materials
(May Subd Geog)
    UF Children's non-book materials
        Juvenile nonbook materials
    BT Nonbook materials

Children's plays[†]
    RT Children as actors

Children's television programs
(May Subd Geog)
    [PN1992.8.C46]
    This heading is used as a topical heading for works about television programs produced especially for children. When used as a topical heading it is subdivided by the appropriate geographical, topical, and/or form subdivisions.
    UF Television programs for children
    BT Television programs
    —Plots, themes, etc.

Children's television programs
    [LCSH Genre]

Chinese American entertainers
(May Subd Geog)
    UF Entertainers, Chinese American
    BT Entertainers—United States

Chinese American motion picture actors and actresses *(May Subd Geog)*
    UF Motion picture actors and actresses, Chinese American
    BT Motion picture actors and actresses—United States

Chinese Americans and mass media
(May Subd Geog)
    UF Mass media and Chinese Americans
    BT Mass media

Chinese Americans in mass media
(Not Subd Geog)
    BT Mass media

Chinese drama[†]
    NT Motion picture plays, Chinese
        Television plays, Chinese

Chinese film posters
    USE Film posters, Chinese

Chinese motion picture plays
    USE Motion picture plays, Chinese

Chinese motion pictures

[†]**Subject headings noted with a dagger contain additional access points and subheadings that are not pertinent to this text and are not included here.**

USE Motion pictures, Chinese
Chinese television plays
     USE Television plays, Chinese
Chinese Theatre (Los Angeles, Calif.)
     UF Grauman's Chinese Theatre (Los Angeles, Calif.)
          Mann's Chinese Theatre (Los Angeles, Calif.)
     BT Motion picture theaters—California
Chocobo's Dungeon (Game)
     [GV1469.35.C56]
     BT Video games
Choice of nonbook materials
     USE Selection of nonbook materials
Christian education[†]
     NT Motion pictures in Christian education
          Television in Christian education
Christian films (May Subd Geog)
     BT Religious films
Christian films [LCSH Genre]
Christian television programs
     [LCSH Genre]
Christianity in motion pictures (Not Subd Geog)
     BT Motion pictures
Christians in motion pictures
     (Not Subd Geog)
     BT Motion pictures
Christmas films (May Subd Geog)
     BT Motion pictures
Christmas films [LCSH Genre]
Christmas in motion pictures
     (Not Subd Geog)
     [PN1995.9.C5113]
     BT Motion pictures
Christmas television programs
     (May Subd Geog)
     BT Television programs
Christmas television programs
     [LCSH Genre]
Chromophotography
     USE Color photography
Chronophotography (May Subd Geog)
     NT Time-lapse cinematography
     BT Sequence photography
Church and mass media (May Subd Geog)
     UF Mass media and the church
     BT Mass media
Church work[†]
     NT Motion pictures in church work
          Video recording in church work
Cine El Cairo (Rosario, Santa Fe, Argentina)
     UF Cairo Theater (Rosario, Santa Fe, Argentina)
          El Cairo Theater (Rosario, Santa Fe, Argentina)

     BT Motion picture theaters—Argentina
Cineangiography (May Subd Geog)
     [RC683.5.C54]
     UF Videoangiocardiography
          Videometry
     BT Angiography
          Cineradiography
          Medical cinematography
Cinefluorography (May Subd Geog)
     BT Medical cinematography
          Radiology, Medical
Cinema
     USE Motion pictures
Cinema Brazil Grand Prize
     USE Grande Prêmio Cinema Brasil
Cinéma Capitole Lausanne (Lausanne, Switzerland)
     USE Capitole (Lausanne, Switzerland)
Cinema composers
     USE Film composers
Cinéma noir
     USE Film noir
Cinema organ
     USE Theater organ
Cinema Studio 4 (Zurich, Switzerland)
     USE Kino "Studio 4" (Zurich, Switzerland)
Cinema, The (Akron, Ohio)
     USE Akron Civic Theatre (Akron, Ohio)
Cinéma vérité (May Subd Geog)
     UF Direct cinema
          Truth cinema
     BT Documentary films
Cinéma vérité films [LCSH Genre]
Cinemas
     USE Motion picture theaters
Cinemascope
     USE Wide-screen processes (Cinematography)
Cinemamatographic films
     USE Motion picture films
Cinematographers (May Subd Geog)
     Here are entered works on the directors of photography who are in charge of all aspects of photography, including the lighting, for a film, television, or video production. Works on the members of a film, television, or video production crew who are responsible for the focus and movement of the camera and for composing the picture are entered under Camera operators.

[†]**Subject headings noted with a dagger contain additional access points and subheadings that are not pertinent to this text and are not included here.**

UF   Cameramen, Lighting
      Directors of photography (Cinematographers)
      Lighting cameramen
NT   Digital cinematographers
      Wildlife cinematographers
      Women cinematographers
BT   Photographers
—Credits
      UF   Credits of cinematographers
            Film credits of cinematographers
Cinematographers (Camera operators)
   USE   Camera operators
Cinematographic film
   USE   Motion picture film
Cinematographic processing
   USE   Cinematography—Processing
Cinematography *(May Subd Geog)*
   [TR845–TR899]
      Here are entered works on the technical aspects
   of making motion pictures and their projection
   onto a screen. General works on motion pictures
   themselves, including motion pictures as an art
   form, copyrighting, distribution, editing, plots,
   production, etc., are entered under Motion pictures.
   Works on the depiction of photography in motion
   pictures are entered under Photography in motion
   pictures. Works on the technical aspects of making
   video recordings, i.e., creating and storing moving
   images in an electronic form and displaying them
   on an electronic display, are entered under Video
   recording. Works on the artistic aspects of making
   video recordings are entered under Video recordings—
   Production and direction.
   UF   Home movies
         Photography—Animated pictures
         Photography—Motion pictures
   BT   Chronophotography
         Photography
   NT   Aerial cinematography
         Animation (Cinematography)
         Chronophotography
         Color cinematography
         Digital cinematography
         Front screen projection
         Industrial cinematography
         Kinetograph
         Kinetoscope
         Microcinematography
         Military cinematography
         Sports cinematography
         Television film
         Time lapse cinematography
         Trick cinematography

Wide-screen processes
   (Cinematography)
—Darkroom techniques
   USE   Cinematography—Processing
—Digital techniques
   USE   Digital cinematography
—Electronic equipment *(May Subd Geog)*
—Electronic methods
   USE   Video recording
—Equipment and supplies
   NT   Motion picture camera stabilization
         systems
         Motion picture cameras
         Motion picture film
—Exposure
   UF   Exposure, Cinematographic
—Failures *(May Subd Geog)*
   UF   Failures in cinematography
—Industrial applications
   USE   Industrial cinematography
—Lighting *(May Subd Geog)*
   UF   Motion pictures—Lighting
—Military applications
   USE   Military cinematography
—Printing processes *(May Subd Geog)*
   UF   Printing processes in cinematography
   BT   Cinematography—Processing
—Processing *(May Subd Geog)*
   UF   Cinematographic processing
         Cinematography—Darkroom technique
         Darkroom technique in cinematography
         Processing, Cinematographic
   BT   Photographic chemistry
   NT   Cinematography—Printing processes
—Scientific applications *(May Subd Geog)*
   [TR893–TR893.8]
   UF   Motion pictures—Scientific applications
   RT   Cinematography, High-speed
         Medical cinematography
—Special effects
   [TR858]
   UF   Motion pictures—Special effects
         Special effects (Cinematography)
   RT   Trick cinematography
Cinematography, Abstract
   UF   Abstract cinematography
   BT   Experimental films
Cinematography, High-speed
   UF   High-speed cinematography

†**Subject headings noted with a dagger contain
additional access points and subheadings that
are not pertinent to this text and are not
included here.**

BT Cinematography—Scientific applications
Cinematography, Industrial
    USE Industrial cinematography
Cinematography, Medical
    USE Medical cinematography
Cinematography, Submarine
    USE Underwater cinematography
Cinematography, Time-lapse
    USE Time lapse cinematography
Cinematography, Trick
    USE Trick cinematography
Cinematography, Underwater
    USE Underwater cinematography
Cinematography, Wide-screen
    USE Wide-screen processes (Cinematography)
Cinematography, Wildlife
    USE Wildlife cinematography
Cinematomicography
    USE Microcinematography
Cinemicrography
    USE Microcinematography
Cinephotomicrography
    USE Microcinematography
Cineradiography (May Subd Geog)
    [TR896.8]
    NT Cineangiography
    BT Radiography
Cinerama
    USE Wide-screen processes
           (Cinematography)
Circulation of audio-visual materials
    USE Audio-visual materials—
           Circulation
Circulation of motion pictures
    USE Motion pictures—Distribution
Circus in motion pictures (Not Subd Geog)
    BT Motion pictures
Ciro-flex camera (Not Subd Geog)
    [TR263.C5]
    BT Cameras
Cisco Kid films
    [PN1995.9.C5125]
    BT Western films
Cisco Kid films [LCSH Genre]
Cities and towns in mass media
    (Not Subd Geog)
    BT Mass media
Cities and towns in motion pictures
    (Not Subd Geog)
    [PN1995.9.C513]
    BT Motion pictures
Cities and towns in television
    USE Cities and towns on television

Cities and towns on television
    (Not Subd Geog)
    UF Cities and towns in television
    BT Television
City and town life in motion pictures
    (Not Subd Geog)
    [PN1995.9.C513]
    BT Motion pictures
City symphonies (Motion pictures)
    (May Subd Geog)
    This heading is used as a topical heading for
works about films that use a montage of images of
a city and city life to capture the essence of a
particular city. When used as a topical heading it is
subdivided by the appropriate geographical,
topical, and/or form subdivisions.
    UF City symphony films
    BT Nonfiction films
City symphonies (Motion pictures) [LCSH Genre]
City symphony films
    USE City symphonies (Motion pictures)
Cityscape photography
    USE Street photography
Civic Theatre (Akron, Ohio)
    USE Akron Civic Theatre (Akron, Ohio)
Civic Theatre (Portland, Me.)
    UF B. F. Keith's (Portland, Me.)
         Keith's (Portland, Me.)
    BT Theaters—Maine
Civilization, Ancient, in motion pictures
    (Not Subd Geog)
    BT Motion pictures
Civilization, Western[†]
    NT Motion pictures—Western influences
Civilization in motion pictures (Not Subd Geog)
    BT Motion pictures
Claremont Theater Building
  (New York, N.Y.)
    BT Commercial buildings—New York (State)
Motion picture theaters—New York (State)
Clark Kent (Fictitious character)
    USE Superman (Fictitious character)
Classification[†]
    SA subdivision Classification under subjects, e.g.,
         Language and languages—Classification;
         Stars—Classification
  —Archives
    UF Archives—Classification

[†]**Subject headings noted with a dagger contain
additional access points and subheadings that
are not pertinent to this text and are not
included here.**

—Motion pictures
    UF Motion pictures—Classification
—Non-book materials
    USE Classification—Nonbook materials
—Nonbook materials
    [Z697.N64]
    UF Classification—Non-book
        materials
Clay animation films *(May Subd Geog)*
    UF Claymation films
        Sculptmation films
    RT Animated films
Clay animation films *[LCSH Genre]*
Clay animation television programs
    [LCSH Genre]
Claymation films
    USE Clay animation films
Clergy in motion pictures *(Not Subd Geog)*
    BT Motion pictures
Clergy on television *(Not Subd Geog)*
    BT Television
Clichés in motion pictures *(Not Subd Geog)*
    BT Motion pictures
Cliffhanger films
    USE Film serials
Clio Awards
    UF American Television and Radio
        Commercials Awards
    BT Radio advertising—Awards—United States
        Television advertising—Awards—
        United States
Clips, Film
    USE Film clips
Cloak and dagger films
    USE Spy films
Close captioning
    USE Closed captioning
Close range photography
    USE Photography, Close-up
Close-up photography
    USE Photography, Close-up
Closed caption television
    USE Closed captioning
Closed caption video recordings
    USE Closed captioning
        Video recordings for the hearing impaired
Closed captioning *(May Subd Geog)*
    UF Captioning, Closed
        Close captioning
        Closed caption television
        Closed caption video recordings
        Television captioning (Closed captioning)
        Video captioning (Closed captioning)

    BT Hearing impaired—Services for
    RT Translating and interpreting
    NT Real-time closed captioning
Closed-circuit television *(May Subd Geog)*
    [TK6680]
    UF CCTV (Closed-circuit
        television)
        Television, Closed-circuit
    BT Television
    RT Intercommunication systems
        Microwave communication systems
    NT Industrial television
        Television in education
        Television in police work
Clothing and dress in motion pictures
    (Not Subd Geog)
    BT Motion pictures
Clothing and dress on television *(Not Subd Geog)*
    BT Television
Co-production (Motion pictures,
    television, etc.)
    USE Coproduction (Motion pictures,
        television, etc.)
Cocktails in motion pictures
    (Not Subd Geog)
    BT Motion pictures
Cold War in mass media *(Not Subd Geog)*
    BT Motion pictures
Cold War in motion pictures
    (Not Subd Geog)
    BT Motion pictures
Collection development (Libraries)[†]
    NT Selection of nonbook materials
Collective agreements
    USE Collective labor agreements
Collective bargaining[†]
    RT Collective labor agreements
    —Motion picture industry
        UF Motion picture industry—Collective
            bargaining
    —Television broadcasting
        (May Subd Geog)
        UF Television broadcasting—Collective
            bargaining
Collective bargaining agreements
    USE Collective labor agreements
Collective labor agreements[†]
    —Actors
        UF Actors—Collective labor agreements

[†]**Subject headings noted with a dagger contain
additional access points and subheadings that
are not pertinent to this text and are not
included here.**

————Law and legislation
    USE Collective labor agreements
—Motion picture industry
    (May Subd Geog)
    UF Motion picture industry—Collective
        labor agreements
—Television broadcasting
    (May Subd Geog)
    UF Television broadcasting—Collective
        labor agreements
College facilities[†]
    NT College television stations
College football films
    USE Football films
College life films *(May Subd Geog)*
    [PN1995.9.C543]
    BT Motion pictures
College life films *[LCSH Genre]*
College teachers in motion pictures
    (Not Subd Geog)
    [PN1995.9.C544]
    BT Motion pictures
College teachers on television
    (Not Subd Geog)
    BT Television
College television stations
    (May Subd Geog)
    UF University television stations
    BT College facilities
        Television stations
Colonel Gordon (Fictitious character)
    USE Gordon, Flash (Fictitious character)
Colonel Robert Gordon (Fictitious character)
    USE Gordon, Flash (Fictitious character
Colony wars (Game)
    [GV1469.35.C64]
    BT Video games
Color cinematography *(May Subd Geog)*
    [TR853]
    BT Cinematography
—Darkroom technique
    USE Color cinematography—
        Processing
—Printing processes *(May Subd Geog)*
    UF Color prints (Cinematography)
        Printing processes in color
           cinematography
        Prints, Color (Cinematography)
    BT Color cinematography—Processing
——Dye transfer *(May Subd Geog)*
    UF Dye transfer process in color
        cinematography
—Processing *(May Subd Geog)*

    UF Color cinematography—Darkroom
        technique
    BT Photographic chemistry
    NT Color cinematography—Printing
        processes
Color films
    USE Color photography—Films
Color motion pictures *(May Subd Geog)*
    Here are entered works on motion pictures filmed
in color, as opposed to black and white. Works on
the use of specific colors, such as red, blue, or
yellow, as an element in motion pictures are entered
under Colors in motion pictures.
    UF Colored motion pictures
        Technicolor pictures
    BT Motion pictures
Color photography *(May Subd Geog)*
    [TR510—TR525]
    UF Chromophotography
        Heliochromy
        Photography, Color
    BT Photography
    NT Hillotype
—Autochrome process
—Darkroom techniques
    USE Color photography—
        Processing
—Developing and developers
— Digital techniques
—Films
    UF Color films
        Films, Color
—Lippmann process
—Printing papers
—Printing processes
——Dye transfer
——Pigment
    USE Photography—Printing processes—
        Pigment
—Processing
—Three-color process
Color prints (Cinematography)
    USE Color cinematography—
        Printing processes
Color television *(May Subd Geog)*
    [TK6670]
    UF Television, Color
    BT Television
—Apparatus and supplies

[†]**Subject headings noted with a dagger contain
additional access points and subheadings that
are not pertinent to this text and are not
included here.**

USE   Color television—Equipment and
      supplies

—Circuits
    BT Electronic circuits
        Television circuits

—Equipment and supplies
    UF Color television—Apparatus and
        supplies

—Picture quality

—Receivers and reception
    UF Color television receivers
  — —Tariff
    USE Tariff on color television receivers

Color television receivers
   USE Color television—Receivers and reception

Colored motion pictures
   USE Color motion pictures

Coloring of motion pictures, Computer
   USE Colorization of motion pictures

Colorization of motion pictures
  (May Subd Geog)
   UF Coloring of motion pictures, Computer
      Computer coloring of motion pictures
      Motion pictures—Colorization
   BT Motion pictures

Combat television
   USE Military television

Combination televisions
   USE Television/video combinations

Comedies, Television
   USE Television comedies

Comedy[†]
   NT Comedy films

Comedy fantasy films
   USE Fantasy comedies (Motion pictures)

Comedy films *(May Subd Geog)*
   BT Motion pictures
   NT Carry On films
      Fantasy comedies (Motion pictures)
      Parody films
      Romantic comedy films
      Rural comedies
      Screwball comedy films
      Three Stooges films
      Trapalhões films

Comedy films *[LCSH Genre]*

Comedy programs
   USE Television comedies

Comedy programs, Television
   USE elevision comedies

Comedy television programs
   USE Television comedies

Comedy videos *(May Subd Geog)*

   BT Video recordings

Comedy writers, Television
   USE Television comedy writers

Comic books, strips, etc.[†]
   NT Comic strip characters in motion pictures

—Influence on mass media
    (May Subd Geog)
    NT Mass media—Influence of comic books,
        strips, etc., on

Comic strip characters in motion pictures
  (Not Subd Geog)
  [PN1995.9.C36]
   BT Comic books, strips, etc.
      Motion pictures

Comic strip superhero films
   USE Superhero films

Comic strip superheroes films
   USE Superhero films

Coming-of-age films *(May Subd Geog)*
   UF Bildungsfilms
      Rite of passage films
   BT Motion pictures

Coming-of-age films *[LCSH Genre]*

Coming-of-age television programs
  (May Subd Geog)
   BT Television programs

Coming-of-age television programs
  [LCSH Genre]

Commercial buildings[†]
   NT Claremont Theater Building
      (New York, N.Y.)

Commercial films, Television
   USE Television commercial films

Commercials, Singing
   USE Singing commercials

Commercials, Television (Advertisements)
   USE Television commercials (Advertisements)

Commercials, Television (Advertising)
   USE Television advertising

Commissario Montalbano
  (Fictitious character)
   USE Montalbano, Salvo (Fictitious character)

Commissario Montalbano television programs
  [PN1992.8.C67]
   BT Television programs

Commissario Montalbano television programs
  [LCSH Genre]

Commodore (New York, N.Y.)

[†]**Subject headings noted with a dagger contain
additional access points and subheadings that
are not pertinent to this text and are not
included here.**

USE Fillmore East (New York, N.Y.)

Communication†
   NT Local mass media
       Mass media
   SA *subdivision* Communication *under*
       ethnic roups
—Internal cooperation†
    UF Mass media—International cooperation
—Religious aspects
    NT Mass media in religion
Communication and traffic†
   NT Broadcasting
Communication in architectural design†
   NT Mass media and architecture
Communication in birth control†
   NT Mass media in birth control
Communication in politics†
   NT Mass media—Political aspects
Communication policy†
   NT Mass media policy
Communications, Military†
   NT Military television
Communism and mass media *(May Subd Geog)*
   [HX550.M35]
   BT Mass media
Communism and motion pictures
   (May Subd Geog)
   [HX550.M65]
   UF Communism and moving-pictures
       Motion pictures and communism
   BT Motion pictures
Communism and moving-pictures
   USE Communism and motion pictures
Communists in motion pictures *(Not Subd Geog)*
   BT Motion pictures
Communities in motion pictures *(Not Subd Geog)*
   BT Motion pictures
Community-access television
   USE Public-access television
Community antenna television
   USE Cable television
Community development†
   NT Mass media in community development
       Television in community development
Community media
   USE Local mass media
Community television
   USE Public-access television
Compact disc digital video
   USE Video CDs
Compact discs†
   NT Video CDs
Companies, Motion picture

USE Motion picture studios
Compilation films *[LCSH Genre]*
Compilation television programs
   [LCSH Genre]
Composers†
   NT Film composers
Composers in motion pictures
   (Not Subd geog)
   [PN 1995.9.C553]
   BT Motion pictures
Composite films
   USE Anthology films
Compulsive behavior†
   NT Television addiction
       Video game addiction
Compulsive gambling in motion pictures
   (Not Subd Geog)
   BT Motion pictures
Computer adventure games *(May Subd Geog)*
   [GV1469.22–GV1469.25]
   UF Adventure and adventurers—Computer
       games
       Adventure games, Computer
       Games, Computer adventure
   BT Adventure games
       Computer games
   SA *subdivision* Computer games *under subjects*
Computer animation *(May Subd Geog)*
   [TR897.7]
   UF Animated cartoons by computer
       Animation, Computer
       Computer-assisted film making
       Computer generated animation
   BT Animation (Cinematography)
       Computer drawing
Computer animation films
   [LCSH Genre]
Computer animation television programs
   [LCSH Genre]
Computer-assisted film making
   USE Computer animation
Computer-based multimedia information
  systems
   USE Multimedia systems
Computer coloring of motion pictures
   USE Colorization of motion pictures
Computer drawing†
   NT Computer animation
Computer games *(May Subd Geog)*

†**Subject headings noted with a dagger contain
additional access points and subheadings that
are not pertinent to this text and are not
included here.**

Here are entered works on games played on a computer. Works on the application of computers and data processing techniques to games in general, including recording statistics, setting up tournaments, etc., are entered under Games—Data processing.
   [GV1469.15–GV1469.25]
  BT Application software
      Electronic games
  NT Computer adventure games
      Computer war games
Computer-generated animation
  USE Computer animation
Computer graphics *(May Subd Geog)*†
  BT Digital video
Computer software†
  NT Interactive multimedia
Computer war games *(May Subd Geog)*
   [U310]
  UF Video war games
      War—Computer games
  BT Computer games
      War—Computer simulation
      War games
Concert films *(May Subd Geog)*
  UF In-concert films
      Live concert films
      Live-in-concert films
  BT Documentary films
  RT Musical films
  NT Rock concert films
Concert films *[LCSH Genre]*
Concert television programs *(May Subd Geog)*
This heading is used for works about television programs of musical concert performances recorded in front of a live audience. When used as a topical heading it is subdivided by the appropriate geographic, topical, and/or form subdivisions.
  UF Television concerts
  BT Television programs
Concert television programs *[LCSH Genre]*
Concrete films
  USE Abstract films
Conduct of court proceedings†
  NT Television broadcasting of court proceedings
Conferencing, Video
  USE Videoconferencing
Conflict of generations in motion pictures
  (Not Subd Geog)
  BT Motion pictures
Conspiracy in motion pictures
  (Not Subd Geog)
  BT Motion pictures

Consultants†
  NT Motion picture consultants
Consumer education†
  NT Television in consumer education
Contaflex camera *(Not Subd Geog)*
  BT Cameras
      Zeiss cameras
Contarex camera *(Not Subd Geog)*
  BT Single-lens reflex cameras
Contax camera *(Not Subd Geog)*
  RT Zeiss cameras
Contax real time system camera
  USE Contax RTS camera
Contax RTS camera *(Not Subd Geog)*
   [TR263.C]
  UF Contax real time system camera
  RT Yashica camera
      Zeiss cameras
Contests†
  NT Television game shows
      Television quiz shows
Continuity (Motion pictures, television, etc.)
  RT Motion pictures—Production and direction
      Television—Production and direction
      Video recordings—Production and direction
Continuity clerks
  USE Script clerks
Continuity girls
  USE Script clerks
Continuous motion pictures
  USE Loop films
Control (Psychology) in motion pictures
  (Not Subd Geog)
  BT Motion pictures
Conversion in motion pictures *(Not Subd Geog)*
  BT Motion pictures
Cooking shows, Television
  USE Television cooking shows
Cooking television programs
  USE Television cooking shows
Cop films
  USE Police films
Cop shows
  USE Television cop shows
Cop television shows
  USE Television cop shows
Coproduction (Motion pictures, television, etc.)
  (May Subd Geog)

†Subject headings noted with a dagger contain additional access points and subheadings that are not pertinent to this text and are not included here.

UF Co-production (Motion pictures,
        television, etc.)
    BT Motion pictures—Production and direction
        Radio—Production and direction
        Television—Production and direction
        Video recordings—Production and direction
Copyright[†]
—Audio-visual materials
        UF Audio-visual materials—Copyright
    —Broadcasting rights *(May Subd Geog)*
        UF Copyright—Radio rights
            Copyright—Television rights
            Copyright and radio
            Copyright and television
            Radio and copyright
            Television and copyright
        RT Video recordings—Fair use (Copyright)
        NT Copyright—Drama
            Copyright—Music
            Copyright—Performing rights
—Fair use
        USE Fair use (Copyright)
    —Interactive multimedia
        (May Subd Geog)
        UF Interactive multimedia—Copyright
    —Motion picture music *(May Subd Geog)*
        UF Motion picture music—Copyright
    —Motion pictures *(May Subd Geog)*
        [Z655]
        UF Copyright—Sound motion pictures
            Motion pictures—Copyright
        NT Copyright—Silent films
    —Silent films *(May Subd Geog)*
        UF Copyright—Silent motion pictures
            Silent films—Copyright
        BT Copyright—Motion pictures
—Silent motion pictures
        USE Copyright—Silent films
—Sound motion pictures
        USE Copyright—Motion pictures
—Television rights
        USE Copyright—Broadcasting rights
—Unauthorized reproduction of video
    recordings
        USE Video recordings—Pirated editions
    —Video recordings *(May Subd Geog)*
        UF Video recordings—Copyright
        RT Video recordings—Fair use (Copyright)
Copyright and audio-visual education
    (May Subd Geog)
    UF Audio-visual education and copyright
    BT Copyright infringement
        Fair use (Copyright)

Copyright and television
    USE Copyright—Broadcasting rights
Copyright infringement[†]
    NT Copyright and audio-visual education
        Fair use (Copyright)
Corporate television
    USE Industrial television
Cosmorex camera
    USE Zenith camera
Costume[†]
    Here are entered works on clothing treated as an
    artistic object, as well as works on clothing created
    for the stage, screen, or special events. Works on the
    utilitarian aspects of clothing, including works on
    how to dress, are entered under Clothing and dress.
    UF Motion pictures—Costume
Costume spectacles (Motion pictures)
    USE Epic films
Counseling[†]
    NT Mass media in counseling
        Television in counseling
Count Dracula (Fictitious character)
    USE Dracula, Count (Fictitious character)
Counterculture in motion pictures
    (Not Subd Geog)
    [PN1995.9.C57]
    BT Motion pictures
Counterculture on television
    (Not Subd Geog)
    BT Television
Country homes in motion pictures
    (Not Subd Geog)
    BT Motion pictures
Country life in motion pictures
    (Not Subd Geog)
    [PN1995.9.C58]
    BT Motion pictures
Courtroom art[†]
    BT Television broadcasting of news
Courtroom films
    USE Legal films
Courtroom television programs
    USE Legal television programs
Countercultural mass media
    USE Alternative mass media
Craps (Game)[†]
    NT Video craps
Crash-and-wreck films
    USE Car-crash films

[†]**Subject headings noted with a dagger contain
additional access points and subheadings that
are not pertinent to this text and are not
included here.**

Crash Bandicoot (Game)
    BT Video games
Crazy comedy films
    USE Screwball comedy films
Crazy Taxi (Game)
    BT Video games
Creation (Literary, artistic, etc.) in motion pictures
    (Not Subd Geog)
    BT Motion pictures
Creature features (Motion pictures)
    USE Monster films
Credit titles (Motion pictures, television, etc.)
    (May Subd Geog)
    [PN1995.9.C65 (Motion pictures)]
    Here are entered works on the lists appearing
on screen before or after a motion picture or
television program that give the names of the actors,
directors, etc. Works on lists of projects in which
actors, directors, etc., were involved are entered
under the heading for the class of persons with
subdivision Credits, e.g., Motion picture actors and
actresses—Credits. Works on the identifying words
or phrases used as names of motion pictures are
entered under Titles of motion pictures. Technical
works on the creation or addition of credit titles,
subtitles, or other printed captions for motion
pictures or television are entered under Motion
pictures—Titling or Television programs—
Titling.
    UF Titles, Credit (Motion pictures,
         television, etc.)
    BT Motion pictures
        Television
        Video recordings
Credits for actors
    USE Actors—Credits
Credits of cinematographers
    USE Cinematographers—Credits
Credits of Hispanic American motion picture actors
  and actresses
    USE Hispanic American motion picture actors and
        actresses—Credits
Credits of Hispanic American motion picture
  producers and directors
    USE Hispanic American motion picture producers
        and directors—Credits
Credits of motion picture actors and actresses
    USE Motion picture actors and actresses—
        Credits
Credits of screenwriters
    USE Screenwriters—Credits
Credits of television actors and actresses
    USE Television actors and actresses—Credits

Credits of television producers and directors
    USE Television producers and directors—
        Credits
Credits of women motion picture producers
  and directors
    USE Women motion picture producers and
        directors—Credits
Crime[†]
    NT Mass media and crime
Crime and criminals in mass media
    USE Crime in mass media
Crime and mass media
    USE Mass media and crime
Crime films *(May Subd Geog)*
    [PN1995.9.C66]
    This heading is used as a topical heading for
works about fictional films that feature the
commission and investigation of crimes. When used
as a topical heading it is subdivided by the
appropriate geographic, topical, and/or form
subdivisions.
    UF Criminal films
    BT Motion pictures
    RT Caper films
        Detective and mystery films
        Thrillers (Motion pictures)
    NT Film noir
        Gangster films
        Juvenile delinquency films
        Police films
        Prison films
Crime films *[LCSH Genre]*
Crime in mass media *(Not Subd Geog)*
    [P96.C74]
    UF Crime and criminals in mass media
    BT Mass media
Crime in television
    USE Crime on television
Crime on television *(Not Subd Geog)*
    UF Crime in television
    BT Television
Crime reenactment television programs
    USE True crime television programs
Crime shows
    USE Television crime shows
Crime television programs
    USE Television crime shows
Criminal films
    USE Crime films

[†]**Subject headings noted with a dagger contain
additional access points and subheadings that
are not pertinent to this text and are not
included here.**

Criminal investigation in mass media
  (Not Subd Geog)
    BT Mass media
Criminal justice and mass media
  USE Mass media and criminal justice
Criminal justice, Administration of[†]
    NT Mass media and criminal
          justice
Criminal investigation on television
  (Not Subd Geog)
    BT Television
Criminal shows
  USE Television crime shows
Criminal television programs
  USE Television crime shows
Critical Depth (Game)
    BT Video games
Criticism[†]
    NT Film criticism
          Mass media criticism
          Television criticism
Criticism of the mass media
  USE Mass media criticism
Critics[†]
    NT Film critics
Croft, Lara (Fictitious character) *(Not Subd Geog)*
    UF Lara Croft (Fictitious character)
          Tomb Raider (Fictitious character)
Croft, Lara (Fictitious character) in mass media
  (Not Subd Geog)
    [P96.C77]
    BT Mass media
Crosley televisions *(Not Subd Geog)*
    BT Television—Receivers and reception
Cross-dressers
  USE Male impersonators
Crossdressers
  USE Male impersonators
Crowds in motion pictures
  (Not Subd Geog)
    BT Motion pictures
Cruelty in motion pictures
  (Not Subd Geog)
    [PN1995.9.C7]
    BT Motion pictures
Crusaders of Might and Magic (Game)
    [GV1469.35.C78]
    BT Video games
Crusades in motion pictures
  (Not Subd Geog)
    BT Motion pictures
Cuban American television personalities
  (May Subd Geog)

    UF Television personalities, Cuban
          American
    BT Television personalities—
          United States
Cuban American women television personalities
  (May Subd Geog)
    UF Women television personalities, Cuban
          American
    BT Women television personalities—
          United States
Cuban film posters
  USE Film posters, Cuban
Cult classics
  USE Cult films
Cult films *(May Subd Geog)*
    Here are entered works on fiction or nonfiction
films that acquire a highly devoted but relatively
small group of fans after their release. Works on
fiction films about a particular subculture in society
are entered under the heading Subculture films,
subdivided by the appropriate geographic, topical,
and/or form subdivisions.
    UF Cult classics
          Cult movies
    BT Motion pictures
Cult films, Subculture
  USE Subculture films
Cult movies
  USE Cult films
Cultural industries[†]
    NT Broadcasting
          Motion picture industry
Cultural television programs *(May Subd Geog)*
    [PN1992.8.C84]
    When subdivided by the appropriate geographic,
topical, and/or form subdivisions, this heading is
used for works about cultural television programs.
    UF Arts television programs
    BT Television programs
Cultural television programs
    [LCSH Genre]
Culture[†]
    NT Mass media and culture
Culture and mass media
  USE Mass media and culture
Culture conflict in motion pictures
  (Not Subd Geog)
    BT Motion pictures

[†]**Subject headings noted with a dagger contain
additional access points and subheadings that
are not pertinent to this text and are not
included here.**

Culture in motion pictures *(Not Subd Geog)*
  BT Motion pictures
Curiosities and wonders in motion pictures
  (Not Subd Geog)
  BT Motion pictures
Curriculum laboratories
  USE Instructional materials centers
Cutout animation films *[LCSH Genre]*
Cyborgs in mass media *(Not Subd Geog)*
  BT Mass media
Cyborgs in motion pictures *(Not Subd Geog)*
  BT Motion pictures
Czech drama[†]
  NT Motion picture plays, Czech
Czech film posters
  USE Film posters, Czech
Czech motion picture plays
  USE Motion picture plays, Czech

Dadasaheb Phalke Award
  UF Phalke Award
  BT Motion pictures—wards—India
Dadaism in motion pictures *(Not Subd Geog)*
  BT Motion pictures
Daewoo televisions *(Not Subd Geog)*
  BT Television—Receivers and reception
Daewoo television/video combinations
  (Not Subd Geog)
  BT Television/video combinations
Dailies (Motion pictures)
  UF Rushes (Motion pictures)
Dance films *[LCSH Genre]*
Dance in motion pictures, television, etc.
  (May Subd Geog)
  [GV1779]
  Here are entered works on professional dance in motion pictures, television, etc. Works on telecast dance parties are entered under Television dance parties.
  UF Dance in television
    Dance on television
    Dancing in motion pictures, television, etc.
  BT Motion pictures
    Television
Dance in television
  USE Dance in motion pictures, television, etc.
Dance on television
  USE Dance in motion pictures, television, etc.
Dance parties[†]
  NT Television dance parties
Dance television programs *[LCSH Genre]*
Dancing in motion pictures, television, etc.
  USE Dance in motion pictures, television, etc.

Danish drama[†]
  NT Television plays, Danish
Danish television plays
  USE Television plays, Danish
Danmarks Radio Film Collection
  BT Motion picture film collections
Daredevils *(May Subd Geog)*
  BT Adventure and adventurers
    Stunt performers
Dark comedy films *[LCSH Genre]*
Dark comedy television programs
  [LCSH Genre]
Dark crime films
  USE Film noir
Dark Seed II (Game)
  [GV1469.35.D37]
  UF Darkseed II (Game)
  BT Video games
Darkroom technique in cinematography
  USE Cinematography—Processing
Darkseed II (Game)
  USE Dark Seed II (Game)
Data terminals
  USE Computer terminals
Data transmission systems[†]
  NT Automatic picture transmission
    Video telephone
De Jur motion picture camera
  (Not Subd Geog)
  BT Motion picture cameras
Dead End Kids films
  USE Bowery Boys films
Dead or Alive (Game)
  [GV1469.35.D39]
  BT Video games
Dead teenager movies
  USE Slasher films
Deaf, Films for the
  USE Films for the hearing impaired
Deaf, Video recordings for the
  USE Video recordings for the hearing impaired
Deaf in motion pictures *(Not Subd Geog)*
  [PN1995.9.D35]
  BT Motion pictures
Death in mass media *(Not Subd Geog)*
  BT Mass media
Death in motion pictures
  (Not Subd Geog)
  [PN1995.9.D37]

[†]**Subject headings noted with a dagger contain additional access points and subheadings that are not pertinent to this text and are not included here.**

BT Motion pictures
Death on television *(Not Subd Geog)*
　　[PN1992.8.D4]
　　BT Television
Deathtrap Dungeon (Game)
　　[GV1469.35.D4]
　　BT Video games
Debates and debating in mass media
　　(Not Subd Geog)
　　[P96.D38]
　　BT Mass media
Deception (Game)
　　[GV1469.35.D43]
　　BT Video games
Decision making in motion pictures
　　(Not Subd Geog)
　　BT Motion pictures
Deejays, Video
　　USE Video jockeys
Deep-sea photography
　　USE Underwater photography
Defeat (Psychology) in motion pictures
　　(Not Subd Geog)
　　BT Motion pictures
Degrassi television programs
　　[PN1992.8.D43]
　　BT Television programs
DeGrassi television programs
　　[LCSH Genre]
Demonology in motion pictures
　　(Not Subd Geog)
　　UF Demons in motion pictures
　　BT Motion pictures
Demons in motion pictures
　　USE Demonology in motion pictures
Dentistry[†]
　　NT Motion pictures in dentistry
　　　　Television in dentistry
Descriptive video (Service for people with visual
　　disabilities)
　　USE Video description
Design[†]
　—Awards[†]
　　　NT BDA International Design Awards
Desire in motion pictures *(Not Subd Geog)*
　　BT Motion pictures
Destrega (Game)
　　[GV1469.35.D46]
　　BT Video games
Detective and mystery films
　　(May Subd Geog)
　　RT Crime films
　　　　Police films

　　NT Charlie Chan films
　　　　Sherlock Holmes films
Detective and mystery films *[LCSH Genre]*
Detective and mystery television programs
　　(May Subd Geog)
　　[PN1992.8.D48]
　　BT Television programs
　　NT Sherlock Holmes television programs
Detective and mystery television programs
　　[LCSH Genre]
Detective teams in motion pictures
　　(Not Subd Geog)
　　BT Motion pictures
Detective teams on television *(Not Subd Geog)*
　　BT Television
Detectives in mass media *(Not Subd Geog)*
　　[P96.D4]
　　BT Mass media
Developmental reading[†]
　　NT Reading films
Deviant behavior in mass media *(Not Subd Geog)*
　　BT Mass media
Devil in motion pictures *(Not Subd Geog)*
　　[PN1995.9.D46]
　　BT Motion pictures
Devil May Cry 2 (Game)
　　UF DMC2 (Game)
　　BT Video games
Diagnostic services[†]
　　NT Medical screening
Dialogue in motion pictures *(Not Subd Geog)*
　　[PN1995.9.D49]
　　UF Film dialogue
　　　　Movie dialogue
　　BT Motion pictures
Diddy Kong Racing (Game)
　　[GV1469.35.D54]
　　BT Video games
Difference (Philosophy) in motion pictures
　　(Not Subd Geog)
　　BT Motion pictures
Digital cameras *(May Subd Geog)*
　　[TR256]
　　UF Digital imaging cameras
　　BT Cameras
　　　　Photography—Electrical equipment
　　NT Apple QuickTake camera
　　　　Canon digital cameras

[†]**Subject headings noted with a dagger contain
additional access points and subheadings that
are not pertinent to this text and are not
included here.**

Konica Minolta digital cameras
Leica digital cameras
Nikon digital cameras
Sigma digital cameras
Sony digital cameras
—**Modification** *(May Subd Geog)*
UF Modification of digital cameras
Digital cinematographers
(May Subd Geog)
BT Cinematographers
Digital cinematography *(May Subd Geog)*
[TR860]
Here are entered works on using digital
technology to assist in making motion pictures.
Works on using digital technology to create or
process moving images for inclusion in computer
programs are entered under Digital video. Works on
using digital technology to send moving images one
way over a communication or information system
through cable or electromagnetic waves are
entered under Digital television.
UF Cinematography—Digital techniques
Digital filmmaking
Digital moviemaking
BT Cinematography
Digital communications[†]
NT Digital television
RT Digital media
Digital compact discs
USE Compact discs
Digital electronics[†]
NT Portable media players
Digital filmmaking
USE Digital cinematography
Digital imaging cameras
USE Digital cameras
Digital media *(May Subd Geog)*
UF Electronic media
BT Mass media

RT Digital communications
Online journalism
NT Digital video
—**Editing**
BT Editing
Digital motion video
USE Digital video
Digital moviemaking
USE Digital cinematography
Digital television *(Not Subd Geog)*
BT Digital communications
Television
NT Apple TV (Digital media receiver)

Digital versatile discs
USE DVDs
Digital video *(May Subd Geog)*
[TK6680.5–TK6687]
UF Digital motion video
PC video
Video, Digital
BT Computer graphics
Digital media
Image processing—Digital techniques
Interactive multimedia
Multimedia systems
NT Interactive video
—**Standards**
MT MPEG (Video coding standard)
Digital video discs
USE DVD-Video discs
Digital video jockeys
USE Video jockeys
Digital video recorders
USE Digital video tape recorders
Digital video tape recorders
(May Subd Geog)
UF Digital video recorders
Digital VTR
DVTR (Video tape recorders)
BT Video tape recorders
Digital videodiscs
USE DVD-Video discs
Digital VTR
USE Digital video tape recorders
Dinners and dining in motion pictures
(Not Subd Geog)
[PN1995.9.D52]
BT Motion pictures
Dino Crisis (Game)
[GV1469.35.D58]
BT Video games
Dinosaurs in mass media *(Not Subd Geog)*
[P96.M6]
BT Mass media
Dinosaurs in motion pictures
(Not Subd Geog)
[PN1995.9.D53]
BT Motion pictures
Direct broadcast satellite television
(May Subd Geog)
[TK6677]

[†]**Subject headings noted with a dagger contain
additional access points and subheadings that
are not pertinent to this text and are not
included here.**

UF Direct-to-home satellite television
    Home satellite television
    Satellite television, Direct broadcast
    Satellite television, Home
BT Earth stations (Satellite
       telecommunication)
    Home video systems
    Television broadcasting

—Scrambling systems
    BT Scrambling systems
        (Telecommunication)

Direct cinema
   USE Cinéma vérité
Direct to home satellite television
   USE Direct broadcast satellite television
Direction of motion pictures
   USE Motion pictures—Production and direction
Direction (Performing arts)
   USE Performing arts—Production and direction
Directors, Motion picture
   USE Motion picture producers and directors
Directors, Television
   USE Television producers and directors
Directors of photography (Cinematographers)
   USE Cinematographers

Disaster films *(May Subd Geog)*
   This heading is used as a topical heading for works about films that feature a man-made or natural calamity that places people in imminent danger. When used as a topical heading it is subdivided by the appropriate geographical, topical, and/or form subdivisions.
   UF Catastrophe films
      Disaster movies
   BT Motion pictures

—History and criticism
    UF Disasters in motion pictures

Disaster films *[LCSH Genre]*
Disaster movies
   USE Disaster films

Disaster television programs *[LCSH Genre]*
Disasters in motion pictures
   USE Disaster films—History and criticism
Disc jockeys, Video
   USE Video jockeys
Discs, Compact
   USE Compact discs
Discs, Video
   USE Video discs

Diseases in motion pictures
  (Not Subd Geog)
  [PN1995.9.D56]
  BT Motion pictures

Disk jockeys, Video
   USE Video jockeys
Disks, Compact
   USE Compact discs
Disks, Video
   USE Videodiscs
Display cards (Motion picture advertising)
   USE Lobby cards
Display systems, Television
   USE Television display systems
Display terminals, Video
   USE Video display terminals
Display terminals, Visual
   USE Video display terminals

Disposable cameras *(May Subd Geog)*
   UF Single-use cameras
   BT Cameras

Distance education[†]
   NT Television in education
Distribution of motion pictures
   USE Motion pictures—Distribution
DJs, Video
   USE Video jockeys
DMC2 (Game)
   USE Devil May Cry 2 (Game)
Doctor films (Motion pictures)
   USE Medical films (Motion pictures)
Doctor Frankenstein (Fictitious character)
   USE Frankenstein (Fictitious character)

Doctor Mabuse films *(May Subd Geog)*
   [PN1995.9.D58]
   UF Doktor Mabuse films
      Dr. Mabuse films
   BT Motion pictures

Doctor Mabuse films *[LCSH Genre]*
Doctor television programs
   USE Medical television programs
Doctrine of fairness (Broadcasting)
   USE Fairness doctrine (Broadcasting)
Documentaries (Motion pictures)
   USE Documentary films
Documentaries, Fake (Motion pictures)
   USE Documentary-style films
Documentaries, Television
   USE Documentary television programs
Documentaries, Video
   USE Documentary videos

Documentary films *(May Subd Geog)*

[†]**Subject headings noted with a dagger contain additional access points and subheadings that are not pertinent to this text and are not included here.**

This heading is used as a topical heading for works about films that are intended to impart knowledge and information, including those for classroom viewing. When used as a topical heading it is subdivided by the appropriate geographic, topical, and/or form subdivisions. Works about the use of motion pictures in education are entered under Motion pictures in education.

  UF Documentaries, Motion picture
      Factual films
      Motion picture documentaries
  NT Cinéma vérité
      Concert films
      Educational films
      Ethnographic films
      Industrial films
      Travelogues (Motion pictures)
  BT Documentary mass media
      Nonfiction films
  RT Actualities (Motion pictures)
—Direction
      USE Documentary films—Production
           and direction
—**Distribution**
—**Production and direction**
      (May Subd Geog)
      UF Documentary films—Direction
Documentary films *[LCSH Genre]*
Documentary films, Fake
  USE Documentary-style films
Documentary films, Fictionalized
  USE Documentary-style films
Documentary films, Mock
  USE Documentary-style films
Documentary mass media
  (May Subd Geog)
  [P96.D62]
  BT Mass media
  RT Documentary films
  NT Documentary television programs
      Documentary videos
      Photography, Documentary
      Reportage literature
Documentary mass media and the arts
  (May Subd Geog)
  [NX180.D63]
  UF Arts and documentary mass media
  BT Arts
Documentary programs, Television
  USE Documentary television programs
Documentary-style films *(May Subd Geog)*
  [PN1995.9.D62]

This heading is used as a topical heading for works about fictional films made to resemble documentary films. When used as a topical heading it is subdivided by the appropriate geographical, topical, and/or form subdivisions.

  UF Documentaries, Fake (Motion pictures)
      Documentary films, Fake
      Documentary films, Fictionalized
      Documentary films, Mock
      Fake documentaries (Motion pictures)
      Fake documentary films
      Fictionalized documentary films
      Mock documentary films
      Mockumentaries
      Mockumentary films
      Pseudo-documentary films
      Semidocumentary films
  BT Motion pictures
Documentary-style films *[LCSH Genre]*
Documentary-style television programs
      [LCSH Genre]
Documentary television programs
  (May Subd Geog)
  UF Bias in documentary television programs
      Documentaries, Television
      Documentary programs, Television
      Documentary videos
      Telementaries
      Television documentaries
      Television documentary programs
      Video recordings, Documentary
  BT Documentary mass media
      Nonfiction television programs
  RT Educational television programs
      Ethnographic television programs
      Travelogues (Television programs)
—Direction
      USE Documentary television programs—
           Production and direction
—**Objectivity** *(May Subd Geog)*
      UF Bias in documentary television programs
      BT Objectivity
—**Production and direction**
      (May Subd Geog)
      UF Documentary television programs—
           Direction
Documentary television programs
  [LCSH Genre]
Documentary videos *(May Subd Geog)*

†**Subject headings noted with a dagger contain additional access points and subheadings that are not pertinent to this text and are not included here.**

UF Documentaries, Video
Factual videos
Nonfiction videos
Video documentaries
BT Documentary mass media
Video recordings
RT Travelogues (Motion pictures)
—**Authorship**
Dogs in motion pictures *(Not Subd Geog)*
BT Motion pictures
Dogs in television
USE Dogs on television
Dogs on television *(Not Subd Geog)*
UF Dogs in television
BT Animals on television
Television
Working dogs
Doktor Mabuse films
USE Doctor Mabuse films
Domestics on television *(Not Subd Geog)*
BT Television
Don Camillo films
[PN1995.9.D625]
BT Motion pictures
Don Giovanni (Legendary character)
USE Don Juan (Legendary character)
Don Juan
USE Don Juan (Legendary character)
Don Juan (Legendary character)
(Not Subd Geog)
UF Don Giovanni (Legendary character)
Don Juan
Juan, Don (Legendary character)
Maraña, Don Juan de (Legendary
character)
Tenorio, Don Juan de (Legendary character)
BT Folklore—Spain
Don Juan films *(May Subd Geog)*
[PN1995.9.D63]
BT Motion pictures
Don Juan television programs
(May Subd Geog)
BT Television programs
Donkey Kong (Game)
[GV1469.35.D66]
BT Video games
Doom 64 (Game)
[GV1469.35.D68]
BT Nintendo video games)
Doppelgänger in motion pictures
USE Doubles in motion pictures
Doppelgängers in motion pictures
USE Doubles in motion pictures

Doubles in motion pictures
(Not Subd Geog)
NT Doppelgänger in motion pictures
Doppelgängers in motion pictures
BT Motion pictures
Dr. Frankenstein (Fictitious character)
USE Frankenstein (Fictitious character)
Dr. Mabuse films
USE Doctor Mabuse films
Dracula, Count (Fictitious character)
(Not Subd Geog)
UF Count Dracula
(Fictitious character)
Dracula films *(May Subd Geog)*
[PN1995.9.D64]
BT Vampire films
Drag kings
USE Male impersonators
Dragon Force (Game)
[GV1469.35.D72]
BT Video games
Dragon Warrior (Game)
BT Video games
Dragon's Lair (Game)
[GV1469.35.D73]
BT Video games
Drama[†]
RT Acting
NT Motion picture plays
Television plays
—**Publishing** *(May Subd Geog)*
NT Photoplay editions
—**Therapeutic use**
UF Acting—Therapeutic use
Drama and education[†]
RT Child actors
Drama in education[†]
RT Acting
Dramatic criticism[†]
NT Television criticism
Dramatic education
USE Acting—Study and teaching
Dramatic films
USE Feature films
Dramatic music[†]
RT Motion picture music
Musicals
Dramatic-narrative films
USE Fiction films

[†]**Subject headings noted with a dagger contain
additional access points and subheadings that
are not pertinent to this text and are not
included here.**

Dramatists[†]
  BT Authors
Dreams in motion pictures
  (Not Subd Geog)
  BT Motion pictures
Drifters in motion pictures
  (Not Subd Geog)
  [PN1995.9.D68]
  BT Motion pictures
Drinking in motion pictures
  (Not Subd Geog)
  [PN1995.9.D75]
  BT Motion pictures
Drinking in television
  USE Drinking on television
Drinking of alcoholic beverages in motion pictures
  (Not Subd Geog)
  BT Motion pictures
Drinking of alcoholic beverages in television
  USE Drinking on television
Drinking on television *(Not Subd Geog)*
  UF Drinking in television
      Drinking of alcoholic beverages
        in television
  BT Television
Drive-in facilities
  USE Drive-in theaters
Drive-in theaters *(May Subd Geog)*
  UF Drive-in facilities
  BT Motion picture theaters
Drug abuse[†]
  NT Drugs and mass media
Drug abuse in mass media
  USE Drugs and mass media
Drugs and mass media
  (May Subd Geog)
  UF Drug abuse in mass media
  BT Drug abuse
      Mass media
Drugs and motion pictures *(May Subd Geog)*
  UF Motion pictures and drugs
  BT Motion pictures
Drugs in motion pictures *(Not Subd Geog)*
  [PN1995.9.D78]
  BT Motion pictures
Dryden Theater (Rochester, N.Y.)
  USE Dryden Theatre (Rochester, N.Y.)
Dryden Theatre (Rochester, N.Y.)
  UF Dryden Theater (Rochester, N.Y.)
      Dryden Theatre at George Eastman House
        (Rochester, N.Y.)
  BT Motion picture theaters—
      New York (State)

Dryden Theatre at George Eastman House
  (Rochester, N.Y.)
  USE Dryden Theatre (Rochester, N.Y.)
Dubbing of motion pictures
  (May Subd Geog)
  [TR886.7]
  UF Dubbing of motion pictures
      Motion pictures—Dubbing
  BT Motion pictures
      Translating and interpreting
Dubbing of television programs
  (May Subd Geog)
  BT Television programs
      Translating and interpreting
Duke Nukem (Game)
  [GV1469.35.D84]
  BT Video games
DVD players *(May Subd Geog)*
  [TK7882.D93]
  UF Players, DVD
  BT High-fidelity sound systems
      Home video systems
      Television/video combinations
DVD technology
  USE DVDs
DVD-Video discs *(May Subd Geog)*
  UF Digital video discs
      Digital videodiscs
      DVD videodiscs
  BT DVDs
      Videodiscs
DVD videodiscs
  USE DVD-Video discs
DVDs *(May Subd Geog)*
  UF Digital versatile discs
      DVD technology
  BT Optical discs
  NT Cataloging of DVDs
      DVD-Video discs
  —Handling *(May Subd Geog)*
      UF Handling of DVDs
DVTR (Video tape recorders)
  USE Digital video tape recorders
Dwarfs in motion pictures *(Not Subd Geog)*
  UF Midgets in motion pictures
  BT Motion pictures
Dye transfer process in color cinematography
  USE Color cinematography—Printing processes—
      Dye transfer

[†]**Subject headings noted with a dagger contain
additional access points and subheadings that
are not pertinent to this text and are not
included here.**

Dynasty Warriors (Game)
  [GV1469.35.D95]
  BT Video games
Dystopia films
  USE Dystopian films
Dystopian films *(May Subd Geog)*
  UF Dystopia films
  BT Science fiction films
  NT Planet of the Apes films
Dystopian films *[LCSH Genre]*

Earth stations (Satellite telecommunication)[†]
  NT Direct broadcast satellite television
Earth Worm Jim (Game)
  [G1469.35.E72]
  UF Earthworm Jim (Game)
  BT Video games
East and West in motion pictures
  (Not Subd Geog)
  BT Motion pictures
East Europeans in motion pictures
  (Not Subd Geog)
  BT Motion pictures
East Indian diaspora in motion pictures
  (Not Subd Geog)
  BT Motion pictures
East Indian motion pictures
  USE Motion pictures, Indic
Eastside Kids films
  USE Bowery Boys films
Ecology in motion pictures *(Not Subd Geog)*
  BT Motion pictures
Economic development[†]
  NT Mass media in economic development
Editing[†]
  Here are entered works on the editing of books
  and texts. Works on editing of newspapers and
  periodicals are entered under Journalism—Editing.
  Works on edition of other materials are entered
  under the subject with subdivision Editing.
  NT Digital media—Editing
      Motion picture plays—Editing
      Motion pictures—Editing
      Television commercial films—Editing
      Television commercials (Advertisements)—
        Editing
      Television scripts—Editing
      Video tapes—Editing
Editing of television commercial films
  USE Television commercial films—Editing
Editing of television commercials
  USE Television commercials (Advertisements)—
        Editing

Editors *(May Subd Geog)*
  NT Motion picture editors
      Story editors (Motion pictures)
Editors, Motion pictures
  USE Motion picture editors
Edixa camera *(Not Subd Geog)*
  BT Cameras
Education[†]
  NT Mass media and education
      Mass media in education
      Video discs in education
      Video tapes in education
  —Audio-visual aids
      NT Filmstrips in education
  —Broadcasting
      USE Educational broadcasting
Education, Elementary[†]
  NT Television in elementary education
Education, Higher[†]
  NT Motion pictures in higher education
      Television in higher education
Education, Secondary[†]
  NT Television in secondary education
Education and mass media
  USE Mass media and education
Education in mass media *(May Subd Geog)*
  [P96.E29]
  BT Mass media
Education in motion pictures
  (Not Subd Geog)
  BT Motion pictures
Education, Higher[†]
  NT Motion pictures in higher education
Educational broadcasting *(May Subd Geog)*
  [LB1044.8]
  UF Broadcasting, Educational
      Education—Broadcasting
  BT Public broadcasting
  —Law and legislation *(May Subd Geog)*
      BT Educational law and legislation
Educational broadcasting in adult education
  (May Subd Geog)
  BT Radio in adult education
      Television in adult education
Educational films *(May Subd Geog)*
  This heading is used as a topical heading for
  works about films that are intended to impart
  knowledge and information, including those for

[†]**Subject headings noted with a dagger contain
additional access points and subheadings that
are not pertinent to this text and are not
included here.**

classroom viewing. When used as a topical heading it is subdivided by the appropriate geographic, topical, and/or form subdivisions. Works about the use of motion pictures in education are entered under Motion pictures in education.

    UF Informational films
    BT Documentary films
    NT Science films
        Social guidance films

Educational films *[LCSH Genre]*
Educational law and legislation†
    NT Audio-visual education—Law and legislation
        Educational broadcasting
        Television in education—Law and legislation
        Video tapes in education—Law and legislation

Educational materials industry
    USE Instructional materials industry
Educational media
    USE Teaching—Aids and devices
Educational media, Cataloging of
    USE Cataloging of educational media
Educational media centers
    USE Instructional materials centers
Educational media personnel
    USE Instructional materials personnel
Educational media programs
    USE Media programs (Education)
Educational technology†
    NT Audio-visual education
        Media programs (Education)
Educational television broadcasting
    USE Television in education
Educational television programs
(May Subd Geog)

This heading is used as a topical heading for works about television programs that are intended to impart knowledge and information, including those for classroom viewing. Works about television programs that use a structured format to teach or train the audience are entered under Instructional television programs. When used as topical headings they are subdivided by the appropriate geographic, topical, and/or form subdivisions.

    UF Informational television programs
    RT Documentary television programs
    NT Science television programs

Educational television programs
[LCSH Genre]
Educational television stations *(May Subd Geog)*
    BT Television in education

    RT Television stations
Educational videos *(May Subd Geog)*

Here are entered video recordings intended for teaching and informational purposes, especially those made for classroom viewing. Video recordings designed to impart skills or techniques to general audiences, typically in a "how-to" manner, are entered under Instructional videos. Works on the use of video tapes in education are entered under Video tapes in education.

    UF Informational videos
    BT Video recordings
    NT Nature videos
Educators†
    NT Mass media and educators
Educators and mass media
    USE Mass media and educators
Egyptian Theater (Boise, Idaho)
    USE Egyptian Theatre (Boise, Idaho)
Egyptian Theatre (Boise, Idaho)
    UF Ada Theatre (Boise, Idaho)
        Egyptian Theater (Boise, Idaho)
    BT Motion picture theaters—Idaho
Egyptian Theatre (Coos Bay, Ore.)
    BT Motion picture theaters—Oregon
Ehrgeiz (Game)
    [GV1469.35.E74]
    BT Video games
El Cairo Theater (Rosario, Santa Fe, Argentina)
    USE Cine El Cairo (Rosario, Santa Fe, Argentina)
Election law†
    NT Equal time rule (Broadcasting)
Electric eye cameras
    UF Automatic cameras
    BT Cameras
    NT Fujica camera
Electric lamps†
    NT Motion picture projectors—Light sources
Electrography
    USE Electronography
Electron beams
    NT Television—Magnetic deflection systems
Electronic art
    USE Video art
Electronic Arts Urban Strike (Game)
    USE Urban Strike (Game)

†**Subject headings noted with a dagger contain additional access points and subheadings that are not pertinent to this text and are not included here.**

Electronic cameras
   [TR882]
   UF Electronic motion picture cameras
   BT Electronography
       Motion picture cameras
       Photography—Electronic equipment
   NT Television cameras
Electronic cinematography
   USE Video recording
Electronic circuits†
   NT Color television—Circuits
Electronic flash photography
   [TR606]
   UF Flash photography, Electronic
       Photography, Electronic flash
   BT Photography, Flash-light
       Photography, High-speed
Electronic games *(May Subd Geog)*
   [GV1469.15–GV1469.25]
   BT Electronic toys
       Games
   NT Computer games
       Video games
Electronic games industry
   BT Electronic industries
       Toy industry
Electronic industries†
   NT Audio-visual equipment industry
       Electronic games industry
Electronic interference†
   NT Television—Interference
Electronic media
   USE Digital media
Electronic motion picture cameras
   USE Electronic cameras
Electronic moviemaking
   USE Video recordings—Production and direction
Electronic photography
   USE Electronography
Electronic program guides (Television)
   (May Subd Geog)
   UF Electronic television program guides
       EPGs (Electronic program guides)
       Interactive program guides (Television)
       IPGs (Interactive program guides)
   BT Information display systems
   RT Television programs
Electronic systems†
   NT Television
Electronic television program guides
   USE Electronic program guides (Television)
Electronic video endoscopy
   USE Video endoscopy

Electronography
   UF Electrography
       Electronic photography
       Photography, Electronic
   BT Electrooptical photography
       Image intensifiers
       Phototypesetting
   NT Electronic cameras
Electrooptical photography *(May Subd Geog)*
   UF Photoelectronic imaging
       Photography, Electrooptical
   BT Optoelectronics
       Photography
   NT Electronography
Electrophotography *(May Subd Geog)*
   [TR1035–TR1045]
   BT Optoelectronics
       Photography
       Photomechanical processes
Elocution†
   RT Acting
Embassy Theatre (Fort Wayne, Ind.)
   UF Embassy Theater and Indiana Hotel
         (Fort Wayne, Ind.)
       Emboyd Theatre (Fort Wayne, Ind.)
   BT Hotels—Indiana
       Motion picture theaters—Indiana
Embassy Theater and Indiana Hotel
  (Fort Wayne, Ind.)
   USE Embassy Theatre (Fort Wayne, Ind.)
Emboyd Theatre (Fort Wayne, Ind.)
   USE Embassy theatre (Fort Wayne, Ind.)
Emerson televisions *(Not Subd Geog)*
   BT Television—Receivers and reception
Emerson videocassette recorders
   (Not Subd Geog)
   BT Videocassette recorders
Emigration and immigration in motion pictures
   (Not Subd Geog)
   [PN1995.9.E44]
   BT Motion pictures
Emmy awards *(May Subd Geog)*
   NT Television broadcasting—Awards—
         United States
Emotions in motion pictures
   (Not Subd Geog)
   BT Motion pictures
Emperors in motion pictures *(Not Subd Geog)*

†**Subject headings noted with a dagger contain
additional access points and subheadings that
are not pertinent to this text and are not
included here.**

BT Motion pictures

Endoscopy[†]
NT Video endoscopy

English drama[†]
NT Motion picture plays, English
Television plays, English

English fiction[†]
—Film adaptations
USE English fiction—Film and video
adaptations
—Film and video adaptions
UF English fiction—Film adaptations

English language[†]
—Audio-visual instruction
USE English language—Study and teaching—
Audio-visual instruction
—Films for foreign speakers
BT English language—Study and teaching—
Foreign speakers—Audio-visual aids
—Films for French [Spanish, etc.]
BT English language—Study and teaching—
Foreign speakers—Audio-visual aids
—Study and teaching
— —Audio-visual aids
Here are entered films and sound or video
recordings as media of language instruction.
BT English language—Study and
teaching—
Audio-visual instruction
—Audio-visual instruction
Here are entered discussions of films and of
sound or video recordings as media of language
instruction.
UF English language—Audio-visual
instruction
BT Audio-visual education
NT English language—Study and teaching—
Audio-visual aids
—Foreign speakers—Audio-visual aids
NT English language—Films for foreign
speakers
English language—Films for French
[Spanish, etc.] speakers

English literature[†]
—Adaptations
NT English literature—Film and video
adaptations
—Film and video adaptations
UF English literature—Television adaptations
English literature—Films for French
Spanish, etc.] speakers
BT English literature—Adaptations
—Television adaptations

USE English literature—Film and video
adaptations
—Video and film adaptations
USE English literature—Film and video
adaptations
English motion picture plays
USE Motion picture plays, English
English television plays
USE Television plays, English

Entertainers[†]
NT Actors
Blackface entertainers
Blacklisting of entertainers
Children of entertainers
Collective bargaining—Entertainers
—Blacklisting
USE Blacklisting of entertainers
—Collective bargaining
USE Collective bargaining—Entertainers
—United States
NT Chinese American entertainers
Entertainers, Blackface
USE Blackface entertainers
Entertainers, Chinese American
USE Chinese American entertainers
Entertainers' children
USE Children of entertainers

Entertainers in motion pictures *(Not Subd Geog)*
[PN1995.9.E77]
BT Motion pictures
Entertainment films
USE Fiction films
Entertainment systems, Home
USE Home entertainment systems
Environment and mass media
USE Mass media and the environment

Environmental films *(May Subd Geog)*
BT Motion pictures

Environmental films *[LCSH Genre]*

Environmentalism in mass media
(Not Subd Geog)
BT Mass media

Environmentalism in motion pictures
(Not Subd Geog)
BT Motion pictures
EPGs (Electronic program guides)
USE Electronic program guides (Television)

Epic films *(May Subd Geog)*

[†]**Subject headings noted with a dagger contain
additional access points and subheadings that
are not pertinent to this text and are not
included here.**

This heading is used as a topical heading for works about films that employ large casts and lavish sets to depict action on a grand scale. When used as a topical heading it is subdivided by the appropriate geographical, topical, and/or form subdivisions.

    UF Costume spectacles (Motion pictures)
        Film epics
        Heroic films
        Monumental films
        Spectacles (Motion pictures)
        Spectaculars (Motion pictures
    BT Motion pictures

Epic films *[LCSH Genre]*

Epic television programs *[LCSH Genre]*

Episode films
  USE Film serials
       Anthology films

Episodic films
  USE Anthology films

Equal time rule (Broadcasting)
  (May Subd Geog)

    Here are entered works dealing with the requirement that equal opportunities for broadcasting be afforded to all legally qualified candidates for public office if any one such candidate is permitted to broadcast. Works dealing with the requirement that broadcasters presenting one side of a controversial issue of public importance must afford reasonable opportunity for the presentation of contrasting views are entered under Fairness doctrine (Broadcasting).

    UF Equal time rule (Broadcasting)—Law and
        legislation
        Rule of equal time (Broadcasting)
    BT Broadcasting policy
        Election law
        Radio in politics
        Right of reply
        Television in politics
    RT Fairness doctrine (Broadcasting)
—Law and legislation
    USE Equal time rule (Broadcasting)

Ernemann cameras *(Not Subd Geog)*
  [TR263.E75]
    BT Cameras

Erotic film festivals *(May Subd Geog)*
    BT Film festivals

Erotic films *(May Subd Geog)*
  [PN1995.9.S45]
    UF Adult films (Erotic films)
    BT Erotica
        Motion pictures

    RT Pornographic films
        Sex in motion pictures
—Direction
    USE Erotic films—Production and direction
—Production and direction
  (May Subd Geog)
    UF Erotic films—Direction

Erotic films *[LCSH Genre]*

Erotic television programs
  [LCSH Genre]

Erotic videos *(May Subd Geog)*
    UF Adult videos
        Porn videos
        X-rated videos
    BT Erotica
        Video recordings
    NT Gay erotic videos

Erotica[†]
    UF Eroticism
    NT Erotic films
        Erotic videos

Eroticism
  USE Erotica

Errors[†]
    NT Motion picture errors

Eskimos in motion pictures *(Not Subd Geog)*
  [PN1995.9.E83]
    BT Motion pictures

Espionage films
  USE Spy films

Espionage television programs
  USE Spy television programs

Ethics in motion pictures *(Not Subd Geog)*
    BT Motion pictures

Ethnic broadcasting *(May Subd Geog)*
  [PN1990.9.E74]
    UF Minority broadcasting
    BT Broadcasting
        Ethnic mass media
    NT Ethnic television broadcasting

Ethnic television programs
  [LCSH Genre]

Ethnic mass media *(May Subd Geog)*
  [PN94.5.M55]
    UF Minority mass media
        Multicultural mass media
    BT Mass media
    NT Ethnic broadcasting
—United States

[†]**Subject headings noted with a dagger contain additional access points and subheadings that are not pertinent to this text and are not included here.**

NT   African American mass media
     Asian American mass media
     Hispanic American mass media

Ethnic relations[†]
   NT   Mass media and ethnic relations
Ethnic relations and mass media
   USE   Mass media and ethnic relations

Ethnic television broadcasting
   (May Subd Geog)
   [PN1992.8.E84]
   UF   Minority television
      broadcasting
   BT   Ethnic broadcasting
      Television broadcasting

Ethnic television programs
   [LCSH Genre]

Ethnicity in motion pictures
   (Not Subd Geog)
   BT   Motion pictures

Ethnographic films *(May Subd Geog)*
   When subdivided by the appropriate geographic, topical, and/or form subdivisions, this heading is used for works about ethnographic films.
   UF   Anthropological films
      Ethnological films
   BT   Documentary films

Ethnographic films *[LCSH Genre]*

Ethnographic television programs
   (May Subd Geog)
   UF   Anthropological television programs
      Ethnological television
       programs
   RT   Documentary television programs

Ethnographic television programs
   [LCSH Genre]

Ethnographic videos
   (May Subd Geog)
   UF   Anthropological videos
      Ethnological videos
   BT   Documentary videos

Ethnological films
   USE   Ethnographic films

Ethnological television programs
   USE   Ethnographic television programs

Ethnological videos
   USE   Ethnographic videos

Etiquette[†]
   NT   Motion picture theater etiquette
   ETV   (Educational television)
   USE   Television in education

Eugenics in motion pictures *(Not Subd Geog)*
   BT   Motion pictures

Europe[†]

NT   Motion pictures—European influences

European drama[†]
   NT   Motion picture plays, European
European motion picture plays
   USE   Motion picture plays, European
Eurowesterns
   USE   Spaghetti Westerns

Evangelistic work[†]
   NT   Motion pictures in evangelistic work
      Video tapes in evangelistic work

Evidence (Law)[†]
   NT   Video tapes in courtroom proceedings

Evil in motion pictures *(Not Subd Geog)*
   BT   Motion pictures
      Good and evil

Evolution in motion pictures *(Not Subd Geog)*
   [PN1995.9.E94]
   BT   Motion pictures

Evolution on television *(Not Subd Geog)*
   BT   Television

EXA camera *(Not Subd Geog)*
   BT   Cameras
Excerpts, Film
   USE   Film excerpts
Exhibitor's campaign manuals (Motion picture advertising)
   USE   Pressbooks
Exiled motion picture actors and actresses
   USE   Expatriate motion picture actors and actresses

Exiles[†]
   NT   Expatriate motion picture actors and actresses
      Expatriate motion picture producers and directors

Existentialism in motion pictures
   (Not Subd Geog)
   BT   Motion pictures

Exoticism in motion pictures
   (Not Subd Geog)
   BT   Motion pictures

Expatriate motion picture actors and actresses
   (May Subd Geog)
   Here are entered works on expatriate motion picture actors and actresses in general and, with local subdivision, works on expatriate motion picture actors and actresses in a particular place. For the latter, an additional heading of the type Motion picture actors and actresses—[place of origin] is assigned, e.g., 1. Expatriate motion picture

[†]**Subject headings noted with a dagger contain additional access points and subheadings that are not pertinent to this text and are not included here.**

actors and actresses—United States; 2. Motion
picture actors and actresses—Germany.
  UF Exiled motion picture actors and actresses
  BT Exiles
      Motion picture actors and actresses

Expatriate motion picture producers and directors
(May Subd Geog)
  Here are entered works on expatriate motion
picture producers and directors in general and, with
local subdivision, works on expatriate motion
picture producers and directors in a particular
place. For the latter, an additional heading of the
type Motion picture producers and directors—
[place of origin] is assigned; e.g., 1. Expatriate
motion picture producers and directors—United
States; 2. Motion picture producers and directors—
Germany.
  UF Exiled motion picture producers and
      directors
  BT Exiles
      Motion picture producers and directors

Experimental films *(May Subd Geog)*
  [PN1995.9.E96]
  UF Avant-garde films
      Experimental videos
      Personal films
      Underground films
  BT Motion pictures
  NT Cinematography, Abstract
  RT Abstract films

Experimental films *[LCSH Genre]*
Experimental television
  USE Video art
Experimental videos
  USE Experimental films

Exploitation films *(May Subd Geog)*
  This heading is used as a topical heading
for works about films of a sensational nature,
usually offering subject matter taboo in mainstream
cinema, usually produced on a low budget and
often presented in the guise of preachy exposés
or pseudo-documentaries. When used as a topical
heading it is subdivided by the appropriate geographical, topical, and/or form subdivisions.
  BT Motion pictures
  RT Sensationalism in motion pictures

Exploitation films *[LCSH Genre]*
Exploitation films, Black
  USE Blaxploitation films
Exposure, Cinematographic
  USE Cinematography—Exposure
Expression†
  RT Acting

Expressionism in motion pictures *(Not Subd Geog)*
  BT Motion pictures
Extras (Actors) *(May Subd Geog)*
  UF Background artists (Actors)
      Supernumeraries (Actors)
  BT Actors
Extraterrestrial beings in motion pictures
(Not Subd Geog)
  BT Motion pictures
Eyeglasses in motion pictures *(Not Subd Geog)*
  BT Motion pictures

Face in motion pictures *(Not Subd Geog)*
  [PN1995.9.F27]
  BT Motion pictures
Factual films
  USE Documentary films
Factual videos
  USE Documentary videos
Failures in cinematography
  USE Cinematography—Failures
Failures in photography
  USE Photography—Failures
Fair Deal (London, England)
  USE Carling Academy Brixton (London, England)
Fair use (Copyright) *(May Subd Geog)*
  UF Copyright—Fair use
      Fair use (Copyright)—Law and legislation
  BT Copyright infringement
  RT Library copyright policies
  NT Copyright and audio-visual education
      Video recordings— Fair use (Copyright)
  USE Fair use (Copyright)
Fairness doctrine (Broadcasting)
(May Subd Geog)
  [HE8689.7.F34]
  Here are entered works dealing with the
requirement that broadcasters presenting one side of
a controversial issue of public importance must
afford reasonable opportunity for the presentation
of contrasting views. Works dealing with
the requirement that equal opportunities for
broadcasting be afforded to all legally qualified
candidates for public office if any one such
candidate is permitted to broadcast are entered
under Equal time rule (Broadcasting).
  UF Doctrine of fairness (Broadcasting)
  BT Broadcasting—Law and legislation
      Broadcasting policy

†**Subject headings noted with a dagger contain
additional access points and subheadings that
are not pertinent to this text and are not
included here.**

NT Equal time rule (Broadcasting)

Fairy tales[†]

—Film and video adaptations

Fairy tales in motion pictures

(Not Subd Geog)

BT Motion pictures

Fake documentaries (Motion pictures)

USE Documentary-style films

Fake documentary films

USE Documentary-style films

Families[†]

UF Family

NT Families in mass media

Families in motion pictures

Families on television

Mass media and families

Television and families

Families and mass media

USE Mass media and families

Families and television

USE Television and families

Families in mass media *(Not Subd Geog)*

UF Family in mass media

BT Mass media

Families in motion pictures *(Not Subd Geog)*

UF Family in motion pictures

BT Motion pictures

Families on television *(Not Subd Geog)*

UF Family on television

BT Television

Family

USE Families

Family in mass media

USE Families in mass media

Family in motion pictures

USE Families in motion pictures

Family on television

USE Families on television

Family violence in motion pictures

BT Motion pictures

Famines in mass media

BT Mass media

Fan films *(May Subd Geog)*

[PN1995.9.F355]

Here are entered works on a film or video inspired by a film, television program, comic book, or a similar source, created by fans rather than the source's copyright holders or creators.

BT Amateur films

Fan films *[LCSH Genre]*

Fantastic comedies (Motion pictures)

USE Fantasy comedies (Motion pictures)

Fantastic films

USE Fantasy films

Fantastic television programs

USE Fantasy television programs

Fantasy comedies (Motion pictures)

(May Subd Geog)

UF Comedy fantasy films

Fantastic comedies (Motion pictures)

Ghost comedies (Motion pictures)

Heavenly comedies (Motion pictures)

BT Comedy films

Fantasy films

Fantasy comedies (Motion pictures)

[LCSH Genre]

Fantasy comedies (Television programs)

[LCSH Genre]

Fantasy films *(May Subd Geog)*

UF Fantastic films

BT Motion pictures

NT Fantasy comedies (Motion pictures)

Lord of the Rings films

Superhero films

Wizard of Oz films

Fantasy films *[LCSH Genre]*

Fantasy in mass media *(Not Subd Geog)*

[P96.F36]

BT Mass media

Fantasy in motion pictures

(Not Subd Geog)

BT Motion pictures

Fantasy television programs

(May Subd Geog)

This heading is used as a topical heading for works about television programs that feature elements of the fantastic, often including magic, supernatural forces, or exotic fantasy worlds. When used as a topical heading it is subdivided by the appropriate geographic, topical, and/or form subdivisions.

UF Fantastic television programs

BT Television programs

Fantasy television programs *[LCSH Genre]*

Fantômas films *[LCSH Genre]*

Fantozzi, Ugo (Fictitious character)

(Not Subd Geog)

UF Ugo Fantozzi (Fictitious character)

Fantozzi films

[PN1995.9.F39]

[†]**Subject headings noted with a dagger contain additional access points and subheadings that are not pertinent to this text and are not included here.**

BT Motion pictures
Fantozzi films *[LCSH Genre]*
Farce[†]
   BT Comedy
   NT Comedy films
      Commedia dell'arte
Farm comedies
   USE Rural comedies
Farm life in mass media
   (Not Subd Geog)
   BT Mass media
Farm life in motion pictures *(Not Subd Geog)*
   BT Motion pictures
Fascism and motion pictures
   (May Subd Geog)
   UF Motion pictures and fascism
   BT Motion pictures
Fascism in motion pictures *(Not Subd Geog)*
   BT Motion pictures
Fashion in motion pictures *(Not Subd Geog)*
   BT Motion pictures
Fatherhood in motion pictures
   (Not Subd Geog)
   BT Motion pictures
Fathers and sons in motion pictures
   (Not Subd Geog)
   BT Motion pictures
Fathers in motion pictures *(Not Subd Geog)*
   BT Motion pictures
Fathers on television *(Not Subd Geog)*
   BT Television
Fear Effect (Game)
   [GV1469.35.F4]
   BT Video games
Feature films *(May Subd Geog)*
   This heading is used as a topical heading for works about individual full-length films with a running time of 40 minutes or more. When used as a topical heading it is subdivided by the appropriate geographical, topical, and/or form subdivisions.
   UF Features (Motion pictures)
   BT Motion pictures
   NT Musicals
      Made-for-TV movies
  —History and criticism
     USE Motion pictures
Feature films *[LCSH Genre]*
Feature stories[†]
   NT Television feature stories
Features, Television
   USE Made-for-TV movies
Federal aid to the motion picture industry
   USE Motion picture industry—Subsidies

Female actors
   USE Actresses
Female friendship in motion pictures
   (Not Subd Geog)
   BT Motion pictures
Female gangs in motion pictures
   (Not Subd Geog)
   BT Motion pictures
Female impersonators in motion pictures
   (Not Subd Geog)
   BT Motion pictures
Feminine beauty (Aesthetics) in motion pictures
   (Not Subd Geog)
   BT Motion pictures
Femininity in motion pictures
   (Not Subd Geog)
   BT Motion pictures
Feminism and mass media
   (May Subd Geog)
   UF Mass media and feminism
   BT Mass media
Feminism and motion pictures
   (May Subd Geog)
   [PN1995.9.W6]
   UF Motion pictures and feminism
   BT Motion pictures
Feminist cinema
   USE Feminist films
Feminist criticism[†]
   NT Feminist film criticism
      Feminist television criticism
Feminist film criticism *(May Subd Geog)*
   BT Feminist criticism
      Film criticism
Feminist films *(May Subd Geog)*
   [PN1995.9.W6]
   UF Feminist cinema
      Feminist motion pictures
      Women's liberation films
   BT Motion pictures
Feminist motion pictures
   USE Feminist films
Feminist films *[LCSH Genre]*
Feminist television criticism *(May Subd Geog)*
   BT Feminist criticism
      Television criticism
Femmes fatales in motion pictures
   (Not Subd Geog)
   BT Motion pictures

[†]**Subject headings noted with a dagger contain additional access points and subheadings that are not pertinent to this text and are not included here.**

Festival de Cannes
USE Cannes Film Festival
Festival international du film
  (Cannes, France)
USE Cannes Film Festival
Fiction[†]
NT Film novelizations
—Publishing *(May Subd Geog)*
NT Photoplay editions
Fiction films *(May Subd Geog)*
UF Dramatic-narrative films
Entertainment films
Fictional films
Fictive films
BT Motion pictures
Fiction films *[LCSH Genre]*
Fiction television programs
  (May Subd Geog)
UF Fictional television programs
BT Television programs
NT Television crime shows
Fiction television programs *[LCSH Genre]*
Fictional films
USE Fiction films
Fictionalized documentary films
USE Documentary-style films
Fictive films
USE Fiction films
Field cameras
USE View cameras
Fight films
USE Boxing films
Fighter's Edge (Game)
  [GV1469.35.F52]
BT Video games
Fighting Force (Game)
  [GV1469.35.F54]
BT Video games
Fillmore (New York, N.Y.)
USE Fillmore East (New York, N.Y.)
Fillmore East (New York, N.Y.)
UF Bill Graham's Fillmore East
    (New York, N.Y.)
Commodore (New York, N.Y.)
Fillmore (New York, N.Y.)
Loew's Commodore (New York, N.Y.)
Village Theater (New York, N.Y.)
BT Music-halls—New York (State)
Film, Cinematographic
USE Motion picture film
Film, Motion picture
USE Motion picture film
Film, Television

USE Television film
Film acting
USE Motion picture acting
Film actors
USE Motion picture actors and actresses
Film adaptations
  [PN1997.85]
UF Adaptations, Films
Books, Filmed
Filmed books
Films from books
Literature—Film and video adaptations
Motion picture adaptations
BT Literature—Adaptations
Motion pictures
NT Fairy tales—Film and video adaptations
Operas—Film and video adaptations
SA *subdivision* Film and video adaptations *under*
    individual literatures, individual literary
    works entered under title, and names
    of individual persons, e.g., English
    literature—Film and video adaptations;
    Beowulf—Film and video adaptations;
    Shakespeare, William, 1564–1616—Film
    and video adaptations
Film adaptations *[LCSH Genre]*
Film and video festivals
USE Film festivals
Film archive acquisitions
USE Film archives—Acquisitions
Film archives *(May Subd Geog)*
  [PN1993.4]
UF Archives, Motion picture
Motion picture archives
BT Archives
RT Motion picture film collections
—Acquisitions *(May Subd Geog)*
UF Acquisitions (Film archives)
    Film archive acquisitions
Film audiences
USE Motion picture audiences
Film authorship
USE Motion picture authorship
Film billboards
USE Motion picture billboards
Film biographies
USE Biographical films
Film catalogs

**[†]Subject headings noted with a dagger contain
additional access points and subheadings that
are not pertinent to this text and are not
included here.**

USE Motion pictures—Catalogs

Film credits of motion picture actors and actresses
　USE Motion picture actors and actresses—Credits

Film clips *(May Subd Geog)*
　This heading is used as a topical heading for works about short segments, usually incomplete scenes, of films. Works about parts, usually complete scenes or sequences, extracted from a complete film are entered under Film excerpts. When used as topical headings, these headings are subdivided by the appropriate geographic, topical, and/or form subdivisions.
　UF Clips, Film
　BT Motion pictures

Film clips *[LCSH Genre]*

Film collectibles
　USE Motion pictures—Collectibles

Film collections
　USE Motion picture film collections

Film companies
　USE Motion picture studios

Film composers *(May Subd Geog)*
　UF Cinema composers
　　Motion picture composers
　　Movie composers
　BT Composers

Film consultants
　USE Motion picture consultants

Film coupons, UNESCO
　USE UNESCO film coupons

Film credits of cinematographers
　USE Cinematographers—Credits

Film credits of Hispanic American actors and actresses
　USE Hispanic American actors and actresses—Credits

Film credits of Hispanic American motion picture producers and directors
　USE Hispanic American motion picture producers and directors—Credits

Film credits of motion picture actors and actresses
　USE Motion picture actors and actresses—Credits

Film credits of motion picture producers and directors
　USE Motion picture producers and directors—Credits

Film credits of screenwriters
　USE Screenwriters—Credits

Film credits of television actors and actresses
　USE Television actors and actresses—Credits

Film credits of television producers and directors
　USE Television producers and directors—Credits

Film credits of women motion picture producers and directors
　USE Women motion picture producers and directors—Credits

Film criticism *(May Subd Geog)*
　[PN1995]
　UF Motion picture criticism
　　Motion pictures—Criticism
　　Moving-pictures—Evaluation
　BT Criticism
　RT Motion pictures—Evaluation
　NT Feminist film criticism

Film critics *(May Subd Geog)*
　UF Motion picture critics
　　Moving-picture critics
　BT Critics
　NT Women film critics
　—United States
　　NT African American film critics

Film critics, African American
　USE African American film critics

Film dialogue
　USE Dialogue in motion pictures

Film directors
　USE Motion picture producers and directors

Film distribution
　USE Motion pictures—Distribution

Film editing (Cinematography)
　USE Motion pictures—Editing

Film editors
　USE Motion picture editors

Film epics
　USE Epic films

Film editing (Cinematography)
　USE Motion pictures—Editing

Film excerpts *(May Subd Geog)*
　This heading is used as a topical heading for works about parts, usually complete scenes or sequences, extracted from a complete film. Works about short segments, usually incomplete scenes, of films are entered under Film clips. When used as topical headings, these headings are subdivided by the appropriate geographic, topical, and/or form subdivisions.
　UF Excerpts, Film
　　Motion picture excerpts
　　Motion pictures—Excerpts

†**Subject headings noted with a dagger contain additional access points and subheadings that are not pertinent to this text and are not included here.**

BT Motion pictures
SA *subdivision* Excerpts *under motion picture*
forms and genres, e.g., Horror films—
Excerpts
Film excerpts *[LCSH Genre]*
Film festivals *(May Subd Geog)*
UF Film and video festivals
Motion picture festivals
Moving-picture festivals
Video and film festivals
BT Performing arts festivals
NT Erotic film festivals
Gay and lesbian film festivals
Indian film festivals
Jewish film festivals
Film genre parodies
USE Parody films
Film genres *(May Subd Geog)*
Here are entered works on the theory of film
genres and works discussing film genres collectively.
Works on a specific film genre are entered under the
heading for the genre, e.g., Western films.
UF Genre films
Genres, Film
Motion picture genres
BT Motion pictures
RT Motion pictures—Plots, themes, etc.
Film hairstyling *(May Subd Geog)*
[PN1995.9.H25]
BT Hairdressing
Film historians *(May Subd Geog)*
UF Motion picture historians
BT Historians
Film industry (Motion pictures)
USE Motion picture industry
Film installations (Art)
(May Subd Geog)
UF Video installations (Art)
BT Installations (Art)
Motion pictures
Film kinesics
USE Nonverbal communication in motion pictures
Film libraries
USE Motion picture film collections
Film literature
USE Motion picture literature
Film loops
USE Loop films
Film make-up
USE Film makeup
Film makeup
UF Film make-up
Make-up, Film

Makeup, Film
Motion picture makeup
BT Theatrical makeup
Film music
USE Motion picture music
Silent film music
Film musicals
USE Musical films
Film noir *(May Subd Geog)*
[PN1995.9.F54]
UF Cinéma noir
Dark crime films
Film noirs
Films noirs
Noir films
BT Crime films
Film noir *[LCSH Genre]*
Film noirs
USE Film noir
Film novelizations *(May Subd Geog)*
Here are entered works on novels adapted
from motion pictures.
UF Motion picture novelizations
Movie novels
Novelizations, Film
BF Fiction
Film parodies
USE Parody films
Film plays
USE Motion picture plays
Film posters *(May Subd Geog)*
[PN19955.9.P5]
UF Motion picture posters
Motion pictures—Posters
Movie posters
BT Playbills
Posters
NT Half-sheet posters
Insert posters
Lobby cards
One-sheet posters
Six-sheet posters
Three-sheet posters
Twenty-four-sheet posters
Film posters, African *(May Subd Geog)*
UF African film posters
Film posters, American *(May Subd Geog)*
UF American film posters

†**Subject headings noted with a dagger contain**
additional access points and subheadings that
are not pertinent to this text and are not
included here.

Film posters, Argentine *(May Subd Geog)*
UF Argentine film posters
Film posters, Armenian *(May Subd Geog)*
UF Armenian film posters
Film posters, Australian *(May Subd Geog)*
UF Australian film posters
Film posters, Belgian *(May Subd Geog)*
UF Belgian film posters
Film posters, Brazilian *(May Subd Geog)*
UF Brazilian film posters
Film posters, Chinese *(May Subd Geog)*
UF Chinese film posters
Film posters, Cuban *(May Subd Geog)*
UF Cuban film posters
Film posters, Czech *(May Subd Geog)*
UF Czech film posters
Film posters, French *(May Subd Geog)*
UF French film posters
Film posters, German *(May Subd Geog)*
UF German film posters
Film posters, Greek *(May Subd Geog)*
UF Greek film posters
Film posters, Hungarian
 (May Subd Geog)
UF Hungarian film posters
Film posters, Indic *(May Subd Geog)*
UF Indic film posters
Film posters, Italian *(May Subd Geog)*
UF Italian film posters
Film posters, Japanese *(May Subd Geog)*
UF Japanese film posters
Film posters, Korean *(May Subd Geog)*
UF Korean film posters
Film posters, Mexican *(May Subd Geog)*
UF Mexican film posters
Film posters, Polish *(May Subd Geog)*
UF Polish film posters
Film posters, Russian *(May Subd Geog)*
UF Russian film posters
Film posters, Slovak *(May Subd Geog)*
UF Slovak film posters
Film posters, Spanish *(May Subd Geog)*
UF Spanish film posters
Film posters, Swedish *(May Subd Geog)*
UF Swedish film posters
Film posters, Swiss *(May Subd Geog)*
UF Swiss film posters
Film posters, Tagalog *(May Subd Geog)*
UF Tagalog film posters
Film posters, Turkish *(May Subd Geog)*
UF Turkish film posters
Film posters, Ukrainian *(May Subd Geog)*
UF Ukrainian film posters

Film producers
USE Motion picture producers and directors
Film programs
USE Motion picture programs
Film remakes *(May Subd Geog)*
[PN1995.9.R45]
UF Motion picture remakes
Motion pictures—Remakes
Moving-picture remakes
Remakes, Film
BT Motion pictures
Film remakes [LCSH Genre]
Film scripts
USE Motion picture plays
Film scriptwriting
USE Motion picture authorship
Film sequels *(May Subd Geog)*
[PN1995.9.S29]
UF Motion picture sequels
Motion pictures—Sequels
Moving-picture sequels
Sequels, Film
BT Film series
Film sequels [LCSH Genre]
Film serials *(May Subd Geog)*
   This heading is used as a topical heading for works about films that were shown in weekly installments and usually featured cliffhanger endings. Works about successive films that feature the same characters and remain true to a common premise are entered under Film series. When used as topical headings they are subdivided by the appropriate geographic, topical, and/or form subdivisions.
UF Chapterplay films
Cliffhanger films
Episode films
Motion picture serials
Moving-picture serials
Serials, Film
BT Motion pictures
Film serials [LCSH Genre]
Film series *(May Subd Geog)*
[PN1995.9.S34]
BT Motion pictures
NT Film sequels
Film series [LCSH Genre]
Film stars
USE Motion picture actors and actresses

†**Subject headings noted with a dagger contain additional access points and subheadings that are not pertinent to this text and are not included here.**

Film studios
  USE Motion picture studios
Film sync discs[†]
  BT Motion picture soundtracks
Film thrillers
  USE Thrillers (Motion pictures)
Film trailers *(May Subd Geog)*
  UF Motion picture previews
      Motion picture trailers
      Previews, Movie
      Trailers, Film
      Trailers, Movie
  BT Advertising—Motion pictures
Film trailers *[LCSH Genre]*
Film travelogues
  USE Travelogues (Motion pictures)
Filmed ballets *[LCSH Genre]*
Filmed books
  USE Film adaptations
Filmed boxing matches *[LCSH Genre]*
Filmed dance *[LCSH Genre]*
Filmed football games *[LCSH Genre]*
Filmed interviews *[LCSH Genre]*
Filmed lectures *[LCSH Genre]*
Filmed musicals *[LCSH Genre]*
Filmed operas *[LCSH Genre]*
Filmed operettas *[LCSH Genre]*
Filmed performances *[LCSH Genre]*
Filmed plays *[LCSH Genre]*
Filmed speeches *[LCSH Genre]*
Filmed sports events *[LCSH Genre]*
Filmed stand-up comedy routines *[LCSH Genre]*
Filmgoers
  USE Motion picture audiences
Filming on location
  USE Motion picture locations
Filmography
  USE Motion pictures—Catalogs
Films
  USE Motion pictures
      Photography—Films
Films, Cinematographic
  USE Motion picture film
Films, Color
  USE Color photography—Films
Films, Foreign
  USE Foreign films
Films by children
  BT Children
      Motion pictures
Films for foreign speakers
  SA *subdivisions* Films for foreign speakers;
      and Films for French, [Spanish, etc.]

speakers *under individual and groups of languages for instructional films about a language or languages designed for speakers of other languages, e.g.,* English language—Films for French, [Spanish, etc.] speakers
Films for people with visual disabilities
  (May Subd Geog)
  UF Films for the visually handicapped
  BT People with visual disabilities
Films for people with visual disabilities
  [LCSH Genre]
Films for the deaf
  USE Films for the hearing impaired
Films for the hearing impaired
  (May Subd Geog)
  UF Deaf, Films for the
      Films for the deaf
      Motion pictures for the deaf
      Motion pictures for the hearing impaired
      Moving-pictures for the deaf
  BT Hearing impaired
      Motion pictures
Films for the hearing impaired
  [LCSH Genre]
Films for the visually handicapped
  USE Films for people with visual disabilities
Films for TV commercials
  USE Television commercial films
Films from books
  USE Film adaptations
Films noirs
  USE Film noir
Filmscripts
  USE Motion picture plays
Finnish drama[†]
  NT Motion picture plays, Finnish
Finnish motion picture plays
  USE Motion picture plays, Finnish
Fire fighters in mass media *(Not Subd Geog)*
  BT Mass media
Fire fighters on television
  (Not Subd Geog)
  BT Television
Fisher televisions *(Not Subd Geog)*
  BT Television—Receivers and reception
Fisher videocassette recorders
  (Not Subd Geog)

Subject headings noted with a dagger contain additional access points and subheadings that are not pertinent to this text and are not included here.

BT Videocassette recorders

Flagellation in motion pictures
   (Not Subd Geog)
   [PN1995.9.F55]
   BT Motion pictures

Flaneurs in motion pictures
   (Not Subd Geog)
   BT Motion pictures

Flash Gordon (Fictitious character)
   USE Gordon, Flash (Fictitious character)

Flash Gordon films *(May Subd Geog)*
   [PN1995.9.F558]
   BT Action and adventure films
      Superhero films

Flash Gordon films *[LCSH Genre]*

Flash photography, Electronic
   USE Electronic flash photography

Flight in motion pictures
   (Not Subd Geog)
   [PN1995.9.F58]
   UF Aeronautics in motion pictures
   BT Motion pictures

Foca camera *(Not Subd Geog)*
   [TR263.F]
   BT Cameras

Folk art in motion pictures
   (Not Subd Geog)
   BT Motion pictures

Folklore[†]
   NT Mass media and folklore
   —Great Britain
      NT Robin Hood (Legendary character)
   —Middle East
      NT Scheherazade (Legendary character)
   —Spain[†]
      NT Don Juan (Legendary character)

Folklore and mass media
   USE Mass media and folklore

Folklore in motion pictures *(Not Subd Geog)*
   BT Motion pictures

Folklore on television *(Not Subd Geog)*
   BT Television

Food in motion pictures *(Not Subd Geog)*
   BT Motion pictures

Food on television *(Not Subd Geog)*
   [PN1992.8.F66]
   BT Television

Food shows (Television programs)
   USE Television cooking shows

Football films *(May Subd Geog)*
   UF College football films
      Grid films
      Gridiron films

BT Sports films

Football films *[LCSH Genre]*

Football television programs *[LCSH Genre]*

Foreign films *(May Subd Geog)*
   [PN1995.9.F67]
   Here are entered works on motion pictures produced by foreign film companies. When the heading is subdivided by place, the subdivision refers to the locality where the films are available or viewed. Works on motion pictures produced by film companies in a specific country and available or viewed in another country or countries are entered under the heading Motion pictures qualified by the country of origin, e.g., Motion pictures, American. Works on motion pictures in a foreign language produced for the export market are entered under the heading Foreign language films.
   UF Films, Foreign
      Motion pictures, Foreign
   BT Motion pictures
   NT Motion pictures, African
      Motion pictures, American
      Motion pictures, Arab
      Motion pictures, Australian
      Motion pictures, Brazilian
      Motion pictures, British
      Motion pictures, Canadian
      Motion pictures, Central Asian
      Motion pictures, Chinese
      Motion pictures, French
      Motion pictures, German
      Motion pictures, Hungarian
      Motion pictures, Indic
      Motion pictures, Irish
      Motion pictures, Italian
      Motion pictures, Japanese
      Motion pictures, Korean
      Motion pictures, Mexican
      Motion pictures, New Zealand
      Motion pictures, Russian
      Motion pictures, Singaporean
      Motion pictures, Soviet
      Motion pictures, Spanish
      Motion pictures, Swiss

Foreign language films
   (May Subd Geog)
   Here are entered works on motion pictures in a foreign language produced for the export market. Works on motion pictures produced by foreign film

[†]**Subject headings noted with a dagger contain additional access points and subheadings that are not pertinent to this text and are not included here.**

companies are entered under the heading Foreign films. Instructional films about a language or languages designed for speakers of other languages are entered under the language being taught with subdivisions Films for foreign speakers or Films for French [Spanish, etc.] speakers, e.g., English language
—Films for foreign speakers; French language—Films for English speakers.
  BT Motion pictures

Foreign language television programs
(May Subd Geog)
  Here are entered works on television programs in languages not widely spoken in the area where they are broadcast. Works on television programs produced in foreign countries are entered under Foreign television programs. This heading is not used for individual television programs, which are entered under headings appropriate to the content, genre, and/or form of the program.
  BT Television programs

Foreign motion picture actors and actresses
  USE Motion picture actors and actresses, Foreign

Foreign television programs *(May Subd Geog)*
  Here are entered works on television programs produced in foreign countries. Works on television programs in languages not widely spoken in the area where they are broadcast are entered under Foreign language television programs. This heading is not used for individual television programs, which are entered under headings appropriate to the content, genre, and/or form of the program.
  UF Television programs, Foreign
  BT Television programs

Forensic sciences on television
(Not Subd Geog)
  BT Television

Forests and forestry[†]
  NT Motion pictures in forestry

Forgiveness in motion pictures
(Not Subd Geog)
  BT Motion pictures

Found footage (Motion pictures, television, etc.)
  USE Stock footage

Fox Theater (Atlanta, Ga.)
  USE Fox Theatre (Atlanta, Ga.)

Fox Theater Building (Detroit, Mich.)
  USE Fox Theatre Building (Detroit, Mich.)

Fox Theater (Detroit, Mich.)
  USE Fox Theatre Building (Detroit, Mich.)

Fox Theatre (Atlanta, Ga.)
  UF Fox Theater (Atlanta, Ga.)

  BT Motion picture theaters—Georgia

Fox Theatre (San Francisco, Calif.)
  BT Motion picture theaters—California

Fox Theatre Building (Detroit, Mich.)
  UF Fox Theater Building (Detroit, Mich.)
      Fox Theatre (Detroit, Mich.)
  BT Motion picture theaters—Michigan

France[†]
  —Civilization
      NT Motion pictures—French influences

Frankenstein (Fictitious character)
  UF Doctor Frankenstein (Fictitious character)
      Dr. Frankenstein (Fictitious character)
      Frankenstein, Doctor (Fictitious character)
      Frankenstein, Dr. (Fictitious character)
      Victor Frankenstein (Fictitious character)

Frankenstein, Doctor (Fictitious character)
  USE Frankenstein (Fictitious character)

Frankenstein, Dr. (Fictitious character)
  USE Frankenstein (Fictitious character)

Frankenstein films *(May Subd Geog)*
  [PN1995.9.F8]
  BT Monster films

Frankenstein films *[LCSH Genre]*

French-Canadian drama[†]
  NT Motion picture plays, French-Canadian
      Television plays, French-Canadian

French-Canadian motion picture plays
  USE Motion picture plays, French-Canadian

French-Canadian motion picture producers and directors
  USE Motion picture producers and directors, French-Canadian

French-Canadian television plays
  USE Television plays, French-Canadian

French-Canadians and mass media
  (May Subd Geog)
  UF Mass media and French-Canadians
  BT Mass media

French drama[†]
  NT Motion picture plays, French
      Television plays, French

French film posters
  USE Film posters, French

French motion picture plays
  USE Motion picture plays, French

French motion pictures
  USE Motion pictures, French

[†]**Subject headings noted with a dagger contain additional access points and subheadings that are not pertinent to this text and are not included here.**

French television plays

Friday the 13th films
 [PN1995.9.F83]
  UF Friday the Thirteenth films
  BT Slasher films

Friday the 13th films *[LCSH Genre]*
Friday the Thirteenth films
  USE Friday the 13th films

Front-screen projection
 [TR859]
  UF Alekon-Gerard process
      Jenkins process
      Scotchlite process
  BT Cinematography
      Lantern projection

Fugitives from justice in motion pictures
 (Not Subd Geog)
  BT Motion pictures

Fujica camera *(Not Subd Geog)*
  BT Electric eye cameras

Funai televisions *(Not Subd Geog)*
  BT Television—Receivers and reception

Future in motion pictures *(Not Subd Geog)*
  BT Motion pictures

Game Boy video games *(Not Subd Geog)*
 [GV1469.32]
  UF Nintendo Game Boy video games
  BT Nintendo video games
  NT Mario Kart Super Circuit (Game)
      Super Mario Advance (Game)
Game Shark (Game)
  USE GameShark (Game)
Game shows
  USE Television game shows
Game shows (Television programs)
  USE Television game shows
GameCube video games
  USE Nintendo GameCube video games
Games[†]
  NT Adventure games
      Electronic games
Games, Adventure
  USE Adventure games
Games, Computer adventure
  USE Computer adventure games
GameShark (Game)
 [GV1469.35.G36]
  UF Game Shark (Game)
  BT Video games
Gang films
  USE Gangster films
      Juvenile delinquency films

Gangland films
  USE Gangster films
Gangster films *(May Subd Geog)*
  UF Bandit gangster films
      Gang films
      Gangland films
      Hoodlum drama (Motion pictures)
      Mafia films
      Organized crime films
      Outlaw-couple films
      Outlaw gangster films
      Rural bandit films
      Syndicate films
      Syndicate-oriented films
  BT Crime films
Gangster films *[LCSH Genre]*
Gangster television programs *[LCSH Genre]*
Gauntlet (Game)
 [GV1469.35.G38]
  BT Video games
Gay actors *(May Subd Geog)*
  BT Actors
      Gay motion picture actors and
        actresses
 —United States
      NT African American gay actors
Gay actors, African American
  USE African American gay actors
Gay adult videos
  USE Gay erotic videos
Gay and lesbian film festivals *(May Subd Geog)*
 [PN1993.44.G39]
  UF Gay film festivals
      Lesbian and gay film festivals
  BT Film festivals
      Gays—Social life and customs
Gay Afro-American actors
  USE African American gay actors
Gay erotic films *(May Subd Geog)*
  BT Erotic films
      Gay erotica
  RT Lesbian erotic films
Gay erotic films *[LCSH Genre]*
Gay erotic videos *(May Subd Geog)*
  UF Gay adult videos
  BT Erotic videos
      Gay erotica
Gay erotica[†]
  NT Gay erotic films

[†]**Subject headings noted with a dagger contain
additional access points and subheadings that
are not pertinent to this text and are not
included here.**

Gay erotic videos
Gay film festivals
   USE Gay and lesbian film festivals
Gay man-heterosexual woman relationships in
   motion pictures *(Not Subd Geog)*
   UF Heterosexual woman-gay man relationships
       in motion pictures
   BT Motion pictures
Gay man-heterosexual woman relationships
   on television *(Not Subd Geog)*
   UF Heterosexual woman-gay men relationships
       on television
   BT Television
Gay men[†]
   NT Motion pictures and gay men
Gay men and motion pictures
   USE Motion pictures and gay men
Gay men and musicals *(May Subd Geog)*
   UF Musicals and gay men
   BT Musicals
Gay men in mass media *(Not Subd Geog)*
   BT Mass media
Gay men in motion pictures
   (Not Subd Geog)
   BT Motion pictures
Gay men on television *(Not Subd Geog)*
   BT Television
Gay motion picture actors and actresses
   (May Subd Geog)
   BT Gay actors
       Motion picture actors and actresses
Gay motion picture producers and directors
   (May Subd Geog)
   BT Motion picture producers and directors
   RT Lesbian motion picture producers and
       directors
Gay skinheads in motion pictures
   (Not Subd Geog)
   BT Motion pictures
Gays[†]
   NT Mass media and gays
       Television and gays
       Television programs for gays
  —Social life and customs
       NT Gay and lesbian film festivals
Gays and mass media
   USE Mass media and gays
Gays and television
   USE Television and gays
Gays in motion pictures *(Not Subd Geog)*
   BT Motion pictures
Gays on television
   USE Homosexuality on television

Gaze in motion pictures *(Not Subd Geog)*
   BT Motion pictures
GE televisions
   USE General Electric televisions
GE videocassette recorders
   USE General Electric videocassette recorders
Gekido (Game)
   [GV1469.35.G44]
   BT Video games
Gender identity in mass media
   (Not Subd Geog)
   [P96.G44]
   BT Mass media
Gender identity in motion pictures
   (Not Subd Geog)
   BT Motion pictures
General Electric televisions *(Not Subd Geog)*
   UF GE televisions
   BT Television—Receivers and reception
General Electric videocassette recorders
   (Not Subd Geog)
   UF GE videocassette recorders
   BT Videocassette recorders
Genetic engineering in motion pictures
   (Not Subd Geog)
   BT Motion pictures
Genetics in mass media *(Not Subd Geog)*
   BT Mass media
Genetics in motion pictures *(Not Subd Geog)*
   BT Motion pictures
Genie Awards
   UF Canadian Film Awards
   BT Motion pictures—Awards—Canada
Genma Onimusha (Game)
   BT Video games
Genocide in mass media *(Not Subd Geog)*
   BT Mass media
Genre films
   USE Film genres
Genre parodies (Motion pictures)
   USE Parody films
Genre parody films
   USE Parody films
Genre videos
   USE Video genres
Genres, Film
   USE Genre films
Genres, Mass media

[†]**Subject headings noted with a dagger contain**
additional access points and subheadings that
are not pertinent to this text and are not
included here.

USE Mass media genres
Genres, Television program
USE Television program genres
Genres, Video
USE Video genres
Gentleman detective stories, [films, etc.]
USE *headings of the type* Detective and mystery
stories; Detective and mystery films; *etc.*
Geographical myths in mass media *(Not Subd Geog)*
[P96.G46]
BT Mass media
Geography[†]
—**Study ad teaching**[†]
NT Television in geography education
Geometry in motion pictures
(Not Subd Geog)
BT Motion pictures
Geopolitics in motion pictures
(Not Subd Geog)
[PN1995.9.G39]
BT Motion pictures
George Foster Peabody Awards
USE Peabody Awards
George Foster Peabody Broadcasting Awards
USE Peabody Awards
George Foster Peabody Radio and Television Awards
USE Peabody Awards
German drama[†]
NT Motion picture plays, German
Television plays, German
German film posters
USE Film posters, German
German motion picture plays
USE Motion picture plays, German
German motion pictures
USE Motion pictures, German
German reunification question (1949–1990) in
motion pictures *(Not Subd Geog)*
[PN1995.9.G43]
BT Motion pictures
German television plays
USE Television plays, German
Germans in motion pictures *(Not Subd Geog)*
[PN1995.9.G45]
BT Motion pictures
Germany[†]
—**Civilization**
NT Motion pictures—German influences
Motion pictures—Netherlands—German
influences
—**On television**
UF Germany on television
Germany on television

USE Germany—On television
Gesture[†]
BT Acting
Movement (Acting)
Gesture in motion pictures *(Not Subd Geog)*
BT Motion pictures
GEX (Game)
[GV1469.35.G48]
BT Video games
Ghost comedies
USE Fantasy comedies (Motion pictures)
Ghost films *[LCSH Genre]*
Ghost in the Shell (Game)
[GV1469.35.G52]
BT Video games
Ghost shows (Television programs)
USE Ghost television programs
Ghost stories (Television programs)
USE Ghost television programs)
Ghost television programs
(May Subd Geog)
UF Ghost shows (Television programs)
Ghost stories (Television programs)
BT Monster television programs
RT Haunted house television programs
Ghost television programs *[LCSH Genre]*
Ghosts in motion pictures *(Not Subd Geog)*
BT Motion pictures
Giovanni, Don (Legendary character)
USE Don Juan (Legendary character)
Girls[†]
NT Mass media and girls
Girls and mass media
USE Mass media and girls
Girls in motion pictures *(Not Subd Geog)*
[PN1995.9.G57]
BT Motion pictures
Gladiator films
USE Peplum films
Global Conquest (Game)
[GV1469.35.G55]
BT Video games
Global Operations (Game)
BT Video games
Globalization[†]
NT Motion pictures and globalization
Television and globalization

[†]**Subject headings noted with a dagger contain**
additional access points and subheadings that
are not pertinent to this text and are not
included here.

Globalization and motion pictures
　USE Motion pictures and globalization
Globalization and television
　USE Television and globalization
Globalization in motion pictures
　(Not Subd Geog)
　　Here are entered works on globalization as a
　theme in motion pictures. Works on the relationship
　between economic and social globalization and
　motion pictures are entered under Motion pictures
　and globalization.
　　BT Motion pictures
Gloria-Palast (Berlin, Germany)
　　UF Romanische Haus (Berlin, Germany)
　　BT Motion picture theaters—Germany
Glover (Game)
　　[PN1469.35.G58]
　　BT Video games
Godfather films
　　[PN1995.9.G8]
　　BT Motion pictures
Godfather films *[LCSH Genre]*
Godzilla films *(May Subd Geog)*
　　[PN1995.9.G63 (History and criticism)]
　　BT Monster films
Godzilla films *[LCSH Genre]*
Golden Globe Awards
　　[PN1993.92]
　　UF Golden Globes
　　BT Motion pictures—Awards—
　　　　United States
Golden Globes
　USE Golden Globe Awards
GoldenEye 007 (Game)
　　[PN1469.35.G64]
　　UF Prima's GoldenEye 007 (Game)
　　BT Video games
Golden Rose of Montreux
　　UF Goldene Rose von Montreux
　　　　Rose d'Or de Montreux
　　BT Television broadcasting—Awards
Goldene Rose von Montreux
　USE Golden Rose of Montreux
Golf television programs *[LCSH Genre]*
Good and evil[†]
　　RT Evil in motion pictures
Gordon, Flash (Fictitious character)
　　UF Colonel Gordon (Fictitious character)
　　　　Colonel Robert Gordon (Fictitious character)
　　　　Flash Gordon (Fictitious character)
　　　　Gordon, Robert (Fictitious character)
　　　　Robert Gordon (Fictitious character)
Gordon, Robert (Fictitious character)

　USE Gordon, Flash (Fictitious character)
Gossip in mass media *(Not Subd Geog)*
　　[P96.G85]
　　UF Gossip industry
　　BT Mass media
Gossip industry
　USE Gossip in mass media
Government aid to the motion picture industry
　USE Motion picture industry—Subsidies
Goya Awards
　USE Premios Anuales de la Academia Goya
Goyas (Awards)
　USE Premios Anuales de la Academia Goya
Graflex camera *(Not Subd Geog)*
　　BT Cameras
Grail in motion pictures *(Not Subd Geog)*
　　BT Motion pictures
Gran Turismo (Game)
　　[GV1469.35.G73]
　　BT Video games
Grand Prix racing in motion pictures
　(Not Subd Geog)
　　BT Motion pictures
Grand Theft Auto games
　　[GV1469.35.G738]
　　UF GTA games
　　BT Video games
Grand Theft Auto: San Andreas (Game)
　　BT Video games
Grande Prêmio BR do Cinema Brasileiro
　USE Grande Prêmio Cinema Brasil
Grande Prêmio Cinema Brasil
　　UF Cinema Brazil Grand Prize
　　　　Grande Prêmio BR do Cinema Brasileiro
　　BT Motion pictures—Awards—Brazil
Grandia (Game)
　　[GV1469.35.G74]
　　BT Video games
Granstream Saga (Game)
　　BT Video games
Graphic arts[†]
　　NT Television graphics
Graphics, Television
　USE Television graphics
Grauman's Chinese Theatre (Los Angeles, Calif.)
　USE Chinese Theatre (Los Angeles, Calif.)
Grazing (Television) *(May Subd Geog)*

[†]**Subject headings noted with a dagger contain
additional access points and subheadings that
are not pertinent to this text and are not
included here.**

Here are entered works on the use of a remote control device to look briefly at television programs.
UF Channel Surfing (Television)
Channel switching (Television)
BT Television
Zapping (Television)

Greek Americans and mass media
(May Subd Geog)
UF Mass media and Greek Americans
BT Mass media

Grid films
USE Football films

Gridiron films
USE Football films

Grief in motion pictures
(Not Subd Geog)
BT Motion pictures

Grimme-Preis
USE Adolf-Grimme-Preis

Grips (Persons) *(May Subd Geog)*
BT Motion picture industry—Employees
Stagehands
Television broadcasting—Employees

Grotesque in motion pictures *(Not Subd Geog)*
BT Motion pictures

GTA games
USE Grand Theft Auto games

Guidance films, Social
USE Social guidance films

Guitar Hero (Game)
BT Video games)

Gun (Game)
BT Video games

H.263 (Video coding standard)
UF ITU H.263 (Video coding standard)
ITU-T Recommendation H.263
(Video coding standard)
BT Digital video—Standards
Video compression—Standards

Hairdressing[†]
NT Film hairstyling

Haitian Americans and mass media
(May Subd Geog)
UF Mass media and Haitian Americans
BT Mass media

Half-sheet posters *(May Subd Geog)*
BT Advertising—Motion pictures
Film posters

Hallucinations and illusions in motion pictures
(Not Subd Geog)
BT Motion pictures

Halo (Game)

BT Video games

Ham television
USE Amateur television stations

Hand-to-hand fighting, Oriental, in motion pictures
USE Martial arts films—History and criticism

Handicapped in mass media
USE People with disabilities in mass media

Handicapped in motion pictures
USE People with disabilities in motion pictures

Handicapped in television
USE People with disabilities on television

Handicapped on television
USE People with disabilities on television

Handling of DVDs
USE DVDs—Handling

Happiness in motion pictures *(Not Subd Geog)*
BT Motion pictures

Harry Potter films *[LCSH Genre]*

Hasselblad camera *(Not Subd Geog)*
BT Cameras

Haunted house films *(May Subd Geog)*
UF Old dark house mysteries (Motion pictures)
Old house thrillers (Motion pictures)
BT Motion pictures
RT Horror films

Haunted house films *[LCSH Genre]*

Haunted house television programs
(May Subd Geog)
UF Old dark house mysteries (Television programs)
Old house thrillers (Television programs)
RT Ghost television programs
Horror television programs

Haunted house films *[LCSH Genre]*

HD video recording
USE High definition video recording

HDTV (Television)
USE High definition television

HDTV sets
USE High definition television—Receivers and reception

HDTVs (Television)
USE High definition television—Receivers and reception

Head cameras
USE Wearable video devices

Headcams
USE Wearable video devices

[†]**Subject headings noted with a dagger contain additional access points and subheadings that are not pertinent to this text and are not included here.**

Healers in mass media *(Not Subd Geog)*
 [P96.H42]
 BT Mass media
Health education[†]
 NT Mass media in health education
Health in mass media *(Not Subd Geog)*
 [P96.H43]
 BT Mass media
Health risk assessment[†]
 NT Medical screening
Hearing impaired[†]
 NT Films for the hearing impaired
  Television for the hearing impaired
  Video recordings for the hearing impaired
 —Services for[†]
  NT Closed captioning
Heavenly comedies (Motion pictures)
 USE Fantasy comedies (Motion pictures)
Heimat films
 USE Heimatfilme
Heimatfilme *(May Subd Geog)*
 [PN1995.9.H4]
  This heading is used as a topical heading for works about films produced in Germany that present an idealized view of country life in southern Germany. When used as a topical heading it is subdivided by the appropriate geographic, topical, and/or form subdivisions.
  UF Heimat films
   Heimatfilms
   Homeland films
Heimatfilme *[LCSH Genre]*
Heimatfilms
 USE Heimatfilme
Heist films
 USE Caper films
Heliochromy
 USE Color photography
Hellraiser films
 BT Motion pictures
Hellraiser films *[LCSH Genre]*
Hero-lawyer films
 USE Legal films
Heroes in mass media *(Not Subd Geog)*
 [P96.H46]
 BT Mass media
Heroes in motion pictures *(Not Subd Geog)*
 BT Motion pictures
Heroes on television *(Not Subd Geog)*
 BT Television
Heroines in motion pictures *(Not Subd Geog)*
 BT Motion pictures
Heroines on television *(Not Subd Geog)*

 BT Television
Heroic films
 USE Epic films
Heterosexual men in motion pictures
 (Not Subd Geog)
 BT Motion pictures
Heterosexual women in motion pictures
 (Not Subd Geog)
 BT Motion pictures
Heterosexual women on television
 (Not Subd Geog)
 BT Television
Heterosexuality in motion pictures
 (Not Subd Geog)
 [PN1995.9.H45]
 BT Motion pictures
Hidden camera photography
 (May Subd Geog)
 BT Photography
High definition television *(May Subd Geog)*
 [HE8700.73–HE8700.74 (Economics)]
 [TK6679 (Engineering)]
 UF HDTV (Television)
 BT Television
 —Receivers and reception
  UF HDTV sets
   HDTVs (Television)
  BT High definition television—Equipment and supplies
   Household electronics
High definition video recording
 (May Subd Geog)
 [TR862]
 UF HD video recording
 BT Video recording
High-fidelity sound systems[†]
 NT DVD players
High-speed cinematography
 USE Cinematography, High-speed
High-speed videorecording *(May Subd Geog)*
 BT Video recording
Hillbilly comedies
 USE Rural comedies
Hillotype
 [TR510]
 BT Color photography
Hindi drama [†]

[†]Subject headings noted with a dagger contain additional access points and subheadings that are not pertinent to this text and are not included here.

NT Television plays, Hindi
Hindi motion pictures
USE Motion pictures, Hindi
Hindi television plays
USE Television plays, Hindi
Hip-hop in motion pictures *(Not Subd Geog)*
[PN1995.9.H46]
BT Motion pictures
Hispanic American actors
(May Subd Geog)
UF Actors, Hispanic American
BT Actors—United States
Hispanic American mass media
(May Subd Geog)
[P94.5.H58]
UF Hispanic American media
Mass media, Hispanic American
BT Mass media, Hispanic American
Ethnic mass media—United States
RT Hispanic Americans and mass media
Hispanic American media
USE ispanic American mass media
Hispanic American motion picture actors and
actresses *(May Subd Geog)*
UF Motion pictures actors and actresses,
Hispanic American
—Credits
UF Credits of Hispanic American motion
picture actors and actresses
Film credits of Hispanic American
motion picture actors and actresses
Hispanic American motion picture producers and
directors *(May Subd Geog)*
UF Motion picture producers
and directors, Hispanic American
BT Motion picture producers and directors—
United States
—Credits
UF Credits of Hispanic American motion
picture producers and directors
Film credits of Hispanic American
motion picture producers and
directors
Hispanic American television actors and actresses
(May Subd Geog)
UF Television actors and actresses, Hispanic
American
BT Television actors and actresses—United
States
Hispanic American television personalities
(May Subd Geog)
UF Television personalities,
Hispanic American

BT Television personalities—
United States
Hispanic American television producers and
directors *(May Subd Geog)*
UF Television producers and directors, Hispanic
American
BT Television producers and directors—
United States
Hispanic American women in mass media
(Not Subd Geog)
BT Mass media
Hispanic American women television personalities
(May Subd Geog)
UF Women television personalities, Hispanic
American
BT Women television personalities—
United States
Hispanic Americans and mass media
(May Subd Geog)
UF Mass media and Hispanic Americans
BT Mass media
NT Hispanic American mass media
Hispanic Americans in motion pictures
(Not Subd Geog)
BT Motion pictures
Hispanic Americans in television
USE Hispanic Americans on television
Hispanic Americans in television broadcasting
BT Television broadcasting—United States
Hispanic Americans in the motion picture industry
(May Subd Geog)
BT Motion picture industry—
United States
Hispanic Americans on television
(Not Subd Geog)
UF Hispanic Americans in television
BT Television
Historians[†]
NT Film historians
Historical films *(May Subd Geog)*
BT Motion pictures
Historical films *[LCSH Genre]*
Historical programs, Television
USE Historical television programs
Historical reenactments (Motion pictures)
[LCSH Genre]
Historical reenactments (Television programs)
[LCSH Genre]

[†]**Subject headings noted with a dagger contain**
additional access points and subheadings that
are not pertinent to this text and are not
included here.

Historical television programs
> *(May Subd Geog)*
>> UF Historical programs, Television
>> Television historical programs
>> BT History
>> Television programs

Historical television programs
> [LCSH Genre]

Historiography[†]
>> NT Motion pictures in historiography
>> Video tapes in historiography

History[†]
>> NT Historical television programs
>> Mass media and history
>> Motion pictures and history
>> Television and history

History and mass media
> USE Mass media and history

History and motion pictures
> USE Motion pictures and history

History in mass media *(Not Subd Geog)*
> [P96.H55]
>> BT Mass media

History in motion pictures *(Not Subd Geog)*
> Here are entered works on historical themes in films that are not themselves historical films. Works on films that portray historical events or famous people are entered under Historical films with appropriate geographic, topical, and/or form subdivisions. Works on the relationship and influence of motion pictures on history are entered under Motion pictures and history.
>> BT Motion pictures

Histrionics
> USE Acting

Hockey films *(May Subd Geog)*
>> UF Ice hockey films
>> BT Sports films

Hockey films [LCSH Genre]

Hockey television programs [LCSH Genre]

Hollywood romance films
> USE Romance films

Holmes, Sherlock (Fictitious character)
> *(Not Subd Geog)*
>> UF Sherlock Holmes (Fictitious character)
>> RT Sherlock Holmes films
>> Sherlock Holmes television programs

Holmes, Sherlock (Fictitious character) in mass media *(Not Subd Geog)*
> [P96.H59]
>> BT Mass media

Holocaust, Jewish (1939–1945), in motion pictures
> *(Not Subd Geog)*

>> BT Motion pictures

Holocaust, Jewish (1939–1945) on television
> *(Not Subd Geog)*
> [PN1992.8.H63]
>> BT Television

Holocaust survivors in motion pictures
> *(Not Subd Geog)*
>> BT Motion pictures

Home economics[†]
>> NT Television in home economics

Home entertainment systems
> *(May Subd Geog)*
> [TK7881.3]
>> UF Entertainment systems, Home
>> BT Household electronics
>> NT Home video systems

Home in motion pictures *(Not Subd Geog)*
> [PN1995.9.H54]
>> BT Motion pictures

Home motion picture theaters
> USE Home theaters

Home movies
> USE Amateur films
> Cinematography

Home satellite television
> USE Direct broadcast satellite television

Home shopping television programs
> *(May Subd Geog)*
> This heading is used as a topical heading for works about live television programs that purvey a wide variety of goods that can be purchased by the viewers. Works about program-length television commercials that are devoted to one product, and that usually include a discussion or demonstration, are entered under Infomercials. When used as topical headings they are subdivided by the appropriate geographic, topical, and/or form subdivisions.
>> BT Television programs
>> RT Infomercials

Home shopping television programs
> [LCSH Genre]

Home theaters *(May Sub Geog)*
>> UF Home motion picture theaters
>> Theater rooms
>> BT Rooms

Home video systems *(May Subd Geog)*
>> BT Home entertainment systems

[†]**Subject headings noted with a dagger contain additional access points and subheadings that are not pertinent to this text and are not included here.**

Television
Videocassette recorders
NT Camcorders
Direct broadcast satellite television
DVD players
Television display systems
Television/video combinations

Home video systems industry
BT Television supplies industry
Homeland films
USE Heimatfilme
Homelessness in mass media
(Not Subd Geog)
[P96.H62]
BT Mass media
Homosexuality and motion pictures
(May Subd Geog)
UF Motion pictures and homosexuality
BT Motion pictures
Homosexuality and television
(May Subd Geog)
[PN1992.8.H64]
UF Television and homosexuality
BT Television
Homosexuality in motion pictures
(Not Subd Geog)
[PN1995.9.H55]
BT Motion pictures
Homosexuality in television
USE Homosexuality on television
Homosexuality, Male, in motion pictures
USE Male homosexuality in motion pictures
Homosexuality on television
(Not Subd Geog)
[PN1992.8.H64]
UF Gays on television
Homosexuality in television
BT Television
Hood, Robin (Legendary character)
USE Robin Hood (Legendary character)
Hoodlum drama (Motion pictures)
USE Gangster films
Juvenile delinquency films
Hopalong Cassidy (Fictitious character)
USE Cassidy, Hopalong (Fictitious character)
Hopalong Cassidy films
[PN1995.9.H56]
BT Western films
Hopalong Cassidy films [LCSH Genre]
Horror films (May Subd Geog)
UF Spookfests (Motion pictures)
BT Motion pictures
RT Haunted house films

Monster films
Nightmare on Elm Street films
Slasher films
Splatter films
Television broadcasting of horror films
—Direction
USE Horror films—Production and direction
—Interviews
BT Interviews
—Production and direction
(May Subd Geog)
UF Horror films—Direction
Horror films [LCSH Genre]
Horror in mass media (Not Subd Geog)
[P96.H65]
Horror television programs (May Subd Geog)
BT Television programs
RT Haunted house television programs
Monster television programs
Horror television programs [LCSH Genre]
Horses in motion pictures (Not Subd Geog)
BT Motion pictures
Hospital films
USE Medical films (Motion pictures)
Hospital television programs
USE Medical television programs
Hot Wheels turbo racing (Game)
[GV1469.35.H65]
BT Video games
Hotels[†]
NT Embassy Theatre (Fort Wayne, Ind.)
House of the dead (Game)
[GV1469.35.H67]
BT Video games
Household electronics[†]
NT High definition television—Receivers and
reception
Home entertainment systems
Television—Receivers and reception
Video tape recorders and recording
Housing[†]
—Law and legislation
NT Housing law in mass media
Housing law in mass media
(Not Subd Geog)
BT Housing—Law and legislation
Mass media
How-to videos
USE Instructional videos

**[†]Subject headings noted with a dagger contain
additional access points and subheadings that
are not pertinent to this text and are not
included here.**

HSX (Videotex system)
  BT Videotex systems
**Human-animal relationships in motion
  pictures** *(Not Subd Geog)*
  BT Motion pictures
Human body in mass media *(Not Subd Geog)*
  UF Body, Human, in mass media
  BT Mass media
Human body in motion pictures
  (Not Subd Geog)
  UF Body, Human, in motion pictures
  BT Motion pictures
Human body on television *(Not Subd Geog)*
  [PN1992.8.B64]
  UF Body, Human, on television
  BT Television
Human cloning in mass media *(Not Subd Geog)*
  BT Mass media
Human cloning in motion pictures *(Not Subd Geog)*
  BT Motion pictures
Human reproductive technology in motion pictures
  (Not Subd Geog)
  BT Motion pictures
Human rights in mass media
  (Not Subd Geog)
  [P96.H84]
  BT Mass media
Humor in motion pictures
  USE Wit and humor in motion pictures
Hungarian drama†
  NT Television plays, Hungarian
Hungarian motion pictures
  USE Motion pictures, Hungarian
Hungarian television plays
  USE Television plays, Hungarian
Hunting in motion pictures
  (Not Subd Geog)
  [PN1995.9.H84]
  BT Motion pictures
Hybrid Heaven (Game)
  [GV1469.35.H94]
  BT Nintendo video games
Hypermedia systems
  USE Interactive multimedia
Hypnotism in motion pictures
  (Not Subd Geog)
  [PN1995.9.H95]
  BT Motion pictures
Hysteria in motion pictures *(Not Subd Geog)*
  BT Motion pictures

Icarex camera *(Not Subd Geog)*
  BT Cameras

Ice hockey films
  USE Hockey films
Ichi films
  USE Zatoichi films
Idan-ha Theater (Soda Springs, Idaho)
  USE Idanha Theater (Soda Springs, Idaho)
Idanha Theater (Soda Springs, Idaho)
  UF Idan-ha Theater (Soda Springs, Idaho)
  BT Motion picture theaters—Idaho
Identity (Psychology) and mass media
  (May Subd Geog)
  [P96.I34]
  UF Mass media and identity
  BT Mass media
Identity (Psychology) in motion pictures
  (Not Subd Geog)
  BT Motion pictures
Identity (Psychology) on television *(Not Subd Geog)*
  BT Television
Ideology in motion pictures
  BT Motion pictures
IDPA Awards
  UF IDPA Awards for Documentary, Animation,
    and Advertising Films
    IDPA Awards for Documentary
    & Animation films Indian
    Documentary Producers'
    Association Awards
  BT Motion pictures
IDPA Awards for Documentary, Animation, and
  Advertising Films
  USE IDPA Awards
IDPA Awards for Documentary & Animation films
  USE IDPA Awards
Ikoflex camera *(Not Subd Geog)*
  [TR263]
  BT Cameras
    Zeiss cameras
Ikonta camera *(Not Subd Geog)*
  [TR263.13]
  BT Cameras
    Zeiss cameras
Illusion in motion pictures *(Not Subd Geog)*
  BT Motion pictures
Image intensifiers†
  NT Electronography
Image processing†
  —Digital techniques
    NT Digital video

†**Subject headings noted with a dagger contain
additional access points and subheadings that
are not pertinent to this text and are not
included here.**

Image quality of television cameras
  USE Television cameras—Image quality
Image stabilization†
  NT Motion picture camera stabilization systems
Image transmission†
  NT Automatic picture transmission
        Television—Transmitters and transmission
        Video telephone
Imagery (Psychology) in motion pictures
  (Not Subd Geog)
  BT Motion pictures
Imaginary places in mass media
  (Not Subd Geog)
  BT Mass media
Imagination in motion pictures
  (Not Subd Geog)
  BT Motion pictures
Immigrants†
  NT Mass media and immigrants
Immigrants and mass media
  USE Mass media and immigrants
Immigrants in motion pictures
  (Not Subd Geog)
  BT Motion pictures
Immigrants on television
  (Not Subd Geog)
  BT Television
Impersonation†
  BT Acting
        Comedy
Impersonation in motion pictures
  (Not Subd Geog)
  BT Motion pictures
Impersonators, Female
  BT Actresses
Impersonators, Female, in motion pictures
  (Not Subd Geog)
  BT Motion pictures
Impersonators, Male
  USE Male impersonators
Impersonators of men
  USE Male impersonators
Impressionism in motion pictures
  (Not Subd Geog)
  [PN1995.9.I45]
  BT Motion pictures
Imprisonment in motion pictures
  (Not Subd Geog)
  BT Motion pictures
Improvisation (Acting)†
  BT Acting
In-concert films
  USE Concert films

In-water photography
  USE Underwater photography
Incest in motion pictures
  (Not Subd Geog)
  BT Motion pictures
Independent filmmakers
  (May Subd Geog)
  UF Independent moviemakers
  BT Motion picture producers and directors
Independent films *(May Subd Geog)*
  UF Indie films
  BT Motion pictures
Independent films *[LCSH Genre]*
Independent moviemakers
  USE Independent filmmakers
Indian captivities in motion pictures
  (Not Subd Geog)
  BT Motion pictures
Indian Documentary Producers' Association Awards
  USE IDPA Awards
Indian film festivals *(May Subd Geog)*
  BT Film festivals
Indian mass media *(May Subd Geog)*
  UF Indians of North America—Mass media
        Mass media, Indian
  BT Mass media
Indian motion picture actors and actresses
  (May Subd Geog)
  UF Motion picture actors and actresses, Indian
  BT Motion picture actors and actresses
Indian motion pictures *(May Subd Geog)*
  [P1995.9.I48]
  Here are entered works on motion pictures
  produced by American Indian
  film makers.
  UF Motion pictures, Indian
  BT Motion pictures
Indian women in motion pictures
  (Not Subd Geog)
  BT Motion pictures
Indiana Jones (Fictitious character)
  USE Jones, Indiana (Fictitious character)
Indiana Jones films
  BT Action and adventure films
Indiana Jones films *[LCSH Genre]*
Indiana Jones television programs
  [LCSH Genre]
Indians in mass media *(Not Subd Geog)*
  [P94.5.I53]

†**Subject headings noted with a dagger contain
additional access points and subheadings that
are not pertinent to this text and are not
included here.**

UF Indians of Central America in mass media
 Indians of Mexico in mass media
 Indians of North America in mass media
 Indians of South America in mass media
 Indians of the West Indies in mass media
BT Mass media
Indians in motion pictures *(Not Subd Geog)*
 [PN1995.9.I48]
 UF Indians of Central American in motion
  pictures
  Indians of Mexico in motion pictures
  Indians of North America in motion pictures
  Indians of South America in motion pictures
  Indians in the West Indies in motion pictures
 BT Motion pictures
Indians in the motion picture industry
 (May Subd Geog)
 [PN1995.9.I48]
 BT Motion picture industry
Indians of Central America in mass media
 USE Indians in mass media
Indians of Central America in motion pictures
 USE Indians in motion pictures
Indians of Mexico in mass media
 USE Indians in mass media
Indians of Mexico in motion pictures
 USE Indians in motion pictures
Indians of North America†
 —Mass media
  USE Indian mass media
Indians of North America in motion pictures
 USE Indians in motion pictures
Indians of South America in mass media
 USE Indians in mass media
Indians of South America in motion pictures
 USE Indians in motion pictures
Indians of the West Indies in mass media
 USE Indians in mass media
Indians of the West Indies in motion pictures
 USE Indians in motion pictures
Indians on television *(Not Subd Geog)*
 BT Television
Indic film posters
 USE Film posters, Indic
Indic motion pictures
 USE Motion pictures, Indic
Indie films
 USE Independent films
Indigenous films *(May Subd Geog)*
 Here are entered general works on the films
of indigenous filmmakers, not limited to a
particular racial or ethnic group. Works on the
portrayal of indigenous peoples in films are

entered under Indigenous peoples in motion
pictures.
 BT Motion pictures
Indigenous peoples and mass media
 (May Subd Geog)
 UF Mass media and indigenous peoples
 BT Mass media
Indigenous peoples in motion peoples
 (Not Subd Geog)
 Here are entered general works on the films of
indigenous filmmakers, not limited to a particular
racial or ethnic group. Works on the portrayal of
indigenous peoples in films are entered under
Indigenous peoples in motion pictures.
 BT Motion pictures
**Individuation (Psychology) in motion
pictures**
 (Not Subd Geog)
 BT Motion pictures
Indonesian drama†
 NT Motion picture plays, Indonesian
Indonesian motion picture plays
 USE Motion picture plays, Indonesian
Industrial cinematography *(May Subd Geog)*
 UF Cinematography—Industrial
  applications
  Cinematography, Industrial
 BT Cinematography
  Photography, Industrial
Industrial films *(May Subd Geog)*
 UF Business films
  Industry-sponsored films
  Motion pictures—Industrial applications
  Motion pictures in business
  Motion pictures in industry
  Moving-pictures in industry
 BT Documentary films
Industrial films *[LCSH Genre]*
Industrial television *(May Subd Geog)*
 UF Business television
  Corporate television
  Television—Industrial applications
  Television, Business
  Television, Corporate
  Television, Industrial
  Television in industry
 BT Closed-circuit television
 RT Television in management

---

†**Subject headings noted with a dagger contain
additional access points and subheadings that
are not pertinent to this text and are not
included here.**

Industrial television programs
  [LCSH Genre]
Industry†
  NT Motion pictures in industry
Industry sponsored films
  USE Industrial films
Information literacy†
  NT Media literacy
Infomercials *(May Subd Geog)*
  UF Informercials
  BT Broadcast advertising
  RT Home shopping television programs
Infomercials *[LCSH Genre]*
Information display systems†
  RT Vacuum-tubes
  NT Cathode ray tubes
       Electronic program guides (Television)
       Television display systems
Information storage and retrieval systems†
  NT Multimedia systems
  SA *individual makes of information storage and*
       retrieval systems
Informational films
  USE Educational films
Informational television programs
  USE Educational television programs
       Instructional television programs
Informational videos
  USE Educational videos
       Instructional videos
Informercials
  USE Infomercials
Infringement of copyright
  USE Copyright infringement
Insert cards (Film posters)
  USE Insert posters
Insert posters *(May Subd Geog)*
  UF Cards, Insert (Film posters)
       Insert cards (Film posters)
  BT Advertising—Motion pictures
       Film posters
Insight in motion pictures
  (Not Subd Geog)
  BT Motion pictures
Inspector Charlie Chan (Fictitious character)
  USE Chan, Charlie (Fictitious character)
Inspector Montalbano (Fictitious character)
  USE Montalbano, Salvo (Fictitious character)
Installations (Art)†
  NT Film installations (Art)
       Video installations (Art)
Instamatic camera
  [TR263.1]

  UF Pocket instamatic camera
  BT Cameras
       Kodak camera
  BT Cameras
Instant camera, Kodak
  USE Kodak instant camera
Instant photography
  [TR269]
  —Films
       UF Films, Instant photography
Instructional films *[LCSH Genre]*
Instructional materials centers
  (May Subd Geog)
  [LB3044.7–LB3077.74]
  UF Audio visual materials centers
       Curriculum laboratories
       Educational media centers
       Instructional media centers
       Laboratories, Curriculum
       Learning resource centers
       Media centers (Education)
       School media centers
  RT Audio-visual library service
       School libraries
  —Acquisitions
       BT Acquisitions (Libraries)
  —Book selection
       BT Book selection
  —Collection development
       BT Collection development (Libraries)
  —Public relations
       UF Public relations—Instructional materials
            centers
  —Services to minorities
       BT Minorities—Services for
  —Services to people with disabilities
       UF Instructional materials centers—Services
            to the handicapped
       BT People with disabilities—Services for—
            Services to the handicapped
       USE Instructional materials centers—Services
            to the handicapped
  —User education
       UF User education (Instructional materials
            centers)
       BT Library orientation
Instructional materials industry
  (May Subd Geog)
  [HD9810]

†**Subject headings noted with a dagger contain
additional access points and subheadings that
are not pertinent to this text and are not
included here.**

UF Audio-visual materials industry
     Educational materials industry
BT Audio-visual materials
Instructional materials personnel[†]
   NT Audio-visual education
Instructional media centers
   USE Instructional materials centers
Instructional television programs
   USE Media programs (Education)
Instructional television programs
   [LCSH Genre]
Instructional videos *(May Subd Geog)*
   Here are entered video recordings designed to impart skills or techniques to general audiences, typically in a "how-to" manner. Video recordings intended for teaching and informational purposes, especially those made for classroom viewing, are entered under Educational videos. Works on the use of video tapes in education are entered under Video tapes in education.
   UF How-to videos
       Informational videos
       Skill videos
       Training videos
   BT Video recordings
Insurance[†]
   NT Motion picture insurance
Insurance, Motion picture
   USE Motion picture insurance
Intangible property[†]
   NT Copyright
Intellect on television *(Not Subd Geog)*
   [PN1992.8.I66]
   BT Television
Intellectual freedom
   USE Censorship
Intellectual property[†]
   NT Copyright
Intellectuals in motion pictures
   (Not Subd Geog)
   BT Motion pictures
Intelligence levels in mass media
   (Not Subd Geog)
   BT Mass media
Interactive computer systems[†]
   UF Computer systems, Interactive
   NT Computer terminals—Interactive terminals
Interactive terminals
   USE Computer terminals—Interactive terminals
Interactive media
   USE Interactive multimedia
Interactive multimedia *(May Subd Geog)*
   [QA76.76.I59]

Here are entered works on media containing information that may be interactively manipulated by individual users through the use of software or microprocessing capabilities. Works on computer systems that integrate and present diverse media, such as text, graphics, still and moving images, and audio, are entered under Multimedia systems.
   UF Hypermedia systems
       Interactive media
   BT Computer software
   RT Cataloging of interactive multimedia
       Digital video
       Video recordings
   NT Interactive video
   SA *subdivision* Interactive multimedia *under subjects*
—Copyright
   USE Copyright—Interactive multimedia
Interactive program guides (Television)
   USE Electronic program guides (Television)
Interactive television *(May Subd Geog)*
   [HE8700.95 (Telecommunication industry)]
   [TK6679.3 (Engineering)]
   BT Television
Interactive video *(May Subd Geog)*
   [LB1028.75 (Computer-assisted instruction)]
   [TK6687 (Technology)]
   UF Video systems, Interactive
   BT Digital video
       Interactive multimedia
       Video recordings
   NT Video dial tone
Intercommunication systems[†]
   NT Closed-circuit television
Intercultural communication in motion pictures
   (Not Subd Geog)
   BT Motion pictures
Interior decoration[†]
   NT Audio-visual equipment in interior decoration
International Festival of the Cinema (Cannes, France)
   USE Cannes Film Festival
International Film Festival (Cannes, France)
International relations[†]
   NT Mass media and international relations
International relations and mass media
   USE Mass media and international relations
International relations in motion pictures
   (Not Subd Geog)

[†]**Subject headings noted with a dagger contain additional access points and subheadings that are not pertinent to this text and are not included here.**

BT Motion pictures

International relations on television
(Not Subd Geog)
BT Television

**International Standard Bibliographic Description
for Non-Book Materials**
[Z695.66]
BT Cataloging of nonbook materials

Internet television *(May Subd Geog)*
[TK5105.887]
UF Internet TV
Net television
Net TV
Web television
Web TV
BT Television
Webcasting

Internet TV
USE Internet television

Internet videoconferencing
(May Subd Geog)
BT Videoconferencing

Internet videos *(May Subd Geog)*
[TK105.8867]
UF Net videos
Online videos
Web videos
BT Video recordings
Web sites

Interpersonal conflict in motion pictures
(Not Subd Geog)
BT Motion pictures

Interpersonal relations on television
(Not Subd Geog)
BT Television

Interracial marriage in mass media
(Not Subd Geog)
BT Mass media

Interviewing in mass media
(May Subd Geog)
[P96.I]
BT Mass media—Methodology

Interviewing in television
USE Interviewing on television

Interviewing on television *(Not Subd Geog)*
[PN1992.8.I68]
UF Interviewing in television
Television interviewing
BT Television
RT Television talk shows

Interviews[†]
NT Horror films—Interviews
Motion pictures—Interviews

Intimacy (Psychology) in motion pictures
(Not Subd Geog)
BT Motion pictures

Introspection in motion pictures
(Not Subd Geog)
[PN1995.9.I58]
BT Motion pictures

Inuit in motion pictures *(Not Subd Geog)*
BT Motion pictures

IPGs (Interactive program guides)
USE Electronic program guides (Television)

Iris Theater (American Falls, Idaho)
BT Motion picture theaters—Idaho

Irish Americans in motion pictures *(Not Subd Geog)*
[PN1995.9.I67]
BT Motion pictures

Irish Americans in the motion picture industry
(May Subd Geog)
BT Motion picture industry—United States

Irish drama[†]
NT Television plays, Irish

Irish in motion pictures *(Not Subd Geog)*
BT Motion pictures

Irish motion pictures
USE Motion pictures, Irish

Irish question in motion pictures
(Not Subd Geog)
[PN1995.9.I68]
BT Motion pictures

Irish television plays
USE Television plays, Irish

**Irish Travellers (Nomadic people)
in motion pictures**
BT Motion pictures

Irony in motion pictures *(Not Subd Geog)*
BT Motion pictures

Islam in mass media *(Not Subd Geog)*
[P96.I84]
BT Mass media

Islam in motion pictures *(Not Subd Geog)*
BT Motion pictures

Islamic law[†]
NT Mass media (Islamic law)
Motion pictures (Islamic law)

Israel-Arab War, 1973[†]
—Motion pictures and the war
UF Israel-Arab War, 1973, in motion
pictures

[†]**Subject headings noted with a dagger contain
additional access points and subheadings that
are not pertinent to this text and are not
included here.**

Italian Americans in mass media
(Not Subd Geog)
BT Mass media
Italian Americans in motion pictures
(Not Subd Geog)
[PN1995.9.I73]
BT Motion pictures
Italian Americans in the motion picture industry
(May Subd Geog)
[PN1995.9.I73]
BT Motion picture industry—United States
Italian drama[†]
NT Motion picture plays, Italian
Italian film posters
USE Film posters, Italian
Italian motion picture plays
USE Motion picture plays, Italian
Italian motion pictures
USE Motion pictures, Italian
Italians in mass media *(Not Subd Geog)*
BT Mass media
Italians in motion pictures *(Not Subd Geog)*
BT Motion pictures
Itinerant motion picture theaters
USE Traveling motion picture theaters
ITU H.263 (Video coding standard)
USE H.263 (Video coding standard)
ITU-T Recommendation H.263
(Video coding standard)
USE H.263 (Video coding standard)

J. D. films
USE Juvenile delinquency films
Jade Cocoon (Game)
[GV1469.35.J34]
BT Video games
James Bond (Fictitious character)
USE Bond, James (Fictitious character)
James Bond films *(May Subd Geog)*
[PN1995.9.J3]
UF Bond films
BT Action and adventure films
RT Spy films
Bond, James (Fictitious character)
James Bond films *[LCSH Genre]*
Japanese drama[†]
NT Motion picture plays, Japanese
Television plays, Japanese
Japanese film posters
USE Film posters, Japanese
Japanese motion picture plays
USE Motion picture plays, Japanese
Japanese motion pictures

USE Motion pictures, Japanese
Japanese television plays
USE Television plays, Japanese
Jazz in motion pictures *(Not Subd Geog)*
[PN1995.9.J37]
BT Motion pictures
Jealousy in motion pictures
(Not Subd Geog)
BT Motion pictures
Jean Vigo, Prix
USE Prix Jean Vigo
Jedi Power Battles (Game)
[GV1469.35.J42]
BT Video games
Jenkins process
USE Front-screen projection
Jerry (Fictitious character: Hanna and Barbera)
(Not Subd Geog)
Jesus Christ[†]
—In motion pictures
UF Jesus Christ in motion pictures
BT Motion pictures
Jesus Christ in motion pictures
USE Jesus Christ—In motion pictures
Jet Force Gemini (Game)
[GV1469.35.J48]
BT Video games
Jet Moto (Game)
[GV1469.35.J52]
BT Video games
Jewish actors *(May Subd Geog)*
UF Actors, Jewish
BT Actors
Jewish-Arab relations in motion pictures *(Not Subd Geog)*
[PN1995.9.J45]
BT Motion pictures
Jewish film festivals *(May Subd Geog)*
BT Film festivals
Jewish motion picture producers and directors
(May Subd Geog)
BT Motion picture producers and directors
Jewish women in motion pictures
(Not Subd Geog)
BT Motion pictures
Jews[†]
—Biography
NT Actors, Jewish

[†]**Subject headings noted with a dagger contain additional access points and subheadings that are not pertinent to this text and are not included here.**

Jews in motion pictures *(Not Subd Geog)*
  [PN1995.9.J46]
  BT Motion pictures
Jews in television
  USE Jews on television
Jews in the motion picture industry
  (May Subd Geog)
  BT Motion picture industry
Jews on television *(Not Subd Geog)*
  UF Jews in television
  BT Television
Jinseiza (Tokyo, Japan)
  BT Motion picture theaters—Japan
Joints (Engineering)†
  NT Motion picture film—Splicing
Jones, Indiana (Fictitious character)
  (Not Subd Geog)
  UF Indiana Jones (Fictitious character)
Journalism†
  NT Broadcast journalism
    Motion picture journalism
  —Editing
    NT Editing
Journalism and motion pictures
  UF Motion pictures and journalism
  BT Motion pictures
Journalism films *[LCSH Genre]*
Journalism television programs
  [LCSH Genre]
Journalists†
  NT Motion picture journalists
    Television journalists
Journalists in motion pictures *(Not Subd Geog)*
  BT Motion pictures
Juan, Don (Legendary character)
  USE Don Juan (Legendary character)
Judicial power†
  NT Mass media and judicial power
Judicial power and mass media
  USE Mass media and judicial power
Juggernaut (Game)
  [GV1469.35.J83]
  BT Video games
Jungle films *(May Subd Geog)*
  This heading is used as a topical heading for
  works about adventure films that feature a jungle
  background.
    BT Action and adventure films
Jungle films *[LCSH Genre]*
Jungle television programs *(May Subd Geog)*
  This heading is used as a topical heading for
  works about adventure television programs that
  feature a jungle background.

  NT Television programs
Jungle television programs *[LCSH Genre]*
Jury in motion pictures *(Not Subd Geog)*
  BT Motion pictures
Justice, Administration of, in motion pictures
  (Not Subd Geog)
  [PN1995.9.J8]
  BT Motion pictures
Justice, Administration of, on television
  (Not Subd Geog)
  [PN1992.8.J87]
  BT Television
Juvenile delinquency films *(May Subd Geog)*
  [PN1995.9.J87]
  UF Gang films
    Hoodlum drama (Motion pictures)
    J. D. films
    Juvenile delinquent films
    Youth gang films
    Youth street films
  BT Teen films
  RT Crime films
Juvenile delinquency films *[LCSH Genre]*
Juvenile delinquent films
  USE Juvenile delinquency films
Juvenile films
  USE Children's films
JVC televisions *(Not Subd Geog)*
  BT Television—Receivers and reception

Kabuki Warriors (Game)
  BT Video games
Kagero: Deception II (Game)
  [GV1469.35.K35]
  BT Video games
Kalee motion picture projectors
  (Not Subd Geog)
  BT Motion picture projectors
Kannada drama†
  NT Motion picture plays, Kannada
    Television plays, Kannada
Kannada motion picture plays
  USE Motion picture plays, Kannada
Kannada television plays
  USE Television plays, Kannada
Karat camera *(Not Subd Geog)*
  [TR263.K]
  BT Cameras

†**Subject headings noted with a dagger contain
additional access points and subheadings that
are not pertinent to this text and are not
included here.**

Karate in motion pictures
  (Not Subd Geog)
    BT Motion pictures
Kardon camera *(Not Subd Geog)*
  [TR263.K]
    BT Cameras
        Leica camera
Kartia (Game)
  [GV1469.35.K37]
    BT Video games
Keith's (Portland, Me.)
    USE Civic Theatre (Portland, Me.)
Ken Theater (Frankenmuth, Mich.)
    BT Motion picture theaters—Michigan
Keno[†]
    NT Video keno
Kent, Clark (Fictitious character)
    USE Superman (Fictitious character)
Kerala Samsthana Calaccitra Avard
    USE Kerala State Film Awards
Kerala State Film Award
    USE Kerala State Film Awards
Kerala State Film Awards
    UF Kerala Samsthena Calaccitra Avard
        Kerala State Film Award
    BT Motion pictures—Awards—India
Keystone motion picture camera
  (Not Subd Geog)
    BT Motion picture cameras
Kibbutzim[†]
    NT Mass media and kibbutzim
Kibbutzim and mass media
    USE Mass media and kibbutzim
Kiev camera *(Not Subd Geog)*
  [TR263.K]
    BT Cameras
Killer Instinct (Game)
  [GV1469.35.K54]
    BT Video games
Kinescope recording
    USE Television film recording
Kinetograph
  [TR885]
    BT Cinematography
        Motion picture cameras
Kinetoscope
  [TR885]
    BT Cinematography
King Kong (Fictitious character)
  (Not Subd Geog)
    UF Kong, King (Fictitious character)
King Kong films
  [PN1995.9.K55]

    BT Monster films
King Kong films *[LCSH Genre]*
Kings, Drag
    USE Male impersonators
Kings and rulers in motion pictures
  (Not Subd Geog)
    BT Motion pictures
King's Field (Game)
  [GV1469.35.K58]
    BT Video games
Kino "Studio 4" (Zurich, Switzerland)
    UF Cinema Studio 4 (Zurich, Switzerland)
        Studio 4 (Zurich, Switzerland)
    BT Motion picture theaters—Switzerland
Kino Xenix (Zurich Switzerland)
    UF Xenix (Zurich, Switzerland)
    BT Motion picture theaters—Switzerland
Kirby 64 (Game)
    UF Kirby Sixty-four (Game)
    BT Nintendo video games
Kirby Sixty-four (Game)
    USE Kirby 64 (Game)
Kissing in motion pictures *(Not Subd Geog)*
  [PN1995.9.K57]
    BT Motion pictures
Knockout Kings 2000 (Game)
  [GV1469.35.K62]
    UF Knockout Kings Two Thousand (Game)
    BT Video games
Knockout Kings Two Thousand (Game)
    USE Knockout Kings 2000 (Game)
Kodak camera *(Not Subd Geog)*
    BT Cameras
    NT Instamatic camera
        Kodak instant camera
        Retina camera
Kodak instant camera *(Not Subd Geog)*
    UF Instant camera, Kodak
    BT Cameras
        Kodak camera
    NT Brownie camera
Kodak motion picture camera
  (Not Subd Geog)
    BT Motion picture cameras
Kong, King (Fictitious character)
    USE King Kong (Fictitious character)
Konica camera *(Not Subd Geog)*

[†]**Subject headings noted with a dagger contain additional access points and subheadings that are not pertinent to this text and are not included here.**

BT Cameras

Konka televisions *(Not Subd Geog)*
　　BT Television—Receivers and reception

Korean American motion picture actors and actresses *(May Subd Geog)*
　　UF Motion picture actors and actresses, Korean American
　　BT Motion picture actors and actresses—United States

Korean drama[†]
　　NT Motion picture plays, Korean
　　　　Television plays, Korean

Korean film posters
　　USE Film posters, Korean

Korean motion picture plays
　　USE Motion picture plays, Korean

Korean motion pictures
　　USE Motion pictures, Korean

Korean television plays
　　USE Television plays, Korean

Korelle camera *(Not Subd Geog)*
　　[TR263K]
　　BT Cameras

Kosmos-Kino (Vienna, Austria)
　　UF Kosmos-Lichtspiele (Vienna, Austria)
　　　　Kosmos-Theater (Vienna, Austria)
　　　　Rex-Kino (Vienna, Austria)
　　BT Motion picture theaters—Austria

Kosmos-Lichtspiele (Vienna, Austria)
　　USE Kosmos-Kino (Vienna, Austria)

Kosmos-Theater (Vienna, Austria)
　　USE Kosmos-Kino (Vienna, Austria)

Kung fu films
　　USE Martial arts films

Kurds in mass media *(Not Subd Geog)*
　　BT Mass media

Labor agreements
　　USE Collective labor agreements

Labor and laboring classes in motion pictures
　　USE Working class in motion pictures

Labor and laboring classes in television
　　USE Working class on television

Labor contract[†]
　　NT Collective labor agreements

Labor unions and mass media *(May Subd Geog)*
　　[P96.T7]
　　UF Mass media and labor unions
　　　　Trade-unions and mass media
　　BT Mass media

Laboratories, Curriculum
　　USE Instructional materials centers

Ladies, Leading (Actresses)
　　USE Leading ladies (Actresses)

Landmark Theatre (Syracuse, N.Y.)
　　USE Loew's State Theatre (Syracuse, N.Y.)

Landscape in motion pictures
　　(Not Subd Geog)
　　BT Motion pictures

Language and languages[†]
　　NT Mass media and language
　　　　Motion pictures and language
　　—Study and teaching[†]
　　　　NT Television in foreign language education

Language and languages in motion pictures
　　(Not Subd Geog)
　　BT Motion pictures

Language and motion pictures
　　USE Motion pictures and language

Lantern projection[†]
　　UF Projection, Lantern
　　BT Projection
　　NT Front-screen projection
　　　　Motion picture projection
　　　　Motion picture projectors

Lara Croft (Fictitious character)
　　USE Croft, Lara (Fictitious character)

Latin Americans in motion pictures
　　(Not Subd Geog)
　　[PN1995.9.L37]
　　BT Motion pictures

Latin lovers in motion pictures
　　(Not Subd Geog)
　　[PN1995.9.L38]
　　BT Motion pictures

Law films
　　USE Legal films

Law in mass media *(Not Subd Geog)*
　　BT Mass media

Law television programs
　　USE Legal television programs

Lawyer films
　　USE Legal films

Lawyer television programs
　　USE Legal television programs

Lawyers in motion pictures
　　(Not Subd Geog)
　　BT Motion pictures

Lawyers on television *(Not Subd Geog)*
　　BT Television

[†]**Subject headings noted with a dagger contain additional access points and subheadings that are not pertinent to this text and are not included here.**

LC-A camera
  USE Lomo Kompakt Automat camera
Lease and rental services†
  NT Video recordings industry
Leadership in motion pictures
  (Not Subd Geog)
  BT Motion pictures
Leading ladies (Actresses) *(May Subd Geog)*
  UF Ladies, Leading (Actresses)
  BT Actresses
Leading men (Actors) *(May Subd Geog)*
  UF Men, Leading (Actors)
  BT Male actors
Learning resource centers
  USE Instructional materials centers
Legacy of Kain (Game)
  [GV1469.L28]
  BT Video games
Legal films *(May Subd Geog)*
  This heading is used as a topical heading for
  works about fiction and/or nonfiction films that
  feature the interaction of lawyers, prosecutors,
  clients, witnesses, and judges. When used as a
  topical heading it is subdivided by the appropriate
  geographic, topical, and/or form subdivisions.
  UF Courtroom films
      Hero-lawyer films
      Law films
      Lawyer films
      Legal films (Drama)
      Trial films
  BT Motion pictures
Legal films (Drama)
  USE Legal films
Legal films *[LCSH Genre]*
Legal television programs *(May Subd Geog)*
  This heading is used as a topical heading for works
  about fiction and/or nonfiction television programs
  that feature the interaction of lawyers, prosecutors,
  clients, witnesses, and judges. When used as a topical
  heading it is subdivided by the appropriate
  geographic, topical, and/or form subdivisions.
  UF Courtroom television programs
      Law television programs
      Lawyer television programs
      Legal television programs (Drama)
      Trial television programs
  BT Television programs
Legal television programs *[LCSH Genre]*
Legal television programs (Drama)
  USE Legal television programs
Legend of Legaia (Game)
  [GV1469.35.L42]

  BT Video games
Legend of Zelda (Game)
  [GV1469.35.L43]
  UF Adventure of Link (Game)
      Legend of Zelda II (Game)
      Zelda II (Game)
      Zelda (Game4)
  BT Video games
Legend of Zelda II (Game)
  USE Legend of Zelda
Legislative bodies†
  —Television broadcasting of proceedings
    (May Subd Geog)
    UF Television coverage of legislative
        proceedings
    BT Television broadcasting
    SA *subdivision* Television broadcasting of
        proceedings *under names of individual
        legislative bodies, e.g.,* United States.
        Congress – Television broadcasting of
        proceedings
Leica camera *(Not Subd Geog)*
  BT Cameras
  NT Kardon camera
      Leica digital cameras
      Leicaflex camera
Leica digital cameras *(Not Subd Geog)*
  BT Digital cameras
      Leica camera
Leicaflex camera *(Not Subd Geog)*
  BT Leica camera
      Single-lens reflex cameras
Lemmings (Game)
  [GV1469.35.L]
  BT Video games
Lesbian actresses *(May Subd Geog)*
  BT Actresses
Lesbian and gay film festivals
  USE Gay and lesbian film festivals
Lesbian bars in motion pictures
  (Not Subd Geog)
  BT Motion pictures
Lesbian erotic films *(May Subd Geog)*
  BT Gay erotic films
      Lesbian erotica
Lesbian erotic films *[LCSH Genre]*
Lesbian erotica†
  NT Lesbian erotic films

†**Subject headings noted with a dagger contain
additional access points and subheadings that
are not pertinent to this text and are not
included here.**

Lesbian motion picture producers and directors
(May Subd Geog)
    BT Gay motion picture producers and directors
       Women motion picture producers and
       directors

Lesbian vampires in motion pictures
(Not Subd Geog)
    BT Motion pictures

Lesbianism in motion pictures
(Not Subd Geog)
    [PN1995.9.L48]
    BT Motion pictures

Lesbianism on television *(Not Subd Geog)*
    [PN1992.8.L47]
    UF Lesbians on television
    BT Television

Lesbians in mass media *(Not Subd Geog)*
    BT Mass media

Lesbians in motion pictures
(Not Subd Geog)
    Here are entered works on the portrayal of
lesbians in motion pictures. Works on all aspects of
lesbian involvement in motion pictures are entered
under Lesbians in the motion picture industry.
Works on specific aspects of lesbian involvement
are entered under the specific subject, e.g., Lesbian
actresses.
    BT Motion pictures

Lesbians in the motion picture industry
(May Subd Geog)
    Here are entered works on all aspects of lesbian
involvement in motion pictures. Works on the
portrayal of lesbians in motion pictures are entered
under Lesbians in motion pictures. Works on
specific aspects of lesbian involvement are entered
under the specific subject, e.g., Lesbian actresses.
    BT Motion picture industry

Lesbians on television
    USE Lesbianism on television

Letter writing in motion pictures *(Not Subd Geog)*
    BT Motion pictures

Letters in motion pictures
(Not Subd Geog)
    BT Motion pictures

Liberty in motion pictures
(Not Subd Geog)
    BT Motion pictures

Librarians in motion pictures
(Not Subd Geog)
    BT Motion pictures

Libraries†
—Special collections
— —Nonbook materials

    NT Nonbook materials

Libraries, Broadcasting
    USE Broadcasting libraries

Libraries, Film
    USE Motion picture film collections

Libraries, Motion pictures
    USE Motion picture film collections

Libraries, Special
    NT Broadcasting libraries
       Motion picture film collections

Libraries and home video systems
    USE Home video systems—Library applications

Libraries and mass media
(May Subd Geog)
    BT Mass media
    NT Libraries and television

Libraries and motion pictures
(May Subd Geog)
    UF Motion pictures and libraries
       Motion pictures in libraries
    BT Motion pictures

Libraries and television *(May Subd Geog)*
    [Z716.8]
    UF Television and libraries
    BT Audio-visual library service
       Libraries and mass media
       Television
    NT Video tape recorders and recording—Library
       applications

Libraries and video discs
    USE Video discs—Library applications

Libraries and video recording
(May Subd Geog)
    UF Video recording and libraries
    BT Video recording

Libraries and video tape recorders
and recording
    USE Video tape recorders and recording—Library
       applications

Libraries and videotex systems
    USE Videotex systems—Library applications

Libraries in motion pictures
(Not Subd Geog)
    BT Motion pictures

Library applications of home video systems
    USE Home video systems—Library applications

Library application of video discs
    USE Video discs—Library applications

†**Subject headings noted with a dagger contain
additional access points and subheadings that
are not pertinent to this text and are not
included here.**

Library applications of video tape recorders and
recordings
   USE Video tape recorders and recording—Library
      applications
Library applications of videotex systems
   USE Videotex systems—Library applications
Library copyright policies[†]
   RT Fair use (Copyright)
Library film
   USE Stock footage
Library materials[†]
   NT Nonbook materials
Library shelving[†]
   NT Shelving for nonbook materials
Library shots (Motion pictures, television, etc.)
   USE Stock footage
Lichtburg (Essen, Germany)[†]
   UF Lichtburg Cinema (Essen, Germany)
      Lichtburg Essen (Essen, Germany)
      Lichtburg Filmpalast (Essen, Germany)
      Lichtburg Theater (Essen, Germany)
   BT Motion picture theaters—Germany
Lichtburg Cinema (Essen, Germany)
   USE Lichtburg (Essen, Germany)
Lichtburg Essen (Essen, Germany)
   USE Lichtburg (Essen, Germany)
Lichtburg Filmpalast (Essen, Germany)
   USE Lichtburg (Essen, Germany)
Lichtburg Theater (Essen, Germany)
   USE Lichtburg (Essen, Germany)
Light sources for motion picture projectors
   USE Motion picture projectors—Light sources
Lighting cameramen
   USE Cinematographers
Liminality on television *(Not Subd Geog)*
   BT Television
Limited serials (Television programs)
   USE Television mini-series
Limited serials (Video recordings)
   USE Video mini-series
Linhof cameras *(Not Subd Geog)*
   USE Cameras
Lions in motion pictures *(Not Subd Geog)*
   BT Motion pictures
Literature[†]
   NT Copyright
      Criticism
      Mass media and literature
      Motion pictures and literature
      Television and literature
  —Adaptations
      USE Film and video adaptations Literature,
         Film

   USE Motion picture literature Literature,
      Motion pictures
   USE Motion picture literature Literature and
      motion pictures
   USE Motion pictures and literature
Literature and television
   USE Television and literature
Little Rascals films
   USE Our Gang films
Live captioning (Closed captioning)
   USE Real-time closed captioning
Live concert films
   USE Concert films
Live-in-concert films
   USE Concert films
Live television programs *(May Subd Geog)*
   UF Television programs, Live
   BT Television programs
Live television programs *[LCSH Genre]*
Lobby cards *(May Subd Geog)*
   NT Cards, Lobby
      Display cards (Motion picture advertising
      Scene cards (Motion picture advertising)
      Title cards (Motion picture advertising)
      Title lobby cards
   BT Advertising—Motion pictures
      Film posters
Local communication
   USE Local mass media
Local mass media *(May Subd Geog)*
   UF Community media
      Local communication
      Local media
   BT Communication
      Mass media
   NT Public-access television
Local media
   USE Local mass media
Locations (Motion pictures)
   USE Motion picture locations
Locations (Television programs)
   USE Television program locations
Loew's Commodore (New York, N.Y.)
   USE Fillmore East (New York, N.Y.)
Loew's Paradise Theater
(New York, N.Y.)
   UF Paradise Twins 1 and 2
      (New York, N.Y.)

[†]**Subject headings noted with a dagger contain
additional access points and subheadings that
are not pertinent to this text and are not
included here.**

Paradise Twins One and Two
(New York, N.Y.)
BT Motion picture theaters—New York (State)
Loew's State Theater (Syracuse, N.Y.)
USE Loew's State Theatre (Syracuse, N.Y.)
Loew's State Theatre (Syracuse, N.Y.)
UF Landmark Theatre (Syracuse, N.Y.)
Loew's State Theater (Syracuse, N.Y.)
Syracuse Area Landmark Theatre and Loew
Building (Syracuse, N.Y.)
BT Motion picture theaters—New York (State)
Loew's Theatre (Akron, Ohio)
USE Akron Civic Theatre (Akron, Ohio)
Lomo Compact Automat camera
USE Lomo Kompakt Automat camera
Lomo Kompact Automat camera
USE Lomo Kompakt Automat camera
Lomo Kompakt Automat camera
(Not Subd Geog)
UF LC-A camera
Lomo Compact Automat camera
Lomo Kompact Automat camera
BT Cameras
Lone Ranger films
BT Western films
Lone Ranger films *[LCSH Genre]*
Loop films
UF Continuous motion pictures
Film loops
Motion picture loops
Moving-pictures, Loop
BT Motion pictures
Loop films *[LCSH Genre]*
Lord of the Rings films
[PN1995.9.L58]
BT Fantasy films
Lord of the Rings (Game)
[GV1469.35.L67]
BT Video games
Los Angeles Theatre (Los Angeles, Calif.)
BT Motion picture theaters—California
Loss (Psychology) in motion pictures
(Not Subd Geog)
[PN1995.9.L59]
BT Motion pictures
Lost architecture in mass media *(Not Subd Geog)*
BT Mass media
Lost films *(May Subd Geog)*
Here are entered works on films thought to be no longer in existence. This heading is not used for individual films formerly believed to be lost, which are entered under headings appropriate to the content, genre, and/or form of the film.

UF Lost films—History and criticism
BT Motion pictures
—History and criticism
USE Lost films
Lost television programs
(May Subd Geog)
Here are entered works on television programs that were broadcast live and not recorded or for which the recordings no longer exist. This heading is not used for individual television programs formerly believed to be lost, which are entered under headings appropriate to the content, genre, and/or form of the program.
UF Missing television programs
BT Television programs
Love films
USE Romance films
Love in mass media *(Not Subd Geog)*
BT Mass media
Love in motion pictures *(Not Subd Geog)*
[PN1995.9.L6]
BT Motion pictures
Low budget films *(May Subd Geog)*
UF Low budget motion pictures
Low budget movies
Low budget pictures
BT Motion pictures
Low budget films *[LCSH Genre]*
Low budget motion pictures
USE Low budget films
Low budget movies
USE Low budget films
Low budget pictures
USE Low budget films
Low budget television programs
(May Subd Geog)
BT Television programs
Low power television *(May Subd Geog)*
[HE8700.7–HE8700.72 (Broadcasting)]
UF LPTV
Television, Low power
BT Television broadcasting
Lowell Theater (Eugene, Ore.)
USE McDonald Theater (Eugene, Ore.)
Lowell Theatre (Eugene, Ore.)
USE McDonald Theater (Eugene, Ore.)
LPTV
USE Low power television

†Subject headings noted with a dagger contain additional access points and subheadings that are not pertinent to this text and are not included here.

Lunar (Game)
  [GV1469.35.L84]
  BT Video games
Lyrical films *[LCSH Genre]*

Machinima films *(May Subd Geog)*
  UF 3D game-based animated films
      3D game-based films
      Machinimas
  BT Animated films
Machinima films *[LCSH Genre]*
Machismo in motion pictures
  BT Motion pictures
Mad scientist films *(May Subd Geog)*
  [PN1995.9.M2]
  BT Monster films
Mad scientist films *[LCSH Genre]*
Madcap comedy films
  USE Screwball comedy films
Madcap romantic comedies
  USE Screwball comedy films
Made-for-television films
  USE Made-for-TV movies
Made-for-television motion pictures
  USE Made-for-TV movies
Made-for-television movies
  USE Made-for-TV movies
Made-for-TV films
  USE Made-for-TV movies
Made-for-TV motion pictures
  USE Made-for-TV movies
Made-for-TV movies *(May Subd Geog)*
  UF Features, Television
      Made-for-television films
      Made-for-television motion
        pictures
      Made-for-television movies
      Made-for-TV films
      Made-for-TV motion pictures
      Tele-features
      Telefeatures
      Telefilms
      Telemovies
      Telepics
      Television features
      Television films
      Television movies
      Vidpics
  BT Feature films
      Television programs
  RT Television broadcasting of films
  NT Film make-up
Made-for-TV movies *[LCSH Genre]*

Mafia films
  USE Gangster films
Mafia in motion pictures *(Not Subd Geog)*
  [PN1995.9.M23]
  BT Motion pictures
Magazine format programming (Television)
  USE Magazine format television programs
Magazine format television programs
  (May Subd Geog)
  [PN1992.3.M33]
  UF Magazine format programming (Television)
      Magazines (Television programs)
      News magazines (Television programs)
      Newsmagazines (Television programs)
  BT Nonfiction television programs
Magazine format television programs
  [LCSH Genre]
Magazines (Television programs)
  USE Magazine format television programs
Magic in motion pictures
  (Not Subd Geog)
  BT Motion pictures
Magnavox televisions *(Not Subd Geog)*
  BT Television—Receivers and reception
Magnavox videocassette recorders
  (Not Subd Geog)
  BT Videocassette recorders
Magnetic deflection systems (Television)
  USE Television—Magnetic deflection systems
Magnetic devices[†]
  NT Television—Magnetic deflection systems
Magnetic recorders and recording[†]
  NT Video recordings
      Video tape recorders
Magnetic tapes[†]
  NT Video tapes
Majestic Theatre (Eureka, Mont.)
  BT Motion picture theaters—Montana
Make-up, Film
  USE Film makeup
Make-up, Television
  USE Television makeup
Makeover reality television programs
  USE Makeover television programs
Makeover shows (Television programs)
  USE Makeover television programs
Makeover television programs
  (May Subd Geog)
  UF Makeover reality television programs

[†]**Subject headings noted with a dagger contain
additional access points and subheadings that
are not pertinent to this text and are not
included here.**

Makeover shows (Television programs)
Makeover television shows
  BT Reality television programs
Makeover television programs
  [LCSH Genre]
Makeover television shows
  USE Makeover television programs
Makeup, Film
  USE Film makeup
Makeup, Television
  USE Television makeup
Malayalam drama[†]
  NT Motion picture plays, Malayalam
Malayalam motion picture plays
  USE Motion picture plays, Malayalam
Male actors *(May Subd Geog)*
  Here are entered works on male actors
  collectively. Works on female actors collectively are
  entered under Actresses. General works on both
  male and female actors collectively, works on both
  male and female state actors collectively and works
  on individual male and female state actors are
  entered under Actors. Works on actors, collectively
  or individually, specializing in particular media are
  entered under the appropriate specific heading, e.g.,
  Television actors and actresses, with an additional
  heading Male actors or Actresses, assigned as
  appropriate to works of collective biography.
  UF Men actors
  BT Actors
  NT Leading men (Actors)
Male actors' wives
  USE Actors' spouses
Male friendship in motion pictures
  (Not Subd Geog)
  BT Motion pictures
Male homosexuality in motion pictures
  (Not Subd Geog)
  [PN1995.9.H55]
  UF Homosexuality, Male, in motion pictures
  BT Motion pictures
Male impersonators *(May Subd Geog)*
  Here are entered works on women who
  impersonate men, generally for purposes of
  entertainment or comic effect. Works on men who
  impersonate women, generally for purposes of
  entertainment or comic effect, are entered under
  Female impersonators. Works on persons, especially
  males, who assume the dress and manner of the
  opposite sex for psychological gratification are
  entered under Transvestites.
  UF Cross-dressers
      Crossdressers

Drag kings
Impersonators, Male
Impersonators of men
Kings, Drag
  BT Actresses
      Transgender people
  BT Actresses
Male impersonators in motion pictures
  (Not Subd Geog)
  BT Motion pictures
Maler Video-Installations-Preis
  BT Video art—Awards—Germany
Maler Video-Kunst-Preis
  BT Video art—Awards—Germany
Mamiya camera *(Not Subd Geog)*
  BT Twin-lens cameras
Man-woman relationships in motion pictures
  (Not Subd Geog)
  [PN1995.9.M27]
  BT Motion pictures
Man-woman relationships on television
  (Not Subd Geog)
  BT Television
Management[†]
  NT Television in management
Managers, Motion picture theater
  USE Motion picture theater managers
Mann's Chinese Theatre (Los Angeles, Calif.)
  USE Chinese Theatre (Los Angeles, Calif.)
Maori (New Zealand people) in motion pictures
  (Not Subd Geog)
  BT Motion pictures
Maps in motion pictures *(Not Subd Geog)*
  [PN1995.9.M28]
  BT Motion pictures
Maraña, Don Juan de (Legendary character)
  USE Don Juan (Legendary character)
Marginality, Social, in motion pictures
  (Not Subd Geog)
  BT Motion pictures
Mario Kart Super Circuit (Game)
  BT Game Boy video games
Mario Party (Game)
  [GV1469.35.M35]
  BT Video games
Mario Tennis (Game)
  [GV1469.35.M36]
  BT Video games

[†]**Subject headings noted with a dagger contain
additional access points and subheadings that
are not pertinent to this text and are not
included here.**

Marionette films
    USE Puppet films
Marionette television programs
    USE Puppet television programs
Marionettes in motion pictures
    (Not Subd Geog)
    [PN1995.9.M285]
    BT Motion pictures
Marriage in motion pictures
    (Not Subd Geog)
    [PN1995.0.M3]
    BT Motion pictures
Martial arts films *(May Subd Geog)*
    [PN1995.9.H3]
    UF Kung fu films
        Spaghetti Easterns
    BT Action and adventure films
  —History and criticism
        UF Hand-to-hand fighting, Oriental, in
            motion pictures
Martial arts films *[LCSH Genre]*
Martial arts television programs
    [LCSH Genre]
Martians in mass media *(Not Subd Geog)*
    [P96.M38–P96.M382]
    BT Mass media
Martyrdom in motion pictures
    (Not Subd Geog)
    BT Motion pictures
Mary Pickford Theater (Library of Congress
  James Madison Memorial Building,
  Washington, D.C.)
    UF Pickford Theater (Library of Congress
        James Madison Memorial Building,
        Washington, D.C.)
    BT Motion picture theaters—Washington (D.C.)
Masculinity in motion pictures
    (Not Subd Geog)
    BT Motion pictures
Masculinity on television
    (Not Subd Geog)
    BT Television
Masks in motion pictures
    (Not Subd Geog)
    BT Motion pictures
Masochism in motion pictures
    (Not Subd Geog)
    [PN1995.9.M]
    BT Motion pictures
Mass media *(May Subd Geog)*
    UF Mass communication
        Media, Mass
        Media, The

    BT Communication
    NT Aboriginal Australians and mass media
        Aboriginal Australians in mass media
        African Americans and mass media
        African Americans in mass media
        African Americans in the mass media
          industry
        AIDS (Disease) and mass media
        AIDS (Disease) in mass media
        Air power in mass media
        Air warfare in mass media
        Alcoholism in mass media
        Alternative mass media
        Animals in mass media
        Apartheid in mass media
        Apocalypse in mass media
        Arabs in mass media
        Armed Forces and mass media
        Asian Americans and mass media
        Asians in mass media
        Astronautics in mass media
        Astronomy in mass media
        Athletes in mass media
        Automobiles in mass media
        Batman (Fictitious character) in mass media
        Bioterrorism and mass media
        Black English in mass media
        Black mass media
        Blacks and mass media
        Blacks in mass media
        Body (Human) in mass media
        Capitalism and mass media
        Celebrities in mass media
        Characters and characteristics in mass media
        Charisma (Personality trait) in mass media
        Child sexual abuse in mass media
        Children's mass media
        Chinese Americans and mass media
        Chinese Americans in mass media
        Church and mass media
        Cities and towns in mass media
        Cold War in mass media
        Communism and mass media
        Crime in mass media
        Criminal investigation in mass media
        Croft, Lara (Fictitious character) in mass
          media
        Cyborgs in mass media

†**Subject headings noted with a dagger contain**
additional access points and subheadings that
are not pertinent to this text and are not
included here.

Death in mass media
Debates and debating in mass media
Detectives in mass media
Deviant behavior in mass media
Digital media
Dinosaurs in mass media
Documentary mass media
Drugs and mass media
Education in mass media
Environmentalism in mass media
Ethnic mass media
Families in mass media
Famines in mass media
Fantasy in mass media
Farm life in mass media
Feminism and mass media
Fire fighters in mass media
French-Canadians and mass media
Gay men in mass media
Gender identity in mass media
Genetics in mass media
Genocide in mass media
Geographical myths in mass media
Gossip in mass media
Greek Americans and mass media
Haitian Americans and mass media
Healers in mass media
Health in mass media
Heroes in mass media
Hispanic American women in mass media
Hispanic Americans and mass media
History in mass media
Holmes, Sherlock (Fictitious character) in
    mass media
Homelessness in mass media
Horror in mass media
Housing law in mass media
Human cloning in mass media
Human rights in mass media
Identity (Psychology) and mass media
Imaginary places in mass media
Indian mass media
Indians in mass media
Indigenous peoples and mass media
Intelligence levels in mass media
Interracial marriage in mass media
Islam in mass media
Italian Americans in mass media
Italians in mass media
Kurds in mass media
Labor unions and mass media
Law in mass media
Lesbians in mass media

Libraries and mass media
Local mass media
Lost architecture in mass media
Love in mass media
Magic in motion pictures
Martians in mass media
Mass media genres
Massacres in mass media
Men in mass media
Men's mass media
Mental illness in mass media
Mexican Americans and mass media
Mickey Mouse (Fictitious character) in mass
    media
Militia movements in mass media
Minorities in mass media
Minorities in the mass media industry
Monsters in mass media
Multiculturalism in mass media
Mummies in mass media
Murder in mass media
Myth in mass media
National characteristics in mass media
Nurses in mass media
Nutrition in mass media
Obesity in mass media
Older people in mass media
Operation Desert Shield, 1990–1991, in mass
    media
Oppression (Psychology) in mass media
Pacific Islanders in mass media
Pedophilia in mass media
People with disabilities in mass media
Pinocchio (Fictitious character) in mass
    media
Pirates in mass media
Police and mass media
Police in mass media
Police violence in mass media
Popeye (Fictitious character) in mass media
Prisoners of war in mass media
Prisons in mass media
Product placement in mass media
Protest movements in mass media
Public welfare in mass media
Race relations in mass media
Racism in mass media
Radicalism in mass media

†**Subject headings noted with a dagger contain
additional access points and subheadings that
are not pertinent to this text and are not
included here.**

Radioactive waste disposal in mass media
Rape in mass media
Reality in mass media
Reproductive health in mass media
Ritual abuse in mass media
Ritual in mass media
Scandals in mass media
Science in mass media
September 11 Terrorist Attacks, 2001, in
    mass media
Serial murders in mass media
Sex differences in mass media
Sex in mass media
Sex role in mass media
Sexism in mass media
Social classes in mass media
Social conflict in mass media
Social problems in mass media
Social sciences in mass media
Sound in mass media
South Asians in mass media
Space and time in mass media
Stereotypes (Social psychology) in mass
    media
Storytelling in mass media
Suburbs in mass media
Suicide in mass media
Superman (Fictitious character) in mass
    media
Surfing in mass media
Surrealism in mass media
Tarzan (Fictitious character) in mass
    media
Teenagers in mass media
Terrorism and mass media
Terrorism in mass media
Vampires in mass media
Veils in mass media
Victims of crimes in mass media
Villains in mass media
Violence in mass media
Voyages, Imaginary, in mass media
War in mass media
War on Terrorism, 2001–, in mass media
West Indian Americans in mass media
Women detectives in mass media
Women in mass media
Women in the mass media industry
Women's mass media
Xenophobia in mass media
Youth in mass media
SA *subdivision* In mass media *under names of
      countries, cities, etc., and under names of*

*individual persons, families, and corporate
bodies; and headings of the type* [topic] *in
mass media, e.g.,* Alcoholism in mass
media.
—Aesthetics
    BT Aesthetics
—Audiences
    [P96.A83]
    UF Audiences, Mass media
    BT Audiences
        Mass media—Social aspects
    NT Television viewers
—Awards
— —United States
        NT Unity Awards in Media
—Censorship *(May Subd Geog)*
    NT Blacklisting of authors
—Employees
— —Labor unions *(May Subd Geog)*
—Evaluation
    USE Mass media criticism
—Government policy
    USE Mass media policy
—Influence
    [P94]
—Influence of comic books, strips, etc., on
    USE Comic books, strips, etc.—Influence
         on mass media
—International cooperation
    USE Communication—International
         cooperation
—Law and legislation *(May Subd Geog)*
    NT Right of reply
—Methodology
    NT Interviewing in mass media
—Moral and ethical aspects
    (May Subd Geog)
    UF Mass media—Moral and religious
        aspects
—Moral and religious aspects
    USE Mass media—Moral and ethical
         aspects
         Mass media—Religious aspects
—Objectivity *(May Subd Geog)*
    UF Bias in mass media
    BT Objectivity
—Political aspects *(May Subd Geog)*
    BT Communication in politics

†**Subject headings noted with a dagger contain
additional access points and subheadings that
are not pertinent to this text and are not
included here.**

—Public opinion
  [P96.P83]
    Here are entered works on public opinion about the mass media. Works on general relations between the media and public opinion, including the influence of the mass media on the formation of public opinion, are entered under the heading Mass media and public opinion.
—Rankings
    USE Mass media—Ratings and rankings
—Ratings
    USE Mass media—Ratings and rankings
—Ratings and rankings
  (May Subd Geog)
    [P96.R36–P96.R362]
    UF Mass media—Rankings
        Mass media—Ratings
        Rankings of mass media
        Ratings of mass media
—Religious aspects
    UF Mass media—Moral and religious
        aspects
    BT Communication—Religious aspects
    NT Mass media in religion
—Selling
    USE Selling—Mass media
—Semiotics *(May Subd Geog)*
    BT Semiotics
—Social aspects *(May Subd Geog)*
    RT Mass media—Audiences
—Surveys
    USE Mass media surveys
—Technological innovations
    (May Subd Geog)
—United States
    NT African American mass media
Mass media (Islamic law)
  (May Subd Geog)
    [KBP3482–KBP3512]
    BT Islamic law
Mass media, African American
  USE African American mass media
Mass media, Asian American
  USE Asian American mass media
Mass media, Hispanic American
  USE Hispanic American mass media
Mass media, Indian
  USE Indian mass media
Mass media and African Americans
  USE African Americans and mass media
Mass media and AIDS (Disease)
  USE AIDS (Disease) and mass media

Mass media and alien labor
  USE Mass media and foreign workers
Mass media and anthropology
  (May Subd Geog)
    [P96.A58]
    UF Anthropology and mass media
    BT Anthropology
Mass media and architecture
  (May Subd Geog)
    BT Architecture
        Communication in architectural design
Mass media and art *(May Subd Geog)*
    [N72.M28]
    UF Art and mass media
    BT Art
Mass media and Asian Americans
  USE Asian Americans and mass media
Mass media and bioterrorism
  USE Bioterrorism and mass media
Mass media and Blacks
  USE Blacks and mass media
Mass media and business
  (May Subd Geog)
    BT Business
        Public relations
Mass media and capitalism
  USE Capitalism and mass media
Mass media and children
  (May Subd Geog)
    UF Children and mass media
    BT Children
Mass media and Chinese Americans
  USE Chinese Americans and mass media
Mass media and communism
  USE Communism and mass media
Mass media and crime *(May Subd Geog)*
    [P96.C74]
    UF Crime and mass media
    BT Crime
Mass media and criminal justice
  (May Subd Geog)
    UF Criminal justice and mass media
    BT Criminal justice, Administration of
Mass media and culture
  (May Subd Geog)
    [P94.6]
    UF Culture and mass media
    BT Culture

†**Subject headings noted with a dagger contain additional access points and subheadings that are not pertinent to this text and are not included here.**

Mass media and education *(May Subd Geog)*
  UF Education and mass media
  BT Education
Mass media and educators *(May Subd Geog)*
  UF Educators and mass media0
  BT Educators
Mass media and ethnic relations
  (May Subd Geog)
  UF Ethnic relations and mass media
  BT Ethnic relations
Mass media and families
  (May Subd Geog)
  UF Families and mass media
    Mass media and the family
  BT Families
Mass media and feminism
  USE Feminism and mass media
Mass media and folklore
  (May Subd Geog)
  [P96.F65]
  UF Folklore and mass media
  BT Folklore
Mass media and foreign workers
  (May Subd Geog)
  UF Mass media and alien labor
Mass media and French-Canadians
  USE French-Canadians and mass media
Mass media and gays *(May Subd Geog)*
  [P94.5.G38]
  UF Gays and mass media
  BT Gays
Mass media and girls *(May Subd Geog)*
  [P94.5.G57–P94.5.G572]
  UF Girls and mass media
  BT Girls
Mass media and Greek Americans
  USE Greek Americans and mass media
Mass media and Haitian Americans
  USE Haitian Americans and mass media
Mass media and Hispanic Americans
  USE Hispanic Americans and mass media
Mass media and history
  (May Subd Geog)
  [P96.H55]
  UF History and mass media
  BT History
Mass media and identity
  USE Identity (Psychology) and mass media
Mass media and immigrants
  (May Subd Geog)
  [P94.5.I48]
  UF Immigrants and mass media
  BT Immigrant

Mass media and indigenous peoples
  USE Indigenous peoples and mass media
Mass media and international relations
  (May Subd Geog)
  [P96.I53]
  UF International relations and mass media
  BT International relations
Mass media and judicial power *(May Subd Geog)*
  [P96.J83]
  UF Judicial power and mass media
  BT Judicial power
Mass media and kibbutzim *(May Subd Geog)*
  [P96.K52]
  UF Kibbutzim and mass media
  BT Kibbutzim
Mass media and labor unions
  USE Labor unions and mass media
Mass media and language *(May Subd Geog)*
  BT Language and languages
Mass media and literature *(May Subd Geog)*
  [P96.L5]
  BT Literature
Mass media and Mexican Americans
  USE Mexican Americans and mass media
Mass media and minorities
  (May Subd Geog)
  Here are entered works discussing all aspects of the involvement of minorities in the mass media. Works discussing the employment of minorities in the mass media are entered under Minorities in the mass media industry. Works discussing the portrayal of minorities in the mass media are entered under Minorities in mass media.
  BT Minorities
  RT Ethnic press
Mass media and music *(May Subd Geog)*
  [ML3849]
  UF Music and mass media
  BT Music
Mass media and nationalism
  (May Subd Geog)
  UF Nationalism and mass media
  BT Nationalism
Mass media and older people
  (May Subd Geog)
  [P94.5.A38]
  UF Mass media and the aged
    Older people and mass media

†**Subject headings noted with a dagger contain additional access points and subheadings that are not pertinent to this text and are not included here.**

BT Older people
Mass media and peace *(May Subd Geog)*
    [P96.P33]
    UF Peace and mass media
    BT Peace
Mass media and police
    USE Police and mass media
Mass media and propaganda
    (May Subd Geog)
    UF Propaganda and mass media
    BT Propaganda
Mass media and public opinion *(May Subd Geog)*
    Here are entered works on general relations
    between the mass media and public opinion,
    including the influence of the mass media
    on the formation of public opinion. Works
    on public opinion about the media are entered
    under the heading Mass media—Public
    opinion.
    UF Public opinion and mass media
    BT Public opinion
Mass media and publicity
    (May Subd Geog)
    [P96.P85]
    UF Publicity and mass media
    BT Publicity
Mass media and race problems
    USE Mass media and race relations
Mass media and race relations
    (May Subd Geog)
    UF Mass media and race problems
        Race relations and mass media
    BT Race relations
Mass media and sex *(May Subd Geog)*
    UF Sex and mass media
    BT Sex
Mass media and social integration
    (May Subd Geog)
    [P96.S64]
    UF Social integration and mass media
    BT Social integration
Mass media and social service
    (May Subd Geog)
    [HV42]
    UF Social service and mass media
    BT Social service
Mass media and sports
    (May Subd Geog)
    [GV742]
    BT Popular culture
        Sports
Mass media and state
    USE Mass media policy

Mass media and technology
    (May Subd Geog)
    UF Technology and mass media
    BT Technology
Mass media and teenagers *(May Subd Geog)*
    [HQ799.2.M35]
    UF Teenagers and mass media
    BT Teenagers
Mass media and terrorism
    USE Terrorism and mass media
Mass media and the aged
    USE Mass media and older people
Mass media and the Amish *(May*
    Subd Geog)
    [P94.5.A46–P94.5.A462]
    UF Amish and mass media
    BT Amish
Mass media and the arts *(May Subd Geog)*
    UF Arts and mass media
    BT Arts
Mass media and the church
    USE Church and mass media
Mass media and the environment
    (May Subd Geog)
    UF Environment and mass media
Mass media and the family
    USE Mass media and families
Mass media and theater *(May Subd Geog)*
    [PN2041.M37]
    UF Theater and mass media
    BT Theater
Mass media and war *(May Subd Geog)*
    UF War and mass media
    BT War
    RT War in mass media
    SA *subdivision* Mass media and the war,
        [revolution, etc.] *under individual wars,*
        e.g., World War, 1939–1945—Mass media
        and the war
Mass media and women *(May Subd Geog)*
    [P94.5.W65]
    Here are entered works discussing all aspects of
    women's involvement in the mass media. Works
    discussing women's employment in the mass media
    are entered under Women in the mass media
    industry. Works discussing the portrayal of women
    in the mass media are entered under Women in
    mass media.

†**Subject headings noted with a dagger contain
additional access points and subheadings that
are not pertinent to this text and are not
included here.**

UF Women and mass media
BT Women
RT Women in the mass media industry

Mass media and world politics
(May Subd Geog)
[P96.W62–P96.W622]
UF World politics and mass media
BT World politics

Mass media and young adults
(May Subd Geog)
UF Young adults and mass media
BT Young adults

Mass media and youth
(May Subd Geog)
[HQ799.2.M35]
UF Youth and mass media
BT Youth

Mass media and Zionism
(May Subd Geog)
UF Zionism and mass media
BT Zionism

Mass media coverage of . . .
USE *subdivision* In mass media
*under name of countries, cities, etc., and
under names of individual persons,
families, and corporate bodies; and
headings of the type [topic] in mass media,
e.g.,* Alcoholism in mass media

Mass media criticism *(May Subd Geog)*
[P96.C76]
Here are entered works on the principles and
techniques of criticism of the mass media.
UF Criticism of the mass media
Mass media—Evaluation
BT Criticism

Mass media for children
USE Children's mass media

Mass media for women
USE Women's mass media

Mass media in agricultural extension work
(May Subd Geog)
BT Agricultural extension work

Mass media in birth control
USE Mass media in family planning

Mass media in breast feeding promotion
USE Mass media in breastfeeding promotion

Mass media in breastfeeding promotion
(May Subd Geog)
UF Mass media in breast feeding promotion
BT Breastfeeding promotion

Mass media in community development
(May Subd Geog)
BT Community development

Mass media in counseling *(May
Subd Geog)*
[RC466.3 (Mental health counseling)]
BT Counseling

Mass media in economic development
(May Subd Geog)
BT Economic development

Mass media in education *(May
Subd Geog)*
BT Education

Mass media in family planning
UF Mass media in birth control

Mass media in health education
(May Subd Geog)
BT Health education

Mass media in literature *(Not Subd Geog)*

Mass media in mental health education
(May Subd Geog)
[RA790.87]
BT Mental health education

Mass media in missionary work
(May Subd Geog)
[BV2082.M3]
BT Missions

Mass media in motion pictures
(Not Subd Geog)
BT Motion pictures

Mass media in religion *(May Subd Geog)*
[BV652.95]
BT Communication—Religious aspects
Mass media—Religious aspects
Religious broadcasting

Mass media in traffic safety *(May Subd Geog)*
BT Traffic safety

Mass media genres *(May Subd Geog)*
[P96.G455–P96.G4552]
UF Genres, Mass media
BT Mass media

Mass media literacy
USE Media literacy

Mass media policy *(May Subd Geog)*
[P95.8]
UF Mass media—Government policy
Mass media and state
State and mass media
BT Communication policy
NT Broadcasting policy

Mass media scholars

†**Subject headings noted with a dagger contain
additional access points and subheadings that
are not pertinent to this text and are not
included here.**

USE Mass media specialists

Mass media specialists *(May Subd Geog)*
 UF Mass media scholars
 BT Specialists

Mass media surveys *(May Subd Geog)*
 UF Mass media—Surveys
 BT Surveys

Mass medical screening
 USE Medical screening

Mass screening, Medical
 USE Medical screening

Massacres in mass media *(Not Subd Geog)*
 [P96.M39–P96.M392]
 BT Mass media

Master antenna television
 USE Television, Master antenna

Masters of Teräs Käsi (Game)
 [GV1469.35.M37]
 BT Video games

Mathematics[†]
 —Study and teaching[†]
 NT Television in mathematics education

MATV
 USE Television, Master antenna

McDonald Theater (Eugene, Ore.)
 UF Lowell Theater (Eugene, Ore.)
 Lowell Theatre (Eugene, Ore.)
 McDonald Theatre (Eugene, Ore.)
 BT Motion picture theaters—Oregon

McDonald Theatre (Eugene, Ore.)
 USE McDonald Theater (Eugene, Ore.)

Media centers (Education)
 USE Instructional materials centers

Media literacy *(May Subd Geog)*
  Here are entered works on a person's knowledge and ability to use, interpret and evaluate modern means of communication, such as radio, television, newspapers, and magazines.
 UF Mass media literacy
 BT Information literacy

Media planning in advertising
 USE Advertising media planning

Media programs (Education)
 (May Subd Geog)
 [LB1028.4]
 UF Educational media programs
 Instructional materials programs
 Multi media programs
 Programs, Media
 School media programs
 BT Educational technology
 Teaching—Aids and devices

Media selection

USE Selection of nonbook materials

Medical cinematography *(May Subd Geog)*
 UF Cinematography, Medical
 BT Medical photography
 NT Cineangiography
 Cinefluorography

Medical examinations
 USE Medical screening

Medical films
 USE Motion pictures in medicine

Medical films (Drama)
 USE Medical films (Motion pictures)

Medical films (Motion pictures)
 (May Subd Geog)
  This heading is used as a topical heading for works about fiction and/or nonfiction films that feature medical personnel and the practice of medicine. When used as a topical heading it is subdivided by the appropriate geographic, topical, and/or form subdivisions.
 UF Doctor films (Motion pictures)
 Hospital films
 Medical films (Drama)
 BT Motion pictures
 RT Medicine in motion pictures

Medical films (Motion pictures)
 [LCSH Genre]

Medical personnel in motion pictures
 (Not Subd Geog)
 BT Motion pictures

Medical personnel on television
 (Not Subd Geog)
 BT Television

Medical photography[†]
 NT Medical cinematography

Medical television
 USE Television in medicine

Medical television programs
 (May Subd Geog)
  This heading is used as a topical heading for works about fiction and/or nonfiction television programs that feature medical personnel and the practice of medicine. When used as a topical heading it is subdivided by the appropriate geographic, topical, and/or form subdivisions.
 UF Doctor television programs
 Hospital television programs
 Medical television programs (Drama)

[†]**Subject headings noted with a dagger contain additional access points and subheadings that are not pertinent to this text and are not included here.**

BT Television programs
Medical television programs
  [LCSH Genre]
Medical television programs (Drama)
  USE Medical television programs
Medicine[†]
  NT Motion pictures and medicine
      Motion pictures in medicine
      Television in medicine
      Video recording in medicine
  —**Study and teaching**
      NT Television in medical education
Medicine and motion pictures
  USE Motion pictures and medicine
Medicine in motion pictures
  (Not Subd Geog)
  RT Medical films (Motion pictures)
Medicine in television
  USE Medicine on television
Medicine on television *(Not Subd Geog)*
  [PN1992.8.M43]
  UF Medicine in television
  BT Television
Medieval (Game)
  [GV1469.35.M4]
  BT Video games
Medium format cameras
  [TR257]
  Here are entered works on cameras which
  produce images on film larger than 35mm but
  smaller than 2 1/4 x 3 1/4 sheet film.
  UF Roll film cameras
  BT Cameras
Meet the Robinsons (Game)
  BT Video games
Mega Man Battle Network (Game)
  USE MegaMan Battle Network (Game)
Mega Man X (Game)
  [GV1469.35.M43]
  BT Video games
MegaMan Battle Network (Game)
  UF Mega Man Battle Network (Game)
  BT Video games
Melodrama in motion pictures *(Not Subd Geog)*
  [PN1995.9.M45]
  BT Motion pictures
Melodrama in television
  USE Melodrama on television
Melodrama on television *(Not Subd Geog)*
  UF Melodrama in television
  BT Television
Melodramas (Motion pictures)
  [LCSH Genre]

Memorex televisions *(Not Subd Geog)*
  BT Televisions—Receivers and reception
Memory in motion pictures *(Not Subd Geog)*
  BT Motion pictures
Men[†]
  NT Motion pictures and men
      Motion pictures for men
Men, Leading (Actors)
  USE Leading men (Actors)
Men actors
  USE Male actors
Men and motion pictures
  USE Motion pictures and men
Men in mass media *(Not Subd Geog)*
  BT Mass media
Men in motion pictures *(Not Subd Geog)*
  [PN1995.9.M46]
  BT Motion pictures
Men in television
  USE Men on television M
Men on television *(Not Subd Geog)*
  UF Men in television
  BT Television
Men (White) in motion pictures
  (Not Subd Geog)
  [PN1995.9.M4615]
  BT Motion pictures
Men's mass media *(May Subd Geog)*
  BT Mass media
      Men's products
Men's products[†]
  NT Men's mass media
Mental health education[†]
  NT Mass media in mental health education
Mental hygiene films
  USE Social guidance films
Mental illness in mass media
  (Not Subd Geog)
  [P96.M45]
  BT Mass media
Mental illness in motion pictures
  (Not Subd Geog)
  [PN1995.9.M463]
  BT Motion pictures
Messiah (Game)
  BT Video games
Metal Gear Solid (Game)
  [GV1469.35.M46]

[†]**Subject headings noted with a dagger contain
additional access points and subheadings that
are not pertinent to this text and are not
included here.**

BT Video games
Metal Gear Solid 2: Sons of Liberty (Game)
    BT Video games
Metamorphosis in motion pictures
    (Not Subd Geog)
    BT Motion pictures
Metaphor in motion pictures
    (Not Subd Geog)
    [PN1995.9.M472]
    BT Motion pictures
Meteorologists, Television
    USE Television weathercasters
Metroid Prime (Game) *(Not Subd Geog)*
    BT Nintendo GameCube video games
Mexican American actors
    (May Subd Geog)
    UF Actors, Mexican American
    BT Actors—United States
**Mexican American motion picture producers
and directors** *(May Subd Geog)*
    UF Motion picture producers and directors,
        Mexican American
    BT Motion picture producers and directors—
        United States
Mexican American women in motion pictures
    (Not Subd Geog)
    BT Motion pictures
Mexican Americans and mass media
    (May Subd Geog)
    UF Mass media and Mexican Americans
    BT Mass media
Mexican Americans and television
    (May Subd Geog)
    BT Television
Mexican Americans in motion pictures
    (Not Subd Geog)
    [PN1995.9.M49]
    BT Motion pictures
Mexican Americans in television broadcasting
    (May Subd Geog)
    BT Television broadcasting—United States
Mexican Americans in the motion picture industry
    (May Subd Geog)
    BT Motion picture industry—United States
Mexican Americans on television *(Not Subd Geog)*
    BT Television
Mexican drama†
    NT Motion picture plays, Mexican
Mexican motion picture plays
    USE Motion picture plays, Mexican
Mexican motion pictures
    USE Motion pictures, Mexican
Mickey Mouse (Cartoon character)

    USE Mickey Mouse (Fictitious character)
Mickey Mouse (Cartoon character)
  in mass media
    USE Mickey Mouse (Fictitious character) in mass
        media
Mickey Mouse (Fictitious character)
    (Not Subd Geog)
    UF Mickey Mouse (Cartoon character)
        Mouse, Mickey (Fictitious character
Mickey Mouse (Fictitious character) in mass media
    (Not Subd Geog)
    UF Mickey Mouse (Cartoon character) in mass
        media
    BT Mass media
Micro Maniacs (Game)
    BT Video games
Microcinematography *(May Subd Geog)*
    [QH255]
    UF Cinematomicrography
        Cinemicrography
        Cinephotomicrography
        Moving photomicrography
    BT Cinematography
        Photomicrography
Microsoft Xbox video games
    USE Xbox video games
Microwave communication systems†
    RT Closed-circuit television
Middle age in motion pictures
    (Not Subd Geog)
    BT Motion pictures
Middle Ages in motion pictures
    (Not Subd Geog)
    [PN1995.9.M52]
    BT Motion pictures
Middle Ages on television *(Not Subd Geog)*
    BT Television
Middle class in motion pictures
    (Not Subd Geog)
    BT Motion pictures
Midgets in motion pictures
    USE Dwarfs in motion pictures
Midnight Club: Los Angeles (Game)
    BT Video games
Military cinematography
    (May Subd Geog)
    UF Cinematography—Military applications

†**Subject headings noted with a dagger contain
additional access points and subheadings that
are not pertinent to this text and are not
included here.**

BT Cinematography
     Photography, Military
Military education[†]
  NT Motion pictures in military education
       Television in military education
Military films [LCSH Genre]
Military television
  [UG623]
  UF Combat television
       Television, Military
  BT Communications, Military
       Television
Military television programs
  [LCSH Genre]
Militia movements in mass media
  (Not Subd Geog)
  [P96.M54]
  BT Mass media
Mime
  BT Acting
Mimes
  BT Actors
Mimesis in motion pictures (Not Subd Geog)
  [PN1995.9.M53]
  BT Motion pictures
Miners in motion pictures (Not Subd Geog)
  [PN1995.9.M54]
  BT Motion pictures
Mini-series, Television
  USE Television mini-series
Mini-series, Video
  USE Video mini-series
Miniature cameras (May Subd Geog)
  UF Subminiature cameras
       Ultra-miniature came5ras
  BT Cameras
  NT Bolsey camera
       Retina camera
Mining engineering[†]
  NT Motion pictures in mining
Miniseries, Television
  USE Television mini-series
Minolta camera (Not Subd Geog)
  BT Cameras
Minorities[†]
  NT Ethnic mass media
       Mass media and minorities
Minorities in broadcasting (May Subd Geog)
  BT Broadcasting
Minorities in films
  USE Minorities in motion pictures
Minorities in mass media (Not Subd Geog)
  BT Mass media

Minorities in motion pictures (Not Subd Geog)
  [PN1995.9.M]
  UF Minorities in films
  BT Motion pictures
  SA specific minority groups in motion pictures
Minorities in the motion pictures industry
  (May Subd Geog)
  BT Motion picture industry
Minorities in television
  USE Minorities on television
Minorities in television broadcasting
  (May Subd Geog)
  UF Minorities in the television industry
  BT Television broadcasting
Minorities in the mass media industry
  (May Subd Geog)
  BT Mass media
Minorities in the motion picture industry
  (May Subd Geog)
  BT Motion picture industry
Minorities on television
  (Not Subd Geog)
  [PN1992.6.M54]
  UF Minorities in television
  BT Television
Minority broadcasting
  USE Ethnic broadcasting
Minority mass media
  USE Ethnic mass media
Minority television broadcasting
  USE Ethnic television broadcasting
Minority women in motion pictures
  (Not Subd Geog)
  BT Motion pictures
Minstrel shows[†]
  UF Blackfaced minstrel shows
  NT Blackface entertainers
Miranda camera (Not Subd Geog)
  BT Single-lens reflex cameras
Misadventures of Tron Bonne (Game)
  [GV1469.35.M54]
  BT Video games
Miscegenation in motion pictures
  (Not Subd Geog)
  BT Motion pictures
Misogyny in motion pictures (Not Subd Geog)
  BT Motion pictures
Missing television programs

[†]**Subject headings noted with a dagger contain
additional access points and subheadings that
are not pertinent to this text and are not
included here.**

USE Lost television programs

Mission Impossible (Game)
   [GV1469.35.M57]
   BT Video games

Missions[†]
   NT Mass media in missionary work
       Motion pictures in missionary work

Mitsubishi televisions *(Not Subd Geog)*
   BT Television—Receivers and reception

Mock documentary films
   USE Documentary-style films

Mockumentaries
   USE Documentary-style films

Mocumentary films
   USE Documentary-style films

Money in motion pictures
   (Not Subd Geog)
   [PN1995.9.M59]
   BT Motion pictures

Monkey Hero (Game)
   [GV1469.35.M65]
   BT Video games

Monster films *(May Subd Geog)*
   UF Creature features (Motion pictures)
   RT Horror films
   NT King Kong films
       Mad scientist films
       Mothra films
       Vampire films
       Werewolf films

Monster films *[LCSH Genre]*

Monster television programs
   (May Subd Geog)
   BT Television programs
   RT Ghost television programs
       Horror television programs

Monster television programs
   [LCSH Genre]

Monsters in mass media *(Not Subd Geog)*
   [P96.M6]
   BT Mass media

Monsters in motion pictures
   (Not Subd Geog)
   [PN1995.9.M6]
   BT Motion pictures

Montage[†]
   NT Motion pictures—Editing

Montalbano, Salvo (Fictitious character)
   (Not Subd Geog)
   UF Commissario Montalbano (Fictitious
       character)
       Inspector Montalbano (Fictitious character)
       Salvo Montalbano (Fictitious character)

Monumental films
   USE Epic films

Mormons in motion pictures *(Not Subd Geog)*
   BT Motion pictures

Morning news talk shows *(May Subd Geog)*
   UF Breakfast television
   BT Television talk shows
       Television broadcasting of news

Mortal Kombat (Game)
   [GV1469.35.M67]
   BT Video games

Motherhood in motion pictures
   (Not Subd Geog)
   BT Motion pictures

Mothers and daughters in motion pictures
   (Not Subd Geog)
   [PN1995.9.63]
   BT Motion pictures

Mothers in motion pictures
   (Not Subd Geog)
   [PN1995.9.M63]
   BT Motion pictures

Mothers on television
   (Not Subd Geog)
   [PN1992.8.M58]
   BT Television

Mothra films *(May Subd Geog)*
   [PN1995.9.M64]
   BT Monster films

Mothra films *[LCSH Genre]*

Motion picture acting
   UF Film acting
       Moving-picture acting
   BT Acting
   —Auditions
       USE Screen tests

Motion picture actors and actresses
   (May Subd Geog)
   UF Film actors
       Film stars
       Motion pictures stars
       Movie stars
       Stars, Movie
   BT Actors
       Actresses
   NT African American motion picture actors
       and actresses
       Austrian American motion picture actors
       and actresses

[†]**Subject headings noted with a dagger contain
additional access points and subheadings that
are not pertinent to this text and are not
included here.**

Children of motion picture actors and
actresses
Chinese American motion picture actors
and actresses
Expatriate motion picture actors and actresses
Gay motion picture actors and actresses
Hispanic American motion picture actors
and actresses
Indian motion picture actors and actresses
Korean American motion picture actors
and actresses

—**Credits**
UF Credits of motion picture actors and
actresses
Film credits of motion picture actors and
actresses
Motion picture actors and actresses,
African American
USE African American motion picture actors
and actresses
Motion picture actors and actresses, Austrian
American
USE Austrian American motion picture actors
and actresses
Motion picture actors and actresses, Chinese
American
USE Chinese American motion picture actors
and actresses
Motion picture actors and actresses, Foreign
(*May Subd Geog*)
UF Foreign motion picture actors and actresses
Motion picture actors and actresses, Hispanic
American
USE Hispanic American motion picture actors
and actresses
Motion picture actors and actresses, Indian
USE Indian motion picture actors and actresses
Motion picture actors and actresses, Korean American
USE Korean American motion picture actors
and actresses
Motion picture actors and actresses in literature
(*Not Subd Geog*)
**Motion picture actors and actresses on postage
stamps**
[HE6183.M7]
BT Postage stamps
Motion picture adaptations
USE Film adaptations
Motion picture anachronisms
USE Motion picture errors
Motion picture archives
USE Film archives
Motion picture art directors (*May Subd Geog*)

UF Art directors, Motion picture
Motion picture production designers
Moving-picture art directors
Production designers, Motion picture
BT Motion picture producers and directors
Motion picture audience etiquette
USE Motion picture theater etiquette
Motion picture audiences (*May Subd Geog*)
UF Film audiences
Filmgoers
Moviegoers
Moving-picture audiences
BT Performing arts—Audiences
Motion picture authorship (*May Subd Geog*)
[PN1996]
UF Film authorship
Film scriptwriting
Motion picture plays—Authorship
Motion picture scriptwriting
Motion picture writing
Motion pictures—Play-writing
Moving-picture authorship
Screen writing
Screenplay writing
Screenwriting
Scriptwriting, Film
Scriptwriting, Motion picture
BT Authorship
RT Scriptwriters
NT Motion picture plays—Technique
Treatments (Motion pictures, television, etc.)
SA *subdivision* Authorship *under motion picture
forms and genres, e.g.,* Comedy films—
Authorship
Motion picture billboards (*May Subd Geog*)
UF Film billboards
BT Billboards
Motion picture bloopers
USE Motion picture errors
Motion picture camera operators
USE Cinematographers
Motion picture camera stabilization systems
(*May Subd Geog*)
BT Cinematography—Equipment and supplies
Image stabilization
Motion picture cameras
[TR880]
UF Moving-picture cameras

†**Subject headings noted with a dagger contain
additional access points and subheadings that
are not pertinent to this text and are not
included here.**

BT Cameras
    Cinematography—Equipment and supplies
NT AK 8 motion picture camera
    Akeley motion picture camera
    Arriflex 16SR motion picture camera
    Arriflex 35 motion picture cameras
    Bell and Howell motion picture camera
    Bolex motion picture cameras
    De Jur motion picture camera
    Electronic cameras
    Framing cameras
    Keystone motion picture camera
    Kinetograph
    Kodak motion picture camera
    Panaflex motion picture camera
    Red One motion picture cameras
    Revere motion picture camera

Motion picture cartoons
  USE Animated films

Motion picture characters
  USE Characters and characteristics in motion
      pictures

Motion picture circulation
  USE Motion pictures—Distribution

Motion picture collections
  USE Motion picture film collections

Motion picture companies
  USE Motion picture studios

Motion picture composers
  USE Film composers

Motion picture consultants
  (May Subd Geog)
    UF Film consultants
    BT Consultants

Motion picture credits of actors and actresses
  USE Motion picture actors and actresses—Credits

Motion picture credits of producers and directors
  USE Motion picture producers and directors—
      Credits

Motion picture criticism
  USE Film criticism

Motion picture critics
  USE Film critics

Motion picture direction
  USE Motion pictures—Production and direction

Motion picture directors
  USE Motion picture producers and directors

Motion picture distribution
  USE Motion pictures—Distribution

Motion picture documentaries
  USE Documentary films

Motion picture editing
  USE Motion pictures—Editing

Motion picture editors *(May Subd Geog)*
  UF Film editors
    Moving-picture editors
  BT Editors

Motion picture errors *(May Subd Geog)*
  UF Motion picture anachronisms
    Motion picture bloopers
  BT Errors

Motion picture excerpts
  USE Film excerpts

Motion Picture Experts Group standard
  USE MPEG (Video coding
      standard)

Motion picture festivals
  USE Film festivals

Motion picture film
  UF Cinematographic film
    Film, Cinematographic
    Film, Motion picture
    Films, Cinematographic
    Motion pictures—Film
    Moving-picture film
  BT Cinematography—Equipment and supplies
    Photography—Films
—Conservation and restoration
  USE Motion picture film—Preservation
—Preservation *(May Subd Geog)*
  UF Motion picture film—Conservation
      and restoration
    Motion picture film—Preservation
      and storage
    Motion pictures—Conservation
      and restoration
—Preservation and storage
  USE Motion picture film—Preservation
—Splicing
  [TR886.5]
  UF Splicing (Motion picture film)
  BT Joints (Engineering)

Motion picture film collections
  (May Subd Geog)
    UF Film collections
    Film libraries
    Motion picture collections
    Motion picture libraries
    Moving-picture film collections
    BT Special libraries
    RT Film archives

†**Subject headings noted with a dagger contain
additional access points and subheadings that
are not pertinent to this text and are not
included here.**

NT Danmarks Radio Film Collection
    Tyler, Texas, Black Film Collection
    Stock footage collections
Motion picture film coupons
  USE UNESCO film coupons
Motion picture film editing
  USE Motion pictures—Editing
Motion picture genres
  USE Film genres
Motion picture historians
  USE Film historians
Motion picture industry
  (May Subd Geog)
    UF Film industry (Motion pictures)
        Moving-picture industry
    BT Cultural industries
    NT African Americans in the moving-picture
        industry
        Indians in the motion picture industry
        Jews in the motion picture industry
        Minorities in the motion picture industry
        Video recordings industry
        Women in the motion picture industry
  —Accidents *(May Subd Geog)*
  — —Investigation *(May Subd Geog)*
  —Collectibles
        USE Motion pictures—Collectibles
  —Collective bargaining
        USE Collective bargaining—Motion
             picture industry
  —Collective labor agreements
        USE Collective labor agreements—Motion
             picture industry
  —Employees
        BT Grips (persons)
  — —Biography
        USE Motion pictures—Biography
  —Finance
        UF Motion pictures—Finance
  —India
  — —Bombay
        UF Bollywood
  —Public relations *(May Subd Geog)*
        UF Public relations—Motion picture
             industry
             Public relations—
             Moving-picture industry
  —Strikes and lockouts
        USE Strikes and lockouts—Motion
             picture industry
  —Subsidies *(May Subd Geog)*
        UF Federal aid to the motion
             picture industry

        Government aid to the motion
             picture industry
  —United States
        NT African Americans in the motion
             picture industry
             Asian Americans in the motion
             picture industry
             Hispanic Americans in the motion
             picture industry
             Irish Americans in the motion
             picture industry
             Italian Americans in the motion
             picture industry
             Mexican Americans in the motion
             picture industry
  —Wages
        USE Wages—Motion picture industry
Motion picture industry in literature
  (Not Subd Geog)
Motion picture industry in motion pictures
  (Not Subd Geog)
  [PN1995.9.M65]
    BT Motion pictures
Motion picture insurance *(May Subd Geog)*
  [HG9993–HG9993.4]
    UF Insurance, Motion picture
    BT Insurance
Motion picture journalism *(May Subd Geog)*
    UF Newsreel
    BT Journalism
        Newsreels
Motion picture journalists *(May Subd Geog)*
    BT Journalists
Motion picture libraries
  USE Motion picture film collections
Motion picture literature *(May Subd Geog)*
    UF Film literature
    BT Motion pictures—Bibliography
    NT Cataloging of motion picture literature
Motion picture locations *(May Subd Geog)*
  [PN1995.67]
    UF Filming on location
        Locations (Motion pictures)
    BT Motion pictures—Setting and scenery
Motion picture loops
  USE Loop films
Motion picture makeup
  USE Film makeup

†**Subject headings noted with a dagger contain
additional access points and subheadings that
are not pertinent to this text and are not
included here.**

Motion picture music *(May Subd Geog)*

Here are entered musical works composed for sound films or performed on soundtracks. Unaltered motion picture soundtracks that may include speech, sound effects, music, etc., are entered under Motion picture soundtracks. Musical works composed or adapted to accompany silent films are entered under Silent film music.

UF Background music for motion pictures
    Film music
    Motion pictures—Musical accompaniments

BT Dramatic music
    Music

RT Silent film music

—Copyright
    USE Copyright—Motion picture music

Motion picture music, Arranged

Motion picture musicals
    USE Musical films

Motion picture novelizations
    USE Film novelizations

Motion picture parodies
    USE Parody films

Motion picture plays

[PN1996–PN1997]

UF Film plays
    Film scripts
    Filmscripts
    Motion picture scripts
    Moving-picture plays
    Photoplays
    Scenarios
    Screen plays
    Screenplays
    Scripts (Motion pictures)

BT Drama

SA *subdivision* Motion picture plays *under names of individual literary authors, e.g.,* Shakespeare, William, 1564–1616—Motion picture plays

—Authorship
    USE Motion picture authorship

—**Editing**
    BT Editing

—**History and criticism**
    Here are entered works on criticism of screenplays. Works dealing with the technique of motion picture reviewing are entered under Film criticism. Collections of motion picture reviews are entered under Motion pictures—Reviews.

—Production and direction
    USE Motion pictures—Production and direction

—Reviews
    USE Motion pictures—Reviews

—Stories, plots, etc.
    USE Motion pictures—Plots, themes, etc.

—**Technique**
    BT Motion picture authorship

—**Women authors**
    [PN1997]

Motion picture plays, American *(May Subd Geog)*

UF American motion picture plays

BT American drama

Motion picture plays, Argentine
(May Subd Geog)

UF Argentine motion picture plays

BT Argentine drama

Motion picture plays, Australian *(May Subd Geog)*

UF Australian motion picture plays

BT Australian drama

Motion picture plays, Austrian *(May Subd Geog)*

UF Austrian motion picture plays

BT Austrian drama

Motion picture plays, Bengali *(May Subd Geog)*

UF Bengali motion picture plays
    Bengali drama

Motion picture plays, Brazilian *(May Subd Geog)*

UF Brazilian motion picture plays

BT Brazilian drama

Motion picture plays, Burmese *(May Subd Geog)*

UF Burmese motion picture plays

BT Burmese drama

Motion picture plays, Canadian *(May Subd Geog)*

UF Canadian motion picture plays

BT Canadian drama

Motion picture plays, Chinese *(May Subd Geog)*

UF Chinese motion picture plays

BT Chinese drama

Motion picture plays, Czech *(May Subd Geog)*

UF Czech motion picture plays

BT Czech drama

Motion picture plays, English *(May Subd Geog)*

UF English motion picture plays

BT English drama

—Philippines
    USE Motion picture plays, Philippine (English)

Motion picture plays, European

UF European motion picture plays

BT European drama

†Subject headings noted with a dagger contain additional access points and subheadings that are not pertinent to this text and are not included here.

Motion picture plays, Finnish *(May Subd Geog)*
  UF Finnish motion picture plays
  BT Finnish drama
Motion picture plays, French *(May Subd Geog)*
  UF French motion picture plays
  BT French drama
Motion picture plays, French-Canadian
  (May Subd Geog)
  UF French-Canadian motion picture plays
  BT French-Canadian drama
Motion picture plays, German *(May Subd Geog)*
  UF German motion picture plays
  BT German drama
Motion picture plays, Indonesian *(May Subd Geog)*
  UF Indonesian motion picture plays
  BT Indonesian drama
Motion picture plays, Italian *(May Subd Geog)*
  UF Italian motion picture plays
  BT Italian drama
Motion picture plays, Japanese *(May Subd Geog)*
  UF Japanese motion picture plays
  BT Japanese drama
Motion picture plays, Kannada *(May Subd Geog)*
  UF Kannada motion picture plays
  BT Kannada drama
Motion picture plays, Korean *(May Subd Geog)*
  UF Korean motion picture plays
  BT Korean drama
Motion picture plays, Malayalam
  (May Subd Geog)
  UF Malayalam motion pictures plays
  BT Malayalam drama
Motion picture plays, Mexican *(May Subd Geog)*
  UF Mexican motion picture plays
  BT Mexican drama
Motion picture plays, Persian *(May Subd Geog)*
  UF Persian motion picture plays
  BT Persian drama
Motion picture plays, Philippine (English)
  (May Subd Geog)
  UF Motion picture plays, English—Philippines
      Philippine motion picture plays (English)
  BT Philippine drama (English)
Motion picture plays, Russian
  (May Subd Geog)
  UF Russian motion picture plays
  BT Russian drama
Motion picture plays, Slovak *(May Subd Geog)*
  UF Slovak motion picture plays
  BT Slovak drama
Motion picture plays, Spanish *(May Subd Geog)*
  UF Spanish motion picture plays
  BT Spanish drama

Motion picture plays, Swedish *(May Subd Geog)*
  UF Swedish motion picture plays
  BT Swedish drama
Motion picture plays, Telugu *(May Subd Geog)*
  UF Telugu motion picture plays
  BT Telugu drama
Motion picture plays, Turkish *(May Subd Geog)*
  UF Turkish motion picture plays
  BT Turkish drama
Motion picture plays, Ukrainian
  (May Subd Geog)
  UF Ukrainian motion picture plays
  BT Ukrainian drama
Motion picture plays, Urdu *(May Subd Geog)*
  UF Urdu motion picture plays
  BT Urdu drama
Motion picture plays, Vietnamese
  (May Subd Geog)
  UF Vietnamese motion picture plays
  BT Vietnamese drama
Motion picture plots
  USE Motion pictures—Plots, themes, etc.,
Motion picture posters
  USE Film posters
Motion picture previews
  USE Film trailers
Motion picture producers and directors
  (May Subd Geog)
  BT Directors, Motion picture
      Film directors
      Film producers
      Motion picture directors
      Moving-picture producers and directors
      Producers, Motion picture
  NT Casting directors
      Expatriate motion picture producers and
        directors
      Gay motion picture producers and directors
      Independent filmmakers
      Jewish motion picture producers and directors
      Motion picture art directors
      Women motion picture producers and
        directors
—**Credits**
    UF Credits of motion picture producers
        and directors
        Film credits of motion picture producers
        and directors

†Subject headings noted with a dagger contain additional access points and subheadings that are not pertinent to this text and are not included here.

—United States
    NT African American motion picture
          producers and directors
         Asian American motion picture
          producers and directors
         Hispanic American motion picture
          producers and directors
         Mexican American motion picture
          producers and directors
         Pacific Islander American motion picture
          producers and directors
         Palestinian American motion picture
          producers and directors
         Tunisian American motion picture
          producers and directors
Motion picture producers and directors, African
  American
    USE African American motion picture producers
        and directors
Motion picture producers and directors, Asian
  American
    USE Asian American motion picture producers
        and directors
**Motion picture producers and directors, French-
Canadian** *(May Subd Geog)*
    UF French-Canadian motion picture producers
        and directors
Motion picture producers and directors, Hispanic
  American
    USE Hispanic American motion picture producers
        and directors
Motion picture producers and directors, Mexican
  American
    USE Mexican American motion picture producers
        and directors
Motion picture producers and directors, Pacific
  Islander American
    USE Pacific Islander American motion picture
        producers and directors
Motion picture producers and directors, Palestinian
  American
    USE Palestinian American motion picture
        producers and directors
Motion picture producers and directors, Tunisian
  American
    USE Tunisian American motion picture producers
        and directors
Motion picture producers' and directors' spouses
  (May Subd Geog)
    BT Spouses
Motion picture production
    USE Motion pictures—Production and direction
Motion picture production companies

    USE Motion picture studios
Motion picture production designers
    USE Motion picture art directors
Motion picture programs *(May Subd Geog)*
    [PN1995.9.P5]
    UF Film programs
    BT Playbills
Motion picture projection *(May Subd Geog)*
    [TR890]
    UF Bioscope
        Projection, Motion picture
    BT Lantern projection
  —Safety regulations *(May Subd Geog)*
Motion picture projectionists *(May Subd Geog)*
    UF Projectionists, Motion picture
    BT Motion picture theaters—Employees
Motion picture projectors *(May Subd Geog)*
    BT Projectors
    NT Bolex motion picture projectors
        Kalee motion picture projectors
  —Light sources
      UF Light sources for motion picture
         projectors
      BT Electric lamps
  ——**Power supply** *(May Subd Geog)*
Motion picture remakes
  USE Film remakes
Motion picture reviews
  USE Motion pictures—Reviews
Motion picture script clerks
  USE Script clerks
Motion picture scripts
  USE Motion picture plays
Motion picture scriptwriting
  USE Motion picture authorship
Motion picture sequels
  USE Film sequels
Motion picture serials
  USE Film serials
Motion picture set designers *(May Subd Geog)*
    BT Set designers
Motion picture soundtracks *(May Subd Geog)*
  Here are entered recordings of unaltered motion
picture soundtracks that may include speech, sound
effects, music, etc., and that may be complete
soundtracks or selected portions of soundtracks. For
those that include music, an additional subject entry
is made under the heading Motion picture music.

†**Subject headings noted with a dagger contain
additional access points and subheadings that
are not pertinent to this text and are not
included here.**

UF Soundtracks, Motion picture
BT Sound recordings
Motion picture stars
  USE Motion picture actors and actresses
Motion picture stock materials
  USE Stock footage
Motion picture story editors
  USE Story editors (Motion pictures)
Motion picture studios *(May Subd Geog)*
  UF Companies, Motion picture
    Film companies
    Film studios
    Motion picture companies
    Motion picture production companies
    Production companies, Motion picture
    Studios, Motion picture
  BT Business enterprises
Motion picture stunt men and women
  USE Stunt performers
Motion picture theater etiquette *(May Subd Geog)*
  [PN1995.9.E86]
  UF Motion picture audience etiquette
  BT Etiquette
Motion picture theater managers
  (May Subd Geog]
  UF Managers, Motion picture theater
    Theater managers, Motion picture
  BT Theatrical managers
Motion picture theaters
  (May Subd Geog) †
  [NA6845 (Architecture)]
  UF Cinemas
    Movie theaters
    Theaters, Motion picture
  BT Theaters
  NT Adult movie theaters
    Drive-in theaters
    Multiplex theaters
    Traveling motion picture theaters
—Access for the physically handicapped
    USE Motion picture theaters—Barrier-free design
—**Argentina**
    NT Cine El Cairo (Rosario, Santa Fe, Argentina)
—**Austria**
    NT Kosmos-Kino (Vienna, Austria)
—**Barrier-free design**
    UF Motion picture theaters—Access for the physically handicapped
—**California**
    NT Chinese Theatre (Los Angeles, Calif.)
    Fox Theatre (San Francisco, Calif.)

    Los Angeles Theatre (Los Angeles, Calif.)
    Paramount Theatre (Oakland, Calif.)
—**Conservation and restoration**
—**Employees**
    NT Motion picture projectionists
—**England**
    NT Botchergate Picture House (Carlisle, England)
    Carling Academy Brixton (London, England)
    Odeon (Sheffield, England)
—**Georgia**
    NT Fox Theatre (Atlanta, Ga.)
—**Germany**
    NT Gloria-Palast (Berlin, Germany)
    Lichtburg (Essen, Germany)
    Tatiana-Palast (Berlin, Germany)
—**Idaho**
    NT Bovill Opera House (Bovill, Idaho)
    Egyptian Theatre (Boise, Idaho)
    Idanha Theater (Soda Springs, Idaho)
    Iris Theater (American Falls, Idaho)
—**Illinois**
    NT Oriental Theatre (Chicago, Ill.)
—**Indiana**
    NT Embassy Theatre (Fort Wayne, Ind.)
—**Italy**
    NT Anteo spazioCinema (Milan, Italy)
—**Japan**
    NT Jinseiza (Tokyo, Japan)
    Subaruza (Tokyo, Japan)
—**Mexico**
    NT Teatro Alameda (Querétaro, Mexico)
—**Michigan**
    NT Fox Theatre Building (Detroit, Mich.)
    Ken Theater (Frankenmuth, Mich.)
—**Montana**
    NT Majestic Theatre (Eureka, Mont.)
—**Netherlands**
    NT Theater Tuschinski (Amsterdam, Netherlands)
—**New York (State)**
    NT Claremont Theater Building (New York, N.Y.)
    Dryden Theatre (Rochester, N.Y.)
    Loew's Paradise Theater (New York, N.Y.)
    Loew's State Theatre (Syracuse, N.Y.)

†**Subject headings noted with a dagger contain additional access points and subheadings that are not pertinent to this text and are not included here.**

—Ohio
> NT   Akron Civic Theatre (Akron, Ohio)
> Utopia Theatre (Painesville, Ohio)

—Oregon
> NT   Bagdad Theater (Portland, Or.)
> Egyptian Theatre (Coos Bay, Or.)
> McDonald Theater (Eugene, Or.)

—Reconstruction *(May Subd Geog)*
> UF   Reconstruction of motion picture theaters

—Remodeling for other use

—Scotland
> NT   Picture House (Campbeltown, Scotland)

—South Carolina
> NT   Richardson Theatre (Seneca, S.C.)

—Switzerland
> NT   Capitole (Lausanne, Switzerland)
> Kino "Studio 4" (Zurich, Switzerland)
> Kino Xenix (Zurich, Switzerland)

—Wages
> USE   Wages—Motion picture theaters

—Washington (D.C.)
> NT   Mary Pickford Theater (Library of
> Congress James Madison Memorial
> Building, Washington, D.C.)

Motion picture theaters in art *(Not Subd Geog)*

Motion picture theaters in literature
(Not Subd Geog)

Motion picture titles
> USE   Titles of motion pictures

Motion picture titling
> USE   Motion pictures—Titling

Motion picture trailers
> USE   Film trailers

Motion picture writing
> USE   Motion picture authorship

Motion pictures *(May Subd Geog)*
[PN1993–PN1999]

This heading is used as a topical heading for general works about motion pictures themselves, including motion pictures as an art form, copyrighting, distribution, editing, plots, production, etc. Works about the technical aspects of making motion pictures and their projection onto a screen are entered under Cinematography. Works about the technical aspects of making video recordings, i.e., creating and storing moving images in an electronic form and displaying them on an electronic display are entered under Video recording. Works about the artistic aspects of making video recordings are entered under Video recordings—Production and direction.
> UF   Cinema
> Feature films—History and criticism

Films
Movies
> BT   Audio-visual materials
> Mass media
> Performing arts
> NT   3-D films
> Abjection in motion pictures
> Aboriginal Australians in motion pictures
> Action and adventure films
> Advertising in motion pictures
> African American men in motion pictures
> African American women heroes in motion
> pictures
> African American women in motion pictures
> African American yuppies in motion pictures
> African Americans in the motion picture
> industry
> Aging in motion pictures
> AIDS (Disease) in motion pictures
> Alcoholism in motion pictures
> Aliens in motion pictures
> Amateur films
> Ambiguity in motion pictures
> Amusement ride films
> Anarchism in motion pictures
> Andy Hardy films
> Angélique films
> Angels in motion pictures
> Animal films
> Animals in motion pictures
> Animated films
> Anthology films
> Anti-Jewish films
> Anti-Nazi movement in motion pictures
> Anti-war films
> Antichrist in motion pictures
> Antiheroes in motion pictures
> Antipsychiatry in motion pictures
> Antisemitism in motion pictures
> Apartments in motion pictures
> Apes in motion pictures
> Apocalypse in motion pictures
> Appalachians (People) in motion pictures
> Arabs in motion pictures
> Archaeology in motion pictures
> Archetype (Psychology) in motion pictures
> Architects in motion pictures
> Architecture in motion pictures

†**Subject headings noted with a dagger contain additional access points and subheadings that are not pertinent to this text and are not included here.**

Armed Forces in motion pictures
Armor in motion pictures
Art and motion pictures
Art in motion pictures
Arthurian romances in motion pictures
Artists in motion pictures
Asian American men in motion pictures
Asian American women in motion pictures
Asian Americans in motion pictures
Asians in motion pictures
Atomic bomb victims in motion pictures
Auteur theory (Motion pictures)
Authority in motion pictures
Authors in motion pictures
Automobiles in motion pictures
Autonomy (Psychology) in motion pictures
Ballet in motion pictures, television, etc.
Basques in motion pictures
Baths in motion pictures
Beauty, Personal, in motion pictures
Beheading in motion pictures
Big bands in motion pictures
Bioethics in motion pictures
Biographical films
Biology in motion pictures
Bisexuality in motion pictures
Black men in motion pictures
Blacks in motion pictures
Blaxploitation films
Blind in motion pictures
Blockbusters (Motion pictures)
Blondes in motion pictures
Blood in motion pictures
Blues (Music) in motion pictures
Boats and boating in motion pictures
Body (Human) in motion pictures
Bondage (Sexual behavior) in motion pictures
Bookstores in motion pictures
Boundaries in motion pictures
Bowery Boys films
Boys in motion pictures
Brainwashing in motion pictures
Buddy films
Bullfights in motion pictures
Bureaucracy in motion pictures
Business ethics in motion pictures
Business in motion pictures
Cannibalism in motion pictures
Cantors (Judaism) in motion pictures
Caper films
Captivity in motion pictures
Car-chase films
Carmen films

Carnival in motion pictures
Catastrophical, The, in motion pictures
Cataloging of motion pictures
Catholics in motion pictures
Cats in motion pictures
Chance in motion pictures
Characters and characteristics in motion pictures
Child sexual abuse in motion pictures
Childhood in motion pictures
Children in motion pictures
Christianity in motion pictures
Christians in motion pictures
Christmas films
Christmas in motion pictures
Circus in motion pictures
Cities and towns in motion pictures
City and town life in motion pictures
Civilization, Ancient, in motion pictures
Civilization in motion pictures
Clergy in motion pictures
Clichés in motion pictures
Clothing and dress in motion pictures
Cocktails in motion pictures
Cold War in motion pictures
College life films
College teachers in motion pictures
Color motion pictures
Colorization of motion pictures
Comic strip characters in motion pictures
Coming-of-age films
Communism and motion pictures
Communists in motion pictures
Communities in motion pictures
Composers in motion pictures
Compulsive gambling in motion pictures
Conflict of generations in motion pictures
Conspiracy in motion pictures
Control (Psychology) in motion pictures
Conversion in motion pictures
Counterculture in motion pictures
Country homes in motion pictures
Country life in motion pictures
Creation (Literary, artistic, etc.) in motion pictures
Credit titles (Motion pictures, television, etc.)
Crime films
Crowds in motion pictures

†**Subject headings noted with a dagger contain additional access points and subheadings that are not pertinent to this text and are not included here.**

Cruelty in motion pictures
Crusades in motion pictures
Cult films
Culture conflict in motion pictures
Culture in motion pictures
Curiosities and wonders in motion pictures
Cyborgs in motion pictures
Dance in motion pictures, television, etc.
Deaf in motion pictures
Death in motion pictures
Decision making in motion pictures
Defeat (Psychology) in motion pictures
Demonology in motion pictures
Desire in motion pictures
Detective teams in motion pictures
Devil in motion pictures
Dialogue in motion pictures
Difference (Philosophy) in motion pictures
Dinners and dining in motion pictures
Dinosaurs in motion pictures
Disaster films
Diseases in motion pictures
Doctor Mabuse films
Documentary-style films
Dogs in motion pictures
Don Camillo films
Don Juan films
Doubles in motion pictures
Dreams in motion pictures
Drifters in motion pictures
Drinking in motion pictures
Drinking of alcoholic beverages in motion
  pictures
Drugs and motion pictures
Drugs in motion pictures
Dubbing of motion pictures
Dwarfs in motion pictures
East and West in motion pictures
East Europeans in motion pictures
East Indian diaspora in motion pictures
Ecology in motion pictures
Education in motion pictures
Emigration and immigration in motion
  pictures
Emotions in motion pictures
Emperors in motion pictures
Entertainers in motion pictures
Environmental films
Environmentalism in motion pictures
Epic films
Erotic films
Eskimos in motion pictures
Ethics in motion pictures

Ethnicity in motion pictures
Eugenics in motion pictures
Evil in motion pictures
Evolution in motion pictures
Existentialism in motion pictures
Exoticism in motion pictures
Experimental films
Exploitation films
Expressionism in motion pictures
Extraterrestrial beings in motion pictures
Eyeglasses in motion pictures
Face in motion pictures
Fairy tales in motion pictures
Families in motion pictures
Family violence in motion pictures
Fantasy films
Fantasy in motion pictures
Fantozzi films
Farm life in motion pictures
Fascism and motion pictures
Fascism in motion pictures
Fashion in motion pictures
Fatherhood in motion pictures
Fathers and sons in motion pictures
Fathers in motion pictures
Female friendship in motion pictures
Female gangs in motion pictures
Female impersonators in motion pictures
Feminine beauty (Aesthetics) in motion
  pictures
Femininity in motion pictures
Feminism and motion pictures
Femmes fatales in motion pictures
Fiction films
Film adaptations
Film clips
Film excerpts
Film genres
Film installations (Art)
Film remakes
Film serials
Film series
Films for the hearing impaired
Flagellation in motion pictures
Flaneurs in motion pictures
Flight in motion pictures
Folk art in motion pictures
Folklore in motion pictures

†**Subject headings noted with a dagger contain additional access points and subheadings that are not pertinent to this text and are not included here.**

Food in motion pictures
Foreign films
Foreign language films
Forgiveness in motion pictures
Fugitives from justice in motion pictures
Future in motion pictures
Gay man-heterosexual woman in motion
  pictures
Gay men in motion pictures
Gay skinheads in motion pictures
Gays in motion pictures
Gaze in motion pictures
Gender identity in motion pictures
Genetic engineering in motion pictures
Genetics in motion pictures
Geometry in motion pictures
Geopolitics in motion pictures
German reunification question (1949–1990)
  in motion pictures
Germans in motion pictures
Gesture in motion pictures
Ghosts in motion pictures
Girls in motion pictures
Globalization in motion pictures
Godfather films
Grail in motion pictures
Grand Prix racing in motion pictures
Grief in motion pictures
Grotesque in motion pictures
Hallucinations and illusions in motion
  pictures
Happiness in motion pictures
Haunted house films
Heimatfilme
Hellraiser films
Heroes in motion pictures
Heroines in motion pictures
Heterosexual men in motion pictures
Heterosexual women in motion pictures
Heterosexuality in motion pictures
Hip-hop in motion pictures
Hispanic Americans in motion pictures
Historical films
History in motion pictures
Holocaust, Jewish (1939–1945),
  in motion pictures
Holocaust survivors in motion pictures
Home in motion pictures
Homosexuality and motion pictures
Homosexuality in motion pictures
Horror films
Horses in motion pictures

Human-animal relationships in motion
  pictures
Human cloning in motion pictures
Human reproductive technology in motion
  pictures
Human rights in motion pictures
Humor in motion pictures
Hunting in motion pictures
Hypnotism in motion pictures
Hysteria in motion pictures
Identity (Psychology) in motion pictures
Ideology in motion pictures
Illusion in motion pictures
Imagery (Psychology) in motion pictures
Imagination in motion pictures
Immigrants in motion pictures
Impersonation in motion pictures
Impressionism in motion pictures
Imprisonment in motion pictures
Incest in motion pictures
Independent films
Indian captivities in motion pictures
Indian motion pictures
Indian women in motion pictures
Indians in motion pictures
Indigenous films
Indigenous peoples in motion pictures
Individuation (Psychology) in motion pictures
Insight in motion pictures
Intellectuals in motion pictures
Intercultural communication in motion
  pictures
International relations in motion pictures
Interpersonal conflict in motion pictures
Intimacy (Psychology) in motion pictures
Introspection in motion pictures
Inuit in motion pictures
Irish Americans in motion pictures
Irish in motion pictures
Irish question in motion pictures
Irish Travellers (Nomadic people) in motion
  pictures
Irony in motion pictures
Islam in motion pictures
Italian Americans in motion pictures
Italians in motion pictures
Jazz in motion pictures
Jealousy in motion pictures

**Subject headings noted with a dagger contain
additional access points and subheadings that
are not pertinent to this text and are not
included here.**

Jesus Christ in motion pictures
Jewish-Arab relations in motion pictures
Jewish women in motion pictures
Jews in motion pictures
Journalism and motion pictures
Journalists in motion pictures
Jury in motion pictures
Justice, Administration of, in motion pictures
Karate in motion pictures
Kings and rulers in motion pictures
Kissing in motion pictures
Latin Americans in motion pictures
Latin lovers in motion pictures
Lawyers in motion pictures
Leadership in motion pictures
Legal films
Lesbian bars in motion pictures
Lesbian vampires in motion pictures
Lesbianism in motion pictures
Lesbians in motion pictures
Letter writing in motion pictures
Letters in motion pictures
Liberty in motion pictures
Librarians in motion pictures
Libraries and motion pictures
Libraries in motion pictures
Lions in motion pictures
Loop films
Loss (Psychology) in motion pictures
Lost films
Love in motion pictures
Low budget films
Machismo in motion pictures
Mafia in motion pictures
Male friendship in motion pictures
Male homosexuality in motion pictures
Male impersonators in motion pictures
Man-woman relationships in motion pictures
Maori (New Zealand people) in motion
    pictures
Maps in motion pictures
Marginality, Social, in motion pictures
Marionettes in motion pictures
Marriage in motion pictures
Martyrdom in motion pictures
Masculinity in motion pictures
Masks in motion pictures
Masochism in motion pictures
Mass media in motion pictures
Medical films (Motion pictures)
Medical personnel in motion pictures
Medicine in motion pictures
Melodrama in motion pictures

Memory in motion pictures
Men in motion pictures
Men (White) in motion pictures
Mental illness in motion pictures
Metamorphosis in motion pictures
Metaphor in motion pictures
Mexican American women in motion pictures
Mexican Americans in motion pictures
Middle age in motion pictures
Middle Ages in motion pictures
Middle class in motion pictures
Miners in motion pictures
Minorities in motion pictures
Minority women in motion pictures
Miscegenation in motion pictures
Misogyny in motion pictures
Money in motion pictures
Monster films
Monsters in motion pictures
Mormons in motion pictures
Motherhood in motion pictures
Mothers and daughters in motion pictures
Mothers in motion pictures
Motion picture industry in motion pictures
Motion pictures and socialism
Motor vehicles in motion pictures
Motorcycle films
Mountaineering in motion pictures
Mountains in motion pictures
Murder in motion pictures
Museums and motion pictures
Music-halls (Variety-theaters, cabarets, etc.)
    in motion pictures
Musical films
Muslim women in motion pictures
Muslims in motion pictures
Myth in motion pictures
Mythology in motion pictures
National characteristics, American, in motion
    pictures
National characteristics, Argentine, in motion
    pictures
National characteristics, Australian, in motion
    pictures
National characteristics, British, in motion
    pictures
National characteristics, East Asian, in
    motion pictures

†**Subject headings noted with a dagger contain additional access points and subheadings that are not pertinent to this text and are not included here.**

National characteristics, French, in motion
  pictures
National characteristics, German, in motion
  pictures
National characteristics, Mexican, in motion
  pictures
National characteristics, Russian, in motion
  pictures
National characteristics, Spanish, in motion
  pictures
National characteristics in motion pictures
National socialism and motion pictures
National socialism in motion pictures
Nature in motion pictures
New Deal, 1933–1939, in motion pictures
New wave films
Nihilism (Philosophy) in motion pictures
Niskavuori films
Nonfiction films
Nonverbal communication in motion pictures
North Africans in motion pictures
Nostalgia in motion pictures
Nuclear warfare in motion pictures
Nudity in motion pictures
Nuns in motion pictures
Occultism in motion pictures
Oedipus complex in motion pictures
Ontology in motion pictures
Opera in motion pictures
Organizational behavior in motion pictures
Our Gang films
Outlaws in motion pictures
Outsiders in motion pictures
Outtakes
Pacifism in motion pictures
Painting and motion pictures
Palestinian Arabs in motion pictures
Paradise in motion pictures
Paranoia in motion pictures
Paraphilias in motion pictures
Parody in motion pictures
Passing (Identity) in motion pictures
Pathos in motion pictures
Patriarchy in motion pictures
Patriotism in motion pictures
Peasants in motion pictures
People with disabilities in motion pictures
People with mental disabilities in motion
  pictures
Peronism and motion pictures
Personal space in motion pictures
Philosophy in motion pictures
Photography in motion pictures

Physicians in motion pictures
Pink panther films
Pinocchio (Fictitious character) in motion
  pictures
Pioneers in motion pictures
Pirates in motion pictures
Polish people in motion pictures
Politics in motion pictures
Popular music in motion pictures
Populist films
Pornographic films
Portraits in motion pictures
Postage stamps in motion pictures
Postcolonialism in motion pictures
Power (Social sciences) in motion pictures
Pregnancy in motion pictures
Prehistoric animals in motion pictures
Prehistoric peoples in motion pictures
Presidents in motion pictures
Printing and motion pictures
Prisoners of war in motion pictures
Prostitutes in motion pictures
Prostitution in motion pictures
Psychiatry in motion pictures
Psychic trauma in motion pictures
Psychoanalysis and motion pictures
Psychoanalysis in motion pictures
Psychopaths in motion pictures
Public health in motion pictures
Public toilets in motion pictures
Puerto Ricans in motion pictures
Punk culture in motion pictures
Puppet films
Queens in motion pictures
Race awareness in motion pictures
Race films
Race in motion pictures
Race relations in motion pictures
Racially mixed people in motion pictures
Racism in motion pictures
Railroads in motion pictures
Rap (Music) in motion pictures
Rape in motion pictures
Rats in motion pictures
Realism in motion pictures
Reconciliation in motion pictures
Reconstruction (U.S. history, 1865–1877) in
  motion pictures

†**Subject headings noted with a dagger contain
additional access points and subheadings that
are not pertinent to this text and are not
included here.**

Redemption in motion pictures
Rednecks in motion pictures
Regeneration in motion pictures
Religion in motion pictures
Religious films
Repetition in motion pictures
Restrooms in motion pictures
Resurrection in motion pictures
Revolutions in motion pictures
Rites and ceremonies in motion pictures
Road films
Roadblocks (Police methods) in motion
    pictures
Robin Hood (Legendary character) in motion
    pictures
Robots in motion pictures
Rocky films
Romance films
Romanies in motion pictures
Rubble films
Rural-urban migration in motion pictures
Rural women in motion pictures
Rushes (Motion pictures)
Russians in motion pictures
Sacrifice in motion pictures
Sadism in motion pictures
Saints in motion pictures
Sami (European people) in motion pictures
San (African people) in motion pictures
Scapegoat in motion pictures
Scheherazade (Legendary character) in
    motion pictures
Schizophrenia in motion pictures
Schlemiels in motion pictures
Schools in motion pictures
Science fiction films
Science in motion pictures
Scientists in motion pictures
Sculpture in motion pictures
Sea in motion pictures
Secularism in motion pictures
Security (Psychology) in motion pictures
Seduction in motion pictures
Self in motion pictures
Self-presentation in motion pictures
Sensationalism in motion pictures
Senses and sensation in motion pictures
Sentimentalism in motion pictures
Serial murderers in motion pictures
Sex discrimination in motion pictures
Sex role in motion pictures
Sexism in motion pictures
Shamanism in motion pictures

Sick in motion pictures
Silence in motion pictures
Silent films
Single mothers in motion pictures
Sisters in motion pictures
Skin in motion pictures
Skyscrapers in motion pictures
Slavery in motion pictures
Smoking in motion pictures
Soccer in motion pictures
Social change in motion pictures
Social classes in motion pictures
Social problem films
Social problems in motion pictures
Social psychology in motion pictures
Socialism and motion pictures
Socialist realism in motion pictures
Soldiers in motion pictures
Sound in motion pictures
Sound motion pictures
Space and time in motion pictures
Space vehicles in motion pictures
Sports films
Spy films
Stamp collecting in motion pictures
Stereotypes (Social psychology) in motion
    pictures
Stock footage
Stores, Retail, in motion pictures
Strangers in motion pictures
Street films
Strikes and lockouts in motion pictures
Strong men in motion pictures
Subculture films
Subjectivity in motion pictures
Submarines (Ships) in motion pictures
Suburbs in motion pictures
Subways in motion pictures
Suffering in motion pictures
Super-8 motion pictures
Supernatural in motion pictures
Surrealism in motion pictures
Suspense in motion pictures, television, etc.
Swordplay in motion pictures
Swordsmen in motion pictures
Symbolism in motion pictures
Taboo in motion pictures
Tango (Dance) in motion pictures

†**Subject headings noted with a dagger contain
additional access points and subheadings that
are not pertinent to this text and are not
included here.**

Tarzan films
Tattooing in motion pictures
Teachers in motion pictures
Technology in motion pictures
Teen films
Teenage boys in motion pictures
Teenage girls in motion pictures
Teenagers in motion pictures
Telephone in motion pictures
Television broadcasting of films
Television in motion pictures
Terror in motion pictures
Terrorism in motion pictures
Theater announcements (Motion pictures)
Theater in motion pictures
Thrillers (Motion pictures)
Time in motion pictures
Time travel in motion pictures
Titanic (Steamship) in motion pictures
Titles of motion pictures
Toilets in motion pictures
Torchy Blane films
Torres Strait Islanders I motion pictures
Torture in motion pictures
Totalitarianism and motion pictures
Touch in motion pictures
Tourism in motion pictures
Transgender people in motion pictures
Translating and interpreting in motion
    pictures
Transportation in motion pictures
Transsexuals in motion pictures
Transvestism in motion pictures
Travel in motion pictures
Trials in motion pictures
Trick films
Tricksters in motion pictures
Turks in motion pictures
Twins in motion pictures
Underground movements in motion pictures
Unfinished films
Unidentified flying objects motion pictures
Urban African Americans in motion pictures
Utopias in motion pictures
Veterans in motion pictures
Villains in motion pictures
Violence in motion pictures
Vision in motion pictures
Voice in motion pictures
Voodooism in motion pictures
Walking in motion pictures
Weddings in motion pictures
Western films

Whites in motion pictures
Wine in motion pictures
Wit and humor in motion pictures
Witches in motion pictures
Women, Black, in motion pictures
Women, Romani, in motion pictures
Women, White, in motion pictures
Women heroes in motion pictures
Women in motion pictures
Women jazz musicians in motion pictures
Women journalists in motion pictures
Women lawyers in motion pictures
Women murderers in motion pictures
Women presidents in motion pictures
Women scientists in motion pictures
Women spies in motion pictures
Work in motion pictures
Working class in motion pictures
Working women in motion pictures
Wrestlers in motion pictures
Writing in motion pictures
Xenophobia in motion pictures
Yiddish films
Youth in motion pictures

SA *subdivision* In motion pictures *under names*
    of countries, cities, etc., and under names
    of individual persons, families, and
    corporate bodies, and heading of the type
    [topic] in motion pictures, *e.g.,* Children in
    motion pictures; Death in motion pictures;
    and titles of individual motion pictures
—Advertising
    USE Advertising—Motion pictures
—Aesthetics
    BT Aesthetics
—Appreciation *(May Subd Geog)*
    UF Appreciation of motion
        pictures
— —Study and teaching (Secondary)
    (May Subd Geog)
—Art direction *(May Subd Geog)*
    [PN1995.9.A74]
    BT Art direction
        Motion pictures—Production and direction
        Motion pictures—Setting and scenery
—Asia, Central
    Here are entered general works on motion
    pictures shown in Central Asia or produced by
    Central Asian film companies. Works on motion

†**Subject headings noted with a dagger contain
additional access points and subheadings that
are not pertinent to this text and are not
included here.**

pictures produced by Central Asian film companies and shown outside of Central Asia are entered under Motion pictures, Central Asian.

—Australia

Here are entered general works on motion pictures shown in Australia or produced by Australian film companies. Works on motion pictures produced by Australian film companies and shown outside of Australia are entered under Motion pictures, Australian.

—Awards *(May Subd Geog)*

——Brazil

NT Grande Prêmio Cinema Brasil

——Canada

NT Genie Awards

——France

NT Prix Jean Vigo

——Germany

NT Bayerischer Filmpreis

——India

NT Dadasaheb Phalke Award
IDPA Awards
Kerala State Film Awards

——Italy

NT Premio Solinas

——Spain

NT Premios Anuales de la Academia Goya

——United States

NT Academy Awards (Motion pictures)
Golden Globe Awards

—Bibliography

BT Motion picture literature

—Biography

UF Motion picture industry—Employees—
Biography

—Brazil

Here are entered general works on motion pictures shown in Brazil or produced by Brazilian film companies. Works on motion pictures produced by Brazilian film companies and shown outside Brazil are entered under Motion pictures, Brazilian.

—Canada

Here are entered general works on motion pictures shown in Canada or produce by Canadian film companies. Works on motion pictures produced by Canadian film companies and shown outside of Canada are entered under Motion pictures, Canadian.

—Casting *(May Subd Geog)*

BT Casting (Performing arts)
Motion pictures—Production and
direction

—Catalogs

UF Catalogs, Film
Film catalogs
Filmography

SA *subdivision* Film catalogs *under subjects for lists of films about those subjects; and subdivision* Catalogs *under individual film genres, e.g.,* Science fiction films—Catalogs.

—Censorship *(May Subd Geog)*

—China

Here are entered general works on motion pictures shown in China or produced by Chinese film companies. Works on motion pictures produced by Chinese film companies and shown outside of China are entered under Motion pictures, Chinese.

—Classification

USE Classification—Moving-pictures

—Collectibles *(May Subd Geog)*

[PN1995.9.C53]

UF Film collectibles
Motion picture industry—Collectibles

—Colorization

USE Colorization of motion pictures

—Conservation and restoration

USE Motion picture film—Preservation

—Copyright

USE Copyright—Motion pictures

—Costume

USE Costume ·

—Criticism

USE Film criticism

—Direction

USE Motion pictures—Production and
direction

—Distribution

UF Circulation of motion pictures
Distribution of motion pictures
Film distribution
Motion picture circulation
Motion picture distribution
Motion pictures—Release
Release of motion pictures

NT Block booking

—Documentaries

USE Documentary films

—Dubbing

†**Subject headings noted with a dagger contain additional access points and subheadings that are not pertinent to this text and are not included here.**

USE Dubbing of motion pictures
—Editing
    UF Film editing (Cinematography)
        Motion picture editing
        Motion picture film editing
        Motion pictures—Montage
    BT Editing
        Montage
—European influences
    BT Europe—Civilization
—Evaluation
    Here are entered works on the methods and
    results of assessing the quality of motion
    pictures. Works on methods and results of
    assessing the suitability of motion pictures for
    specific audiences are entered under Motion
    pictures—Ratings.
    NT Film criticism
—Excerpts
    USE Film excerpts
—Film
    USE Motion picture film
—Finance
    USE Motion picture industry—Finance
—France
    Here are entered general works
    on motion pictures shown in France
    or produced by French film
    companies. Works on motion
    pictures produced by French film companies
    and shown outside of France are entered under
    Motion pictures, French.
—French influences
    BT France—Civilization
—German influences
    BT Germany—Civilization
—Germany
    Here are entered general works on motion
    pictures shown in Germany or produced by
    German film companies. Works on motion
    pictures produced by German film companies
    and shown outside of Germany are entered
    under Motion pictures, German.
—Great Britain
    Here are entered general works on motion
    pictures shown in Great Britain or produced by
    British film companies. Works on motion
    pictures produced by British film companies
    and shown out side of Great Britain are entered
    under Motion pictures, British.
—History
    UF Motion pictures—History and criticism
—History and criticism

USE Motion pictures—History
—Homiletical use
    [BV4235.M68]
    BT Preaching
—Hungary
    Here are entered general works on motion
    pictures shown in Hungary or produced by
    Hungarian film companies. Works on motion
    pictures produced by Hungarian film
    companies and shown outside of Hungary are
    entered under Motion pictures, Hungarian.
—India
    Here are entered general works on motion
    pictures shown in India or produced by Indic
    film companies. Works on motion pictures
    produced by Indic film companies and shown
    outside of India are entered under Motion
    pictures, Indic.
—Industrial applications
    USE Industrial films
—Interviews
    BT Interviews
—Ireland
    Here are entered general works on motion
    pictures shown in Ireland or produced by Irish
    film companies. Works on motion pictures
    produced by Irish film companies and shown
    outside Ireland are entered under Motion
    pictures, Irish.
—Italy
    Here are entered general works on motion
    pictures shown in Italy or produced by Italian
    film companies. Works on motion pictures
    produced by Italian film companies and shown
    outside of Italy are entered under Motion
    pictures, Italian.
—Japan
    Here are entered general works on motion
    pictures shown in Japan or produced by
    Japanese film companies. Works on motion
    pictures produced by Japanese film companies
    and shown outside of Japan are entered under
    Motion pictures, Japanese.
—Lighting
    USE Cinematography—Lighting
—Mexico
    Here are entered general works on motion
    pictures shown in Mexico or produced by
    Mexican film companies. Works on motion

†**Subject headings noted with a dagger contain
additional access points and subheadings that
are not pertinent to this text and are not
included here.**

pictures produced by Mexican film companies and shown outside of Mexico are entered under Motion picture, Mexican.

—Montage

USE Motion pictures—Editing

—**Moral and ethical aspects** *(May Subd Geog)*

[PN1995.9]

—**Music supervision** *(May Subd Geog)*

BT Motion pictures and music

Music supervision

—Musical accompaniments

USE Motion picture music

—**Netherlands**

— —**German influences**

BT Germany—Civilization

—**New Zealand**

Here are entered general works on motion pictures shown in New Zealand or produced by New Zealand film companies. Works on motion pictures produced by New Zealand film companies and shown outside of New Zealand are entered under Motion pictures, New Zealand.

—Play-writing

USE Motion picture authorship

—**Plots, themes, etc.**

UF Motion picture plays—Stories, plots, etc.

Motion picture plots

Motion pictures—Stories, plots, etc.

Motion pictures—Themes, motives

BT Plots (Drama, novel, etc.)

RT Film genres

SA *subdivision* In motion pictures *under names of countries, cities, etc., and under names of individual persons, families, and corporate bodies; also headings for film genres, e.g.,* Horror films ; War films, *and headings of the type [topic] in motion pictures,* e.g., Children in motion pictures; Death in motion pictures

—**Portugal**

Here are entered general works on motion pictures shown in Portugal or produced by Portuguese film companies. Works on motion pictures produced by Portuguese film companies and shown outside of Portugal are entered under Motion pictures, Portuguese.

—Posters

USE Motion picture plays

—**Production and direction** *(May Subd Geog)*

UF Direction of motion pictures

Motion picture direction

Motion picture plays—Production and direction

Motion picture production

Motion pictures—Direction

Production of motion pictures

NT Blocking (Motion pictures)

Continuity (Motion pictures, television, etc.)

Motion pictures—Art direction

Motion pictures—Casting

Motion pictures—Setting and scenery

Storyboards

SA *subdivision* Production and direction *under motion picture forms and genres, e.g.,* Documentary films—Production and direction

—**Ratings** *(May Subd Geog)*

Here are entered works on methods and results of assessing the suitability of motion pictures for specific audiences. Works on the methods and results of assessing the quality of motion pictures are entered under Motion pictures—Evaluation

UF Ratings of motion pictures

—**Registration** *(May Subd Geog)*

UF Registration of motion pictures

BT Recording and registration

—Release

USE Motion pictures—Distribution

—**Religious aspects**

UF Religion and motion pictures

— —**Catholic Church**

UF Catholic Church and motion pictures

Motion pictures and Catholic Church

—Remakes

USE Film remakes

—**Reviews**

UF Motion picture plays—Reviews

Motion picture reviews

Movie reviews

Reviews of motion pictures

—**Russia (Federation)**

Here are entered general works on motion pictures shown in Russia or produced by Russian film companies. Works on motion pictures produced by Russian film companies and shown outside Russia are entered under

†**Subject headings noted with a dagger contain additional access points and subheadings that are not pertinent to this text and are not included here.**

Motion pictures, Russian.
—Scientific applications
　USE　Cinematography—Scientific applications
—**Semiotics** *(May Subd Geog)*
　BT　Semiotics
—Sequels
　USE　Film sequels
—**Setting and scenery** *(May Subd Geog)*
　[PN1995.9.S4]
　UF　Scenery (Motion pictures)
　　　Setting (Motion pictures)
　BT　Motion pictures—Art direction
　　　Motion pictures—Production and
　　　　direction
—**Singapore**
　Here are entered general works on motion
pictures shown in Singapore or produced by
Singaporean film companies. Works on motion
pictures produced by Singaporean film
companies and shown outside of Singapore are
entered under Motion pictures, Singaporean.
—**Sound effects**
　UF　Sound effects (Motion pictures)
—**Soviet Union**
　Here are entered general works on motion
pictures shown in the Soviet Union or
produced by Soviet film companies. Works on
motion pictures produced by Soviet film
companies and shown outside of the Soviet
Union are entered under Motion pictures,
Soviet.
—**Spain**
　Here are entered general works on motion
pictures shown in Spain or produced by
Spanish film companies. Works on motion
pictures produced by Spanish film companies
and shown outside of Spain are entered under
Motion pictures, Spanish.
—Special effects
　USE　Cinematography—Special effects
—Stories, plots, etc.
　USE　Motion pictures—Plots, themes, etc.
—**Switzerland**
　Here are entered general works on motion
pictures shown in Switzerland or produced by
Swiss film companies. Works on motion
pictures produced by Swiss film companies and
shown outside of Switzerland are entered under
Motion pictures, Swiss.
—Themes, motives
　USE　Motion pictures—Plots, themes, etc.
—Therapeutic use
　USE　Motion pictures in psychotherapy

—**Titling**
　[TR886.7]
　UF　Motion picture titling
　　　Titling of motion pictures
—**United States**
　Here are entered general works on motion
pictures shown in the United States or produced
by American film companies. Works on motion
pictures produced by American film companies
and shown outside of the United States entered
under Motion pictures, American.
—**Western influences**
　BT　Civilization, Western
Motion pictures *[LCSH Genre]*
Motion pictures (Islamic law) *(May Subd Geog)*
　BT　Islamic law
Motion pictures, African *(May Subd Geog)*
　Here are entered works on motion pictures
produced by African film companies and shown
outside of Africa. General works on motion
pictures shown in Africa or produced by African film
companies are entered under Motion pictures—
Africa. This heading is not used for individual films,
which are entered under headings appropriate to the
content, genre, and/or form of the film.
　UF　African motion pictures
　BT　Foreign films
Motion pictures, American *(May Subd Geog)*
　UF　American motion pictures
　BT　Foreign films
Motion pictures, Arab *(May Subd Geog)*
　UF　Arab motion pictures
　BT　Foreign films
Motion pictures, Arab countries
Motion pictures, Australian *(May Subd Geog)*
　UF　Australian motion pictures
　BT　Foreign films
Motion pictures, Brazilian *(May Subd Geog)*
　UF　Brazilian motion pictures
　BT　Foreign films
Motion pictures, British *(May Subd Geog)*
　UF　British motion pictures
　BT　Foreign films
Motion pictures, Canadian *(May Subd Geog)*
　UF　Canadian motion pictures
　BT　Foreign films
Motion pictures, Central Asian *(May Subd Geog)*
　UF　Central Asian motion pictures

[†]**Subject headings noted with a dagger contain
additional access points and subheadings that
are not pertinent to this text and are not
included here.**

BT Foreign films
Motion pictures, Chinese *(May Subd Geog)*
    UF Chinese motion pictures
    BT Foreign films
Motion pictures, East Indian
    USE Motion pictures, Indic
Motion pictures, Foreign
    USE Foreign films
Motion pictures, French *(May Subd Geog)*
    UF French motion pictures
    BT Foreign films
Motion pictures, German *(May Subd Geog)*
    UF German motion pictures
    BT Foreign films
Motion pictures, Hindi *(May Subd Geog)*
    UF Hindi motion pictures
Motion pictures, Hungarian *(May Subd Geog)*
    UF Hungarian motion pictures
    BT Foreign films
Motion pictures, Indian
    USE Indian motion pictures
Motion pictures, Indic *(May Subd Geog)*
    UF East Indian motion pictures
        Indic motion pictures
        Motion pictures, East Indian
    BT Foreign films
Motion pictures, Irish *(May Subd Geog)*
    UF Irish motion pictures
    BT Foreign films
Motion pictures, Italian *(May Subd Geog)*
    UF Italian motion pictures
    BT Foreign films
Motion pictures, Japanese *(May Subd Geog)*
    UF Japanese motion pictures
    BT Foreign films
Motion pictures, Korean *(May Subd Geog)*
    UF Korean motion pictures
    BT Foreign films
Motion pictures, Mexican *(May Subd Geog)*
    UF Mexican motion pictures
    BT Foreign films
Motion pictures, New Zealand *(May Subd Geog)*
    UF New Zealand motion pictures
    BT Foreign films
Motion pictures, Portuguese *(May Subd Geog)*
    UF Portuguese motion pictures
    BT Foreign films
Motion pictures, Russian *(May Subd Geog)*
    UF Russian motion pictures
    BT Foreign films
Motion pictures, Singaporean
    (May Subd Geog)
    UF Singaporean motion pictures

BT Foreign films
Motion pictures, Soviet *(May Subd Geog)*
    UF Soviet motion pictures
    BT Foreign films
Motion pictures, Spanish *(May Subd Geog)*
    UF Spanish motion pictures
    BT Foreign films
Motion pictures, Swiss *(May Subd Geog)*
    UF Swiss motion pictures
    BT Foreign films
Motion pictures, Yiddish *(May Subd Geog)*
    [PN1995.9.Y54]
    UF Yiddish motion pictures
Motion pictures and art
    USE Art and motion pictures
Motion pictures and Catholic Church
    USE Motion pictures—Religious aspects—
        Catholic Church
Motion pictures and children *(May Subd Geog)*
    UF Children and motion pictures
    BT Children
Motion pictures and communism
    USE Communism and motion pictures
Motion pictures and fascism
    USE Fascism and motion pictures
Motion pictures and feminism
    USE Feminism and motion pictures
Motion pictures and gay men *(May Subd Geog)*
    UF Gay men and motion pictures
    BT Gay men
Motion pictures and globalization *(May Subd Geog)*
    Here are entered works on the relationship
    between economic and social globalization and
    motion pictures. Works on globalization as a theme
    in motion pictures are entered under Globalization
    in motion pictures.
        UF Globalization and motion pictures
        BT Globalization
Motion pictures and history
    [PN1995.2]
    Here are entered works on the relationship and
    influence of motion pictures on history. Works on
    films that portray historical events or famous people
    are entered under Historical films with appropriate
    geographic, topical, and/or form subdivisions.
    Works on historical themes in films that are not
    themselves historical films are entered under History
    in motion pictures.

†**Subject headings noted with a dagger contain
additional access points and subheadings that
are not pertinent to this text and are not
included here.**

UF History and motion pictures
    History
Motion pictures and homosexuality
  USE Homosexuality and motion pictures
Motion pictures and journalism
  USE Journalism and motion pictures
Motion pictures and language *(May Subd Geog)*
    [PN1995.4]
  UF Language and motion pictures
  BT Language and languages
Motion pictures and libraries
  USE Libraries and motion pictures
Motion pictures and literature *(May Subd Geog)*
    [PN1995.3]
  UF Literature and motion pictures
  BT Literature
Motion pictures and medicine
    (May Subd Geog)
  UF Medicine and motion pictures
  BT Medicine
Motion pictures and men *(May Subd Geog)*
    [PN1995.9.M46]
  UF Men and motion pictures
  BT Men
Motion pictures and museums
  USE Museums and motion pictures
Motion pictures and music
  UF Music and motion pictures
  BT Music
  NT Motion pictures—Music supervision
Motion pictures and national socialism
  USE National socialism and motion pictures
Motion pictures and opera
    (May Subd Geog)
  UF Opera and motion pictures
  BT Opera
Motion pictures and painting
  USE Painting and motion pictures
Motion pictures and Peronism
  USE Peronism and motion pictures
Motion pictures and printing
  USE Printing and motion pictures
Motion pictures and psychoanalysis
  USE Psychoanalysis and motion pictures
Motion pictures and rock music
  UF Rock music and motion pictures
  BT Rock music
Motion pictures and socialism
  USE Socialism and motion pictures
Motion pictures and teenagers *(May Subd Geog)*
  UF Teenagers and motion pictures
  BT Teenagers
Motion pictures and television *(May Subd Geog)*

UF Television and motion pictures
BT Television
Motion pictures and the arts *(May Subd Geog)*
    [PN1995.25]
  UF Arts and motion pictures
  BT Arts
Motion pictures and theater *(May Subd Geog)*
    Here are entered works on the interrelations
    between motion pictures and theater. Works on the
    use of motion pictures in theatrical performances are
    entered under Motion pictures in the theater.
  UF Theater and motion pictures
  BT Theater
Motion pictures and totalitarianism
  USE Totalitarianism and motion pictures
Motion pictures and transnationalism
    (May Subd Geog)
  UF Transnationalism and motion pictures
Motion pictures and war
  USE *subdivision* Motion pictures and the war,
        Motion pictures and the revolution, *etc.,*
        under individual wars, e.g., World War,
        1939–1945—Motion pictures and the war
Motion pictures and women *(May Subd Geog)*
  UF Women and motion pictures
  BT Women
Motion pictures and youth *(May Subd Geog)*
  UF Youth and motion pictures
  BT Youth
Motion pictures for children
  USE Children's films
Motion pictures for men *(May Subd Geog)*
    [PN1995.9.M46]
  BT Men
Motion pictures for the deaf
  USE Films for the hearing impaired
Motion pictures for the hearing impaired
  USE Films for the hearing impaired
Motion pictures for women
  BT Women
Motion pictures for young adult
  USE Young adult films
Motion pictures in ability testing *(May Subd Geog)*
  BT Ability—Testing
Motion pictures in advertising *(May Subd Geog)*
  UF Advertising, Motion pictures in
  BT Advertising

†**Subject headings noted with a dagger contain
additional access points and subheadings that
are not pertinent to this text and are not
included here.**

Motion pictures in aeronautics *(May Subd Geog)*
  BT Aeronautics
Motion pictures in agriculture *(May Subd Geog)*
  BT Agriculture
Motion pictures in art *(Not Subd Geog)*
Motion pictures in business
  USE Industrial films
Motion pictures in chemical engineering
  (Not Subd Geog)
  BT Chemical engineering
Motion pictures in child psychology
  (May Subd Geog)
  BT Child psychology
Motion pictures in Christian education
  (May Subd Geog)
  [BV1535.4]
  BT Christian education
Motion pictures in church work *(May Subd Geog)*
  [BV652.82]
  BT Church work
Motion pictures in dentistry *(May Subd Geog)*
  BT Dentistry
Motion pictures in ethnology *(May Subd Geog)*
  [GN347]
  BT Visual anthropology
Motion pictures in evangelistic work
  (May Subd Geog)
  BT Evangelistic work
Motion pictures in forestry *(May Subd Geog)*
  BT Forests and forestry
Motion pictures in higher education
  (May Subd Geog)
  BT Education, Higher
Motion pictures in historiography *(May Subd Geog)*
  BT Historiography
Motion pictures in industry
  USE Industrial films
Motion pictures in libraries
  USE Libraries and motion pictures
Motion pictures in literature *(Not Subd Geog)*
Motion pictures in medicine
  (May Subd Geog)
  UF Medical films
  BT Medicine
Motion pictures in military education
  (May Subd Geog)
  BT Military education
Motion pictures in mining
  (May Subd Geog)
  BT Mining engineering
Motion pictures in missionary work
  (May Subd Geog)
  BT Missions

Motion pictures in museums
  USE Museums and motion pictures
Motion pictures in nursing education
  (May Subd Geog)
    BT Nursing—Study and teaching—Audio—
        visual aids
Motion pictures in physics *(May Subd Geog)*
  BT Physics
Motion pictures in propaganda
  (May Subd Geog)
  UF Propaganda in motion pictures
  BT Propaganda
Motion pictures in psychology
  (May Subd Geog)
  BT Psychology
Motion pictures in psychotherapy
  (May Subd Geog)
  UF Motion pictures—Therapeutic use
  BT Psychotherapy
Motion pictures in religious education
  (May Subd Geog)
  BT Religious education
Motion pictures in science *(May Subd Geog)*
  BT Science
Motion pictures in sex education
  USE Motion pictures in sex instruction
Motion pictures in sex instruction
  (May Subd Geog)
  UF Motion pictures in sex education
  BT Sex instruction
Motion pictures in sports *(May Subd Geog)*
  BT Sports
Motion pictures in teacher training
  (May Subd Geog)
  BT Teachers—Training of
Motion pictures in technical education
  (May Subd Geog)
  [T65.5.M6]
  BT Technical education
Motion pictures in television
  USE Television broadcasting of films
Motion pictures in the social sciences
  (May Subd Geog)
  BT Social sciences
Motion pictures in the theater *(May Subd Geog)*
  [PN2091.M68]
  Here are entered works on the use of motion
  pictures in theatrical performances. Works on the

†**Subject headings noted with a dagger contain
additional access points and subheadings that
are not pertinent to this text and are not
included here.**

interrelations between motion pictures and the theater are entered under Motion pictures and theater.

    BT Theater

Motor vehicles in motion pictures

(Not Subd Geog)

[PN1995.9.A85]

    BT Motion pictures

Motorcycle films *(May Subd Geog)*

[PN1995.9.M66]

When subdivided by the appropriate geographic, topical, and/or form subdivisions, this heading is used for works about motorcycle films.

    UF Biker films

    BT Motion pictures

Motorcycle films *[LCSH Genre]*

Mountain films *(May Subd Geog)*

    UF Bergfilme

        Mountaineering films

    BT Sports films

Mountain films *[LCSH Genre]*

Mountain whites (Southern States) in motion pictures

    USE Appalachians (People) in motion pictures

Mountaineering films

    USE Mountain films

Mountaineering in motion pictures

(Not Subd Geog)

    BT Motion pictures

Mountains in motion pictures *(Not Subd Geog)*

    BT Motion pictures

Mouse, Mickey (Fictitious character)

    USE Mickey Mouse (Fictitious character)

Movement, Acting

    UF Movement on the stage

    BT Acting

    NT Gesture

        Nonverbal communication in motion pictures

Movement on the stage

    USE Movement, Acting

Movie . . .

    USE *subject headings beginning with the words*

        Motion picture . . .

Movie composers

    USE Film composers

Movie dialogue

    USE Dialogue in motion pictures

Movie editions

    USE Photoplay editions

Movie novels

    USE Film novelizations

Movie parodies

    USE Parody films

Movie stars

    USE Motion picture actors and actresses

Movie reviews

    USE Motion pictures—Reviews

Movie thrillers

    USE Thrillers (Motion pictures)

Movie tie-in books

    USE Photoplay editions

Movies

    USE Motion pictures

Moving photomicrography

    USE Microcinematography

Moving-picture . . .

    USE *headings beginning with*

        Motion picture . . .

MPEG (Video coding standard)

    UF Motion Picture Experts Group standard

    BT Digital video—Standards

        Video compression—Standards

Ms. Pac-Man Maze Madness (Game)

[GV1469.35.M73]

    BT Video games

Multi media programs

    USE Media programs (Education)

Multicultural mass media

    USE Ethnic mass media

Multiculturalism in mass media

(Not Subd Geog)

    BT Mass media

Multimedia computing

    USE Multimedia systems

Multimedia information systems

    USE Multimedia systems

Multimedia knowledge systems

    USE Multimedia systems

Multimedia library services

    BT Audio-visual library service

    RT Instructional materials centers

Multimedia systems *(May Subd Geog)*

[QA76.575]

Here are entered works on computer systems that integrate and present diverse media, such as text, graphics, still and moving images, and audio. Works on media containing information that may be interactively manipulated by individual users through the use of software or microprocessing capabilities are entered under Interactive multimedia.

    UF Computer-based multimedia information

        systems

†**Subject headings noted with a dagger contain additional access points and subheadings that are not pertinent to this text and are not included here.**

Multimedia computing
Multimedia information systems
Multimedia knowledge systems
BT   Information storage and retrieval systems
NT   Digital video

Multiple roles (Acting)
BT   Acting
Multiple story films
USE   Anthology films
Multiplex cinemas
USE   Multiplex theaters
Multiplex theaters *(May Subd Geog)*
UF   Multiplex cinemas
Multiplexes (Motion picture theaters)
BT   Motion picture theaters
Multiplexes (Motion picture theaters)
USE   Multiplex theaters
Mummies in mass media
(Not Subd Geog)
BT   Mass media
Mummies in motion pictures
USE   Mummy films—History and criticism
Mummy films
[PN1995.9.M83]
—History and criticism
UF   Mummies in motion pictures
Mummy films *[LCSH Genre]*
Mummy television programs
[LCSH Genre]
Murder in mass media *(Not Subd Geog)*
BT   Mass media
Murder in motion pictures *(Not Subd Geog)*
BT   Motion pictures
Museums and motion pictures
UF   Motion pictures and museums
Motion pictures in museums
Museums and television *(May Subd Geog)*
UF   Television and museums
BT   Television
Music†
NT   Mass media and music
Motion picture music
Motion pictures and music
Television and music
Television music
Video game music
Music and mass media
USE   Mass media and music
Music and motion pictures
USE   Motion pictures and music
Music and television
USE   Television and music
Music for animated films

USE   Animated film music
Music for animated television programs
USE   Animated television music
Music for silent films
USE   Silent film music
Music for television
USE   Television music
Music-halls†
—England
NT   Carling Academy Brixton (London, England)
—New York (State)
NT   Fillmore East (New York, N.Y.)
Music-halls (Variety-theaters, cabarets, etc.) in motion pictures *(Not Subd Geog)*
BT   Motion pictures
Music in advertising†
NT   Singing commercials
Music supervision
NT   Motion pictures—Music supervision
Music television *(May Subd Geog)*
Here are entered works on television networks, channels, and programs that present primarily music videos and related programming.
BT   Television broadcasting
Music video direction
USE   Music videos—Production and direction
Music video production
USE   Music videos—Production and direction
Music videos *(May Subd Geog)*
UF   Videos, Music
BT   Television programs
Video recordings
RT   Television music
NT   Rock videos
—Direction
USE   Music videos—Production and direction
—Production and direction *(May Subd Geog)*
UF   Music video direction
Music video production
Music videos—Direction
Music videos *[LCSH Genre]*
Musical comedies
USE   Musicals
Musical films *(May Subd Geog)*
[PN1995.9.M86]
UF   Film musicals
Motion picture musicals
Musicals (Motion pictures)

†**Subject headings noted with a dagger contain additional access points and subheadings that are not pertinent to this text and are not included here.**

BT Motion pictures
    Film adaptations
RT Concert films
    Operas—Film and video adaptations
    Rock films

Musical films *[LCSH Genre]*

Musical instruments[†]
    NT Television receivers as musical instruments

Musical plays
    USE Musicals

Musical revues, comedies, etc.
    USE Musicals

Musical shows
    USE Musicals

Musical television programs
    USE Television musicals

Musicals[†]
    NT Television musicals

Musicals (Motion pictures)
    USE Musical films

Muslim women in motion pictures *(Not Subd Geog)*
    BT Motion pictures

Muslims in motion pictures *(Not Subd Geog)*
    BT Motion pictures

Mystery and detective television programs
    USE Detective and mystery television programs

Myth in mass media *(Not Subd Geog)*
    BT Mass media

Myth in motion pictures *(Not Subd Geog)*
    BT Motion pictures

Myth on television *(Not Subd Geog)*
    BT Television

Mythology in motion pictures *(Not Subd Geog)*
    [PN1995.9.M97]
    BT Motion pictures

Nagel camera *(Not Subd Geog)*
    BT Cameras

Nanny television programs *(May Subd Geog)*
    [PN1992.8.N35]
    BT Television programs

Nanny television programs *[LCSH Genre]*

Narration for silent films *(May Subd Geog)*
    Here are entered works on the use of live
    narration to accompany and explain silent films.
    BT Silent films

Narrative television (Service for people with visual
   disabilities)
    USE Video description

**National characteristics, American, in motion
pictures** *(Not Subd Geog)*
    [PN1995.9.N34]
    BT Motion pictures

**National characteristics, Argentine, in motion
pictures** *(Not Subd Geog)*
    BT Motion pictures

**National characteristics, Australian, in motion
pictures** *(Not Subd Geog)*
    [PN1995.9.N35]
    BT Motion pictures

National characteristics, British, in motion pictures
(Not Subd Geog)
    [PN1995.9.N352]
    BT Motion pictures

**National characteristics, East Asian, in motion
pictures** *(Not Subd Geog)*
    [PN1995.9.N353]
    BT Motion pictures

National characteristics, French, in motion pictures
(Not Subd Geog)
    BT Motion pictures

**National characteristics, German, in motion
pictures** *(Not Subd Geog)*
    [PN1995.9.N354]
    BT Motion pictures

**National characteristics, Mexican,
in motion pictures** *(Not Subd Geog)*
    BT Motion pictures

**National characteristics, Russian, in motion
pictures** *(Not Subd Geog)*
    BT Motion pictures

**National characteristics, Spanish, in motion
pictures** *(Not Subd Geog)*
    BT Motion pictures

National characteristics in mass media
(Not Subd Geog)
    [P96.N37]
    BT Mass media

National characteristics in motion pictures
(Not Subd Geog)
    [PN1995.9.N33]
    BT Motion pictures

National Hockey League 2K (Game)
    USE NHL 2K (Game)

**National School Library Media Program of the
Year Award**
    UF AASL National School Library Media
        Program of the Year Award
        NSLMPY Award
        School Library Media Program of the
          Year Award

[†]**Subject headings noted with a dagger contain
additional access points and subheadings that
are not pertinent to this text and are not
included here.**

BT School libraries—Awards—United States
National socialism and motion pictures
  [P1995.9.N36]
  UF Motion pictures and national socialism
  BT Motion pictures
National socialism in motion pictures
  (Not Subd Geog)
  BT Motion pictures
National socialism on television *(Not Sub Geog)*
  [PN1992.8.N37]
  BT Television
Nationalism[†]
  NT Mass media and nationalism
Nationalism and mass media
  USE Mass media and nationalism
Natural history films
  USE Nature films
Natural history motion pictures
  USE Nature films
Natural history movies
  USE Nature films
Natural history television programs
  USE Nature television programs
Natural history videos
  USE Nature videos
Nature cinematography *(May Subd Geog)*
  [TR893.4]
  NT Wildlife cinematography
Nature films *(May Subd Geog)*
  This heading is used as a topical heading for works about nonfiction films that depict or explain the natural world and its phenomena. When used as a topical heading it is subdivided by the appropriate geographic, topical, and/or form subdivisions.
  UF Natural history films
      Natural history motion pictures
      Natural history movies
      Nature motion pictures
      Nature movies
  BT Science films
  NT Wildlife films
Nature films *[LCSH Genre]*
Nature in motion pictures *(Not Subd Geog)*
  [PN1995.9.N38]
  BT Motion pictures
Nature motion pictures
  USE Nature films
Nature movies
  USE Nature films
Nature television programs *(May Subd Geog)*
  This heading is used as a topical heading for works about nonfiction television programs that depict or explain the natural world and its

phenomena. When used as a topical heading it is subdivided by the appropriate geographic, topical, and/or form subdivisions.
  UF Natural history television programs
  BT Science television programs
  NT Wildlife television programs
Nature television programs *[LCSH Genre]*
Nature videos *(May Subd Geog)*
  UF Natural history videos
  BT Educational videos
  NT Wildlife videos
Naval education[†]
  NT Television in naval education
NBA 2K (Game)
  [GV1469.35.N3]
  BT Video games
NBA JAM (Game)
  [GV1469.N33]
  BT Video games
NBA Live 2000 (Game)
  [GV1469.35.N335]
  BT Video games
NBA Showtime (Game)
  [GV1469.35.N336]
  BT Video games
Negro actors
  USE African American actors
       Actors, Black
Negro entertainers
  USE African American entertainers
Negro moving-picture actors and actresses

  USE African American motion picture actors
       and actresses
Negroes in moving-pictures
  USE African Americans in motion pictures
       Blacks in motion pictures
Negroes in the moving picture industry
  USE African Americans in the motion
       picture industry
       Blacks in the motion picture industry
Negroes in the performing arts
  USE African Americans in the performing arts
Net television
  USE Internet television
Net TV
  USE Internet television
Net videos
  USE Internet videos

[†]Subject headings noted with a dagger contain additional access points and subheadings that are not pertinent to this text and are not included here.

New Deal, 1933–1939, in motion pictures
   (Not Subd Geog)
   [PN1995.9.N37]
   BT Motion pictures
New wave (Motion pictures)
   USE New wave films
New wave cinema
   USE New wave films
New wave films *(May Subd Geog)*
   UF New wave (Motion pictures)
      New wave cinema
      Nouvelle vague (Motion pictures)
      Nouvelles vagues (Motion pictures)
   BT Motion pictures
New wave films *[LCSH Genre]*
New Zealand drama[†]
   NT Motion picture plays, New Zealand
      Television plays, New Zealand
New Zealand motion pictures
   USE Motion pictures, New Zealand
New Zealand television plays
   USE Television plays, New Zealand
News magazines (Television programs)
   USE Magazine format television programs
Newscasters
   USE Television journalists
Newsmagazines (Television programs)
   USE Magazine format television programs
Newsreel
   USE Motion picture journalism
Newsreels
   RT Actualities (Motion pictures)
   NT Motion picture journalism
Newsreels *[LCSH Genre]*
NFL 2K1 (Game)
   [GV1469.35.N338]
   BT Video games
NFL Blitz (Game)
   [GV1469.35.N34]
   BT Video games
NHL 2K (Game)
   [GV1469.35.N]
   UF National Hockey League 2K (Game)
   BT Video games
Nigerian drama (English)[†]
   NT Television plays, Nigerian (English)
Nigerian television plays (English)
   USE Television plays, Nigerian (English)
Nightmare Creatures (Game)
   [GV1469.35.N35]
   BT Video games
Nightmare on Elm Street films
   BT Horror films

Nightmare on Elm Street films
   [LCSH Genre]
Nights into Dreams (Game)
   [GV1469.35.N36]
   BT Video games
Nihilism (Philosophy) in motion pictures
   (May Subd Geog)
   [PN1995.9.N55]
   BT Motion pictures
Nihilism (Philosophy) on television
   (Not Subd Geog)
   BT Television
Nikkormat camera *(Not Subd Geog)*
   [TR263.N]
   UF Nikkorex camera
   BT Cameras
      Nikon camera
Nikkorex camera
   USE Nikkormat camera
Nikon camera *(Not Subd Geog)*
   NT Nikkormat camera
      Nikon digital cameras
      Nikonos camera
Nikon digital cameras
   (Not Subd Geog)
   BT Digital cameras
      Nikon camera
Nikonos camera *(Not Subd Geog)*
   [TR263.N]
   BT Cameras
      Nikon camera
      Underwater cameras
Ninja, Shadow of Darkness (Game)
   [GV1469.35.N39]
   BT Video games
Nintendo Game Boy video games
   USE Game Boy video games
Nintendo GameCube video games *(Not Subd Geog)*
   UF GameCube video games
   BT Nintendo video games
   NT Metroid Prime (Game)
Nintendo games
   USE Nintendo video games
Nintendo video games *(Not Subd Geog)*
   [GV1469.32]
   UF Nintendo games
   BT Video games
   NT Blast Corps (Game)

[†]**Subject headings noted with a dagger contain additional access points and subheadings that are not pertinent to this text and are not included here.**

Bomberman 64 (Game)
Castlevania (Game)
Doom 64 (Game)
Game Boy video games
Hybrid Heaven (Game)
Kirby 64 (Game)
Nintendo GameCube video games
Nintendo Wii video games
Ridge Racer 64 (Game)
Rocket (Game)
Shadows of the Empire (Game)
Star Fox 64 (Game)
Super Mario 64 (Game)
Super Mario Bros. (Game)
Super Mario RPG (Game)
Super Smash Bros. (Game)
Tonic Trouble (Game)
Turok (Game)
Turok 2 (Game)
War Gods (Game)
Yoshi's Story (Game)
Nintendo Wii video games *(Not Subd Geog)*
   UF Wii video games
   BT Nintendo video games
Niskavuori films
   [PN1995.9.N57]
   BT Motion pictures
Niskavuori films *[LCSH Genre]*
Nizo camera *(Not Subd Geog)*
   BT Cameras
Noir films
   USE Film noir
Non-book materials
   USE Nonbook materials
Non-commercial broadcasting
   USE Public broadcasting
        Public television
Nonbook materials *(May Subd Geog)*
   [Z688.N6]
   UF Non-book materials
   BT Library materials
   NT Acquisition of nonbook materials
       Audio-visual materials
       Cataloging of nonbook materials
       Children's nonbook materials
       Libraries—Special collections—
         Nonbook materials
       Physical processing of nonbook materials
       Selection of nonbook materials
       Shelving for nonbook materials
Nonbook materials selection
   USE Selection of nonbook materials
Noncommercial broadcasting

   USE Public broadcasting
        Public television
Nonfiction films *(May Subd Geog)*
   UF Nonstory films
   BT Motion pictures
   NT Actualities (Motion pictures)
       City symphonies (Motion pictures)
       Documentary films
       Promotional films
Nonfiction films *[LCSH Genre]*
Nonfiction television programs
   (May Subd Geog)
Nonfiction television programs
   [LCSH Genre]
Nonfiction videos
   USE Documentary videos
Nonobjective films
   USE Abstract films
Nonrepresentational films
   USE Abstract films
Nonstory films
   USE Nonfiction films
Nonverbal communication in motion pictures
   (Not Subd Geog)
   UF Film kinesics
   BT Motion pictures
       Movement (Acting)
Nonverbal communication in television
   USE Nonverbal communication on television
Nonverbal communication on television
   (Not Subd Geog)
   [PN1992.8.N65]
   UF Nonverbal communication in television
   BT Television
North Africans in motion pictures *(Not Subd Geog)*
   [PN1995.9.N66]
   BT Motion pictures
Nostalgia in motion pictures *(Not Subd Geog)*
   [PN1995.9.N67]
   BT Motion pictures
Nouvelle vague (Motion pictures
   USE New wave films
Nouvelles vagues (Motion pictures)
   USE New wave films
Novelizations, Film
   USE Film novelizations
Novelties (Motion pictures)
   USE Novelty films

†**Subject headings noted with a dagger contain
additional access points and subheadings that
are not pertinent to this text and are not
included here.**

Novelty films *(May Subd Geog)*
> This heading is used as a topical heading for works about whimsical or humorous short films designed to catch one's attention momentarily with something with a novel twist. When used as a topical heading it is subdivided by the appropriate geographic, topical, and/or form subdivisions.
>> UF Novelties (Motion pictures)
>> BT Short films

Novelty films *[LCSH Genre]*

Nuclear energy in television
> USE Nuclear energy on television

Nuclear energy on television *(Not Subd Geog)*
> UF Nuclear energy in television
> BT Television

Nuclear Strike (Game)
> *[GV1469.35.N83]*
> BT Video games

Nuclear warfare in motion pictures
(Not Subd Geog)
> UF Atomic warfare in motion pictures
> BT Motion pictures

Nuclear warfare in television
> USE Nuclear warfare on television

Nuclear warfare on television
(Not Subd Geog)
> UF Nuclear warfare in television
> BT Television

Nudity in motion pictures *(Not Subd Geog)*
> BT Motion pictures

Nuns in motion pictures *(Not Subd Geog)*
> BT Motion pictures

Nurses in mass media *(Not Subd Geog)*
> BT Mass media

Nurses in television
> USE Nurses on television

Nurses on television *(Not Subd Geog)*
> *[PN1982.8.N87]*
> UF Nurses in television
> BT Television

Nursing[†]
> **—Study and teaching**[†]
> **— —Audio-visual aids**
>> NT Motion pictures in nursing education
>> Television in nursing education

Nutrition in mass media *(Not Subd Geog)*
> BT Mass media

O.D.T. (Game)
> *[GV1469.35.O2]*
> BT Video games

Oakland Paramount Theatre (Oakland, Calif.)
> USE Paramount Theatre (Oakland, Calif.)

Obesity in mass media *(Not Subd Geog)*
> *[P96.O23–P96.O232]*
> BT Mass media

Objectivity[†]
> NT Documentary television programs—Objectivity
> Mass media—Objectivity
> Television broadcasting of news—Objectivity

Occultism in motion pictures *(Not Subd Geog)*
> BT Motion pictures

Occultism on television *(Not Subd Geog)*
> BT Television

Occupations in television
> USE Occupations on television

Occupations on television *(Not Subd Geog)*
> *[PN1992.8.O27]*
> Here are entered works on the portrayal of occupations on television. Works on the occupational opportunities in the field of television are entered under Television—Vocational guidance.
>> UF Occupations in television
>> BT Television

Ocean in motion pictures
> USE Sea in motion pictures

Oceanography[†]
> NT Television in oceanography

Oddball comedy films
> USE Screwball comedy films

Odeon (Sheffield, England)
> UF Odeon Sheffield (Sheffield, England)
> BT Motion picture theaters—England

Odeon-Astoria, Brixton (London, England)
> USE Carling Academy Brixton (London, England)

Odeon Sheffield (Sheffield, England)
> USE Odeon (Sheffield, England)

Oedipus complex in motion pictures
(Not Subd Geog)
> BT Motion pictures

Ogre Battle (Game)
> *[GV1469.35.O47]*
> BT Video games

Old dark house mysteries (Motion pictures)
> USE Haunted house films

Old dark house mysteries (Television programs)
> USE Haunted house television programs

Old house thrillers (Motion pictures)
> USE Haunted house films

Old house thrillers (Television programs)
> USE Haunted house television programs

[†]**Subject headings noted with a dagger contain additional access points and subheadings that are not pertinent to this text and are not included here.**

Older people[†]
  NT Mass media and older people
    Television and older people
Older people and mass media
  USE Mass media and older people
Older people and television
  USE Television and older people
Older people in mass media *(Not Subd Geog)*
  [P96.A38]
  UF Aged in mass media
  BT Mass media
Older people on television
  (Not Subd Geog)
  UF Aged in television
    Aged on television
  BT Television
Older television viewers *(May Subd Geog)*
  Here are entered works on television viewers who
  are older than middle age.
  BT Television viewers
Olympus camera *(Not Subd Geog)*
  BT Cameras
Omnibus films
  USE Anthology films
One (Game)
  [GV1469.35.O53]
  BT Video games
One Thousand Eighty Degree
  Snowboarding (Game)
  USE 1080 Degree Snowboarding (Game)
One-sheet posters *(May Subd Geog)*
  UF 1-sheet posters
  BT Advertising—Motion pictures
    Film posters
Online journalism *(May Subd Geog)*[†]
  RT Digital media
Online videos
  USE Internet videos
Ontology in motion pictur4es *(Not Subd Geog)*
  BT Motion pictures
Opera[†]
  NT Motion pictures and opera
Opera and motion pictures
  USE Motion pictures and opera
Opera films *[LCSH Genre]*
Opera in motion pictures *(Not*
  Subd Geog)
  [PN1995.9.O64]
  BT Motion pictures
Opera television programs *[LCSH Genre]*
Operas[†]
  NT Television operas
  —Film and video adaptations

  UF Opera—Film and video adaptations
  BT Film adaptations
    Musical films
Operating cameramen
  USE Camera operators
Operation Desert Shield, 1990–1991, in mass media
  (Not Subd Geog)
  BT Mass media
Operators, Camera
  USE Camera operators
Operetta films *[LCSH Genre]*
Operettas
  USE Musicals
Oppression (Psychology) in mass media
  (Not Subd Geog)
  BT Mass media
Optical disks[†]
  NT DVDs
    Videodiscs
Optical oceanography[†]
  NT Underwater television
Optima camera *(Not Subd Geog)*
  BT Cameras
Optoelectronic devices[†]
  NT Television
Optoelectronics[†]
  [TR1035–TR1045]
  NT Electrophotography
  BT Electrooptical photography
Oral histories *[LCSH Genre]*
Organ (Musical instrument)[†]
  NT Theater organ
Organizational behavior in motion pictures
  (Not Subd Geog)
  [PN1995.9.O75]
  BT Motion pictures
Organizational behavior in television
  USE Organizational behavior on television
Organizational behavior on television
  (Not Subd Geog)
  [PN1992.8.O72]
  UF Organizational behavior
    in television
  BT Television
Organized crime films
  USE Gangster films
Oriental Theatre (Chicago, Ill.)
  UF Balaban & Katz Oriental Theatre
    (Chicago, Ill.)

[†]**Subject headings noted with a dagger contain
additional access points and subheadings that
are not pertinent to this text and are not
included here.**

BT Motion picture theaters—Illinois

Orion televisions *(Not Subd Geog)*
    BT Television—Receivers and reception

Orion videocassette recorders *(Not Subd Geog)*
    BT Videocassette recorders

Our Gang films
    [PN1995.9.O8]
    UF Little Rascals films
    BT Motion pictures

Our Gang films *[LCSH Genre]*

Outdoor photography
    NT Street photography

Outlaw-couple films
    USE Gangster films

Outlaw gangster films
    USE Gangster films

Outlaws in motion pictures *(Not Subd Geog)*
    [PN1995.9.O84]
    BT Motion pictures

Outsiders in motion pictures *(Not Subd Geog)*
    BT Motion pictures

Outtakes *(May Subd Geog)*
    This heading is used as a topical heading for
    works about excerpts from films and television
    programs usually excluded from the final versions
    of completed films or programs. When used as a
    topical heading it is subdivided by the appropriate
    geographic, topical, and/or form subdivisions.
    BT Motion pictures
        Television programs

Outtakes *[LCSH Genre]*

Oz (Fictitious character : Baum)
    USE Wizard of Oz (Fictitious character)

Oz films
    USE Wizard of Oz films

P.I. stories, [films, etc.]
    USE *headings of the type* Detective and mystery
        stories, Detective and mystery films, etc.

Pac-Man (Game)
    BT Atari computer
        Video games

Pac-Man World (Game)
    [GV1469.35.P34]
    UF Video games)

**Pacific Islander American motion picture
    producers and directors** *(May Subd Geog)*
    UF Motion picture producers and directors,
        Pacific Islander American
    BT Motion picture producers and directors—
        United States

Pacific Islanders in mass media *(Not Subd Geog)*
    BT Mass media

Pacifism in motion pictures *(Not Subd Geog)*
    [PN1995.9.P23]
    BT Motion pictures

Pacifist films
    USE Anti-war films

Pacifist television programs
    USE Anti-war television programs

Paillard motion picture cameras
    USE Bolex motion picture cameras

Painting and motion pictures *(May Subd Geog)*
    UF Motion pictures and painting
    BT Motion pictures

Paleontology[†]
    NT Prehistoric animals in motion pictures

Palestinian Arabs in motion pictures
    (May Subd Geog)
    BT Motion pictures

Palestinian American motion pictures and directors
    (May Subd Geog)
    UF Motion picture producers and directors,
        Palestinian American
        Motion picture producers and directors—
            United States

Panaflex motion picture camera
    (Not Subd Geog)
    [TR883.P]
    BT Motion picture cameras

Panasonic televisions *(Not Subd Geog)*
    BT Television—Receivers and reception

Panasonic videocassette recorders *(Not Subd Geog)*
    BT Videocassette recorders

Panjabi drama[†]
    NT Television plays, Panjabi

Panjabi television plays
    USE Television plays, Panjabi

Parables in motion pictures *(May Subd Geog)*
    BT Motion pictures

Paradise in motion pictures *(Not Subd Geog)*
    BT Motion pictures

Paradise Twins 1 and 2 (New York, N.Y.)
    USE Loew's Paradise Theater (New York, N.Y.)

Paradise Twins One and Two (New York, N.Y.)
    USE Loew's Paradise Theater (New York, N.Y.)

Paramount Theatre (Oakland, Calif.)
    UF Oakland Paramount Theatre (Oakland, Calif.)
    BT Motion picture theaters—California

Paranoia in motion pictures
    (Not Subd Geog)

[†]**Subject headings noted with a dagger contain
additional access points and subheadings that
are not pertinent to this text and are not
included here.**

BT Motion pictures

Paraphilias in motion pictures *(Not Subd Geog)*
UF Sexual deviation in motion pictures
BT Motion pictures

Parasite Eve (Game)
[GV1469.35.P37]
BT Video games

Parodies[†]
NT Parody films

Parody films *(May Subd Geog)*
UF Film genre parodies
Film parodies
Genre parodies (Motion pictures
Genre parody films
Motion picture parodies
Movie parodies
Send-up films
Spoof films
Spoofs (Motion pictures)
Takeoff films
BT Comedy films
Parodies
SA *subdivision* Parodies, imitations, etc., *under motion picture forms and genres, e.g.,* Thrillers (Motion pictures)—Parodies, imitations, etc.

Parody films *[LCSH Genre]*

Parody in motion pictures *(Not Subd Geog)*
BT Motion pictures

Parody television programs *[LCSH Genre]*

Passing (Identity) in motion pictures
(Not Subd Geog)
BT Motion pictures

Pathos in motion pictures *(Not Subd Geog)*
BT Motion pictures

Patriarchy in motion pictures *(Not Subd Geog)*
BT Motion pictures

Patriotism in motion pictures *(Not Subd Geog)*
BT Motion pictures

Pay-per-view television
USE Subscription television

Pay television
USE Subscription television

Pay TV
USE Subscription television

PC video
USE Digital video

Peabody Awards
UF George Foster Peabody Awards
George Foster Peabody Broadcasting Awards
George Foster Peabody Radio and Television Awards
Peabodys (Awards)

BT Radio broadcasting—Awards—United States
Television broadcasting—Awards—United States

Peabodys (Awards)
USE Peabody Awards

Peace[†]
NT Mass media and peace

Peace and mass media
USE Mass media and peace

Peasantry in motion pictures
USE Peasants in motion pictures

Peasants in motion pictures *(Not Subd Geog)*
UF Peasantry in motion pictures
BT Motion pictures

Pedophilia in mass media
(Not Subd Geog)
BT Mass media

Pentacon camera *(Not Subd Geog)*
BT Single-lens reflex cameras

Pentax camera
USE Pentax cameras

Pentax cameras *(Not Subd Geog)*
[TR263.P]
UF Pentax camera
BT Cameras

Penti camera *(Not Subd Geog)*
BT Cameras

People with disabilities[†]
NT Actors with disabilities

People with disabilities in mass media
(Not Subd Geog)
UF Handicapped in mass media
BT Mass media

People with disabilities in motion pictures
(Not Subd Geog)
UF Handicapped in motion pictures
BT Motion pictures

People with disabilities on television
(Not Subd Geog)
[PN1992.8.H36]
UF Handicapped in television
Handicapped on television
BT Television

People with mental disabilities in motion pictures
(Not Subd Geog)
BT Motion pictures

People with visual disabilities[†]
NT Films for people with visual disabilities

[†]**Subject headings noted with a dagger contain additional access points and subheadings that are not pertinent to this text and are not included here.**

Television for people with visual disabilities
Video recordings for people with visual
disabilities
—**Services for**[†]
NT Audiodescription
Peplum films *(May Subd Geog)*
This heading is used as a topical heading for
works about films that feature mythological,
biblical, or invented strongmen as heroes. When
used as a topical heading it is subdivided by the
appropriate geographic, topical, and/or form
subdivisions.
UF Gladiator films
Sandal-and-spear epics (Motion pictures)
Sex-and-sand films
Sword-and-sandal epics (Motion pictures)
BT Motion pictures
Peplum films *[LCSH Genre]*
Perfect Dark (Game)
[GV1469.35.P47]
BT Video games
Performance art[†]
NT Video art
Performers, Stunt
USE Stunt performers
Performing arts[†]
NT Television and the performing arts
—**United States**
NT African Americans in the performing arts
Performing arts festivals[†]
NT Film festivals
Peronism and motion pictures
(May Subd Geog)
[PN1995.9.P38]
UF Motion pictures and Peronism
BT Motion pictures
Persian drama[†]
NT Motion picture plays, Persian
Persian Gulf War, 1991[†]
—**Mass media and the war**
UF Persian Gulf War, 1991, in mass media
Persian Gulf War, 1991, in mass media
USE Persian Gulf War, 1991—Mass media and
the war
Persian motion picture plays
USE Motion picture plays, Persian
Personal beauty in motion pictures
USE Beauty, Personal, in motion pictures
Personal films
USE Amateur films
Experimental films
Personal space in motion pictures
(Not Subd Geog)

BT Motion pictures
Persons[†]
NT Video gamers
Petri camera *(Not Subd Geog)*
BT Cameras
Phalke Award
USE Dadasaheb Phalke Award
Philippine drama (English)[†]
NT Motion picture plays, Philippine (English)
Philippine motion picture plays (English)
USE Motion picture plays, Philippine (English)
Philips Magnavox television/video combinations
(Not Subd Geog)
BT Television/video combinations
Philips Magnavox televisions
(Not Subd Geog)
BT Television—Receivers and reception
Philips televisions *(Not Subd Geog)*
BT Television—Receivers and reception
Philips videocassette recorders *(Not Subd Geog)*
BT Videocassette recorders
Philosophy in motion pictures
(Not Subd Geog)
BT Motion pictures
Photoelectronic imaging
USE Electrooptical photography
Photographers
RT Camera operators
Cinematographers
Photographic chemistry[†]
NT Cinematography—Processing
Photographic industry *(May Subd Geog)*
[HD9708.5.C35–HD9708.5.C354]
NT Camera industry
Photography[†]
RT Cinematography
NT Electrooptical photography
Electrophotography
Hidden camera photography
Stills (Motion pictures)
—**Electronic equipment**[†]
NT Digital cameras
Electronic cameras
—**Equipment and supplies**[†]
—**Failures** *(May Subd Geog)*
UF Failures in photography
—**Films**
NT Motion picture film

[†]**Subject headings noted with a dagger contain
additional access points and subheadings that
are not pertinent to this text and are not
included here.**

—**Scientific applications**[†]
  NT Underwater photography
Photography, Artistic
  RT Photography, Close-up
Photography, Close-up
  [TR683–TR683.5]
  UF Close range photography
      Close-up photography
  RT Photography, Artistic
Photography, Color
  NT Color photography
Photography, Color
  USE Color photography
Photography, Documentary
  USE Documentary mass media
Photography, Electronic
  USE Electronography
Photography, Electronic flash
  USE Electronic flash photography
Photography, Electrooptical
  USE Electrooptical photography
Photography, Flash-light
  NT Electronic flash photography
Photography, High-speed
  NT Electronic flash photography
Photography, Industrial
  NT Industrial cinematography
Photography, Military
  NT Military cinematography
Photography, Submarine
  USE Underwater photography
Photography, Underwater
  USE Submarine photography
Photography in motion pictures *(Not Subd Geog)*
  Here are entered works on the depiction of
  photography in motion pictures. Works on the
  technical aspects of making motion pictures and
  their projection onto a screen are entered under
  Cinematography.
  BT Motion pictures
Photography of sports[†]
  NT Sports cinematography
Photojournalism[†]
  NT Video journalism
Photomechanical processes
  NT Electrophotography
Photomicrography
  NT Microcinematography
Photoplay books
  USE Photoplay editions
Photoplay editions *(May Subd Geog)*
  Here are entered works on editions of novels or
  plays published with still photographs from a related

motion picture or a stage performance, such as the
fictional work on which the motion picture was
based, a later novelization of the motion picture
script, the text of the stage-play, or a novelization of
the stage-play.
  UF Movie editions
      Movie tie-in books
      Photoplay books
  BT Drama—Publishing
      Fiction—Publishing
Photoplays
  USE Motion picture plays
Phototypesetting
  NT Electronography
Physical education and training[†]
  NT Television in physical education
Physical processing of nonbook materials
  (May Subd Geog)
  BT Nonbook materials
Physically handicapped actors
  USE Actors with disabilities
Physicians in motion pictures *(Not Subd Geog)*
  [PN1995.9.P44]
  BT Motion pictures
Physicians in television
  USE Physicians on television
Physicians on television *(Not Subd Geog)*
  UF Physicians in television
  BT Television
Physics[†]
  NT Motion pictures in physics
Pickford Theater (Library of Congress James Madison
  Memorial Building, Washington, D.C.)
  USE Mary Pickford Theater (Library of Congress.
        James Madison Memorial Building,
        Washington, D.C.
Picture House (Campbeltown, Scotland)
  BT Motion picture theaters—Scotland
Picture telephone
  USE Video telephone
Pilot programs, Television]
  USE Television pilot programs
Pilots (Television programs)
  USE Television pilot programs
Pink Panther (Fictitious character)
  (Not Subd Geog)
Pink Panther films
  BT Motion pictures

[†]**Subject headings noted with a dagger contain
additional access points and subheadings that
are not pertinent to this text and are not
included here.**

Pink Panther films *[LCSH Genre]*
Pink Panther television programs
    BT Animated television programs
Pink Panther television programs
    [LCSH Genre]
Pinocchio (Fictitious character)
    (Not Subd Geog)
Pinocchio (Fictitious character) in mass media
    (Not Subd Geog)
    [P96.P55]
    BT Mass media
Pinocchio (Fictitious character) in motion pictures
    (Not Subd Geog)
    BT Motion pictures
Pioneers in motion pictures *(Not Subd Geog)*
    [PN1995.9.P487]
    BT Motion pictures
Pioneers on television *(Not Subd Geog)*
    BT Television
Piracy (Copyright)[†]
    NT Video recordings—Pirated editions
Pirated video recordings
    USE Video recordings—Pirated editions
Pirates in mass media *(Not Subd Geog)*
    [P94.5.P57–P94.5.P572]
    BT Mass media
Pixilated animation films *[LCSH Genre]*
Placement of products in mass media
    USE Product placement in mass media
Planet of the Apes films
    [PN1995.9.P495]
    BT Dystopian films
Planet of the Apes films *[LCSH Genre]*
Playbills
    NT Film posters
          Motion picture programs
Players, Video game (Persons)
    USE Video gamers
Plays, Television
    USE Television plays
Plots (Drama, novel, etc.)[†]
    NT Motion pictures—Plots, themes, etc.
          Television programs—Plots, themes, etc.
PMPs (Portable media players)
    USE Portable media players
Pocket instamatic camera
    USE Instamatic camera
Pocket monsters (Fictitious characters)
    USE Pokémon (Fictitious characters)
Point of view in motion pictures
    USE Subjectivity in motion pictures
Pokémon (Fictitious characters) *(Not Subd Geog)*
    UF Pocket monsters (Fictitious characters)

Pokémon (Game)
    [GV1469.35.P63]
    BT Video games
Pokémon Stadium (Game)
    [GV1469.35.P636]
    BT Video games
Pokémon Yellow (Game)
    [GV1469.35.P64]
    BT Video games
Poker[†]
    NT Video poker
Polaroid Land camera *(Not Subd Geog)*
    BT Cameras
Poles in motion pictures
    USE Polish people in motion pictures
Police[†]
    NT Wearable video devices in police work
Police and mass media *(May Subd Geog)*
    UF Mass media and police
    BT Mass media
Police films *(May Subd Geog)*
    UF Cop films
    BT Crime films
    RT Detective and mystery films
Police films *[LCSH Genre]*
Police in mass media *(Not Subd Geog)*
    BT Mass Media
Police shows (Television programs)
    USE Television cop shows
Police television shows
    USE Television cop shows
Polish drama[†]
    NT Television plays, Polish
Polish people in motion pictures
    (Not Subd Geog)
    UF Poles in motion pictures
    BT Motion pictures
Polish television plays
    USE Television plays, Polish
Political broadcasting (Television)
    USE Television politics
Political films *[LCSH Genre]*
Political science[†]
    NT Television and politics
Political television commercials
    [LCSH Genre]
Political television programs
    [LCSH Genre]

[†]**Subject headings noted with a dagger contain additional access points and subheadings that are not pertinent to this text and are not included here.**

Political violence in mass media
   (Not Subd Geog)
      BT Mass media
Politics, Practical[†]
      NT Television in politics
Politics and television
      USE Television and politics
Politics in motion pictures *(May Subd Geog)*
      [PN1995.9.P6]
      BT Motion pictures
Politique des auteurs (Motion pictures)
      USE Auteur theory (Motion pictures)
Popeye (Fictitious character) *(Not Subd Geog)*
Popeye (Fictitious character) in mass media
   (Not Subd Geog)
      [P96.p65]
      BT Mass media
Popular culture[†]
      NT Mass media and sports
Popular music in motion pictures *(Not Subd Geog)*
      BT Motion pictures
Populist films *(May Subd Geog)*
      BT Motion pictures
Populist films *[LCSH Genre]*
Porn videos
      USE Erotic videos
Porno films
      USE Pornographic films
Pornographic films *(May Subd Geog)*
      [PN1995.9.S45]
      UF Adult films (Pornographic films)
         Blue movies
         Porno films
         Stag films
         XXX films
      BT Motion pictures
         Pornography
      RT Erotic films
         Sex in motion pictures
         Snuff films
Pornographic films *[LCSH Genre]*
Pornographic television programs *[LCSH Genre]*
Pornography *(May Subd Geog)*[†]
      [NX650.E7 (Arts)]
      NT Pornographic films
Pornography in mass media
      USE Sex in mass media
Portable media players *(May Subd Geog)*
      UF PMPs (Portable media players)
      BT Digital electronics
Portland televisions *(Not Subd Geog)*
      BT Television—Receivers and reception
Portmanteau films

      USE Anthology films
Portraits (Biographical television programs)
      USE Biographical television programs)
Portraits in motion pictures *(Not Subd Geog)*
      [PN1995.9.P65]
      BT Motion pictures
Portuguese motion pictures
      USE Motion pictures, Portuguese
Postage stamps[†]
      NT Motion picture actors and actresses on
         postage stamps
Postage stamps in motion pictures *(Not Subd Geog)*
      [PN1995.9.P653]
      BT Motion pictures
Postage stamps on television
   (Not Subd Geog)
      BT Television
Postcolonialism in motion pictures
   (Not Subd Geog)
      BT Motion pictures
Posters[†]
      NT Film posters
Power (Social sciences) in motion pictures
   (Not Subd Geog)
      BT Motion pictures
Praktica camera *(Not Subd Geog)*
      BT Twin-lens cameras
Praktina camera *(Not Subd Geog)*
      BT Cameras
Preaching[†]
      NT Motion pictures—Homiletical use
Pregnancy in motion pictures *(Not Subd Geog)*
      BT Motion pictures
Prehistoric animals in motion pictures
   (Not Subd Geog)
      [PN1995.9.P67]
      UF Animals, Fossil, in motion pictures
         Animals, Prehistoric, in motion pictures
      BT Motion pictures
         Paleontology
Prehistoric peoples in motion pictures
   (Not Subd Geog)
      [PN1995.9.P674]
      BT Motion pictures
Prehistoric peoples on television
   (Not Subd Geog)
      BT Television
Premio Solinas

[†]**Subject headings noted with a dagger contain
additional access points and subheadings that
are not pertinent to this text and are not
included here.**

BT Motion pictures—Awards—Italy

Premios Anuales de la Academia Goya

   UF Goya Awards

      Goyas (Awards)

      Premios Anuales de la Academia de las Artes y las Ciencias Cinematograficas de Espana

      Premios Goya

   BT Motion pictures—Awards—Spain

Premios Anuales de la Academia de las Artes y las Ciencias Cinematograficas de Espana

   USE Premios Anuales de la Academia Goya

Premios Goya

   USE Premios Anuales de la Academia Goya

Premo camera (Not Subd Geog)

   [TR263.P]

   BT Cameras

Presidents in motion pictures (Not Subd Geog)

   BT Motion pictures

Press†

   NT Broadcast journalism

Press books (Motion picture advertising)

   USE Pressbooks

Press law†

   NT Television broadcasting of news—Law and legislation

Pressbooks (May Subd Geog)

   Here are entered works on advertising and publicity packets produced by motion picture studios to encourage local promotion of their films.

   UF Books, Press (Motion picture advertising)

      Campaign books (Motion picture advertising)

      Exhibitor's campaign manuals (Motion picture advertising)

      Press books (Motion picture advertising)

      Showman's manuals

      Showmen's manuals

   BT Advertising—Motion pictures

Previews, Movie

   USE Film trailers

Primal Rage (Game)

   BT Video games)

Prima's GoldenEye 007 (Game)

   USE GoldenEye 007 (Game)

Printing and motion pictures (May Subd Geog)

   UF Motion pictures and printing

   BT Motion pictures

Printing processes in color cinematography

   USE Color cinematography—Printing processes

Prints, Color

   USE Color cinematography—Printing processes

Prinzflex camera

   USE Zenith camera

Prison films (May Subd Geog)

   Here are entered individual films which depict prison life.

   BT Crime films

Prison films [LCSH Genre]

Prison television programs [LCSH Genre]

Prisoners of war in mass media (Not Subd Geog)

   BT Mass media

Prisoners of war in motion pictures (Not Subd Geog)

   BT Motion pictures

Prisons in mass media (Not Subd Geog)

   BT Mass media

Private investigator stories, [films, etc.]

   USE headings of the type Detective and mystery stories; Detective and mystery films, etc.

Private Snafu (Fictitious character) (Not Subd Geog)

   UF Pvt. Snafu (Fictitious character)

      Snafu, Private (Fictitious character)

Private Snafu films (May Subd Geog)

   When subdivided by the appropriate geographic, topical and/or form subdivisions, this heading is used for works about Private Snafu films.

   UF Snafu films

   RT Animated films

      Short films

      Snafu, Private (Fictitious character)

Private Snafu films [LCSH Genre]

Prix Jean Vigo

   UF Jean Vigo, Prix

   BT Motion pictures—Awards—France

Prize-fight films

   USE Boxing films

Prize-fighting films

   USE Boxing films

Prizefight films

   USE Boxing films

Prizefighting films

   USE Boxing films

Processing, Cinematographic

   USE Cinematography—Processing

Product placement in mass media (May Subd Geog)

   [HF6146.P78]

   Here are entered works on an advertising technique that consists of the use of name-brand

†**Subject headings noted with a dagger contain additional access points and subheadings that are not pertinent to this text and are not included here.**

products as props or as set dressing in motion pictures, television programs, or other mass media.
    UF Placement of products in mass media
         Product placement in motion pictures
         Product placement in television programs
    BT Advertising
         Mass media
  —Law and legislation *(May Subd Geog)*
      BT Advertising laws
Product placement in motion pictures
    USE Produce placement in mass media
Product placement in television programs
    USE Product placement in mass media
Production companies, Motion picture
    USE Motion picture studios
Production designers, Motion picture
    USE Motion picture art directors
Production of motion pictures
    USE Motion pictures—Production and direction
Profiles (Biographical television programs)
    USE Biographical television programs
Program rating, Television
    USE Television programs—Rating
Programs, Media
    USE Media programs (Education)
Programs, Television
    USE Television programs
Projection[†]
    NT Lantern projection
Projection, Motion picture
    USE Motion picture projection
Projection, Television
    USE Television projection
Projectionists, Motion picture
    USE Motion picture projectionists
Projectors[†]
    NT Motion picture projectors
Promo films
    USE Promotional films
Promos (Television commercials) *[LCSH Genre]*
Promotional films *(May Subd Geog)*
   This heading is used as a topical heading for works about films that promote or advertise a product, industry, service, organization, etc. When used as a topical heading it is subdivided by the appropriate geographic, topical, and/or form subdivisions.
    UF Advertising films
         Promo films
         Sales films
    BT Advertising
         Nonfiction films
Promotional films *[LCSH Genre]*
Promotional videos *(May Subd Geog)*

Here are entered video recordings promoting or advertising a product, industry, service, organization, etc.
    UF Video promos
    BT Advertising
         Video recordings
    RT Sponsored videos
Propaganda[†]
    NT Mass media and propaganda
         Motion pictures in propaganda
         Television in propaganda
Propaganda and mass media
    USE Mass media and propaganda
Propaganda and television
    USE Television in propaganda
Propaganda films *[LCSH Genre]*
Propaganda in motion pictures
    USE Motion pictures in propaganda
Propaganda in television
    USE Television in propaganda
Propaganda television programs *[LCSH Genre]*
Properties, Stage
    USE Stage props
Props, Stage
    USE Stage props
Proscan televisions *(Not Subd Geog)*
    BT Televisions—Receivers and reception
Prostitutes in motion pictures *(Not Subd Geog)*
    BT Motion pictures
Prostitution in motion pictures *(Not Subd Geog)*
    BT Motion pictures
Protest movements in mass media *(Not Subd Geog)*
    BT Mass media
Pseudo-documentary films
    USE Documentary-style films
Psychiatric television
    USE Television in psychiatry
Psychiatry[†]
    NT Television in psychiatry
Psychiatry in motion pictures *(Not Subd Geog)* *[PN1995.9.P78]*
    BT Motion pictures
Psychic trauma in motion pictures *(Not Subd Geog)*
    BT Motion pictures
Psycho thrillers (Motion pictures)
    USE Thrillers (Motion pictures)

[†]**Subject headings noted with a dagger contain additional access points and subheadings that are not pertinent to this text and are not included here.**

Psycho thrillers (Television programs)
  USE Thrillers (Television pictures)
Psychoanalysis and motion pictures
  (May Subd Geog)
  UF Motion pictures and psychoanalysis
  BT Motion pictures
Public service television programs
  (May Subd Geog)
    This heading is used as a topical heading for
  works about television programs aired by or on
  behalf of nonprofit or governmental organizations to
  promote the common well-being or general welfare
  of society. Works about television programs about
  public policy or politics are entered under Public
  affairs television programs. When used as topical
  headings they are subdivided by the appropriate
  geographic, topical, and/or form subdivisions.
  UF Public interest television programs
      Television programs, Public service
  BT Nonfiction television programs
      Public television
  NT Public television
Public service television programs *[LCSH Genre]*
Public speaking†
  NT Television public speaking
Public television *(May Subd Geog)*
  [HE8700.78–HE8700.79]
  UF Non-commercial television
      Noncommercial television
  BT Television broadcasting
  RT Public service television programs
Public toilets in motion pictures
  (Not Subd Geog)
  BT Motion pictures
Public welfare in mass media *(Not Subd Geog)*
  [P96.P84]
  BT Mass media
Publicity†
  NT Mass media and publicity
      Television and publicity
Publicity and mass media
  USE Mass media and publicity
Puerto Ricans in motion pictures *(Not Subd Geog)*
  BT Motion pictures
Punk culture in motion pictures
  (Not Subd Geog)
  BT Motion pictures
Puppet films *(May Subd Geog)*
  [PN1995.9.P8]
  UF Marionette films
  BT Motion pictures
      Puppet theater
Puppet films *[LCSH Genre]*

Puppet shows (Television programs)
  USE Puppet television programs
Puppet television programs *(May Subd Geog)*
  UF Marionette television programs
      Puppet shows (Television programs)
      Television puppet shows
  BT Puppet theater
      Television programs
Puppet television programs *[LCSH Genre]*
Puppet theater
  NT Puppet films
Puppets on television *(Not Subd Geog)*
  [PN1992.8.P86]
  UF Puppets and puppet-plays in television
      Puppets in television
  BT Television
Puppets and puppet-plays in television
  USE Puppets on television
Puppets in television
  USE Puppets on television
Pvt. Snafu (Fictitious character
  USE Private Snafu (Fictitious character)
Pyramids (Gymnastics) on television
  BT Television

Quake II (Game)
  [GV1469.35.Q32]
  UF Quake 2 (Game)
      Quake Two (Game)
  BT Video games
Quake 2 (Game)
  USE Quake II (Game)
Quake Two (Game)
  USE Quake II (Game)
Quasar televisions *(Not Subd Geog)*
  BT Television—Receivers and reception
Quasar videocassette recorders *(Not Subd Geog)*
  BT Videocassette recorders
Quasi-documentary films
  USE Documentary-style films
Queens in motion pictures *(Not Subd Geog)*
  BT Motion pictures
Quest 64 (Game)
  [GV1469.35.Q64]
  UF Quest Sixty-four (Game)
  BT Video games
Quest Sixty-four (Game)
  USE Quest 64 (Game)

†**Subject headings noted with a dagger contain
additional access points and subheadings that
are not pertinent to this text and are not
included here.**

Questions and answers[†]
  NT Television quiz shows
QuickTake camera
  USE Apple QuickTake camera
Quiz shows
  USE Television quiz shows
Quiz shows (Television programs)
  USE Television quiz shows

Race awareness in motion pictures
  (Not Subd Geog)
  BT Motion pictures
Race films *(May Subd Geog)*
  This heading is used as a topical heading for
works about films produced with African American
casts specifically for African American audiences
beginning in the late silent-film days and continuing
until the end of the 1940s. When used as a topical
heading it is subdivided by the appropriate geo-
graphic, topical, and/or form subdivisions.
  UF Race films—United States
    Race movies
  BT Motion pictures
  RT African Americans in motion pictures
African Americans in the motion picture industry
Race films *[LCSH Genre]*
Race in motion pictures *(Not Subd Geog)*
  BT Motion pictures
Race movies
  USE Race films
Race relations[†]
  NT Mass media and race relations
Race relations and mass media
  USE Mass media and race relations
Race relations in mass media *(Not Subd Geog)*
  BT Mass media
Race relations in motion pictures
  (Not Subd Geog)
  BT Motion pictures
Race relations in television
  USE Race relations on television
Race relations on television *(Not Subd Geog)*
  UF Race relations in television
  BT Television
Racially mixed people in motion pictures
  (Not Subd Geog)
  BT Motion pictures
Racism in mass media *(Not Subd Geog)*
  BT Mass media
Racism in motion pictures *(Not Subd Geog)*
  BT Motion pictures
Racism in television
  USE Racism on television

Racism on television *(Not Subd Geog)*
  UF Racism in television
  BT Television
Radicalism in mass media *(Not Subd Geog)*
  [P96.R32]
  BT Mass media
Radio[†]
  —Production and direction
    BT Coproduction (Motion pictures,
      television, etc.)
Radio advertising[†]
  NT Singing commercials
  —Awards
  — —United States
    NT Clio Awards
Radio and television towers
  (May Subd Geog)
  UF Radio towers
    Telecommunication masts
    Television towers
    Transmission towers, Radio
    Transmission towers, Television
  BT Towers
Radio broadcasting
  —Awards
  — —United States
    NT Peabody Awards
Radio in adult education[†]
  NT Educational broadcasting in adult
    education
Radio in politics[†]
  NT Equal time rule (Broadcasting)
Radio towers
  USE Radio and television towers
Radio vision
  USE Television
Radioactive waste disposal in mass media
  (Not Subd Geog)
  BT Mass media
Radiography[†]
  NT Cineradiography
Radiology, Medical
  NT Cinefluorography
Railroads in motion pictures *(Not Subd Geog)*
  BT Motion pictures
Rankings of mass media
  USE Mass media—Ratings and rankings

[†]**Subject headings noted with a dagger contain
additional access points and subheadings that
are not pertinent to this text and are not
included here.**

Rap (Music) in motion pictures *(Not Subd Geog)*
    BT Motion pictures
Rape in mass media *(Not Subd Geog)*
    [P96.R35]
    BT Mass media
Rape in motion pictures *(Not Subd Geog)*
    [PN1995.9.R27]
    BT Motion pictures
Rape on television *(Not Subd Geog)*
    [PN1992.8.R26]
    BT Television
Ratings of mass media
    USE Mass media—Ratings and rankings
Rating of motion pictures
    USE Motion pictures—Ratings
Rats in motion pictures *(Not Subd Geog)*
    BT Motion pictures
Rayman (Game)
    [GV1469.35.R38]
    BT Video games
RCA television/video combinations
    (Not Subd Geog)
    BT Television/video combinations
RCA videocassette recorders *(Not Subd Geog)*
    BT Videocassette recorders
Reading[†]
    NT Television and reading
    —Aids and devices[†]
        NT Captioned media in reading
Reading films
    BT Developmental reading
Ready 2 Rumble Boxing (Game)
    [GV1469.35.R43]
    UF Ready to Rumble Boxing (Game)
    BT Video games
Ready to Rumble Boxing (Game)
    USE Ready 2 Rumble Boxing (Game)
Real-time closed captioning *(May Subd Geog)*
    UF CART (Real-time closed captioning)
        Live captioning (Closed captioning)
        Simultaneous closed captioning
    BT Closed captioning
Realism in motion pictures *(Not Subd Geog)*
    [PN1995.9.R3]
    BT Motion pictures
Realism in television
    USE Realism on television
Realism on television *(Not Subd Geog)*
    [PN1992.8.R4]
    UF Realism in television
    BT Television
Reality-based television programs
    USE Reality television programs

Reality in mass media *(Not Subd Geog)*
    BT Mass media
Reality shows (Television programs)
    USE Reality television programs
Reality television programs *(May Subd Geog)*
    UF Reality-based television programs
        Reality shows (Television programs)
    BT Nonfiction television programs
    NT Big Brother television programs
        Makeover television programs
Reality television programs
    [LCSH Genre]
Rebirth in motion pictures
    USE Regeneration in motion pictures
Reconciliation in motion pictures *(Not Subd Geog)*
    BT Motion pictures
**Reconstruction (U.S. history, 1865–1877) in motion
    pictures** *(Not Subd Geog)*
    BT Motion pictures
Reconstruction of motion picture theaters
    USE Motion picture theaters—Reconstruction
Recording and registration[†]
    NT Motion pictures—Registration
Recreation centers[†]
    NT Video arcades
Red One motion picture cameras *(Not Subd Geog)*
    BT Motion pictur4e cameras
Redemption in motion pictures *(Not Subd Geog)*
    BT Motion pictures
Rednecks in motion pictures *(Not Subd Geog)*
    [PN1995.9.R33]
    BT Motion pictures
Reflex cameras
    USE Single-lens reflex cameras
        Twin-lens cameras
Regeneration in motion pictures *(Not Subd Geog)*
    [PN1995.9.R35]
    UF Rebirth in motion pictures
    BT Motion pictures
Registration of motion pictures
    USE Motion pictures—Registration
Release of motion pictures
    USE Motion pictures—Distribution
Religion and motion pictures
    USE Motion pictures—Religious aspects
Religion in motion pictures *(Not Subd Geog)*
    [PN1995.9.R4]
    BT Motion pictures
        Religious films

[†]**Subject headings noted with a dagger contain
additional access points and subheadings that
are not pertinent to this text and are not
included here.**

Religion on television *(Not Subd Geog)*

Here are entered works on the portrayal of religious topics on television. Works on the use of television as a medium of communication in religion are entered under Television in religion. General works on the relationship between television broadcasting and religion, as well as works on television broadcasting from a religious viewpoint, are entered under Television broadcasting—Religious aspects.

    BT Television

Religious broadcasting *(May Subd Geog)*

    UF Broadcasting, Religious

    BT Broadcasting

        Mass media in religion

    NT Television in religion

Religious education[†]

    NT Motion pictures in religious education

Religious films

    BT Motion pictures

    NT Bible films

        Christian films

        Religion in motion pictures

Religious films *[LCSH Genre]*

Religious television

    USE Television in religion

Religious television programs *[LCSH Genre]*

Remakes, Film

    USE Film remakes

Repeats (Television programs)

    USE Television reruns

Repetition in motion pictures *(Not Subd Geog)*

    BT Motion pictures

Reportage literature[†]

    NT Documentary mass media

Reproductive health in mass media *(Not Subd Geog)*

    [P96.R46–P96.R462]

    BT Mass media

Reruns (Television programs)

    USE Television reruns

Resident Evil (Game)

    [GV1469.35.R47]

    BT Video game

Resident Evil 3: Nemesis (Game)

    BT Video games

Restrooms in motion pictures *(Not Subd Geog)*

    BT Motion pictures

Resurrection in motion pictures *(Not Subd Geog)*

    BT Motion pictures

Retina camera *(Not Subd Geog)*

    BT Kodak camera

        Miniature cameras

Retinette camera *(Not Subd Geog)*

    [TR263.R]

    BT Cameras

Revere motion picture camera *(Not Subd Geog)*

    BT Motion picture cameras

Reviews

    USE Television programs—Reviews

Reviews of motion pictures

    USE Motion pictures—Reviews

Revolutions in motion pictures *(Not Subd Geog)*

    BT Motion pictures

Revueflex camera

    USE Zenith camera

Rex-Kino (Vienna, Austria)

    USE Motion picture theaters—Austria

Richardson Theatre (Seneca, S.C.)

    BT Motion picture theaters—South Carolina

Ricoh camera *(Not Subd Geog)*

    BT Cameras

Ride films

    USE Amusement ride films

Ride movies

    USE Amusement ride films

Ridge Racer 64 (Game)

    [GV1469.35.R53]

    UF RR64 (Game)

    BT Nintendo video games

Right of reply[†]

    NT Equal time rule (Broadcasting)

    BT Mass media—Law and legislation

Rite of passage films

    USE Coming-of-age films

Rites and ceremonies in motion pictures *(Not Subd Geog)*

    [PN1995.9.R56]

    BT Motion pictures

Ritual abuse in mass media *(Not Subd Geog)*

    BT Mass media

Ritual in mass media *(Not Subd Geog)*

    BT Mass media

Rival Schools (Game)

    [GV1469.35.R58]

    BT Video games

Road films *(May Subd Geog)*

    [PN1995.9.R63]

This heading is used as a topical heading for works about films that are set on the open road. When used as a topical heading it is subdivided by

[†]**Subject headings noted with a dagger contain additional access points and subheadings that are not pertinent to this text and are not included here.**

the appropriate geographic, topical, and/or form subdivisions.
    UF Road movies
    BT Motion pictures
Road films *[LCSH Genre]*
Road movies
    USE Road films
Road Rash Jailbreak (Game)
    [GV1469.35.R59]
    BT Video games
Road television programs
    [LCSH Genre]
Roadblocks (Police methods) in motion pictures
(Not Subd Geog)
    BT Motion pictures
Robert Gordon (Fictitious character)
    USE Gordon, Flash (Fictitious character)
Robin Hood
    USE Robin Hood (Legendary character)
Robin Hood (Legendary character)
(Not Subd Geog)
    UF Hood, Robin (Legendary character)
        Robin Hood
    BT Folklore—Great Britain
Robin Hood (Legendary character) in motion pictures *(Not Subd Geog)*
    [PN1995.9.R65]
    BT Motion pictures
Robot camera *(Not Subd Geog)*
    BT Cameras
Robots in motion pictures *(Not Subd Geog)*
    BT Motion pictures
Rock concert documentaries
    USE Rock concert films
Rock concert documentary films
    USE Rock concert films
Rock concert films *(May Subd Geog)*
    UF Rock concert documentaries
        Rock concert documentary films
        Rock docs (Motion pictures)
        Rock documentaries
        Rock documentary films
    BT Concert films
        Rock films
Rock docs (Motion pictures)
    USE Rock concert films
Rock documentaries
    USE Rock concert films
Rock documentary films
    USE Rock concert films
Rock films *(May Subd Geog)*
    [PN1995.9.M86]
    BT Musical films

    NT Rock concert films
Rock films *[LCSH Genre]*
Rock music[†]
    NT Motion pictures and rock music
Rock music and motion pictures
    USE Motion pictures and rock music
Rock music on television *(Not Subd Geog)*
    [PN1992.8.M87]
    BT Television
Rock videos *(May Subd Geog)*
    [PN1992.8.M87]
    UF Videos, Rock
    BT Music videos
Rock videos *[LCSH Genre]*
Rocket (Game)
    [GV1469.35.R6]
    BT Nintendo video games
Rocky Balboa (Fictitious character)
    USE Balboa, Rocky (Fictitious character)
Rocky Balboa films
    USE Rocky films
Rocky films
    [PN1995.9.R666]
    UF Rocky Balboa films
    BT Motion pictures
Rocky films *[LCSH Genre]*
Rogue Trip Vacation 2012 (Game)
    [GV1469.35.R64]
    BT Video games
Roll film cameras
    USE Medium format cameras
Rollcage (Game)
    [GV1469.35.R67]
    BT Video games
Rollei camera *(Not Subd Geog)*
    BT Cameras
Rolleicord camera *(Not Subd Geog)*
    BT Cameras
Rolleiflex camera *(Not Subd Geog)*
    BT Cameras
Romance films *(May Subd Geog)*
    UF Chick flicks
        Love films
        Hollywood romance films
        Romance (Motion pictures)
        Romance movies
        Romance pictures (Motion pictures)
        Romantic films

[†]**Subject headings noted with a dagger contain additional access points and subheadings that are not pertinent to this text and are not included here.**

Romantic movies
  BT Motion pictures
Romance films *[LCSH Genre]*
Romance (Motion pictures)
  USE Romance films
Romance movies
  USE Romance films
Romance pictures (Motion pictures)
  USE Romance films
Romance television programs
  [LCSH Genre]
Romanies in motion pictures *(Not Subd Geog)*
  [PN1995.9.R67]
  BT Motion pictures
Romanische Haus (Berlin, Germany)
  USE Gloria-Palast (Berlin, Germany)
Romantic comedies (Motion pictures)
  USE Romantic comedy films
Romantic comedy films *(May Subd Geog)*
  UF Romantic comedies (Motion pictures)
  BT Comedy films
Romantic comedy films *[LCSH Genre]*
Romantic comedy television programs
  [LCSH Genre]
Romantic films
  USE Romance films
Romantic movies
  USE Romance films
Romantic screwball comedy films
  USE Screwball comedy films
Rooms[†]
  NT Home theaters
Rose d'Or de Montreux
  USE Golden Rose of Montreux
Royal Rumble (Game)
  [GV1469.35.R69]
  UF WWF Royal Rumble (Game)
  BT Video games
RR64 (Game)
  USE Ridge Racer 64 (Game)
Rubble films *(May Subd Geog)*
  [PN1995.9.R83]
  This heading is used as a topical heading for
  works about films produced in the years after World
  War II, often featuring exteriors in bombed-out
  cities. When used as a topical heading it is subdi-
  vided by the appropriate geographic, topical, and/or
  form subdivisions.
  BT Motion pictures
Rubble films *[LCSH Genre]*
Rule of equal time (Broadcasting)
  USE Equal time rule (Broadcasting)
Rune scape (Game)

  USE RuneScape (Game)
RuneScape (Game)
  UF Rune scape (Game)
  BT Video games
Rural bandit films
  USE Gangster films
Rural comedies *(May Subd Geog)*
  UF Farm comedies
    Hillbilly comedies
    Rustic comedies
  BT Comedy films
    Television comedies
Rural comedy films *[LCSH Genre]*
Rural comedy television programs
  [LCSH Genre]
Rural development[†]
  NT Television in rural development
**Rural-urban migration in motion
  pictures** *(Not Subd Geog)*
  BT Motion pictures
Rural women in motion pictures *(Not Subd Geog)*
  BT Motion pictures
Rush 2 (Game)
  [GV1469.35.R85]
  BT Video games
Rushes (Motion pictures)
  (May Subd Geog)
  This heading is used as a topical heading for
  works about work prints of a day's shooting of a
  film, usually meant to be shown and studied before
  the next day's shooting begins. When used as a
  topical heading it is subdivided by the appropriate
  geographic, topical, and/or form subdivisions.
  UF Dailies (Motion pictures)
  BT Motion pictures
Rushes (Motion pictures)
  [LCSH Genre]
Rushes (Television programs)
  [LCSH Genre]
Russian drama[†]
  NT Motion picture plays, Russian
    Television plays, Russian
Russian motion picture plays
  USE Motion picture plays, Russian
Russian motion pictures
  USE Motion pictures, Russian
Russian television plays
  USE Television plays, Russian

[†]**Subject headings noted with a dagger contain
additional access points and subheadings that
are not pertinent to this text and are not
included here.**

Russians in motion pictures *(Not Subd Geog)*
[PN1995.9.R87]
BT Motion pictures
Rustic comedies
USE Rural comedies

Sacrifice in motion pictures
(Not Subd Geog)
BT Motion pictures
Sadism in motion pictures *(Not Subd Geog)*
UF Sadism in moving-pictures
BT Motion pictures
Sadism in moving-pictures
USE Sadism in motion pictures
Sailors[†]
NT Actors as sailors
Sailors as actors *(May Subd Geog)*
BT Actors
Saints in motion pictures *(Not Subd Geog)*
[PN1995.9.S234]
BT Motion pictures
Saints on television *(Not Subd Geog)*
BT Television
Sales films
USE Promotional films
Salvo Montalbano (Fictitious character)
USE Montalbano, Salvo (Fictitious character)
Sami (European people) in motion pictures
(Not Subd Geog)
[PN1995.9.S]
BT Motion pictures
Samsung television/video combinations
(Not Subd Geog)
BT Television/video combinations
Samsung televisions *(Not Subd Geog)*
BT Television—Receivers and reception
Samurai films *(May Subd Geog)*
This heading is used as a topical heading for works
about films that feature samurai, usually set in the
Tokugawa period of Japanese history. When used as a
topical heading it is subdivided by the appropriate
geographic, topical, and/or form subdivisions.
BT Motion pictures
NT Zatoichi films
Samurai films *[LCSH Genre]*
San (African people) in motion pictures
(Not Subd Geog)
BT Motion pictures
San Francisco Rush (Game)
[GV1469.35.S33]
BT Video games
Sand-and-surf films
USE Beach party films

Sandal-and-spear epics (Motion pictures)
USE Peplum films
Sansui televisions *(Not Subd Geog)*
BT Television—Receivers and reception
Sanyo televisions *(Not Subd Geog)*
BT Television—Receivers and reception
Sanyo videocassette recorders *(Not Subd Geog)*
BT Videocassette recorders
Satellite master antenna television *(May Subd Geog)*
[HE8700.7]
UF SMATV
BT Cable television
Television, Master antenna
Satellite meteorology[†]
NT Television in satellite meteorology
Satellite television, Direct broadcast
USE Direct broadcast satellite television
Satellite television, Home
USE Direct broadcast satellite television
Scandals in mass media *(Not Subd Geog)*
[P96.S29]
BT Mass media
Scanning systems[†]
NT Television scanning
Scapegoat in motion pictures *(Not Subd Geog)*
BT Motion pictures
Scenarios
USE Motion picture plays
Scenarios, Television
USE Television plays
Scene cards (Motion picture advertising)
USE Lobby cards
Scenery (Motion pictures)
USE Motion pictures—Setting and scenery
Scenery (Television)
USE Television—Stage-setting and scenery
Scheherazade (Legendary character)
(Not Subd Geog)
UF Cheherazade (Legendary character)
Sahahrazad (Legendary character)
Shahrzād (Legendary character)
Sheherazade (Legendary character)
BT Folklore—Middle East
**Scheherazade (Legendary character) in motion
pictures** *(Not Subd Geog)*
BT Motion pictures
Schizophrenia in motion pictures
(Not Subd Geog)
BT Motion pictures

[†]**Subject headings noted with a dagger contain
additional access points and subheadings that
are not pertinent to this text and are not
included here.**

Schlemiels in motion pictures
   (Not Subd Geog)
   UF Shlemiels in motion pictures
   BT Motion pictures
School libraries[†]
   RT Instructional materials centers
   —**Awards**
   ——**United States**
           NT National School Library Media
               Program of the Year Award
School management and organization[†]
   NT Video recording in school management and
       organization
School media centers
   USE Instructional materials centers
School media programs
   USE Media programs (Education)
Schools in motion pictures *(Not Subd Geog)*
   [PN1995.9.S253]
   BT Motion pictures
Schulmädchen-Report films
   BT Erotic films
Schulmädchen-Report films
   [LCSH Genre]
Science[†]
   NT Motion pictures in science
       Television in science
   —**Study and teaching**[†]
       NT Television in science education
Science fiction films *(May Subd Geog)*
   BT Motion pictures
   NT Alien films
       Dystopian films
       Star Trek films
       Star Wars films
       Superhero films
Science fiction films *[LCSH Genre]*
Science fiction television programs
   (May Subd Geog)
   BT Television programs
   NT Star Trek television programs
Science fiction television programs
   [LCSH Genre]
Science films *(May Subd Geog)*
   [PN1995.9.S25]
   This heading is used as a topical heading for
works about films that are intended to educate or
inform about science or scientific topics. When
used as a topical heading it is subdivided by the
appropriate geographic, topical, and/or form
subdivisions. Works on the depiction of science or
scientific topics in motion pictures are entered under
Science in motion pictures.
   BT Educational films
   NT Nature films
Science films *[LCSH Genre]*
Science in mass media *(Not Subd Geog)*
   BT Mass media
Science in motion pictures *(Not Subd Geog)*
   Here are entered works on the depiction of
science or scientific topics in motion pictures.
Works about films that are intended to educate or
inform about science or scientific topics are entered
under Science films with appropriate geographic,
topical, and/or form subdivisions.
   BT Motion pictures
Science television programs *(May Subd Geog)*
   This heading is used as a topical heading for
works about television programs that are intended to
educate or inform about science or scientific topics.
When used as a topical heading it is subdivided by
the appropriate geographic, topical, and/or form
subdivisions.
   BT Educational television programs
   NT Nature television programs
Science television programs *[LCSH Genre]*
Scientists in motion pictures *(Not Subd Geog)*
   [PN1995.9.S267]
   BT Motion pictures
Scooby-Doo (Fictitious character)
   (Not Subd Geog)
Scooby-Doo films *[LCSH Genre]*
Scooby-Doo television programs
   [PN1992.8.S36]
   BT Animated television programs
Scooby-Doo television programs *[LCSH Genre]*
Scotchlite process
   USE Front-screen projection
Scottish drama[†]
   NT Television plays, Scottish
Scottish television plays
   USE Television plays, Scottish
Scrambling systems (Telecommunication)[†]
   NT Cable television—Scrambling systems
Screen biographies
   USE Biographical films
Screen plays
   USE Motion picture plays
Screen-reliant installations (Art)
   USE Video installations (Art)
Screen tests
   UF Motion picture acting—Auditions

[†]**Subject headings noted with a dagger contain
additional access points and subheadings that
are not pertinent to this text and are not
included here.**

RT Acting—Auditions
Screen tests [LCSH Genre]
Screen writing
   USE Motion picture authorship
Screening, Medical
   USE Medical screening
Screenplay writing
   USE Motion picture authorship
Screenplays
   USE Motion picture plays
Screenwriters
   RT Motion picture authorship
Screenwriters, African American
   USE African American screenwriters
Screenwriters as actors (May Subd Geog)
   BT Actors
Screenwriting
   USE Motion picture authorship
Screwball comedies
   USE Screwball comedy films
Screwball comedy films (May Subd Geog)
   UF Crazy comedy films
      Madcap comedy films
      Madcap romantic comedies
      Oddball comedy films
      Romantic screwball comedy films
      Screwball comedies
      Wacky comedy films
      White telephone comedy films
   BT Comedy films
Screwball comedy films [LCSH Genre]
Script clerks (May Subd Geog)
   UF Continuity clerks
      Continuity girls
      Motion picture script clerks
      Script girls
Script girls
   USE Script clerks
Scripts (Motion pictures)
   USE Motion picture plays
Scriptwriting, Film
   USE Motion picture authorship
Scriptwriting, Motion picture
   USE Motion picture authorship
Scriptwriting, Video
   USE Video authorship
Sculptmation films
   USE Clay animation films
Sculpture in motion pictures (Not Subd Geog)
   [PN1995.9.S274]
   BT Motion pictures
Sea & Sea cameras (Not Subd Geog)
   [TR263.S]

   UF Sea and Sea cameras
   BT Underwater cameras
Sea and Sea cameras
   USE Sea & Sea cameras
Sea in motion pictures (Not Subd Geog)
   [PN1995.9.S28]
   UF Ocean in motion pictures
   BT Motion pictures
Secret agent films
   USE Spy films
Secret of Evermore (Game)
   [GV1469.35.S43]
   BT Video games
Secret service films
   USE Spy films
Secularism in motion pictures (Not Subd Geog)
   BT Motion pictures
Security (Psychology) in motion pictures
   (Not Subd Geog)
   BT Motion pictures
Security systems†
   NT Television in security systems
Seduction in motion pictures (Not Subd Geog)
   BT Motion pictures
Sega Dreamcast video games (Not Subd Geog)
   BT Video games
Sega Genesis (Game)
   USE Sega Genesis video games
Sega Genesis video games (Not Subd Geog)
   UF Sega Genesis (Game)
   BT Video games
Sega Saturn (Game)
   USE Sega Saturn video games
Sega Saturn video games (Not Subd Geog)
   [GV1469.335]
   UF Sega Saturn (Game)
   BT Video games
Sega Sports World Series Baseball 2K1 (Game)
   USE World Series Baseball 2K1 (Game)
Selection of non-book materials
   USE Selection of nonbook materials
Selection of nonbook materials
   (May Subd Geog)
   UF Choice of nonbook materials
      Media selection
      Nonbook materials selection
      Selection of non-book materials
   BT Collection development (Libraries)
      Nonbook materials

†**Subject headings noted with a dagger contain
additional access points and subheadings that
are not pertinent to this text and are not
included here.**

Self in motion pictures *(Not Subd Geog)*
  BT Motion pictures
Self-presentation in motion pictures
  (Not Subd Geog)
  BT Motion pictures
Selfix camera *(Not Subd Geog)*
  [TR263.S]
  BT Cameras
Selling[†]
  —Mass media
      UF Mass media—Selling
Semidocumentary films
  USE Documentary-style films
Semiotics[†]
  NT Mass media—Semiotics
      Motion pictures—Semiotics
      Television—Semiotics
Send-up films
  USE Parody films
Sensationalism in motion pictures
  (Not Subd Geog)
  [PN1995.9.S284]
  BT Motion pictures
  RT Exploitation films
Sensationalism in television
  USE Sensationalism on television
Sensationalism on television *(Not Subd Geog)*
  [PN1992.8.S37]
  UF Sensationalism in television
  BT Television
Senses and sensation in motion pictures
  (Not Subd Geog)
  [PN1995.9.S285]
  BT Motion pictures
Sentimentalism in motion pictures
  (Not Subd Geog)
  BT Motion pictures
September 11 Terrorist Attacks, 2001, in mass media *(Not Subd Geog)*
  BT Mass media
September 11 Terrorist Attacks, 2001, on television
  (Not Subd Geog)
  BT Television
Sequels, Film
  USE Film sequels
Sequence photography[†]
  BT Chronophotography
Serbian drama[†]
  NT Television plays, Serbian
Serbian television plays
  USE Television plays, Serbian
Serial murderers in motion pictures
  (Not Subd Geog)

  [PN1995.9.S297]
  BT Motion pictures
Serial murders in mass media
  (Not Subd Geog)
  BT Mass media
Serials, Limited (Television programs)
  USE Television mini-series
Serials, Limited (Video recordings)
  USE Video mini-series
Series, Television
  USE Television series
Set designers[†]
  NT Motion picture set designers
Set props
  USE Stage props
Setting (Motion pictures)
  USE Motion pictures—Setting and scenery
Setting (Television)
  USE Television—Stage-setting and scenery
Sex[†]
  NT Mass media and sex
Sex and law[†]
  NT Sex in mass media—Law and legislation
Sex and mass media
  USE Mass media and sex
Sex-and-sand films
  USE Peplum films
Sex differences in mass media *(Not Subd Geog)*
  BT Mass media
Sex discrimination in motion pictures
  (Not Subd Geog)
  BT Motion pictures
Sex in mass media *(Not Subd Geog)*
  UF Pornography in mass media
  BT Mass media
  —Law and legislation *(May Subd Geog)*
      BT Sex and law
Sex in motion pictures
  [PN1995.9.S45]
  BT Motion pictures
  RT Erotic films
      Pornographic films
Sex in television
  USE Sex on television
Sex instruction[†]
  NT Motion pictures in sex instruction
      Video tapes in sex instruction
Sex on television *(Not Subd Geog)*
  UF Sex in television

[†]**Subject headings noted with a dagger contain additional access points and subheadings that are not pertinent to this text and are not included here.**

BT Television
Sex-oriented businesses[†]
   NT Adult movie theaters
Sex role in mass media *(Not Subd Geog)*
   [P96.S5]
   BT Mass media
Sex role in motion pictures *(Not Subd Geog)*
   [PN1995.9.S47]
   BT Motion pictures
Sex role in television
   USE Sex role on television
Sex role on television *(Not Subd Geog)*
   UF Sex role in television
   BT Television
Sexism in mass media *(Not Subd Geog)*
   BT Mass media
Sexism in motion pictures *(Not Subd Geog)*
   BT Motion pictures
Sexual minorities on television
   (Not Subd Geog)
   BT Television
Shadow Madness (Game)
   [GV1469.35.S47]
   BT Video games
Shadows of the Empire (Game)
   [GV1469.35.S48]
   BT Nintendo video games)
Shahrazad (Legendary character)
   USE Scheherazade (Legendary character)
Shahrzād (Legendary character)
   USE Scheherazade (Legendary character)
Shakespearean actors and actresses
   (May Subd Geog)
   UF Shakespearian actors and actresses
   BT Actors
      Actresses
Shamanism in motion pictures *(Not Subd Geog)*
   [PN1995.9.S48]
   BT Motion pictures
Sharp television/video combinations
   (Not Subd Geog)
   BT Television/video combinations
Sharp televisions *(Not Subd Geog)*
   BT Television—Receivers and reception
Sharp videocassette recorders
   (Not Subd Geog)
   BT Videocassette recorders
Sheherazade (Legendary character)
   USE Scheherazade (Legendary character)
Shelving (for non-book materials)
   USE Shelving for nonbook materials
Shelving for nonbook materials *(May Subd Geog)*
   [Z685]

   UF Shelving (for non-book materials)
   BT Library shelving
      Nonbook materials
Sherlock Holmes (Fictitious character)
   USE Holmes, Sherlock (Fictitious character)
Sherlock Holmes films *(May Subd Geog)*
   This heading is used as a topical heading for works about Sherlock Holmes films discussed collectively. When used as a topical heading it is subdivided by the appropriate geographic, topical, and/or form subdivisions. Works on individual Sherlock Holmes films are entered under the specific title.
   BT Detective and mystery films
   RT Holmes, Sherlock (Fictitious character)
Sherlock Holmes films *[LCSH Genre]*
Sherlock Holmes television programs
   (May Subd Geog)
   BT Detective and mystery television programs
   RT Holmes, Sherlock (Fictitious character)
Sherlock Holmes television programs
   [LCSH Genre]
Shlemiels in motion pictures
   USE Schlemiels in motion pictures
Short feature films
   USE Short films
Short films *(May Subd Geog)*
   This heading is used as a topical heading for works about films usually limited to a running time of less than 40 minutes. When used as a topical heading it is subdivided by the appropriate geographic, topical, and/or form subdivisions.
   UF Short feature films
      Shorts (Motion pictures)
   BT Motion pictures
   RT Animated films
   NT Actualities (Motion pictures)
      Novelty films
      Private Snafu films
—Direction
   USE Short films—Production and direction
—Production and direction
   UF Short films—Direction
Short films *[LCSH Genre]*
Shorts (Motion pictures)
   USE Short films
Show business films *[LCSH Genre]*
Showman's manuals

[†]Subject headings noted with a dagger contain additional access points and subheadings that are not pertinent to this text and are not included here.

USE Pressbooks
Showmen's manuals
USE Pressbooks
Shows, Musical
USE Musicals
Shows, Television
USE Television programs
Sick in motion pictures *(Not Subd Geog)*
BT Motion pictures
Sigma digital cameras *(Not Subd Geog)*
BT Digital cameras
Silence in motion pictures *(Not Subd Geog)*
[PN1995.9.S545]
Silence in film, not silent films.
BT Motion pictures
Silent film music *(May Subd Geog)*
[M176]
Here are entered musical works composed or
adapted to accompany silent films. Works on the
technique of composing, adapting, or performing
musical accompaniments to silent films are entered
under Silent films—Musical accompaniment.
Musical works composed for sound films or
performed on soundtracks are entered under Motion
picture music.
UF Film music
Music for silent films
Silent films—Musical accompaniments
BT Motion picture music
Silent films *(May Subd Geog)*
This heading is used as a
topical heading for works about films produced in
the early days of the motion picture industry before
the advent of talking films. When used as a topical
heading it is subdivided by the appropriate
geographic, topical, and/or form subdivisions.
UF Silent motion pictures
BT Motion pictures
NT Actualities (Motion pictures)
Narration for silent films
—Copyright
USE Copyright—Silent films
—**Musical accompaniment**
[MT737]
Here are entered works on the technique of
composing, adapting, or performing musical
accompaniments to silent films. Musical works
composed or adapted to accompany silent films
are entered under Silent film music.
—Musical accompaniments
USE Silent film music
Silent films *[LCSH Genre]*
Silent Hill (Game)

[GV1469.35.S54]
BT Video games
Silent motion pictures
USE Silent films
Silette camera *(Not Subd Geog)*
BT Cameras
Silhouette animation films *[LCSH Genre]*
Simultaneous closed captioning
USE Real-time closed captioning
Sinar camera *(Not Subd Geog)*
BT View cameras
Sindhi drama[†]
NT Television plays, Sindhi
Sindhi television plays
USE Television plays, Sindhi
Singaporean motion pictures
USE Motion pictures, Singaporean
Singing commercial direction
USE Singing commercials—Production
and direction
Singing commercial production
USE Singing commercials—Production
and direction
Singing commercials *(May Subd Geog)*
[M1977.S5]
[M1978.S5]
UF Commercials, Singing
BT Music in advertising
Radio advertising
Television advertising
—Direction
UF Singing commercials—Production
and direction
—**Production and direction**
(May Subd Geog)
UF Singing commercial direction
Singing commercial production
Singing commercials—Direction
Singing cowboy films *[LCSH Genre]*
Singing cowboy television programs *[LCSH Genre]*
Single-lens reflex cameras *(May Subd Geog)*
[TR261]
UF Reflex cameras
SLR cameras
BT Cameras
NT Contarex camera
Leicaflex camera
Miranda camera
Pentacon camera

[†]**Subject headings noted with a dagger contain
additional access points and subheadings that
are not pertinent to this text and are not
included here.**

Single mothers in motion pictures *(Not Subd Geog)*
  BT Motion pictures
Single-use cameras
  USE Disposable cameras
Sinhalese drama[†]
  NT Television plays, Sinhalese
Sinhalese television plays
  USE Television plays, Sinhalese
Sisters in motion pictures
  (Not Subd Geog)
  [PN1995.9.S55]
  BT Motion pictures
Sitcoms (Television programs)
  USE Situation comedies (Television programs)
Situation comedies (Television programs)
  (May Subd Geog)
  UF Sitcoms (Television programs)
    Television sitcoms
    Television situation comedies
  BT Television comedies
Situation comedies (Television programs)
  [LCSH Genre]
Six-sheet posters *(May Subd Geog)*
  UF 6-sheet posters
  BT Advertising—Motion pictures
    Film posters
Skating films *(May Subd Geog)*
  [PN1995.9.S553]
  BT Sports films
Skating films *[LCSH Genre]*
Sketch films
  USE Anthology films
Skill videos
  USE Instructional videos
Skin in motion pictures *(Not Subd Geog)*
  BT Motion pictures
Skyscrapers in motion pictures
  (Not Subd Geog)
  [PN1995.9.S5535]
  BT Motion pictures
Slapstick comedy films *[LCSH Genre]*
Slapstick comedy television programs
  [LCSH Genre]
Slavery in motion pictures *(Not Subd Geog)*
  [PN1995.9.S557]
  BT Motion pictures
Slasher films *(May Subd Geog)*
  [PN1995.9.S554]
  This heading is used as a topical heading for
  works about films that feature teenagers or young
  adults who are stalked and graphically killed by a
  psychopathic killer, usually in the course of one
  night. Works about films that feature explicit gore

and graphic violence, including mutilation of the
human body are entered under Splatter films. When
used as topical headings they are subdivided by the
appropriate geographical, topical and/or form
subdivisions.
  UF Bodycount films
    Dead teenager movies
    Slashers (Motion pictures)
  BT Horror films
  NT Friday the 13th films
Slasher films *[LCSH Genre]*
Slashers (Motion pictures)
  USE Slasher films
Slovak drama[†]
  NT Motion picture plays, Slovak
Slovak motion picture plays
  USE Motion picture pays, Slovak
Slow-scan television
  BT Television
SLR cameras
  USE Single-lens reflex cameras
SMATV
  USE Satellite master antenna television
Smoking in motion pictures *(Not Subd Geog)*
  [PN1995.9.S58]
  BT Motion pictures
Snafu, Private (Fictitious character)
  USE Private Snafu (Fictitious character)
Sno-cross Championship Racing (Game)
  [GV1469.35.S]
  UF Snocross Championship Racing (Game)
  BT Video games
Snocross Championship Racing (Game)
  USE Sno-cross Championship Racing (Game)
Snuff films *(May Subd Geog)*
  This heading is used as a topical heading for
  works about films that feature a murder as the
  climax of sexual activity. When used as a topical
  heading it is subdivided by the appropriate
  geographic, topical, and/or form subdivisions.
  BT Exploitation films
    Pornographic films
Snuff films *[LCSH Genre]*
Soap operas
  USE Television soap operas
Soap operas, Television
  USE Television soap operas
Soccer films *(May Sub Geog)*

[†]**Subject headings noted with a dagger contain
additional access points and subheadings that
are not pertinent to this text and are not
included here.**

[PN1995.9.S59]
   BT Sports films
Soccer films *[LCSH Genre]*
Soccer in motion pictures *(Not Subd Geog)*
   BT Motion pictures
Soccer television programs *[LCSH Genre]*
Social change[†]
   NT Video recording in social change
Social change in motion pictures *(Not Subd Geog)*
   BT Motion pictures
Social classes in mass media *(Not Subd Geog)*
   BT Mass media
Social classes in motion pictures *(Not Subd Geog)*
   BT Motion pictures
Social conflict in mass media *(Not Subd Geog)*
   BT Mass media
Social consciousness films
   USE Social problem films
Social guidance films *(May Subd Geog)*
   This heading is used as a topical heading for
   works about films that guide people, especially
   teenagers, in proper behavior, dating, personal
   safety, etc. When used as a topical heading it is
   subdivided by the appropriate geographic, topical,
   and/or form subdivisions.
   UF Guidance films, Social
        Mental hygiene films
   BT Educational films
Social guidance films *[LCSH Genre]*
Social integration[†]
   NT Mass media and social integration
Social integration and mass media
   USE Mass media and social integration
Social problem films *(May Subd Geog)*
   This heading is used as a topical heading for
   works about films that dramatize a specific social ill,
   or a contemporary political issue, to draw attention
   to it. When used as a topical heading it is
   subdivided by the appropriate geographic, topical,
   and/or form subdivisions.
   UF Social consciousness films
   BT Motion pictures
Social problem television programs
   [LCSH Genre]
Social problems in mass media *(Not Subd Geog)*
   [P96.S]
   BT Mass media
Social problems in motion pictures *(Not Subd Geog)*
   [PN1995.9.S62]
   BT Motion pictures
Social psychology in motion pictures
   (Not Subd Geog)
   BT Motion pictures

Social sciences[†]
   NT Motion pictures in the social sciences
   —Study and teaching[†]
        NT Television in social science education
Social sciences in mass media *(Not Subd Geog)*
   [P96.S65]
   BT Mass media
Social service[†]
   NT Mass media and social service
        Television in social service
Social service and mass media
   USE Mass media and social service
Social work education[†]
   NT Television in social work education
Socialism and motion pictures *(May Subd Geog)*
   [HX550.M65]
   UF Motion pictures and socialism
   BT Motion pictures
Socialist realism in motion pictures *(Not Subd Geog)*
   [PN1995.9.S63]
   BT Motion pictures
Society and theater
   USE Theater and society
Sociology[†]
   —Research[†]
        NT Television in sociological research
Soldiers[†]
   NT Actors as soldiers
Soldiers as actors *(May Subd Geog)*
   BT Actors
Soldiers in motion pictures *(Not Subd Geog)*
   BT Motion pictures
Solid-state television receivers
   USE Transistor television receivers
Sonic Adventure (Game)
   [GV1469.35.S62]
   BT Video games
Sony cameras *(Not Subd Geog)*
   BT Cameras
   NT Sony digital cameras
Sony digital cameras *(Not Subd Geog)*
   [TR263.S66]
   BT Digital cameras
        Sony cameras
Sony Playstation video games
   USE Sony video games
Sony televisions *(Not Subd Geog)*
   BT Television—Receivers and reception

[†]**Subject headings noted with a dagger contain
additional access points and subheadings that
are not pertinent to this text and are not
included here.**

Sony video games *(Not Subd Geog)*
　UF Sony Playstation video games
　BT Video games
Sophisticated comedy films *[LCSH Genre]*
Sophisticated comedy television programs
　　[LCSH Genre]
Soul Blade (Game)
　BT Video games
Soul Calibur (Game)
　　[GV1469.35.S643]
　BT Video games
Sound effects (Motion pictures)
　USE Motion pictures—Sound effects
Sound effects (Television)
　USE Television broadcasting—Sound effects
Sound in mass media *(Not Subd Geog)*
　BT Mass media
Sound in motion pictures *(Not Subd Geog)*
　　Here are entered works on sounds in motion
　pictures. Works on motion pictures that include
　audio as a central element are entered under Sound
　motion pictures.
　BT Motion pictures
Sound motion pictures *(May Subd Geog)*
　　[PN1995.7]
　　Here are entered works on motion pictures that
　include audio as a central element. Works on sounds
　in motion pictures are entered under Sound in
　motion pictures. This heading is not used for
　individual films.
　UF Moving-pictures, Talking Talkies
　　　Talking motion pictures
　BT Motion pictures
　BT Motion pictures
Soundtracks, Television
　USE Television soundtracks
South Asians in mass media *(Not Subd Geog)*
　　[P94.5.S68]
　BT Mass media
Soviet drama†
　NT Television plays, Soviet
Soviet motion pictures
　USE Motion pictures, Soviet
Soviet television plays
　USE Television plays, Soviet
Soviets (People) in television
　USE Soviets (People) on television
Soviets (People) on television *(Not Subd Geog)*
　UF Soviets (People) in television
　BT Television
Space and time in mass media *(Not Subd Geog)*
　　[P96.S7]
　BT Mass media

Space and time in motion pictures *(Not Subd Geog)*
　BT Motion pictures
Space and time on television *(Not Subd Geog)*
　BT Television
Space television
　USE Television in astronautics
Space vehicles in motion pictures *(Not Subd Geog)*
　BT Motion pictures
Spacestation Silicon Valley (Game)
　　[GV1469.35.S645]
　BT Video games
Spaghetti Easterns
　USE Martial arts films
Spaghetti Western films
　USE Spaghetti Westerns
Spaghetti Westerns *(May Subd Geog)*
　　This heading is used as a topical heading for
　works about Western films usually produced or co-
　produced by Italian companies and filmed in Europe.
　When used as a topical heading it is subdivided by
　the appropriate geographic, topical, and/or form
　subdivisions.
　UF Eurowesterns
　　　Spaghetti Western films
　　　Western films—Europe
　　　Western films—Italy
　BT Western films
Spaghetti Westerns *[LCSH Genre]*
Spanish drama†
　NT Motion picture plays, Spanish
　　　Television plays, Spanish
Spanish film posters
　USE Film posters, Spanish
Spanish motion picture plays
　USE Motion picture plays, Spanish
Spanish motion pictures
　USE Motion pictures, Spanish
Spanish television plays
　USE Television plays, Spanish
Spatter films
　USE Splatter films
Special effects (Cinematography)
　USE Cinematography—Special effects
Special effects (Television)
　USE Television broadcasting—Special effects
Special events television coverage *[LCSH Genre]*
Special libraries†
　NT Motion picture film collections

†**Subject headings noted with a dagger contain
additional access points and subheadings that
are not pertinent to this text and are not
included here.**

Special programs on television
    USE Television specials
Specialists[†]
    NT Mass media specialists
Specials, Television
    USE Television specials
Spectacles (Motion pictures)
    USE Epic films
Spectaculars (Motion pictures)
    USE Epic films
Speech[†]
    —Study and teaching[†]
        NT Television in speech education
Splatter films *(May Subd Geog)*
    UF Gore films
        Spatter films
        Splatter horror films
        Splatter movies
        Torture porn films
    BT Horror films
Splatter horror films
    USE Splatter films
Splatter movies
    USE Splatter films
Splicing (Motion picture film)
    USE Motion picture films—Splicing
Sponsored videos *(May Subd Geog)*
    Here are entered video recordings produced,
    subsidized, financed, or otherwise significantly
    supported by a business, government body,
    organization, etc.
        UF Sponsoring videos
        BT Video recordings
        RT Promotional videos
Sponsoring videos
    USE Sponsored videos
Spoof films
    USE Parody films
Spoofs (Motion pictures)
    USE Spoof films
Spookfests (Motion pictures)
    USE Horror films
Sportcasters
    USE Sportscasters
Sports[†]
    NT Mass media and sports
        Motion pictures in sports
        Television and sports
        Video tapes in sports
Sports and television
    USE Television and sports
Sports broadcasters
    USE Sportscasters

Sports broadcasting
    USE Television broadcasting of sports
Sports Car GT (Game)
    [GV1469.35.S66]
    BT Video games
Sports cinematography *(May Subd Geog)*
    [TR895.6]
    BT Cinematography
        Photography of sports
    RT Sports in motion pictures
Sports films
    [PN1995.9.S67]
    BT Motion pictures
    NT Baseball films
        Basketball films
        Boxing films
        Football films
        Hockey films
        Mountain films
        Skating films
        Soccer films
        Surfing films
Sports films *[LCSH Genre]*
Sports in motion pictures *(Not Subd Geog)*
    [PN1995.9.S67]
    BT Motion pictures
    RT Sports cinematography
Sports in television
    USE Television broadcasting of sports
Sports journalism[†]
    NT Sportscasters
        Television broadcasting of sports
Sports journalists
    USE Sportscasters
Sports personnel[†]
    NT Sportscasters
Sports television programs *[LCSH Genre]*
Sports videos *(May Subd Geog)*
    [GV742.34]
    BT Video recordings
Sportscasters[†]
    UF Sportcasters
        Sports broadcasters
        Sports journalists
    BT Broadcasters
        Sports journalism
        Sports personnel

[†]**Subject headings noted with a dagger contain
additional access points and subheadings that
are not pertinent to this text and are not
included here.**

Spouses[†]
   NT Motion picture producers' and directors' spouses
Television producers' and directors' spouses
Spy films *(May Sub Geog)*
   UF Cloak and dagger films
       Espionage films
       Secret agent films
       Secret service films
   BT Motion pictures
   NT James Bond films
Spy films *[LCSH Genre]*
Spy television programs *(May Subd Geog)*
   UF Espionage television programs
   BT Television programs
Spy television programs *[LCSH Genre]*
Spyro 2: Ripto's rage (Game)
   [GV1469.35.S664]
   BT Video games
Spyro the Dragon (Game) *[GV1469.35.S67]*
   BT Video games
Stage
   USE Acting
Stage properties
   USE Stage props
Stage props *(May Subd Geog)*
   [PN1995.9.S69 (Motion pictures)]
   UF Properties, Stage
       Props, Stage
       Set props
       Stage properties
   BT Motion pictures—Setting and scenery
       Television—Stage-setting and scenery
       Theaters—Stage-setting and scenery
Stag films
   USE Pornographic films
Stage lighting[†]
   RT Television—Lighting
Stagehands
   NT Grips (Persons)
Stamp collecting in motion pictures
   (Not Subd Geog)
   [PN1995.9.P653]
   BT Motion pictures
Stamp collecting on television *(Not Subd Geog)*
   BT Television
Star Fox 64 (Game)
   [GV1469.35.S7]
   UF Star Fox Sixty-four (Game)
   BT Nintendo video games
Star Fox Sixty-four (Game)
   USE Star Fox 64 (Game)
Star Ocean (Game)
   [GV1469.35.S72]

   BT Video games
Star Trek films
   [PN1995.9.S694]
   BT Science fiction films
Star Trek films *[LCSH Genre]*
Star Trek television programs
   [PN1992.8.S74]
   This heading is used as a topical heading for works about Star Trek television programs discussed collectively. When used as a topical heading it is subdivided by the appropriate geographic, topical, and/or form subdivisions. Works on individual Star Trek television programs or series are entered under the specific title.
   BT Science fiction television programs
Star Trek television programs
   [LCSH Genre]
Star Wars films *(May Subd Geog)*
   BT Science fiction films
Star Wars films *[LCSH Genre]*
Stars, Movie
   USE Motion picture actors and actresses
State and mass media
   USE Mass media policy
Stations, Television
   USE Television stations
Stereo cameras
   USE Stereoscopic cameras
Stereoscopic cameras
   [TR259]
   UF Stereo cameras
   BT Cameras
       Verascope cameras
Stereoscopic television
   [TK8643]
   UF Television, Three-dimensional
       Three-dimensional television
   BT Television
       Three-dimensional display systems
Stereotype (Psychology) in mass media
   USE Stereotypes (Social psychology) in
        mass media
Stereotypes (Social psychology) in mass media
   (Not Subd Geog)
   UF Stereotype (Psychology) in mass media
   BT Mass media
Stills (Motion pictures) *(May Subd Geog)*
   BT Photography
Stock footage *(May Subd Geog)*

[†]**Subject headings noted with a dagger contain additional access points and subheadings that are not pertinent to this text and are not included here.**

This heading is used as a topical heading for works about pre-recorded footage used or collected and organized to be used in the production of films, television programs, and video recordings. When used as a topical heading it is subdivided by the appropriate geographic, topical, and/or form subdivisions.

UF Found footage (Motion pictures, television, etc.)
    Library film
    Library shots (Motion pictures, television, etc.)
    Motion picture stock materials
    Stock materials (Motion pictures, television, etc.)
    Stockshots (Motion pictures, television, etc.)
BT Motion pictures
    Television programs
    Video recordings

Stock footage [LCSH Genre]
Stock footage collections (May Subd Geog)
UF Stockshot libraries
BT Motion picture film collections
    Video tape collections

Stock materials (Motion pictures, television, etc.)
USE Stock footage

Stock shots (Motion pictures, television, etc.)
USE Stock footage

Stockshot libraries
USE Stock footage collections

Stockshots (Motion pictures, television, etc.)
USE Stock footage

Stooges (Comedy team)
USE Three Stooges (Comedy team)

Stores, Retail, in motion pictures (Not Subd Geog)
BT Motion pictures

Story boards
USE Storyboards

Story editors (Motion pictures) (May Subd Geog)
UF Motion picture story editors
BT Editors

Storyboards (May Subd Geog)
UF Story boards
BT Motion pictures—Production and direction

Storytelling in mass media (Not Subd Geog)
[P96.S78]
BT Mass media

Strangers in motion pictures (Not Subd Geog)
[PN1995.9.S6968]
BT Motion pictures

Streak cameras (May Subd Geog)
[TR257.5]
BT Cameras
Streaming technology (Telecommunications)†
NT Streaming videos
Streaming videos (May Subd Geog)
BT Streaming (Telecommunications)
    Video recordings
Street Fighter Alpha (Game)
[GV1469.35.S74]
BT Video games
Street films (May Subd Geog)
This heading is used as a topical heading for works about films that represent the downtown street as a dangerous lure. When used as a topical heading it is subdivided by the appropriate geographic, topical, and/or form subdivisions.
BT Motion pictures
Street films [LCSH Genre]
Street photography (May Subd Geog)
[TR659.8]
UF Cityscape photography
BT Outdoor photography
Strikes and lockouts†
—Law and legislation†
RT Collective labor agreements
—Motion picture industry
UF Strikes and lockouts—Moving-picture industry
Strikes and lockouts in motion pictures
(Not Subd Geog)
BT Motion pictures
Strong men in motion pictures (Not Subd Geog)
[PN1995.9.S697]
BT Motion pictures
Structural films [LCSH Genre]
Student television stations (May Subd Geog)
BT Amateur television stations
Studio 4 (Zurich, Switzerland)
USE Kino "Studio 4" (Zurich, Switzerland)
Studios, Motion picture
USE Motion picture studios
Stunt men
USE Stunt performers
Stunt men and women
USE Stunt performers
Stunt performers (May Subd Geog)
[PN1995.9.S7]

†**Subject headings noted with a dagger contain additional access points and subheadings that are not pertinent to this text and are not included here.**

UF Motion picture stunt men
  Performers, Stunt
  Stunt men
  Stunt men and women
  Stuntmen
BT Actors
NT Daredevils
  Women stunt performers

Stuntman (Game)
 BT Video games

Stuntmen
 USE Stunt performers

Subaru Theatre (Tokyo, Japan)
 USE Subaruza (Tokyo, Japan)

Subaruza (Tokyo, Japan)
 UF Subaru Theatre (Tokyo, Japan)
 BT Motion picture theaters—Japan

Subcultural films
 USE Subculture films

Subculture cult films
 USE Subculture cult films

Subculture films (May Subd Geog)
 Under this heading, when subdivided by the appropriate geographic, topical, and/or form subdivisions, are entered works on fiction films about a particular subculture in society. Works on fiction or nonfiction films that acquire a highly devoted but relatively small group of fans after their release are entered under Cult films.
 UF Cult films, Subculture
  Subcultural films
  Subculture cult films
  Subculture movies
 BT Motion pictures

Subculture films [LCSH Genre]

Subculture movies
 USE Subculture films

Subjective camera
 USE Subjectivity in motion pictures

Subjectivity in motion pictures (Not Subd Geog)
 UF Point of view in motion pictures
  Subjective camera
 BT Motion pictures

Submarine cinematography
 USE Underwater cinematography

Submarine films (May Subd Geog)
 UF Submarine movies
  Submarine war films
 BT War films

Submarine films [LCSH Genre]

Submarine movies
 USE Submarine films

Submarine photography

USE Underwater photography

Submarine television
 USE Underwater television

Submarine war films
 USE Submarine films

Submarines (Ships) in motion pictures
 (Not Subd Geog)
 BT Motion pictures

Subminiature cameras
 USE Miniature cameras

Subscription television (May Subd Geog)
 UF Pay-per-view television
  Pay television
  Pay TV
  Television broadcasting, Subscription
 BT Television broadcasting
 RT Cable television

Substance abuse on television (Not Subd Geog)
 BT Television

Suburbs in mass media (Not Subd Geog)
 BT Mass media

Suburbs in motion pictures (Not Subd Geog)
 [PN1995.9.S74]
 BT Motion pictures

Subways in motion pictures (Not Subd Geog)
 BT Motion pictures

Suffering in motion pictures (Not Subd Geog)
 BT Motion pictures

Suffering on television (Not Subd Geog)
 BT Television

Suicide in mass media (Not Subd Geog)
 BT Mass media

Suikoden (Game)
 [GV1469.35.S93]
 BT Video games

Sun and sand films
 USE Beach party films

Sundown Centre (London, England)
 USE Carling Academy Brixton (London, England)

Super-8 motion pictures (May Subd Geog)
 BT Motion pictures

Super Mario 64 (Game)
 [GV1469.35.S967]
 BT Nintendo video games

Super Mario Advance (Game)
 BT Game Boy video games

Super Mario Bros. (Game)
 [GV1469.35.S96]

†**Subject headings noted with a dagger contain additional access points and subheadings that are not pertinent to this text and are not included here.**

UF Super Mario Brothers (Game)
BT Nintendo video games
Super Mario Brothers (Game)
  USE Super Mario Bros. (Game)
Super Mario RPG (Game)
  [GV1469.35.S965]
    UF Super Mario RPG Legend of the Seven
         Stars (Game)
    BT Nintendo video games
Super Mario RPG Legend of the
  Seven Stars (Game)
  USE Super Mario RPG (Game)
Super Metroid (Game)
  [GV1469.35.S97]
    BT Video games
Super Smash Bros. (Game)
  [GV1469.35.S98]
    BT Nintendo video games
Superhero films *(May Subd Geog)*
    UF Comic strip superhero films
         Comic strip superheroes films
         Superheroes films
    BT Fantasy films
         Science fiction films
    NT Batman films
         Flash Gordon films
         Superman films
Superhero films *[LCSH Genre]*
Superhero television programs *(May Subd Geog)*
    BT Television programs
Superhero television programs
  [LCSH Genre]
Superheroes films
  USE Superhero films
Superman (Fictitious character)
  (Not Subd Geog)
    UF Clark Kent (Fictitious character)
         Kent, Clark (Fictitious character)
Superman (Fictitious character) in mass media
  (Not Subd Geog)
  [P96.S94]
    UF Superman in mass media
    BT Mass media
Superman (Game)
  [GV1469.35.S983]
    BT Video games
Superman films *(May Subd Geog)*
  [PN1995.9.S77]
    BT Superhero films
Superman films *[LCSH Genre]*
Superman in mass media
  USE Superman (Fictitious character) in
       mass media

Supernatural in motion pictures
  (Not Subd Geog)
  [PN1995.9.S8]
    BT Motion pictures
Supernumeraries (Actors)
  USE Extras (Actors)
Surfing films *(May Subd Geog)*
    BT Sports films
Surfing films *[LCSH Genre]*
Surfing in mass media *(Not Subd Geog)*
    BT Mass media
Surgery†
    NT Television in surgery
Surrealism in mass media *(Not Subd Geog)*
    BT Mass media
Surrealism in motion pictures *(Not Subd Geog)*
  [PN1995.9.S85]
    BT Motion pictures
Surrealist films *[LCSH Genre]*
Surveys†
    NT Mass media surveys
Survival films *[LCSH Genre]*
Survival television programs
  [LCSH Genre]
Suspense films
  USE Thrillers (Motion pictures)
Suspense in motion pictures, television, etc.
  [PN1995.9.S87]
    Here are entered works on the use of suspense in
  motion pictures, television programs, and video
  recordings. Works about films or television
  programs that feature a buildup of suspense, tension,
  uncertainty, menace, and anxiety as primary
  elements and in which the audience is kept on
  tenterhooks are entered under the appropriate
  specific heading, e.g., Thrillers (Motion pictures);
  Thrillers (Television programs) subdivided by the
  appropriate geographic, topical, and/or form
  subdivisions.
    UF Suspense in motion pictures
    BT Motion pictures
         Television programs
         Video recordings
Suspense television programs
  USE Thrillers (Television programs)
Swashbuckler films *(May Subd Geog)*
    This heading is used as a topical heading for
  works about films that feature heroic characters in
  period costume and have swordplay as a central

**†Subject headings noted with a dagger contain
additional access points and subheadings that
are not pertinent to this text and are not
included here.**

element. When used as a topical heading it is subdivide by the appropriate geographic, topical, and/or form. Works on the depiction of swordplay in motion pictures are entered under Swordplay in motion pictures.
   RT Action and adventure films

Swashbuckler films *[LCSH Genre]*

Swedish drama[†]
   NT Motion picture plays, Swedish
       Television plays, Swedish

Swedish motion picture plays
  USE Motion picture plays, Swedish

Swedish television plays
  USE Television plays, Swedish

Swiss motion pictures
  USE Motion pictures, Swiss

Sword-and-sandal epics (Motion pictures)
  USE Peplum films

Swordplay in motion pictures *(Not Subd Geog)*
   Here are entered works on the depiction of swordplay in motion pictures. Works on films that feature heroic characters in period costume and have swordplay as a central element are entered under Swashbuckler films with appropriate geographic, topical, and/or form subdivisions.
   BT Motion pictures
   RT Swashbuckler films

Swordsmen in motion pictures *(Not Subd Geog)*
   BT Motion pictures

Sylvania televisions *(Not Subd Geog)*
   BT Television—Receivers and reception

Symbolism in motion pictures *(Not Subd Geog)*
   BT Motion pictures

Symphonic televisions *(Not Subd Geog)*
   BT Television—Receivers and reception

Syndicate films
  USE Gangster films

Syndicate-oriented films
  USE Gangster films

Syndication of television programs
  USE Television programs—Syndication

Syphon Filter (Game)
  [GV1469.35.S985]
   BT Video games

Syracuse Area Landmark Theatre and Loew Building (Syracuse, N.Y.)
  USE Loew's State Theatre (Syracuse, N.Y.)

Taboo in motion pictures *(Not Subd Geog)*
   BT Motion pictures

Tactics Ogre (Game)
  [GV1469.35.T3]
   BT Video games

T'ai Fu (Game)
  [GV1469.35.T33]
   BT Video games

Take-off films
  USE Parody films

Talk show hosts, Television
  USE Television talk show hosts

Talk shows
  USE Television talk shows

Talk television programs
  USE Television talk shows

Talk television shows
  USE Television talk shows

Talkies
  USE Sound motion pictures

Talking motion pictures
  USE Sound motion pictures

Tango (Dance) in motion pictures *(Not Subd Geog)*
  [PN1995.9.T27]
   BT Motion pictures

Tape recorders, Video
  USE Video tape recorders

Tape recordings, Video
  USE Video tapes

Tapes, Video
  USE Video tapes

Tariff on audio-visual materials
  (May Subd Geog)
   UF Audio-visual materials—Tariff

Tariff on color television receivers *(May Subd Geog)*
  [HF2651.C]
   UF Color television—Receivers and reception—Tariff

Tarzan (Fictitious character) *(Not Subd Geog)*
   UF Tarzan in literature

Tarzan films
   BT Motion pictures

Tarzan films *[LCSH Genre]*

Tarzan in literature
  USE Tarzan (Fictitious character)

Tarzan (Fictitious character) in mass media
  (Not Subd Geog)
  [P96.T37]
   UF Tarzan in mass media
   BT Mass media

Tarzan in mass media
  USE Tarzan (Fictitious character) in mass media

Tatiana-Palast (Berlin, Germany)

[†]**Subject headings noted with a dagger contain additional access points and subheadings that are not pertinent to this text and are not included here.**

BT Motion picture theaters—Germany
Tattooing in motion pictures (*Not Subd Geog*)
  BT Motion pictures
Tattooing on television (*Not Subd Geog*)
  BT Television
Teachers[†]
  —Training of[†]
    NT Motion pictures in teacher training
      Television in teachers training
Teachers in motion pictures (*Not Subd Geog*)
  [PN1995.9.T4]
  BT Motion pictures
Teachers on television (*Not Subd Geog*)
  [PN1992.8.T43]
  BT Television
Teaching[†]
  NT Audio-visual education
  —Aids and devices[†]
    UF Educational media
    BT Media programs (Education)
      Television in education
    NT Cataloging of educational media
Teatro Alameda (Querétaro, Mexico)
  UF Alameda, Teatro (Querétaro, Mexico)
    Teatro Cine Alameda (Querétaro, Mexico)
  BT Motion picture theaters—Mexico
Teatro Cine Alameda (Querétaro, Mexico)
  USE Teatro Alameda (Querétaro, Mexico)
Technical education[†]
  NT Motion pictures in technical education
    Television in technical education
Technicolor pictures
  USE Color motion pictures
Technology[†]
  NT Mass media and technology
Technology and mass media
  USE Mass media and technology
Technology in motion pictures (*Not Subd Geog*)
  BT Motion pictures
Teen cinema
  USE Teen films
Teen drama (Motion pictures)
  USE Teen films
Teen drama (Television programs)
  USE Teen television programs
Teen films (*May Subd Geog*)
  This heading is used as a topical heading for works about films produced especially for a teenage audience (i.e., the general age range of 13 through 18 years) and films with teenagers and teen issues as the primary subject. When used as a topical heading it is subdivided by the appropriate geographical, topical, and/or form subdivisions.

  UF Teen cinema
    Teen drama (Motion pictures)
    Teen movies
    Teen-targeted films
    Teenage films
    Teenage movies
    Teenpics
    Young adult films
    Youth films
  BT Motion pictures
  NT Juvenile delinquency films
Teen films [LCSH Genre]
Teen movies
  USE Teen films
Teen-targeted films
  USE Teen films
Teen television programs (*May Subd Geog*)
  [PN1992.8.Y68]
  UF Teen drama (Television programs)
    Teenage television programs
    Television programs for youth
    Youth television programs
  BT Television programs
Teen television programs [LCSH Genre]
Teenage actors (*May Subd Geog*)
  UF Teenagers as actors
  BT Actors
Teenage boys in motion pictures (*Not Subd Geog*)
  BT Motion pictures
Teenage boys on television (*Not Subd Geog*)
  BT Television
Teenage films
  USE Teen films
Teenage girls in motion pictures (*Not Subd Geog*)
  BT Motion pictures
Teenage movies
  USE Teen films
Teenage television programs
  USE Teen television programs
Teenagers[†]
  NT Mass media and teenagers
    Motion pictures and teenagers
    Television and teenagers
    Video games and teenagers
Teenagers and mass media
  USE Mass media and teenagers
Teenagers and motion pictures
  USE Motion pictures and teenagers

[†]**Subject headings noted with a dagger contain additional access points and subheadings that are not pertinent to this text and are not included here.**

Teenagers and television
    USE Television and teenagers
Teenagers and video games
    USE Video games and teenagers
Teenagers as actors
    USE Teenage actors
Teenagers in mass media (Not Subd Geog)
    BT Mass media
Teenagers in motion pictures
    (Not Subd Geog)
    BT Motion pictures
Teenpics
    USE Teen films
Tekken (Game)
    [GV1469.35.T37]
    BT Video games
Tele-features
    USE Made-for-TV movies
Telecine film
    USE Television film
Telecommunication†
    NT Broadcasting
        Television
        Video dial tone
Telecommunication masts
    USE Radio and television towers
Teleconferencing†
    NT Videoconferencing
Telefeatures
    USE Made-for-TV movies
Telefilming
    USE Television film recording
Telefilms
    USE Made-for-TV movies
Telejournalists
    USE Television journalists
Telementaries
    USE Documentary television programs
Telemovies
    USE Made-for-TV movies
Telephone†
    NT Video telephone
Telephone in motion pictures
    (Not Subd Geog)
    [PN1995.9.T45]
    BT Motion pictures
Telepics
    USE Made-for-TV movies
Telerecording
    USE Television film recording
Televangelism
    USE Television in religion
Televised ballets [LCSH Genre]

Televised baseball games [LCSH Genre]
Televised basketball games [LCSH Genre]
Televised dance [LCSH Genre]
Televised football games [LCSH Genre]
Televised golf matches [LCSH Genre]
Televised hockey games [LCSH Genre]
Televised martial arts events
    [LCSH Genre]
Televised musicals [LCSH Genre]
Televised operas [LCSH Genre]
Televised performances [LCSH Genre]
Televised plays [LCSH Genre]
Televised soccer games [LCSH Genre]
Televised sports events [LCSH Genre]
Televised stand-up comedy routines
    [LCSH Genre]
Televised tennis matches
    [LCSH Genre]
Television (May Subd Geog)
    [TK6630–TK6685]
    Here are entered general works on television and
general technical works on equipment.
    UF Radio vision
        TV
    BT Artificial satellites in telecommunication
        Electronic systems
        Optoelectronic devices
        Telecommunication
    NT African American women on television
        African Americans on television
        Aggressiveness on television
        Animals on television
        Arabs on television
        Archetype (Psychology) on television
        Art on television
        Arthurian romances on television
        Asian Americans on television
        Ballet in motion pictures, television, etc.
        Biology on television
        Bisexuality on television
        Blacks on television
        Bondage (Sexual behavior) on television
        Businessmen on television
        Characters and characteristics on television
        Cities and towns on television
        Clergy on television
        Closed-circuit television
        Clothing and dress on television

**Subject headings noted with a dagger contain
additional access points and subheadings that
are not pertinent to this text and are not
included here.**

College teachers on television
Color television
Counterculture on television
Credit titles (Motion pictures, television, etc.)
Crime on television
Criminal investigation on television
Dance in motion pictures, television, etc.
Death on television
Detective teams on television
Digital television
Dogs on television
Domestics on television
Drinking on television
Evolution on television
Families on television
Fathers on television
Fire fighters on television
Folklore on television
Food on television
Forensic sciences on television
Gay man-heterosexual woman relationships
  on television
Gay men on television
Grazing (Television)
Heroes on television
Heroines on television
Heterosexual women on television
High definition television
Hispanic Americans on television
Holocaust, Jewish (1939–1945), on television
Home video systems
Homosexuality and television
Homosexuality on television
Human body on television
Identity (Psychology) on television
Immigrants on television
Indians on television
Intellect on television
Interactive television
International relations on television
Internet television
Interpersonal relations on television
Interviewing on television
Jews on television
Justice, Administration of, on television
Lawyers on television
Lesbianism on television
Libraries and television
Liminality on television
Man-woman relationships on television
Masculinity on television
Medical personnel on television
Medicine on television

Melodrama on television
Men on television
Mexican Americans and television
Mexican Americans on television
Middle Ages on television
Military television
Minorities on television
Mothers on television
Motion pictures and television
Museums and television
Myth on television
National socialism on television
Nihilism (Philosophy) on television
Nonverbal communication on television
Nuclear energy on television
Nuclear warfare on television
Nurses on television
Occultism on television
Occupations on television
Older people on television
Organizational behavior on television
People with disabilities on television
Physicians on television
Pioneers on television
Postage stamps on television
Prehistoric peoples on television
Puppets on television
Pyramids (Gymnastics) on television
Race relations on television
Racism on television
Rape on television
Realism on television
Religion on television
Rock music on television
Saints on television
Sensationalism on television
September 11 Terrorist Attacks, 2001,
  on television
Sex on television
Sex role on television
Sexual minorities on television
Slow-scan television
Soviets (People) on television
Space and time on television
Stamp collecting on television
Stereoscopic television
Substance abuse on television
Suffering on television

†**Subject headings noted with a dagger contain
additional access points and subheadings that
are not pertinent to this text and are not
included here.**

Tattooing on television
Teachers on television
Teenage boys on television
Television display systems
Terrorism on television
Transgenderism on television
Travel on television
Tricksters on television
Turks on television
Underwater television
Vampires on television
Video art
Video dial tone
Video telephone
Villains on television
Violence on television
Weddings on television
Whites on television
Witches on television
Women employees on television
Women heroes on television
Women on television
Women presidents on television
Women prophets on television
Women physics on television
Women spies on television
Working class on television
Youth on television
Zapping (Television)
—Aerials
    USE Television—Antennas
—Aesthetics
    BT Aesthetics
—Antennas
    UF Television—Aerials
        Television antennas
    BT Antennas (Electronics)
— —Law and legislation
    (May Subd Geog)
      NT Television, Master antenna
—Apparatus and supplies
    USE Television—Equipment and supplies
—Art direction *(May Subd Geog)*
    UF Television—Production design
    BT Art direction
        Television—Production and direction
    RT Television—Stage-setting and scenery
—Auditions
    USE Television broadcasting—Auditions
—Censorship
    RT V-chips
—Channel selectors
    [TK6655.C5]

    UF Channel selectors for television
—Direction
    USE Television—Production and direction
—Equipment and supplies
    UF Television—Apparatus and supplies
    BT Videodisc players
    RT Television—Receivers and reception
        Television—Transmitters and
          transmission
        Television—Ultrahigh frequency
          apparatus and supplies
        Television cameras
        Used television equipment
    NT Video tape recorders
—Industrial applications
    USE Industrial television
—Interference *(May Subd Geog)*
    UF Television interference
    BT Electric interference
—Law and legislation *(May Subd Geog)*
    UF Television broadcasting—Law and
        legislation
—Lighting *(May Subd Geog)*
    [PN1992.8.L5]
    UF Television broadcasting—Lighting
        Television lighting
    BT Stage lighting
—Locations
    USE Television program locations
—Magnetic deflection systems
    [TK6655.D43]
    UF Magnetic deflection systems (Television)
    BT Electron beams
        Magnetic devices
        Television scanning
—Oceanographic applications
    USE Television in oceanography
—Production design
    USE Television—Art design
—Production and direction *(May Subd Geog)*
    [PN1992.75]
    UF Television—Direction
        Television direction
        Television production
    BT Coproduction (Motion pictures,
        television, etc.)
    RT Continuity (Motion pictures,
        television, etc.)

†Subject headings noted with a dagger contain additional access points and subheadings that are not pertinent to this text and are not included here.

Television—Art direction
Television programs—Casting
Television stage management
—Psychological aspects
    UF Television broadcasting—
        Psychological aspects
—Receivers and reception
    [TK6653]
    UF Television receivers
        Television sets
        Televisions
        TV sets
        TVs
    BT Household electronics
        Television—Equipment and supplies
    RT Television/video combinations
    NT Broksonic televisions
        Crosley televisions
        Daewoo televisions
        Emerson televisions
        Fisher televisions
        Funai televisions
        General Electric televisions
        JVC televisions
        Konka televisions
        Magnavox televisions
        Memorex televisions
        Mitsubishi televisions
        Orion televisions
        Panasonic televisions
        Philips Magnavox televisions
        Philips televisions
        Portland televisions
        Proscan televisions
        Quasar televisions
        Samsung televisions
        Sansui televisions
        Sanyo televisions
        Sharp televisions
        Sony televisions
        Sylvania televisions
        Symphonic televisions
        Television—Tuners
        Transistor television receivers
        V-chips
        Zenith televisions
— —Unit construction
        UF Unit construction
—Repairing *(May Subd Geog)*
—Scientific applications
        USE Television in science
—Semiotics *(May Subd Geog)*
        UF Television programs—Semiotics

    BT Semiotics
—Songs and music
        This heading is assigned to songs and other musical works about television. Music composed or arranged for television programs, such as their theme songs or background music, is entered under Television music.
—Stage-setting and scenery *(May Subd Geog)*
        UF Scenery (Television)
            Setting (Television)
        NT Stage props
            Television—Art direction
            Television program locations
            Television stage management
—Stations
        USE Television stations
—Test patterns *(May Subd Geog)*
        UF Test patterns (Television)
—Transmitters and transmission
        Here are entered works on the technical aspects of television transmission, including television transmitters. Works on the transmission of television programs that are intended for general public reception are entered under Television broadcasting.
        UF Television transmission
        BT Image transmission
            Television—Equipment and supplies
            Television broadcasting
—Tuners
        [TK6655.T8]
        UF Television tuners
            Tuners, Television
        BT Television—Receivers and reception
—Ultrahigh frequency apparatus and supplies
        [TK6655.U6]
        UF UHF television
            Ultrahigh frequency television
        BT Television—Equipment and supplies
—Vocational guidance
        (May Subd Geog)
        UF Television as a profession
            Television broadcasting—Vocational guidance
Television, Business
    USE Industrial television
        Television in management
Television, Cable

---

†**Subject headings noted with a dagger contain additional access points and subheadings that are not pertinent to this text and are not included here.**

USE Cable television
Television, Closed-circuit
   USE Closed-circuit television
Television, Color
   USE Color television
Television, Corporate
   USE Industrial television
Television, Industrial
   USE Industrial television
Television, Low power
   USE Low power television
Television, Master antenna
   [TK6676]
   UF Master antenna television
       MATV
   BT Television—Antennas
   NT Satellite master antenna television
Television, Military
   USE Military television
Television, Religious
   USE Television in religion
Television, Submarine
   USE Underwater television
Television, Three-dimensional
   USE Stereoscopic television
Television acting *(May Subd Geog)*
   UF Acting for television
       Acting for video
       Video acting
   BT Acting
Television actors and actresses *(May Subd Geog)*
   [PN1992.4]
   BT Actors
       Actresses
   NT Television personalities
—Credits
       UF Credits of television actors and actresses
           Film credits of television actors
               and actresses
—United States
       NT Hispanic American television actors
           and actresses
Television adaptations
   UF Adaptations, Television
       Literature—Film and video adaptations
   BT Literature—Adaptations
       Television plays
       Television programs
   RT Television scripts
   SA *Use subdivision* Film and video adaptations
       under individual literatures, individual
       literary works entered under title, and
       names of individual persons, e.g., English

literature—Film and video adaptations;
Beowulf—Film and video adaptations;
Shakespeare, William, 1564–1616—Film
and video adaptations
Television adaptations *[LCSH Genre]*
Television addiction *(May Subd Geog)*
   UF Addiction to television
       Addictive use of television
   BT Compulsive behavior
Television advertising
   (May Subd Geog)
   [HF6146.T42]
   UF Advertising, Television
       Commercials, Television (Advertising)
       Television commercials (Advertising)
       Television in advertising
   BT Advertising
       Broadcast advertising
       Television broadcasting
       Television commercials (Advertisements)
   NT Singing commercials
—Awards
——United States
       UF Television advertising—United States—
           Awards
       NT Clio Awards
—Law and legislation
       BT   Advertising laws
—Religious aspects
—United States
——Awards
       USE Television advertising—
           Awards—United States
Television advertising and children
   (May Subd Geog)
   BT Children
Television advertising directors
   (May Subd Geog)
   BT Television producers and directors
       Television agency journalists
Television anchors
   USE Television news anchors
Television and art *(May Subd Geog)*
   UF Art and television
   BT Art
Television and baseball *(May Subd Geog)*
   UF Baseball and television
   BT Baseball

†**Subject headings noted with a dagger contain**
additional access points and subheadings that
are not pertinent to this text and are not
included here.

Television and children *(May Subd Geog)*
  [HQ784.T4}
  UF Children and television
  BT Children
Television and families *(May Subd Geog)*
  [HQ520]
  UF Families and television
      Family and television
      Television and family
  BT Families
Television and family
  USE Television and families
Television and gays *(May Subd Geog)*
  UF Gays and television
  BT Television
Television and globalization *(May Subd Geog)*
  UF Globalization and television
  BT Globalization
Television and history *(May Subd Geog)*
  [PN1992.56]
  BT History
Television and homosexuality
  USE Homosexuality and television
Television and libraries
  USE Libraries and television
Television and literature *(May Subd Geog)*
  [PN1992.655]
  UF Literature and television
  BT Literature
Television and motion pictures
  USE Motion pictures and television
Television and museums
  USE Museums and television
Television and music *(May Subd Geog)*
  UF Music and television
  BT Music
  NT Television broadcasting of music
Television and older people
  (May Subd Geog)
  UF Older people and television
      Television and the aged
  BT Older people
Television and politics *(May Subd Geog)*
  [PN1992.6]
  Here are entered works on the interrelations
between television and political institutions.
Works on the use of television as a medium of
communication in the political process are entered
under Television in politics.
  UF Television broadcasting—Political aspects
      Politics and television
  BT Political science
Television and propaganda

  USE Television in propaganda
Television and reading *(May Subd Geog)*
  BT Books and reading
      Reading
Television and sports *(May Subd Geog)*
  [GV742.3]
  UF Sports and television
  BT Sports
  RT Television broadcasting of sports
  NT Video tapes in sports
Television and teenagers *(May Subd Geog)*
  UF Teenagers and television
  BT Teenagers
Television and the aged
  USE Television and older people
Television and the arts *(May Subd Geog)*
  [NX180.T44]
  UF Arts and television
  BT Arts
Television and the blind *(May Subd Geog)*
  UF Blind and television
  BT Blind
Television and the performing arts
  [PN1992.66]
  UF Performing arts and television
  BT Performing arts
Television and theater *(May Subd Geog)*
  UF Theater and television
  BT Theater
Television and war
  USE *subdivisions* Television and the war, Television
      and the revolution, *etc., under individual*
      wars, e.g., World War, 1939–1945—
      Television and the war
Television and women *(May Subd Geog)*
  UF Women and television
  BT Women
Television and youth *(May Subd Geog)*
  [HQ799.2.T4]
  UF Youth and television
  BT Youth
Television announcing
  UF Announcing for television
  BT Television broadcasting
  RT Television public speaking
Television antennas
  USE Television—Antennas

†**Subject headings noted with a dagger contain
additional access points and subheadings that
are not pertinent to this text and are not
included here.**

Television archives (*May Subd Geog*)
   [PN1992.16]
   BT Broadcasting archives
Television as a profession
   USE Television—Vocational guidance
Television audiences
   USE Television viewers
Television auditions
   USE Television broadcasting—Auditions
Television authorship (*May Subd Geog*)
   [PN1992.7]
   UF Television programs—Authorship
       Television scripts—Authorship
       Television writing
   BT Authorship
   NT Television plays—Authorship
       Treatments (Motion pictures, television, etc.)
   SA *subdivision* Authorship *under television forms and genres, e.g.,* Television comedies—Authorship
Television book review programs
   USE Book review television programs
Television broadcasters of news
   USE Television journalists
Television broadcasting (*May Subd Geog*)
   [HE8700–HE8700.9]
   Here are entered works on the transmission of television programs that are intended for general public reception. Works on the technical aspects of television transmission, including television transmitters, are entered under Television—Transmitters and transmission.
   UF Telecasting
       Television—Broadcasting
       Television industry
   BT Broadcasting
       Mass media
   RT Cable television
   NT Blacks in television broadcasting
       Direct broadcast satellite television
       Ethnic television broadcasting
       Legislative bodies—Television broadcasting of proceedings
       Low power television
       Minorities in television broadcasting
       Music television
       Public-access television
       Public television
       Subscription television
       Television—Transmitters and transmission
       Television advertising
       Television announcing

       Television broadcasting of news
       Television in agriculture
       Television programs
       Television public speaking
       Television relay systems
       Television scripts
       Television stations
       Women in television broadcasting
—Appreciation (*May Subd Geog*)
   UF Appreciation of television broadcasting
—Audience reaction
   USE Television programs—Rating
—Auditions
   UF Television—Auditions
       Television auditions
   BT Auditions
—Australia
   NT Aboriginal Australians in television broadcasting
—Awards
   NT BDA International Design Awards
—Germany
   NT Bayerischer Fernsehpreis
—United States
   NT Emmy Awards
       Peabody Awards
—Collective bargaining
   USE Collective bargaining—Television broadcasting
—Collective labor agreements
   USE Collective labor agreements—Television broadcasting
—Employees
   NT Grips (Persons)
       Television camera operators
       Television journalists
       Television personalities
       Television producers and directors
       Television writers
       Video jockeys
—Labor unions (*May Subd Geog*)
—Government policy
   USE Television broadcasting policy
—Influence
—International cooperation
—Law and legislation
   USE Television—Law and legislation

†**Subject headings noted with a dagger contain additional access points and subheadings that are not pertinent to this text and are not included here.**

—Licenses
    USE Television stations—Licenses
—Lighting
    USE Television—Lighting
—Music
    USE Television broadcasting of music
—News
    USE Television broadcasting of news
—Political aspects
    USE Television and politics
—Program rating
    USE Television programs—Rating
—Psychological aspects
    USE Television—Psychological aspects
—**Religious aspects**
    Here are entered general works on the relationship between television broadcasting and religion, as well as works on television broadcasting from a religious viewpoint. Works on the portrayal of religious topics on television are entered under Religion on television. Works on the use of television as a medium of communication in religion are entered under Television in religion.
    NT Television in religion
—**Sound effects**
    UF Sound effects (Television)
        Television sound effects
    BT Television broadcasting—Special effects
        Television plays—Technique
—**Special effects**
    UF Special effects (Television)
    RT Television broadcasting—Sound effects
—**United States**
    NT African Americans in television broadcasting
        Asian Americans in television broadcasting
        Hispanic Americans in television broadcasting
        Mexican Americans in television broadcasting
—Vocational guidance
    USE Television—Vocational guidance
Television broadcasting, Subscription
  USE Subscription television
Television broadcasting and state
  USE Television broadcasting and state
Television broadcasting of animated films
  (May Subd Geog)
   [PN1992.8.M6]

    UF Television broadcasting of motion picture cartoons
    BT Animated films
Television broadcasting of court proceedings
  (May Subd Geog)
    BT Conduct of court proceedings
Television broadcasting of films (May Subd Geog)
   [PN1992.8.F5]
    Here are entered works on television broadcasts employing motion picture films. Works on the technical production of film for use in television programming are entered under Television film.
    UF Motion pictures in television
        Motion pictures on television
        Television films
        Television movies
    BT Motion pictures
        Television film
    RT Made-for-TV movies
Television broadcasting of horror films
  (May Subd Geog)
    BT Horror films
Television broadcasting of motion picture cartoons
  USE Television broadcasting of animated films
Television broadcasting of music (May Subd Geog)
   [PN1992.8.M87]
    UF Television broadcasting—Music
    BT Television and music
Television broadcasting of news (May Subd Geog)
    UF Television broadcasting—News
        Television coverage of news
        Television journalism
        Television news
    BT Broadcast journalism
        Television broadcasting
    NT Courtroom art
        Morning news talk shows
        Television feature stories
—**Germany**
—**American influences**
    BT United States—Civilization
—**Law and legislation** (May Subd Geog)
    BT Press law
—**Objectivity** (May Subd Geog)
    BT Objectivity
Television broadcasting of sports (May Subd Geog)
   [GV742.3]

†**Subject headings noted with a dagger contain additional access points and subheadings that are not pertinent to this text and are not included here.**

Here are entered works on the television broadcasting of sports in general as well as works on the television broadcasting of individual sports. For the latter, an additional subject heading is assigned for the specific sport.

UF Sports broadcasting
Sports in television
BT Mass media and sports
Sports journalism
RT Television and sports

Television broadcasting policy
(May Subd Geog)
UF Television broadcasting—Government policy

Television camera operators
(May Subd Geog)
BT Camera operators
Television broadcasting—Employees

Television cameras
[TR882]
NT Electronic cameras
Webcams
—Image quality
UF Image quality of television cameras

Television captioning (Closed captioning)
USE Closed captioning

Television cartoon shows
USE Animated television programs

Television characters
USE Characters and characteristics on television

Television comedies *(May Subd Geog)*
[PN1992.8.C66]
UF Comedies, Television
Comedy programs
Comedy programs, Television
Comedy television programs
Television comedy programs
BT Television programs
NT Rural comedies
Situation comedies (Television programs)

Television comedies *[LCSH Genre]*

Television comedy programs
USE Television comedies

Television comedy writers
(May Subd Geog)
UF Comedy writers, Television
BT Television writers

Television commentators
USE Television journalists

Television commercial films
USE Television commercials (Advertisements)

Television commercials (Advertisements)
(May Subd Geog)
UF Commercials, Television (Advertisements)

Television commercial films
BT Television films
Television advertising
—Editing
UF Editing of television commercials
BT Editing

Television commercials (Advertisements)
[LCSH Genre]

Television concerts
USE Concert television programs

Television cooking shows *(May Subd Geog)*
UF Cooking shows, Television
Cooking television programs
Food shows (Television programs)
BT Nonfiction television programs

Television cooking shows *[LCSH Genre]*

Television cop shows *(May Subd Geog)*
UF Cop shows
Cop television shows
Police shows (Television programs)
Police television shows
Television police shows
BT Television crime shows

Television cop shows *[LCSH Genre]*

Television coverage of legislative proceedings
USE Legislative bodies—Television broadcasting of proceedings

Television coverage of news
USE Television broadcasting of news

Television crime shows *(May Subd Geog)*
UF Crime shows
Crime television programs
Criminal shows
Criminal television programs
BT Fiction television programs
Thrillers (Television programs)
NT Detective and mystery television programs
Television cop shows
Thrillers (Television programs)

Television crime shows *[LCSH Genre]*

Television criticism *(May Subd Geog)*
BT Criticism
Dramatic criticism
NT Feminist television criticism

Television dance parties *(May Subd Geog)*
This heading is used as a topical heading for works about telecast dance parties. When used as a topical heading it is subdivided by the appropriate geographic, topical, and/or form subdivisions.

†**Subject headings noted with a dagger contain additional access points and subheadings that are not pertinent to this text and are not included here.**

Works on professional dance in motion pictures, television, etc., are entered under Dance in motion pictures, television, etc.

    BT Dance parties
         Television programs

Television dance parties *[LCSH Genre]*

Television debates *[LCSH Genre]*

Television direction
    USE Television—Production and direction

Television display systems
    [TK7882.16]
    UF Display systems, Television
    BT Home video systems
         Information display systems
         Television

Television documentaries
    USE Documentary television programs

Television documentary programs
    USE Documentary television programs

Television drama
    USE Television plays

Television/DVD combinations
    USE Television/video combinations

Television editing
    USE Television scripts—Editing

Television endoscopy
    USE Video endoscopy

Television fans
    USE Television viewers

Television feature stories *(May Subd Geog)*
    UF Television news feature stories
    BT Feature stories
         Television broadcasting of news

Television features
    USE Made-for-TV movies

Television film
    [TR898]
    Here are entered works on the technical production of film for use in television programming. Works on television broadcasts employing motion picture films are entered under Television broadcasting of films.
    UF Film, Television
         Telecine film
         Video films
    BT Cinematography
         Television broadcasting of films
    RT Video tapes
    NT Television commercials (Advertisements)

Television film recording
    UF Kinescope recording
         Telefilming
         Telerecording

    BT Video tapes
Television films
    USE Made-for-TV movies
         Television broadcasting of films

Television for people with visual disabilities
    (May Subd Geog)
    BT People with visual disabilities

Television for the deaf
    USE Television for the hearing impaired

Television for the hearing impaired
    (May Subd Geog)
    UF Television for the deaf
    BT Hearing impaired

Television game show hosts *(May Subd Geog)*
    BT Television personalities

Television game shows *(May Subd Geog)*
    [PN1992.8.Q5]
    This heading is used as a topical heading for works about television programs that feature contestants participating in various types of competitive activities for prizes. Works about television programs that feature a question-and-answer format are entered under Television quiz shows. When used as topical headings they are subdivided by the appropriate geographic, topical, and/or form subdivisions.
    UF Game shows
         Game shows (Television programs)
    BT Contests
         Television programs

Television game shows *[LCSH Genre]*

Television genres
    USE Television program genres

Television graphics
    UF Graphics, Television
    BT Graphic arts
    —Awards
         NT BDA International Design Awards
            Golden Rose of Montreaux

Television historical programs
    USE Historical television programs

Television in adult education
    (May Subd Geog)
    BT Adult education
         Television in education
    NT Educational broadcasting in adult education
    —Awards *(May Subd Geog)*
    —Adolf-Grimme-Preis

†**Subject headings noted with a dagger contain additional access points and subheadings that are not pertinent to this text and are not included here.**

Television in agriculture *(May Subd Geog)*
 BT Agricultural extension work
   Agriculture—Study and teaching—Audio—
    visual aids
   Television broadcasting
Television in art *(Not Subd Geog)*
Television in art education *(May Subd Geog)*
 BT Television in education
Television in astronautics *(May Subd Geog)*
 [TL3040]
 UF Space television
 BT Astronautics—Communication systems
Television in astronomy *(May Subd Geog)*
 BT Astronomy
 NT Video astronomy
Television in biology education
 (May Subd Geog)
 BT Biology—Study and teaching
Television in birth control
 USE Television in family planning
 BT Birth control
Television in Christian education *(May Subd Geog)*
 [BV1535.8]
 BT Christian education
Television in community development
 (May Subd Geog)
 BT Community development
Television in counseling *(May Subd Geog)*
 BT Counseling
Television in dentistry *(May Subd Geog)*
 BT Dentistry
Television in education *(May Subd Geog)*
 [LB1044.7]
 This heading is used as a topical heading for
works about television programs that are intended to
impart knowledge and information, including those
for classroom viewing. Works about television
programs that use a structured format to teach or
train the audience are entered under Instructional
television programs.
 UF Educational television broadcasting
   ETV (Educational television)
 BT Audio-visual education
   Closed-circuit television
   Distance education
   Teaching—Aids and devices
 NT Educational television stations
   Television in adult education
   Television in art education
   Video tapes in education
Television in elementary education
 (May Subd Geog)
 BT Education, Elementary

Television in family planning *(May Subd Geog)*
 UF Television in birth control
Television in foreign language education
 (May Subd Geog)
 BT Language and languages—Study and
   teaching
Television in geography education *(May Subd Geog)*
 BT Geography—Study and teaching
Television in health education *(May Subd Geog)*
 [RA440.55]
 BT Mass media in health education
Television in higher education *(May Subd Geog)*
 [LC6571–LC6581]
 BT Education, Higher
Television in home economics *(May Subd Geog)*
 BT Home economics
Television in industry
 USE Industrial television
Television in literature *(Not Subd Geog)*
Television in management *(May Subd Geog)*
 [HD30.34]
 UF Business television
   Television, Business
 BT Management
 RT Industrial television
Television in mathematics education
 (May Subd Geog)
 [QA19.T4]
 BT Mathematics—Study and teaching
Television in medical education *(May Subd Geog)*
 [R835]
 BT Medicine—Study and teaching
Television in medicine *(May Subd Geog)*
 UF Medical television
 BT Medicine
 NT Video endoscopy
Television in military education *(May Subd Geog)*
 BT Military education
Television in motion pictures *(Not Subd Geog)*
 BT Motion pictures
Television in naval education *(May Subd Geog)*
 BT Naval education
Television in nursing education *(May Subd Geog)*
 BT Nursing—Study and teaching
Television in oceanography *(May Subd Geog)*
 UF Television—Oceanographic applications
 BT Oceanography

†**Subject headings noted with a dagger contain
additional access points and subheadings that
are not pertinent to this text and are not
included here.**

Television in physical education *(May Subd Geog)*
  BT   Physical education and training
Television in police work
  RT   Closed-circuit television
Television in politics *(May Subd Geog)*
  [HE8700.75–HB8700.76]
    Here are entered works on the use of television as a medium of communication in the political process. Works on the interrelations between television and political institutions are entered under Television and politics.
  UF   Political broadcasting (Television)
  BT   Politics, Practical
  NT   Equal time rule (Broadcasting)
Television in propaganda *(May Subd Geog)*
  UF   Propaganda and television
      Propaganda in television
      Television and propaganda
  BT   Propaganda
Television in psychiatry *(May Subd Geog)*
  UF   Psychiatric television
  BT   Psychiatry
Television in publicity *(May Subd Geog)*
  BT   Publicity
Television in religion *(May Subd Geog)*
  [BV656.3]
    Here are entered works on the use of television as a medium of communication in religion. Works on the portrayal of religious topics on television are entered under Religion on television. General works on the relationship between television broadcasting and religion, as well as works on television broadcasting from a religious viewpoint, are entered under Television broadcasting—Religious aspects.
  UF   Religious television
      Televangelism
      Television, Religious
  BT   Religious broadcasting
      Television broadcasting—Religious aspects
Television in rural development *(May Subd Geog)*
  BT   Rural development
Television in satellite meteorology *(May Subd Geog)*
  BT   Satellite meteorology
Television in science *(May Subd Geog)*
  UF   Television—Scientific applications
  BT   Science
Television in science education *(May Subd Geog)*
  [Q196]
  BT   Science—Study and teaching
Television in secondary education
  (May Subd Geog)
  BT   Education, Secondary

Television in security systems
  BT   Security systems
Television in social science education
  (May Subd Geog)
  BT   Social sciences—Study and teaching
Television in social service *(May Subd Geog)*
  BT   Social service
Television in social work education
  (May Subd Geog)
  BT   Social work education
Television in sociological research *(May Subd Geog)*
  BT   Sociology—Research
Television in speech education *(May Subd Geog)*
  BT   Speech—Study and teaching
Television in surgery *(May Subd Geog)*
  BT   Surgery
Television in teacher training *(May Subd Geog)*
  BT   Teachers—Training
Television in technical education *(May Subd Geog)*
  [T65.5.T4]
  BT   Technical education
Television in university extension *(May Subd Geog)*
  BT   University extension
Television in vocational education
  (May Subd Geog)
  BT   Vocational education
Television in vocational teacher training
  (May Subd Geog)
  BT   Vocational teachers—Training of
Television interference
  USE   Television—Interference
Television interviewing
  USE   Interviewing on television
Television interviews *[LCSH Genre]*
Television journalism
  USE   Television broadcasting of news
Television journalists *(May Subd Geog)*
  UF   Broadcast journalists
      Newscasters
      Telejournalists
      Television agency journalists
      Television broadcasters of news
      Television commentators
      Television news agency journalists
      Television reporters
  BT   Journalists
      Television broadcasting—Employees
  NT   Television news anchors

†**Subject headings noted with a dagger contain additional access points and subheadings that are not pertinent to this text and are not included here.**

—**United States**
    NT African American television journalists
Television journalists, African American
    USE African American television journalists
Television lectures *[LCSH Genre]*
Television licenses
    USE Television stations—Licenses
Television lighting
    USE Television—Lighting
Television makeup *(May Subd Geog)*
    [PN1992.8.M36]
    UF Make-up, Television
        Makeup, Television
    BT Theatrical makeup
Television melodramas *[LCSH Genre]*
Television meteorologists
    USE Television weathercasters
Television mini-series *(May Subd Geog)*
    UF Limited serials (Television programs)
        Mini-series, Television
        Miniseries, Television
        Serials, Limited (Television programs)
        Television miniseries
    BT Television series
Television mini-series *[LCSH Genre]*
Television miniseries
    USE Television mini-series
Television movies
    USE Made-for-TV movies
        Television broadcasting of films
Television music *(May Subd Geog)*
    This heading is assigned to music composed or
    arranged for television programs, such as their
    theme songs or background music. Songs and other
    musical works about television are entered under
    Television—Songs and music.
    UF Background music for television
        Music for television
    BT Music
        Music videos
    NT Animated television music
        Music videos
Television music, Arranged *(May Subd Geog)*
Television musicals *(May Subd Geog)*
    UF Musical television programs
    BT Musicals
        Television programs
Television musicals *[LCSH Genre]*
Television news
    USE Television broadcasting of news
Television news agency journalists
    USE Television journalists
Television news anchors *(May Subd Geog)*

    UF Anchor men
        Anchor persons
        Anchormen
        Anchorpersons
        Anchors (Television journalism)
        Television anchors
    BT Television journalists
        Television personalities
Television news feature stories
    USE Television feature stories
Television news programs *[LCSH Genre]*
Television operas
    [M1527.7]
    BT Operas
Television panel discussions *[LCSH Genre]*
Television personalities *(May Subd Geog)*
    BT Celebrities
        Television broadcasting—Employees
    NT Catholic television personalities
        Television actors and actresses
        Television game show hosts
        Television news anchors
        Television talk show hosts
        Television weathercasters
        Women in television broadcasting
        Women television personalities
—**United States**
    NT African American television
            personalities
        Cuban American television personalities
        Hispanic American television
            personalities
Television personalities, African American
    USE African American television personalities
Television personalities, Cuban American
    USE Cuban American television personalities
Television personalities, Hispanic American
    USE Hispanic American television personalities
Television pilot programs *(May Subd Geog)*
    UF Pilot programs, Television
        Pilots (Television programs)
        Television pilots
    BT Television series
Television pilot programs *[LCSH Genre]*
Television pilots
    USE Television pilot programs
Television plays *(Not Subd Geog)*
    UF Plays, Television

†**Subject headings noted with a dagger contain
additional access points and subheadings that
are not pertinent to this text and are not
included here.**

Scenarios, Television
Television drama
BT Drama
Television programs
Television scripts
NT Television adaptations
—Reviews
USE Television programs—Reviews
—Stories, plots, etc.
USE Television programs—Plots,
themes, etc.
—Technique
BT Television authorship
Television plays, Akan *(May Subd Geog)*
UF Akan television plays
BT Akan drama
Television plays, American *(May Subd Geog)*
[PS336.T45 (History)]
UF American television plays
BT American drama
Television plays, Arabic *(May Subd Geog)*
UF Arabic television plays
BT Arabic drama
Television plays, Australian *(May Subd Geog)*
UF Australian television plays
BT Australian drama
Television plays, Brazilian *(May Subd Geog)*
BT Brazilian drama
Television plays, Bulgarian *(May Subd Geog)*
UF Bulgarian television plays
BT Bulgarian drama
Television plays, Canadian *(May Subd Geog)*
UF Canadian television plays
BT Canadian drama
Television plays, Chinese *(May Subd Geog)*
[PL2368.T44 (History)]
[PL2579.T44 (Collections)]
UF Chinese television plays
BT Chinese drama
Television plays, Danish *(May Subd Geog)*
UF Danish television plays
BT Danish drama
Television plays, English *(May Subd Geog)*
UF English television plays
BT English drama
—Nigeria
USE Television plays, Nigerian (English)
Television plays, French *(May Subd Geog)*
UF French television plays
BT French drama
Television plays, French-Canadian
(May Subd Geog)
UF French-Canadian television plays

BT French-Canadian drama
Television plays, German *(May Subd Geog)*
UF German television plays
BT German drama
Television plays, Hindi *(May Subd Geog)*
UF Hindi television plays
BT Hindi drama
Television plays, Hungarian *(May Subd Geog)*
UF Hungarian television plays
BT Hungarian drama
Television plays, Irish *(May Subd Geog)*
UF Irish television plays
BT Irish drama
Television plays, Japanese *(May Subd Geog)*
[PL737.8 (History)]
UF Japanese television plays
BT Japanese drama
Television plays, Kannada
(May Subd Geog)
UF Kannada television plays
BT Kannada drama
Television plays, Korean *(May Subd Geog)*
[PL963.5.T44 (History)]
[PL978.5.T44 (Collections)]
UF Korean television plays
BT Korean drama
Television plays, New Zealand *(May Subd Geog)*
UF New Zealand television plays
BT New Zealand drama
Television plays, Nigerian (English) *(May Subd Geog)*
UF Nigerian television plays (English)
Television plays, English—Nigerian
BT Nigerian drama (English)
Television plays, Panjabi *(May Subd Geog)*
UF Panjabi television plays
BT Panjabi drama
Television plays, Polish *(May Subd Geog)*
UF Polish television plays
BT Polish drama
Television plays, Russian *(May Subd Geog)*
UF Russian television plays
BT Russian drama
Television plays, Scottish *(May Subd Geog)*
UF Scottish television plays
BT Scottish drama
Television plays, Serbian *(May Subd Geog)*
UF Serbian television plays
BT Serbian drama

**†Subject headings noted with a dagger contain
additional access points and subheadings that
are not pertinent to this text and are not
included here.**

Television plays, Sindhi *(May Subd Geog)*
　UF　Sindhi television plays
　BT　Sindhi drama
Television plays, Sinhalese *(May Subd Geog)*
　UF　Sinhalese television plays
　BT　Sinhalese drama
Television plays, Soviet *(May Subd Geog)*
　UF　Soviet television plays
　BT　Soviet drama
Television plays, Spanish *(May Subd Geog)*
　UF　Spanish television plays
　BT　Spanish drama
Television plays, Swedish *(May Subd Geog)*
　UF　Swedish television plays
　BT　Swedish drama
Television plays, Urdu *(May Subd Geog)*
　UF　Urdu television plays
　BT　Urdu drama
Television plays, Zulu *(May Subd Geog)*
　UF　Zulu television plays
　BT　Zulu drama
Television plots
　USE　Television programs—Plots, themes, etc.
Television police shows
　USE　Television cop shows
Television press conferences *[LCSH Genre]*
Television producers and directors *(May Subd Geog)*
　NT　Television advertising directors
—Credits
　　　UF　Credits of television producers
　　　　　and directors
　　　　　Film credits of television producers
　　　　　and directors
—United States
　　　　NT　African American television producers
　　　　　and directors
　　　　　Hispanic American television producers
　　　　　and directors
Television producers and directors,
　Hispanic American
　USE　Hispanic American television producers
　　　and directors
Television producers' and directors' spouses
　(May Subd Geog)
　BT　Spouses
Television production
　USE　Television—Production and direction
Television program characters
　USE　Characters and characteristics
　　　on television
Television program clips *[LCSH Genre]*
Television program excerpts *[LCSH Genre]*
Television program genres *(May Subd Geog)*

　UF　Genres, Television program
　　　Television genres
　BT　Television programs
Television program locations *(May Subd Geog)*
　UF　Locations (Television programs)
　　　Television—Locations
　BT　Television—Stage-setting and scenery
Television program rating
　USE　Television programs—Rating
Television programs *(May Subd Geog)*
　UF　Programs, Television
　　　Shows, Television
　　　Television shows
　　　TV shows
　BT　Television broadcasting
　　　Electronic program guides (Television)
　　　Television scripts
　NT　Action and adventure television programs
　　　Animated television programs
　　　Anti-war television programs
　　　Biographical television programs
　　　Children's television programs
　　　Christmas television programs
　　　Coming-of-age television programs
　　　Commissario Montalbano television
　　　　programs
　　　Concert television programs
　　　Cultural television programs
　　　Detective and mystery television programs
　　　Don Juan television programs
　　　Dubbing of television programs
　　　Electronic program guides (Television)
　　　Fantasy television programs
　　　Fiction television programs
　　　Foreign language television programs
　　　Foreign television programs
　　　Historical television programs
　　　Home shopping television programs
　　　Horror television programs
　　　Jungle television programs
　　　Legal television programs
　　　Live television programs
　　　Lost television programs
　　　Low budget television programs
　　　Made-for-TV movies
　　　Medical television programs
　　　Monster television programs
　　　Music videos

†**Subject headings noted with a dagger contain**
additional access points and subheadings that
are not pertinent to this text and are not
included here.

Nanny television programs
Outtakes
Puppet television programs
Science fiction television programs
Spy television programs
Stock footage
Superhero television programs
Suspense in motion pictures, television, etc.
Teen television programs
Television adaptations
Television comedies
Television dance parties
Television game shows
Television musicals
Television plays
Television program genres
Television quiz shows
Television reruns
Television scripts
Television series
Television specials
Thrillers (Television programs)
True crime television programs
War television programs
Western television programs
—Advertising
    USE Advertising—Television programs
—Authorship
    USE Television authorship
—Casting
    BT Casting (Performing arts)
        Television—Production and direction
—Characters
    USE Characters and characteristics
         on television
—Editing
    USE Television scripts—Editing
—Plots, themes, etc.
    UF Television plays—Stories,
        plots, etc.
        Television plots
        Television programs—Stories, plots, etc.
        Television programs—Themes, motives
    BT Plots (Drama, novel, etc.)
—Rating
    [HE8700.65–HE8700.66]
    UF Program rating, Television
        Television broadcasting—Audience
         reaction
        Television broadcasting—Program
         rating
        Television program rating
—Reviews

    UF Reviews
        Television plays—Reviews
        Television reviews
—Semiotics
    USE Television—Semiotics
—Stories, plots, etc.
    USE Television programs—Plots,
        themes, etc.
—Syndication *(May Subd Geog)*
    UF Syndication of television programs
—Themes, motives
    USE Television programs—Plots,
        themes, etc.
—Titling
    UF Titling of television programs
Television programs *[LCSH Genre]*
Television programs, Foreign
  USE Foreign television programs
Television programs, Live
  USE Live television programs
Television programs, Public service
  USE Public affairs television programs
       Public service television programs
Television programs for children
  USE Children's television programs
Television programs for gays *(May Subd Geog)*
  BT Gays
Television programs for people with visual disabilities
    [LCSH Genre]
Television programs for the family
  USE Television and family
Television programs for the hearing impaired
    [LCSH Genre]
Television programs for women *(May Subd Geog)*
    Here are entered works on programs intended to be viewed by women. Works on the portrayal of women on television are entered under Women on television. Works on women's employment in television are entered under Women in television broadcasting.
    UF Women's television programs
    BT Women's mass media
Television programs for youth
  USE Teen television programs
Television projection
  UF Projection, Television

†Subject headings noted with a dagger contain additional access points and subheadings that are not pertinent to this text and are not included here.

Television public service announcements
    [LCSH Genre]
Television public speaking
    BT Public speaking
        Television announcing
        Television broadcasting
    NT Television announcing
Television puppet shows
    USE Puppet television programs
Television quiz shows *(May Subd Geog)*
    [PN1992.8.Q5]
    This heading is used as a topical heading for works about television programs that feature a question-and-answer format. Works about television programs that feature contestants participating in various types of competitive activities for prizes are entered under Television game shows. When used as topical headings they are subdivided by the appropriate geographic, topical, and/or form subdivisions.
    UF Quiz shows
        Quiz shows (Television programs)
    BT Contests
        Questions and answers
        Television programs
Television quiz shows *[LCSH Genre]*
Television rebroadcasting
    USE Television relay systems
Television receiver music *(May Subd Geog)*
    Here are entered compositions not in a specific form or of a specific type consisting of sounds produced by television receivers, and collections of such compositions in several forms or types.
    BT Television receivers as musical instruments
    SA *headings for forms and types of music that include "television receiver" or "television receivers" and headings with medium of performances that include "television receiver" or "television receivers"*
Television receivers
    USE Television—Receivers and reception
Television receivers as musical instruments
    (May Subd Geog)
    BT Musical instruments
    NT Television receiver music
Television relay systems
    UF Television rebroadcasting
        Television repeater stations
    BT Television broadcasting
    BT Television stations
Television remakes *[LCSH Genre]*
Television repeater stations
    USE Television relay systems

Television repeats
    USE Television reruns
Television reporters
    USE Television journalists
Television reruns *(May Subd Geog)*
    This heading is not used for individual television programs, which are entered under headings appropriate to the content, genre, and/or form of the program.
    UF Repeats (Television programs)
        Reruns (Television programs)
        Television repeats
    BT Television programs
Television reviews
    USE Television programs—Reviews
Television scanning
    [TK6643]
    BT Scanning systems
    NT Television—Magnetic deflection systems
Television scripts
    [PN1992.77]
    UF Television transcripts
    BT Television broadcasting
    RT Television adaptations
        Television plays
        Television programs
—Authorship
    USE Television authorship
—Editing
    [PN1992.7]
    UF Television editing
        Television programs—Editing
        Television scripts editing
    BT Editing
Television sequels *[LCSH Genre]*
Television serials
    USE Television series
Television series *(May Subd Geog)*
    UF Series, Television
        Television serials
    BT Television programs
    NT Television mini-series
        Television pilot programs
        Television soap operas
Television series *[LCSH Genre]*
Television sets
    USE Television—Receivers and reception
Television shows
    USE Television programs

†**Subject headings noted with a dagger contain additional access points and subheadings that are not pertinent to this text and are not included here.**

Television sitcoms
    USE Situation comedies (Television programs)
Television situation comedies
    USE Situation comedies (Television programs)
Television soap operas *(May Subd Geog)*
    [PN1992.8.S4]
    UF Soap operas
        Soap operas (Television)
    BT Television series
Television soap operas *[LCSH Genre]*
Television sound effects
    USE Television broadcasting—Sound effects
Television soundtracks *(May Subd Geog)*
    Here are entered recordings containing the actual
    sound used in a television production, either as
    complete soundtracks or as portions of soundtracks.
    For recordings containing only the music used in a
    television production, an additional subject entry is
    made under the heading Television music.
    UF Soundtracks, Television
Television specials *(May Subd Geog)*
    [PN1992.8.S64]
    UF Special programs on television
        Specials, Television
    BT Television programs
Television specials *[LCSH Genre]*
Television speeches *[LCSH Genre]*
Television stage management *(May Subd Geog)*
    BT Television—Production and direction
        Television—Stage-setting and scenery
Television stations *(May Subd Geog)*
    [TK6646]
    UF Stations, Television
        Television—Stations
    BT Television broadcasting
    NT Amateur television stations
        Educational television stations
        College television stations
        Television relay stations
    —Call signs
        UF Call letters (Television stations)
            Call signs (Television stations)
    —Employees
    —Licenses *(May Subd Geog)*
        UF Television broadcasting—Licenses
            Television licenses
    —— Fees *(May Subd Geog)*
Television talk show hosts *(May Subd Geog)*
    UF Talk show hosts, Television
    BT Television personalities
Television talk shows *(May Subd Geog)*
    UF Talk television programs
        Talk shows

        Talk television shows
    BT Nonfiction television programs
        Interviewing on television
Television talk shows *[LCSH Genre]*
Television thrillers
    USE Thrillers (Television programs)
Television towers
    USE Radio and television towers
Television transcripts
    USE Television scripts
Television transmission
    USE Television—Transmitters and transmission
Television tuners
    USE Television—Tuners
Television variety shows
    USE Variety shows (Television programs)
Television/VCR combinations
    USE Television/video combinations
Television/video combinations *(May Subd Geog)*
    UF Combination televisions
        Television/DVD combinations
        Television/VCR combinations
        TV/DVD combinations
        TV/VCR combinations
    BT Home video systems
    NT Daewoo television/video combinations
        DVD players
        Philips Magnavox television/video
            combinations
        RCA television/video combinations
        Samsung television/video combinations
        Sharp television/video combinations
        Television—Receivers and reception
        Videocassette recorders
        Zenith television/video combinations
Television viewers *(May Subd Geog)*
    [HE8700.65–HE8700.66]
    UF Audiences, Television
        Television audiences
        Television fans
        Television watchers
        Viewers, Television
    BT Mass media—Audiences
    NT Older television viewers
Television violence
    USE Violence on television
Television watchers
    USE Television viewers

†**Subject headings noted with a dagger contain
additional access points and subheadings that
are not pertinent to this text and are not
included here.**

Television weather broadcasters
  USE Television weathercasters
Television weather forecasters
  USE Television weathercasters
Television weatherpersons
  USE Television weathercasters
Television weathercasters *(May Subd Geog)*
    [QC877.5]
    UF Meteorologists, Television
        Television meteorologists
        Television weather broadcasters
        Television weather forecasters
        Television weatherpersons
        Weather broadcasters, Television
        Weather forecasters, Television
        Weathercasters, Television
        Weatherpersons, Television
    BT Television personalities
Television writers *(May Subd Geog)*
    BT Authors
        Television broadcasting—Employees
    NT Television comedy writers
        Women television writers
Television writing
  USE Television authorship
Televisions
  USE Television—Receivers and reception
Telugu drama[†]
    NT Motion picture plays, Telugu
Telugu motion picture plays
  USE Motion picture plays, Telugu
Ten Eighty Snowboarding (Game)
  USE 1080 Degree Snowboarding (Game)
Tennis television programs *[LCSH Genre]*
Tenorio, Don Juan de (Legendary character)
  USE Don Juan (Legendary character)
Terror in motion pictures *(Not Subd Geog)*
    BT Motion pictures
Terrorism and mass media
    (May Subd Geog)
    UF Mass media and terrorism
    BT Mass media
Terrorism in mass media *(Not Subd Geog)*
    BT Mass media
Terrorism in motion pictures *(Not Subd Geog)*
    BT Motion pictures
Terrorism in television
  USE Television on television
Terrorism on television *(Not Subd Geog)*
    UF Terrorism in television
    BT Motion pictures
Test patterns (Television)
  USE Television—Test patterns

Theater[†]
    RT Acting
    NT Mass media and theater
        Motion pictures and the theater
        Television and theater
        Theater and society
        Video recording in the theater
Theater and mass media
  USE Mass media and theater
Theater and motion pictures
  USE Motion pictures and theater
Theater and society *(May Subd Geog)*
    UF Actors—Social status
        Society and theater
        Theater—Social aspects
    BT Theater
Theater and television
  USE Television and theater
Theater announcements (Motion pictures)
    [LCSH Genre]
Theater commercials (Motion pictures)
    [LCSH Genre]
Theater in motion pictures
    (Not Subd Geog)
    BT Motion pictures
Theater managers, Motion picture
  USE Motion picture theater managers
Theater organ *(May Subd Geog)*
    [ML597 (History)]
    UF Cinema organ
        Theatre organ
    BT Organ (Musical instrument)
Theater rooms
  USE Home theaters
Theater Tuschinski (Amsterdam, Netherlands)
    UF Tuschinski Theater (Amsterdam,
        Netherlands)
Theaters[†]
    NT Akron Civic Theatre (Akron, Ohio)
        Civic Theatre (Portland, Me.)
        Motion picture theaters
  —Stage-setting and scenery
        NT Stage props
Theaters, Motion picture
  USE Motion picture theaters
Theatre organ
  USE Theater organ
Theatrical makeup[†]

[†]**Subject headings noted with a dagger contain
additional access points and subheadings that
are not pertinent to this text and are not
included here.**

UF Acting—Makeup
NT Film makeup
　　Television makeup
Theatrical managers
NT Motion picture theater managers
Theatrical producers and directors *(May Subd Geog)* †
NT Casting directors
Three-dimensional display systems†
NT Stereoscopic television
Three-dimensional television
USE Stereoscopic television
Three-sheet posters *(May Subd Geog)*
UF 3-sheet posters
BT Advertising—Motion pictures
　　Film posters
Three Stooges (Comedy Team)
UF 3 Stooges (Comedy Team)
　　Stooges (Comedy Team)
Three Stooges films
[PN1995.9.T5]
BT Comedy films
Three Stooges films *[LCSH Genre]*
Thrill ride films
USE Amusement ride films
Thriller films
USE Thrillers (Motion pictures)
Thriller movies
USE Thrillers (Motion pictures)
Thriller movies
USE Thrillers (Motion pictures)
Thriller television programs
USE Thrillers (Television programs)
Thrillers (Motion pictures) *(May Subd Geog)*
[PN1995.9.S87]
　　This heading is used as a topical heading for
works about films that feature a buildup of suspense,
tension, uncertainty, menace, and anxiety as primary
elements and in which the audience is kept on
tenterhooks. Works on the use of suspense in motion
pictures, television programs, and video recordings
are entered under Suspense in motion pictures,
television, etc.
UF Film thrillers
　　Movie thrillers
　　Psycho thrillers (Motion pictures)
　　Psychological thrillers (Motion pictures)
　　Psychothrillers (Motion pictures)
　　Suspense films
　　Thriller films
　　Thriller movies
　　Thrillers (Motion pictures, television, etc.)
BT Motion pictures
　　Crime films

Thrillers (Motion pictures)
[LCSH Genre]
Thrillers (Motion pictures, television, etc.)
USE Thrillers (Motion pictures)
　　Thrillers (Television programs)
Thrillers (Television programs) *(May Subd Geog)*
　　This heading is used as a topical heading for
works about television programs that feature a
buildup of suspense, tension, uncertainty, menace,
and anxiety as primary elements and in which the
audience is kept on tenterhooks. When used as a
topical heading it is subdivided by the appropriate
geographic, topical, and/or form subdivisions.
Works about the use of suspense in motion pictures,
television programs, and video recordings are
entered under Suspense in motion pictures,
television, etc.
UF Psycho thrillers (Television programs)
　　Psychological thrillers (Television programs)
　　Psychothrillers (Television programs)
　　Suspense television programs
　　Television thrillers
　　Thriller television programs
　　Thrillers (Motion pictures, television, etc).
BT Television programs
RT Television crime shows
Thrillers (Television programs)
[LCSH Genre]
Time in motion pictures *(Not Subd Geog)*
[PN1995.9.T55]
BT Motion pictures
Time lapse cinematography
(May Subd Geog)
[TR857]
UF Cinematography, Time-lapse
BT Chronophotography
　　Cinematography
Time-lapse films *[LCSH Genre]*
Time travel in motion pictures *(May Subd Geog)*
BT Motion pictures
Titanic (Steamship) in motion pictures
(Not Subd Geog)
BT Motion pictures
Title cards (Motion picture advertising)
USE Lobby cards
Title lobby cards
USE Lobby cards
Titles, Credit (Motion pictures, television, etc.)

---

†**Subject headings noted with a dagger contain
additional access points and subheadings that
are not pertinent to this text and are not
included here.**

USE Credit titles (Motion pictures, television, etc.)

Titles of motion pictures

[PN1995.9.T57]

Here are entered works on the identifying words or phrases used as names of motion pictures. Works on the lists appearing on screen before or after a motion picture or television program that give the names of the actors, directors, etc., are entered under Credit titles (Motion pictures, television, etc.). Technical works on the creation or addition of credit titles, subtitles, or other printed captions for motion pictures are entered under Motion pictures—Titling.

UF Motion picture titles

BT Motion pictures

Titling of motion pictures

USE Motion pictures—Titling

Titling of television programs

USE Television programs—Titling

Tobal No. 1 (Game)

[GV1469.35.T63]

BT Video games

Toilets in motion pictures *(Not Subd Geog)*

BT Motion pictures

Tom (Fictitious character : Hanna and Barbera)

(Not Subd Geog)

Tom and Jerry films

BT Animated films

Tom and Jerry films *[LCSH Genre]*

Tomb Raider (Fictitious character)

USE Croft, Lara (Fictitious character)

Tomorrow Never Dies (Game)

[GV1469.35.T64]

BT Video games

Tonic Trouble (Game)

[GV1469.35.T65]

BT Nintendo video games

Tony Hawk's Pro Skater (Game)

[GV1469.35.T66]

BT Video games

Torchy Blane films

BT Motion pictures

Torchy Blane films *[LCSH Genre]*

Torres Strait Islanders in motion pictures

(Not Subd Geog)

BT Motion pictures

Torture in motion pictures *(Not Subd Geog)*

BT Motion pictures

Torture porn films

USE Splatter films

Totalitarianism and motion pictures

(May Subd Geog)

UF Motion pictures and totalitarianism

BT Motion pictures

Touch in motion pictures *(Not Subd Geog)*

BT Motion pictures

Tourism in motion pictures *(Not Subd Geog)*

BT Motion pictures

Towers[†]

NT Radio and television towers

Toy commander (Game)

[GV1469.35.T68]

BT Video games

Toy Story 2 (Game)

[GV1469.35.T69]

BT Video games

Trade agreements (Labor)

USE Collective labor agreements

Trade-unions and mass media

USE Labor unions and mass media

Traffic safety *(May Subd Geog)*

NT Mass media in traffic safety

Trailers, Film

USE Film trailers

Trailers, Movie

USE Film trailers

Training videos

USE Instructional videos

Transgender people[†]

NT Male impersonators

Transgender people in motion pictures

(Not Subd Geog)

BT Motion pictures

Transgender people on television

USE Transgenderism on television

Transgenderism on television *(Not Subd Geog)*

UF Transgender people on television

BT Television

Transistor television receivers *(May Subd Geog)*

UF Solid-state television receivers

Transistorized television receivers

BT Television—Receivers and reception

Transistorized television receivers

USE Transistor television receivers

Translating and interpreting[†]

RT Closed captioning

Dubbing of motion pictures

Dubbing of television programs

Translating and interpreting in motion pictures

(Not Subd Geog)

[PN1995.9.T685]

BT Motion pictures

Transmission towers, Radio

[†]**Subject headings noted with a dagger contain additional access points and subheadings that are not pertinent to this text and are not included here.**

USE Radio and television towers
Transmission towers, Television
USE Radio and television towers
Transnationalism[†]
NT Motion pictures and transnationalism
Transnationalism and motion pictures
USE Motion pictures and transnationalism
Transportation in motion pictures *(Not Subd Geog)*
BT Motion pictures
Transsexuals in motion pictures *(Not Subd Geog)*
BT Motion pictures
Transvestism in motion pictures *(Not Subd Geog)*
[PN1995.9.T69]
BT Motion pictures
Trapalhões films
[PN1995.9.T72]
BT Comedy films
Trapalhões films *[LCSH Genre]*
Travel in motion pictures *(Not Subd Geog)*
UF Voyages and travels in motion pictures
BT Motion pictures
Travel on television *(Not Subd Geog)*
[PN1992.8.T75]
BT Television
Traveling motion picture theaters *(May Subd Geog)*
UF Itinerant motion picture theaters
BT Motion picture theaters
Travelogs (Motion pictures)
USE Travelogues (Motion pictures)
Travelogue films
USE Travelogues (Motion pictures)
Travelogues (Motion pictures) *(May Subd Geog)*
UF Film travelogues
Travelogs (Motion pictures)
Travelogue films
Travelogues (Motion pictures, television, etc.)
RT Documentary films
Documentary videos
Travelogues (Motion pictures)
[LCSH Genre]
Travelogues (Motion pictures,
television, etc.)
USE Travelogues (Motion pictures)
Travelogues (Television programs)
(May Subd Geog)
UF Television travelogues
Travel television programs
Travelogs (Television programs)
Travelogues (Motion pictures, television, etc.)
RT Documentary television programs
Travelogues (Television programs)
[LCSH Genre]
Treatments (Motion pictures, television, etc.)

BT Motion picture authorship
Television authorship
Trial films
USE Legal films
Trial television programs
USE Legal television programs
Trials in motion pictures
(Not Subd Geog)
[PN1995.9.T75]
BT Motion pictures
Trick cinematography *(May Subd Geog)*
UF Cinematography, Trick
BT Cinematography
Trick photography
RT Cinematography—Special effects
Trick films *(May Subd Geog)*
This heading is used as a topical heading for works about short films from the early years of cinema that emphasize apparent transformations through the use of trick photography or special optical effects.
BT Motion pictures
Trick films *[LCSH Genre]*
Trick photography
NT Trick cinematography
Tricksters in motion pictures *(Not Subd Geog)*
[PN1995.9.T78]
BT Motion pictures
Tricksters on television *(Not Subd Geog)*
BT Television
Trigger films *[LCSH Genre]*
True crime television programs *(May Subd Geog)*
[PN1992.8.T78]
This heading is used as a topical heading for works about nonfiction television programs that feature actual footage and reenactments of criminal and police activities.
UF Crime reenactment television programs
BT Television programs
True crime television programs *[LCSH Genre]*
Truth cinema
USE Cinéma vérité
Tuners, Television
USE Television—Tuners
Tunisian American motion picture producers and directors *(May Subd Geog)*
UF Motion picture producers and directors, Tunisian American

[†]**Subject headings noted with a dagger contain additional access points and subheadings that are not pertinent to this text and are not included here.**

Motion picture producers and directors—
United States
TurboGrafx video games
BT Video games
Turkish drama[†]
NT Motion picture plays, Turkish
Turkish motion picture plays
USE Motion picture plays, Turkish
Turks in motion pictures *(Not Subd Geog)*
BT Motion pictures
Turks on television *(Not Subd Geog)*
BT Television
Turok (Game)
[GV1469.35.T8]
BT Nintendo video games
Turok 2 (Game)
BT Nintendo video games
Tuschinski Theater (Amsterdam, Netherlands)
USE Theater Tuschinski (Amsterdam,
Netherlands)
TV
USE Television
TV characters
USE Characters and characteristics on
television
TV/DVD combinations
USE Television/video combinations
TV sets
USE Television—Receivers and reception
TV shows
USE Television programs
TVs
USE Television—Receivers and reception
TV/VCR combinations
USE Television/video combinations
TV violence
USE Violence on television
Twenty-four-sheet posters *(May Subd Geog)*
UF 24-sheet posters
BT Advertising—Motion pictures
Film posters
Twin-lens cameras
[TR261]
UF Reflex cameras
Twin-lens reflex cameras
BT Cameras
NT Mamiya camera
Praktica camera
Verascope cameras
Twin-lens reflex cameras
USE Twin-lens cameras
Twins in motion pictures *(Not Subd Geog)*
BT Motion pictures

Twisted Metal 2 (Game)
[GV1469.35.T85]
BT Video games
Twisted Metal 3 (Game)
USE Twisted Metal III (Game)
Twisted Metal III (Game)
[GV1469.35.T86]
UF Twisted Metal 3 (Game)
BT Video games
Tyler, Texas, Black Film Collection
UF Black Film Collection, Tyler, Texas
BT Motion picture film collections

UHF television
USE Television—Ultrahigh frequency apparatus
and supplies
Ukrainian drama[†]
NT Motion picture plays, Ukrainian
Ukrainian motion picture plays
USE Motion picture plays, Ukrainian
Ultra-miniature cameras
USE Miniature cameras
Ultrahigh frequency television
USE Television—Ultrahigh frequency apparatus
and supplies
Underground films
USE Experimental films
Underground mass media
USE Alternative mass media
Underground movements in motion pictures
(Not Subd Geog)
BT Motion pictures
Underground videos
USE Experimental films
Underwater cameras
NT Nikonos camera
Sea & Sea cameras
Underwater cinematography
[TR893.8]
UF Cinematography, Submarine
Cinematography, Underwater
Submarine cinematography
BT Underwater photography
Underwater photography
[TR800]
UF Deep-sea photography
In-water photography
Photography, Submarine

[†]**Subject headings noted with a dagger contain
additional access points and subheadings that
are not pertinent to this text and are not
included here.**

Photography, Underwater
Submarine photography
BT Photography—Scientific applications
Underwater cinematography

Underwater television
UF Submarine television
Television, Submarine
BT Optical oceanography
Television

Unedited footage [LCSH Genre]
UNESCO coupons, Film
USE UNESCO film coupons

UNESCO film coupons
UF Film coupons, UNESCO
Motion picture film coupons
UNESCO coupons (Film)

Unfinished films (May Subd Geog)
UF Unfinished motion pictures
BT Motion pictures

Unfinished films [LCSH Genre]
Unfinished motion pictures
USE Unfinished films

Unholy War (Game)
[GV1469.35.U54]
BT Video games

Unidentified flying objects in motion pictures
(Not Subd Geog)
BT Motion pictures
Union agreements
USE Collective labor agreements

United States[†]
—Civilization[†]
NT Television broadcasting of
news—Germany—American influences

Unity Awards in Media
BT Mass media—Awards—United states

University extension[†]
NT Television in university extension
University television stations
USE College television stations

Urban African Americans in motion pictures
(Not Subd Geog)
BT Motion pictures

Urban Strike (Game)
UF Electronic Arts Urban Strike (Game)
BT Video games

Urdu drama[†]
NT Motion picture plays, Urdu
Television plays, Urdu
Urdu motion picture plays
USE Motion picture plays, Urdu
Urdu television plays
USE Television plays, Urdu

Utopia Theatre (Painesville, Ohio)
BT Motion picture theaters—Ohio
Utopias in motion pictures (Not Subd Geog)
[PN1995.9.U76]
BT Motion pictures

V-chips (May Subd Geog)
UF Violence chips
BT Television—Receivers and reception
RT Television—Censorship
Valkyrie Profile (Game)
[GV1469.35.V34]
BT Video games
BT Video games
Vampire films (May Subd Geog)
UF Vampires in motion pictures
BT Monster films
NT Dracula films
Vampire films [LCSH Genre]
Vampire television programs
[LCSH Genre]
Vampires in mass media (Not Subd Geog)
[P96.V35]
BT Mass media
Vampires on television (Not Subd Geog)
BT Television
Vandal Hearts (Game)
[GV1469.35.V37]
BT Video games
Variety programs (Television programs)
USE Variety shows (Television programs)
Variety shows (Motion pictures)
[LCSH Genre]
Variety shows (Television programs)
(May Subd Geog)
UF Television variety shows
Variety programs (Television programs)
Variety television programs
BT Nonfiction television programs
Variety shows (Television programs) [LCSH Genre]
Variety television programs
USE Variety shows (Television programs)
VCDs (Video compact discs)
USE Video CDs
VCR (Video recorders)
USE Videocassette recorders
VCRs (Video recorders)
USE Videocassette recorders

[†]**Subject headings noted with a dagger contain
additional access points and subheadings that
are not pertinent to this text and are not
included here.**

Veils in mass media *(Not Subd Geog)*
  BT Mass media
Verascope cameras *(Not Subd Geog)*
  BT Stereoscopic cameras
    Twin-lens cameras
Veterans in motion pictures *(Not Subd Geog)*
  [PN1995.9.V44]
  BT Motion pictures
Victims of crimes in mass media
  (May Subd Geog)
  BT Mass media
Victor Frankenstein (Fictitious character)
  USE Frankenstein (Fictitious character)
Video, Digital
  USE Digital video
Video and film festivals
  USE Film festivals
Video animation
  USE Animated videos
Video arcades *(May Subd Geog)*
  UF Amusement arcades (Video arcades)
    Arcades, Video
    Video game arcades
  BT Recreation centers
Video art *(May Subd Geog)*
  [N6494.V53]
  UF Electronic art
    Experimental television
  BT Art
    Art, Modern—20th century
    Performance art
    Television
  —Awards
  — —Germany
      NT Maler Video-Installations-Preis
        Maler Video-Installations-Preis
Video astronomy *(May Subd Geog)*
  [QB126]
  UF Video recording in astronomy
  BT Astronomical photography
    Television in astronomy
Video authorship *(May Subd Geog)*
  UF Scriptwriting, Video
    Video recordings—Authorship
    Video scriptwriting
    Video writing
    Writing for video
  BT Authorship
  SA *subdivision* Authorship *under video forms and genres, e.g.,* Documentary videos—Authorship
Video cameras worn on the body
  USE Wearable video devices

Video cameras/recorders
  USE Camcorders
Video captioning (Closed captioning)
  USE Closed captioning
      Video recordings for the hearing impaired
Video cassette recorders
  USE Videocassette recorders
Video cassettes
  USE Videocassettes
Video CDs *(May Subd Geog)*
  UF Compact disc digital video
    VCDs (Video compact discs)
    Video compact discs
    View CDs
  BT Compact discs
    Videodiscs
  —Authoring programs
      UF Authoring programs for video CDs
Video compact discs
  USE Video CDs
Video compression
  NT MPEG (Video coding standard)
Video conferencing
  USE Videoconferencing
Video craps
  BT Craps (Game)
    Video games
Video deejays
  USE Video jockeys
Video description *(May Subd Geog)*
  [HV1769]
  UF Descriptive video (Service for people with visual disabilities)
    Narrative television (Service for people with visual disabilities)
  BT Audiodescription
  NT Video description
Video devices worn on the body
  USE Wearable video devices
Video dial tone *(May Subd Geog)*
  UF Video dialtone
    Video-on-demand
    Video-to-home
  BT Interactive video
    Telecommunication
    Television
Video dialtone
  USE Video dial tone

†**Subject headings noted with a dagger contain additional access points and subheadings that are not pertinent to this text and are not included here.**

Video direction
USE Video recordings—Production and direction
Video disc jockeys
USE Video jockeys
Video disc players
USE Videodisc players
Video discs
USE Videodiscs
Video discs in education
USE Videodiscs in education
Video disk jockeys
USE Video jockeys
Video disks
USE Videodiscs
Video DJs
USE Video jockeys
Video documentaries
USE Documentary videos
Video endoscopy *(May Subd Geog)*
[RC78.7.V53]
UF Electronic video endoscopy
Television endoscopy
BT Endoscopy
Television in medicine
Video films
USE Television film
Video game addiction *(May Subd Geog)*
[RC569.5.V53]
UF Addiction to video games
Addictive use of video games
BT Compulsive behavior
Video game arcades
USE Video arcades
Video game characters *(May Subd Geog)*
[GV1469.34.C48]
UF Videogame characters
BT Characters and characteristics
Video games
Video game characters in art *(May Subd Geog)*
Video game music *(May Subd Geog)*
BT Music
Video game players (Persons)
USE Video gamers
Video gamers *(May Subd Geog)*
UF Gamers, Video
Players, Video game (Persons)
Video game players (Persons)
BT Persons
Video gamers as businesspeople *(May Subd Geog)*
BT Businesspeople
Video games
NT 1080 Degree Snowboarding (Game)
A-Train (Game)

Ace Combat (Game)
Albert Odyssey (Game)
Alundra (Game)
Army Men World War (Game)
Banjo-Kazooie (Game)
Batman & Robin (Game)
Battle Arena Toshinden (Game)
Battle Tanx Global Assault (Game)
Battletoads (Game)
Beyond the Beyond (Game)
Blitz: the League (Game)
Blood Omen (Game)
Blue Dragon (Game)
Blue Stinger (Game)
Body Harvest (Game)
Bomberman World (Game)
Boogerman (Game)
Brave Fencer Musashi (Game)
Breath of Fire (Game)
Brigandine (Game)
Bubsy Bobcat (Game)
Buck Bumble (Game)
Bugs Bunny, Lost in Time (Game)
Bushido Blade 2 (Game)
Carrier (Game)
Centipede (Game)
Cheating at video games
Chocobo's Dungeon (Game)
Colony Wars (Game)
Crash Bandicoot (Game)
Crazy Taxi (Game)
Critical Depth (Game)
Crusaders of Might and Magic (Game)
Dark Seed II (Game)
Dead or Alive (Game)
Deathtrap Dungeon (Game)
Deception (Game)
Destrega (Game)
Devil May Cry 2 (Game)
Diddy Kong Racing (Game)
Dino Crisis (Game)
Donkey Kong (Game)
Dragon Force (Game)
Dragon Warrior (Game)
Dragon's Lair (Game)
Duke Nukem (Game)
Dynasty Warriors (Game)
Earth Worm Jim (Game)

†**Subject headings noted with a dagger contain additional access points and subheadings that are not pertinent to this text and are not included here.**

Ehrgeiz (Game)
Fear Effects (Game)
Fighter's Edge (Game)
Fighting Force (Game)
GameShark (Game)
Gauntlet (Game)
Gekido (Game)
Genma Onimusha (Game)
GEX (Game)
Ghost in the Shell (game)
Global Conquest (Game)
Global Operations (Game)
Glover (Game)
GoldenEye 007 (Game)
Gran Turismo (Game)
Grand Theft Auto games
Grand Theft Auto: San Andreas (Game)
Grandia (Game)
Granstream Saga (Game)
Guitar Hero (Game)
Gun (Game)
Halo (Game)
Hot Wheels turbo racing (Game)
House of the dead (Game)
Jade Cocoon (Game)
Jedi Power Battles (Game)
Jet Force Gemini (Game)
Jet Moto (Game)
Juggernaut (Game)
Kabuki Warriors (Game)
Kagero: Deception II (Game)
Kartia (Game)
Killer Instinct (Game)
King's Field (Game)
Knockout Kings 2000 (Game)
Legacy of Kain (Game)
Legend of Legaia (Game)
Legend of Zelda (Game)
Lemmings (Game)
Lord of the Rings (Game)
Lunar (Game)
Mario Party (Game)
Mario Tennis (Game)
Masters of Teras Käsi (Game)
MediEvil (Game)
Meet the Robinsons (Game)
Mega Man X (Game)
MegaMan Battle Network (Game)
Messiah (Game)
Metal Gear Solid (Game)
Metal Gear Solid 2: Sons of Liberty (Game)
Micro Maniacs (Game)
Midnight Club: Los Angeles (Game)

Misadventures of Tron Bonne (Game)
Mission Impossible (Game)
Monkey Hero (Game)
Mortal Kombat (Game)
Ms. Pac-Man Maze Madness (Game)
NBA 2K (Game)
NBA JAM (Game)
NBA Live 2000 (Game)
NBA Showtime (Game)
NFL 2K1 (Game)
NFL Blitz (Game)
NHL 2K (Game)
Nightmare Creatures (Game)
Nights into Dreams (Game)
Ninja, Shadow of Darkness (Game)
Nintendo video games
Nuclear Strike (Game)
O.D.T. (Game)
Ogre Battle (Game)
One (Game)
Pac-Man (Game)
Pac-Man World (Game)
Parasite Eve (Game)
Perfect Dark (Game)
Pokémon (Game)
Pokémon Stadium (Game)
Pokémon Yellow (Game)
Primal Rage (Game)
Quake II (Game)
Quest 64 (Game)
Rayman (Game)
Ready 2 Rumble Boxing (Game)
Resident Evil (Game)
Resident Evil 3: Nemesis (Game)
Rival Schools (Game)
Road Rash Jailbreak (Game)
Rogue Trip Vacation 2012 (Game)
Rollcage (Game)
Royal Rumble (Game)
RuneScape (Game)
Rush 2 (Game)
San Francisco Rush (Game)
Secret of Evermore (Game)
Sega Dreamcast video games
Sega Genesis video games
Sega Saturn video games
Shadow Madness (Game)
Silent Hill (Game)
Sno-cross Championship Racing (Game)

†**Subject headings noted with a dagger contain additional access points and subheadings that are not pertinent to this text and are not included here.**

Sonic Adventure (Game)
Sony video games
Soul Blade (Game)
Soul Calibur (Game)
Spacestation Silicon Valley (Game)
Sports Car GT (Game)
Spyro 2: Ripto's rage (Game)
Spyro the Dagon (Game)
Star Ocean (Game)
Street Fighter Alpha (Game)
Stuntman (Game)
Suikoden (Game)
Super Metroid (Game)
Superman (Game)
Syphon Filter (Game)
Tactics Ogre (Game)
T'ai Fu (Game)
Tekken (Game)
Tobal No. 1 (Game)
Tomorrow Never Dies (Game)
Tony Hawk's Pro Skater (Game)
Toy commander (Game)
Toy Story 2 (Game)
TurboGrafx video games
Twisted Metal 2 (Game)
Twisted Metal III (Game)
Unholy War (Game)
Urban Strike (Game)
Valkyrie Profile (Game)
Vandal Hearts (Game)
Video craps
Video game characters
Video keno
Video poker
Video wrestling games
Vigilance (Game)
Vigilante 8 (Game)
Violence in video games
Virtua Fighter 1 (Game)
Virtua Fighter 2 (Game)
Virtua Fighter 3 (Game)
Virtual Bart (Game)
Vs. (Game)
WCW Nitro (Game)
WCW/NWO Revenge (Game)
WCW/NWO Thunder (Game)
WCW vs. the World (Game)
Wild Arms (Game)
World Series Baseball 2K1 (Game)
Worms Armageddon (Game)
Wu-Tang Shaolin Style (Game)
WWE Smackdown vs. Raw (Game)
WWF Smack Down (Game)

X-Men (Game)
X-Men vs. Street Fighter (Game)
Xbox video games
Xena, Warrior Princess (Game)
Xenogears (Game)
Video games and children *(May Subd Geog)*
    UF Children and video games
    BT Children
Video games and teenagers *(May Subd Geog)*
    UF Teenagers and video games
    BT Teenagers
Video games for women *(May Subd Geog)*
    BT Women
Video genres *(May Subd Geog)*
    UF Genre videos
        Genres, Video
    BT Video recordings
Video installations (Art) *(May Subd Geog)*
    UF Screen-reliant installations (Art)
    BT Installations (Art)
        Video art
    RT Film Installations (Art)
Video installations (Art) *[LCSH Genre]*
Video jockeys *(May Subd Geog)*
    UF Deejays, Video
        Digital video jockeys
        Disc jockeys, Video
        Disk jockeys, Video
        DJs, Video
        Video deejays
        Video disc jockeys
        Video disk jockeys
        Video Djs
        VJs (Video jockeys)
    BT Television broadcasting—Employs
Video journalism *(May Subd Geog)*
    UF Videojournalism
    BT Photojournalism
Video keno
    BT Keno
        Video games
Video mini-series *(May Subd Geog)*
    UF Limited serials (Video recordings)
        Mini-series, Video
        Miniseries, Video
        Serials, Limited (Video recordings)
        Video miniseries
    BT Video recordings

†**Subject headings noted with a dagger contain additional access points and subheadings that are not pertinent to this text and are not included here.**

Video miniseries
  USE Video mini-series
Video-on-demand
  USE Video dial tone
Video phone
  USE Video telephone
Video poker *(My Subd Geog)*
  [GV1469.35.P65]
    BT Poker
        Video games
Video production
  USE Video recordings—Production and direction
Video promos
  USE Promotional videos
Video recording *(May Subd Geog)*
  [TR845–TR899]
    Here are entered works on the technical aspects of making video recordings, i.e., creating and storing moving images in an electronic form and displaying them on an electronic display. Works on the artistic aspects of making video recordings are entered under Video recordings—Production and direction. Works on the technical aspects of making motion pictures and their projection onto a screen are entered under Cinematography. General works on motion pictures themselves, including motion pictures as an art form, copyrighting, distribution, editing, plots, production, etc., are entered under Motion pictures.
    UF Cinematography—Electronic methods
        Electronic cinematography
        High definition video recording
        High-speed video recording
        Interactive multimedia
        Libraries and video recording
        Video tape recorders and recording
        Video tape recording
        Video taping
        Videography
        Videorecording
        Videotape recording
        Videotaping
        Zipping (Video recordings)
    BT Magnetic recorders and recording
    RT Wearable video devices
    NT Aerial videography
Video recording and libraries
  USE Libraries and video recording
Video recording in astronomy
  USE Video astronomy
Video recording in church work *(May Subd Geog)*
    BT Church work
Video recording in ethnology *(May Subd Geog)*

  [GN347]
    BT Visual anthropology
Video recording in medicine *(May Subd Geog)*
    BT Medicine
Video recording in school management and organization *(May Subd Geog)*
    BT School management and organization
Video recording in social change
  (May Subd Geog)
    BT Social change
Video recording in the theater
  (May Subd Geog)
    BT Theater
Video recording in wildlife management
  (May Subd Geog)
  [SK356.V53]
    BT Wildlife management
Video recordings
    NT Acquisition of video recordings
        Biographical videos
        Cataloging of video recordings
        Comedy videos
        Credit titles (Motion pictures, television, etc.)
        Documentary videos
        Educational videos
        Erotic videos
        Experimental videos
        Instructional videos
        Interactive video
        Internet videos
        Music videos
        Sponsored videos
        Stock footage
        Streaming videos
        Suspense in motion pictures, television, etc.
        Video genres
        Video mini-series
        Video tapes
        Videodiscs
  —Authorship
    USE Video authorship
—Catalogs
    SA *subdivision* Video catalogs *under subjects for lists of video recordings about those subjects; and subdivision* Catalogs *under individual video genres, e.g.,* Music videos—Catalogs

—Copyright
   USE Copyright—Video recordings
—Direction
   USE Video recordings—Production and
       direction
—Fair use (Copyright) *(May Subd Geog)*
   BT Copyright—Broadcasting rights
       Copyright—Video recordings
       Fair use (Copyright)
—Pirated editions *(May Subd Geog)*
   UF Bootleg video recordings
       Copyright—Unauthorized reproductions
       of video recordings
       Pirated video recordings
   BT Piracy (Copyright)
—Production and direction
      Here are entered works on the artistic aspects
   of making video recordings. Works on the
   technical aspects of making video recordings,
   i.e., creating and storing moving images in an
   electronic form and displaying them on an
   electronic display are entered under Video
   recording. Works on the technical aspects of
   making motion pictures and their projection
   onto a screen are entered under
   Cinematography. General works on motion
   pictures themselves, including motion pictures
   as an art form, copyrighting, distribution,
   editing, plots, production, etc., are entered
   under Motion pictures.
   UF Electronic moviemaking
       Video direction
       Video production
       Video recordings—Direction
   BT Coproduction (Motion pictures,
       television, etc.)
   RT Continuity (Motion pictures, television, etc.)
Video recordings *[LCSH Genre]*
Video recordings for children *(May Subd Geog)*
   UF Videocassettes for children
   BT Children
Video recordings for foreign speakers
   SA *subdivision* Video recordings for foreign
       speakers and Video recordings for French,
       [Spanish, etc.] speakers *under individual*
       languages and groups of languages for
       instructional video recordings about a
       language or languages designed for
       speakers of other languages, e.g., English
       language—Video recordings for French,
       [Spanish, etc.] speakers
Video recordings for people with visual disabilities
   (May Subd Geog)

   UF Video recordings for the visually handicapped
   BT People with visual disabilities
Video recordings for people with visual disabilities
   [LCSH Genre]
Video recordings for the deaf
   USE Video recordings for the hearing impaired
Video recordings for the hearing impaired
   (May Subd Geog)
   UF Closed caption video recordings
       Deaf, Video recordings for the
       Video captioning (Closed captioning)
       Video recordings for the deaf
   BT Hearing impaired
Video recordings for the hearing impaired
   [LCSH Genre]
Video recordings for the visually handicapped
   UF Video recordings for people with visual
       disabilities
Video recordings industry *(May Subd Geog)*
   [HD9697.V54–HD9697.V544]
   UF Video industry
       Video tape production industry
   BT Motion picture industry
   RT Video rental services
Video rental services *(May Subd Geog)*
   BT Lease and rental services
   RT Video recordings industry
Video scriptwriting
   USE Video authorship
Video systems, Interactive
   USE Interactive video
Video tape advertising *(May Subd Geog)*
   [HF6146.V53]
   UF Advertising, Video tape
       Advertising in video tapes
       Video tapes in advertising
   BT Advertising
Video tape collections *(May Subd Geog)*
   BT Video tapes
   NT Stock footage collections
Video tape recorders *(May Subd Geog)*
   [TK6655.V5]
   UF Tape recorders, Video
       Video tape recorders and recording
       Videotape recorders
       VTRs (Video recorders)
   BT Magnetic recorders and recording
       Television—Equipment and supplies

†**Subject headings noted with a dagger contain**
additional access points and subheadings that
are not pertinent to this text and are not
included here.

NT Digital video tape recorders
   Videocassette recorders
Video tape recorders and recording
 USE Video tape recorders
Video tape recording
 USE Video recording
Video tapes *(May Subd Geog)*
 UF Tape recordings, Video
   Tapes, Video
   Videotapes
 BT Magnetic tapes
   Video recordings
 RT Television film
 NT Television film recording
   Video tape collections
   Videocassettes
 —Collections
 SA *subdivision* Video catalogs *under subjects*
 —Editing
  BT Editing
 —Preservation *(May Subd Geog)*
  UF Video tapes—Preservation and storage
 —Preservation and storage
  USE Video tapes—Preservation
Video tapes in advertising
 USE Video tape advertising
Video tapes in education *(May Subd Geog)*
 [LB1044.75]
 Here are entered works on the use of video tapes in education. Video recordings intended for teaching and informational purposes, especially those made for classroom viewing, are entered under Educational videos. Video recordings designed to impart skills or techniques to general audiences, typically in a "how-to" manner, are entered under Instructional videos.
 BT Audio-visual education
  Education
  Television in education
 SA *subdivision* Study and teaching—
   Audio-visual aids *under specific subjects*
 —Law and legislation *(May Subd Geog)*
  BT Educational law and legislation
Video tapes in evangelistic work *(May Subd Geog)*
 BT Evangelistic work
Video tapes in historiography *(May Subd Geog)*
 [D16.18]
 BT Historiography
Video tapes in psychology *(May Subd Geog)*
 BT Psychology
Video tapes in psychotherapy *(May Subd Geog)*
 [RC455.2.T45]
 BT Psychotherapy

Video tapes in sex education
 USE Video tapes in sex instruction
Video tapes in sex instruction *(May Subd Geog)*
 UF Video tapes in sex education
 BT Sex instruction
Video tapes in sports *(May Subd Geog)*
 [GV1469.34]
 BT Sports
  Television and sports
Videotape cassettes
 USE Videocassettes
Video taping
 USE Video recording
Video teleconferencing
 USE Videoconferencing
Video telephone
 [TK6505]
 UF Picture telephone
  Video phone
 BT Automatic picture transmission
  Data transmission systems
  Image transmission
  Telephone
  Television
Video-to-home
 USE Video dial tone
Video war games
 USE Computer war games
Video wrestling games *(May Subd Geog)*
 UF Wrestling video games
 BT Video games
  Wrestling
Video writing
 USE Video authorship
Videoangiocardiography
 USE Cineangiography
Videocassette recorders *(May Subd Geog)*
 [TK6655.V5]
 UF VCR (Video recorders)
  VCRs (Video recorders)
  Video cassette recorders
  Video tape recorders and recording
 BT Home video systems
  Video tape recorders
 RT Television/video combinations
  Videocassette recorders
 NT Emerson videocassette recorders
  Fisher videocassette recorders

†**Subject headings noted with a dagger contain additional access points and subheadings that are not pertinent to this text and are not included here.**

General Electric videocassette recorders

Magnavox videocassette recorders

Orion videocassette recorders

Panasonic videocassette recorders

Philips videocassette recorders

Quasar videocassette recorders

RCA videocassette recorders

Sanyo videocassette recorders

Sharp videocassette recorders

Zenith videocassette recorders

Videocassette recordings
   USE Videocassettes
Videocassette tapes
   USE Videocassettes
Videocassettes *(May Subd Geog)*
      UF Video cassettes
         Videocassette recordings
         Videocassette tapes
         Videotape cassettes
      BT Video tapes
Videocassettes for children
   USE Video recordings for children
Videoconferencing *(May Subd Geog)*
      UF Conferencing, Video
         Internet videoconferencing
         Video conferencing
         Video teleconferencing
      BT Teleconferencing
Videodisc players *(May Subd Geog)*
      [TK8685]
      UF Video disc players
         Videodisk players
         Television—Equipment and supplies
Videodiscs *(May Subd Geog)*
      [TK6685 (Television)]
      UF Discs, Video
         Disks, Video
         Video discs
         Video disks
         Videodisks
      BT Optical disks
         Video recordings
      NT DVD-Video discs
         Video CDs
Videodiscs in education *(May Subd Geog)*
      [LB1044.75]
      UF Video discs in education
      BT Audio-visual education
Videodisk players
   USE Videodisc players
Videodisks
   USE Videodiscs
Videogame characters

USE Video game characters
Videography
   USE Video recording
Videojournalism
   USE Video journalism
Videometry
   USE Cineangiography
Videos, Music
   USE Music videos
Videos, Rock
   USE Rock videos
Videotape recorders
   USE Video tape recorders
Videotape recording
   USE Video recording
Videotapes
   USE Video tapes
Videotaping
   USE Video recording
Vidpics
   USE Made-for-TV movies
Vietnamese drama[†]
      NT Motion picture plays, Vietnamese
Vietnamese motion picture plays
   USE Motion picture plays, Vietnamese
View cameras
      [TR258]
      UF Field cameras
      BT Cameras
      NT Sinar camera
View CDs
   USE Video CDs
Vigilance (Game)
      [GV1469.35.V49]
      BT Video games
Vigilante 8 (Game)
      [GV1469.35.V52]
      UF Vigilante Eight (Game)
      BT Video games
Vigilante Eight (Game)
   USE Vigilante 8 (Game)
Village Theater (New York, N.Y.)
   USE Fillmore East (New York, N.Y.)
Villains in mass media *(Not Subd Geog)*
      BT Mass media
Villains in motion pictures *(Not Subd Geog)*
      [PN1995.9.V47]
      BT Motion pictures

[†]**Subject headings noted with a dagger contain additional access points and subheadings that are not pertinent to this text and are not included here.**

Villains on television *(Not Subd Geog)*
  BT Television
Violence chips
  USE V-chips
Violence in mass media *(Not Subd Geog)*
  [O96.V5]
  BT Mass media
Violence in motion pictures *(Not Subd Geog)*
  BT Motion pictures
Violence in television
  USE Violence on television
Violence in video games *(Not Subd Geog)*
  BT Video games
Violence on television *(Not Subd Geog)*
  [PN1992.8.V55]
  UF Television violence
     TV violence
     Violence in television
  BT Television
Virtual Bart (Game)
  [GV1469.35.V57]
  BT Video games
Virtual Fighter 1 (Game)
  [GV1469.35.V548]
  BT Video games
Virtual Fighter 2 (Game)
  [GV1469.35.V549]
  BT Video games
Virtual Fighter 3 (Game)
  [GV1469.35.V55]
  BT Video games
Vision in motion pictures *(Not Subd Geog)*
  BT Motion pictures
Visual anthropology[†]
  NT Motion pictures in ethnology
     Video recording in ethnology
Visual education[†]
  NT Audio-visual education
Vitomatic camera *(Not Subd Geog)*
  BT Cameras
VJs (Video jockeys)
  USE Video jockeys
Vocational education[†]
  NT Television in vocational education
Vocational teachers[†]
  —Training of[†]
     NT Television in vocational teacher training
Voice actors and actresses
  BT Actresses
Voice in motion pictures *(Not Subd Geog)*
  BT Motion pictures
Voigtlander camera *(Not Subd Geog)*
  BT Cameras

Voodooism in motion pictures *(Not Subd Geog)*
  [PN1995.9.V66]
  BT Motion pictures
Voyages, Imaginary, in mass media
  (Not Subd Geog)
  [P96.V68]
  BT Mass media
Voyages and travels in motion pictures
  USE Travel in motion pictures
Vs. (Game)
  [GV1469.35.V73]
  BT Video games
VTRs (Video recorders)
  USE Video tape recorders

Wacky comedy films
  USE Screwball comedy films
Wages[†]
  —Motion picture industry *(May Subd Geog)*
     UF Motion picture industry—Wages
  —Motion picture theaters *(May Subd Geog)*
     UF Motion picture theaters—Wages
Walking in motion pictures *(Not Subd Geog)*
  BT Motion pictures
War[†]
  NT Computer war games
     Mass media and war
     War films
  —Computer games
     USE Computer war games
  —Computer simulation
     NT Computer war games
War and mass media
  USE Mass media and war
War and motion pictures
  USE *subdivisions* Motion pictures and the war,
     Motion pictures and the revolution, *etc.,*
     under individual wars, e.g., World War,
     1939–1945—Motion pictures and the war
War and television
  USE *subdivisions* Television and the war,
     Television and the revolution, *etc., under*
     individual wars, e.g., World War, 1939–
     1945—Television and the war
War films *(May Subd Geog)*
  This heading is used as a topical heading for
works about films that feature military conflicts.
  BT Motion pictures

[†]Subject headings noted with a dagger contain
additional access points and subheadings that
are not pertinent to this text and are not
included here.

RT Anti-war films
NT Submarine films
SA *subdivisions* Motion pictures and the war;
    Motion pictures and the revolution; *etc.,*
    under individual wars, e.g., World War,
    1939–1945—Motion pictures and the war

War films *[LCSH Genre]*

War games†
NT Computer war games

War Gods (Game)
    [GV1469.35.W37]
BT Nintendo video games

War in mass media *(Not Subd Geog)*
BT Mass media
RT Mass media and war
SA *subdivision* Mass media and the war, Mass
    media and the revolution, etc., *under*
    individual wars, e.g., World War, 1939–
    1945—Mass media and the war

War on Terrorism, 2001–, in mass media
    (Not Subd Geog)
BT Mass media

War television programs *(May Subd Geog)*
BT Television programs
RT Anti-war television programs
SA *subdivisions* Television and the war;
    Television and the revolution; *etc., under*
    individual wars, e.g., World War, 1939–
    1945—Television and the war

War television programs *[LCSH Genre]*

Warrior Princess Xena (Fictitious character)
    USE Xena, Warrior Princess (Fictitious character)

Wayne, Bruce (Fictitious character)
    USE Batman (Fictitious character)

WCW Nitro (Game)
    [GV1469.35.W4]
BT Video games

WCW/NWO Revenge (Game)
    [GV146935.W414]
BT Video games

WCW/NWO Thunder (Game)
    [GV1469.35.W416]
BT Video games

WCW vs. the World (Game)
    [GV1469.35.W42]
BT Video games

Wearable video cameras
    USE Wearable video devices

Wearable video devices *(May Subd Geog)*
UF Body-worn video cameras
    Body-worn video devices
    BWVs (Video recording)
    Head cameras

Headcams
Video cameras worn on the body
Video devices worn on the body
Wearable video cameras
BT Video recording

Wearable video devices in police work
    (May Subd Geog)
BT Police

Weather broadcasters, Television
    USE Television weathercasters

Weather broadcasting *(May Subd Geog)*
    [QC877.5]
UF Weathercasting
BT Broadcasting
    Weather forecasting

Weather forecasters, Television
    USE Television weathercasters

Weather forecasting†
NT Weather broadcasting

Weathercasting
    USE Weather broadcasting

Weatherpersons, Television
    USE Television weathercasters

Web cameras
    USE Webcams

Web sites†
NT Internet videos

Web television
    USE Internet television

Web TV
    USE Internet television

Web videos
    USE Internet videos

Webcams *(May Subd Geog)*
UF Web cameras
BT Television cameras

Webcasting
NT Internet television

Weddings in motion pictures *(Not Subd Geog)*
    [PN1995.9.M3]
BT Motion pictures

Weddings on television *(May Subd Geog)*
BT Television

Werewolf films *(May Subd Geog)*
UF Werwolf films
BT Monster films

Werewolf films *[LCSH Genre]*

†**Subject headings noted with a dagger contain**
additional access points and subheadings that
are not pertinent to this text and are not
included here.

Werewolf television programs
[LCSH Genre]
Werwolf films
USE Werewolf films
West Indian Americans in mass media
(Not Subd Geog)
[P94.5.W47]
BT Mass media
Western films (May Subd Geog)
This heading is used as a topical heading for works about films that feature the American West during the period of westward expansion.
UF Westerns
BT Motion pictures
NT Cisco Kid films
Hopalong Cassidy films
Long Ranger films
Spaghetti Westerns
Zorro films
—**Collectibles** (May Subd Geog)
—Europe
USE Spaghetti Westerns
—Italy
USE Spaghetti Westerns
Western films [LCSH Genre]
Western television programs (May Subd Geog)
This heading is used as a topical heading for works about television programs that feature the American West during the period of westward expansion.
UF Westerns
Westerns (Television programs)
BT Television programs
NT Zorro television programs
Western television programs
[LCSH Genre]
Westerns
USE Western films
Westerns (Television programs)
Westerns (Television programs)
USE Western television programs
White telephone comedy films
USE Screwball comedy films
White women in motion pictures
USE Women, White, in motion pictures
Whites in motion pictures (Not Subd Geog)
[PN1995.9.W45]
BT Motion pictures
Whites in television
UF Whites on television
Whites on television (Not Subd Geog)
UF Whites in television
BT Television

Wide-screen processes (Cinematography)
[TR855]
UF Cinemascope
Cinematography, Wide-screen
Cinerama
BT Cinematography
Wild Arms (Game)
[GV1469.35.W54]
BT Video games
Wildlife cinematographers (May Subd Geog)
BT Cinematographers
Wildlife cinematography (May Subd Geog)
[TR893.5]
UF Cinematography, Wildlife
BT Nature cinematography
Wildlife photography
Wildlife films (May Subd Geog)
This heading is used as a topical heading for works about nonfiction films about animals, insects, and plants.
UF Wildlife motion pictures
Wildlife movies
BT Nature films
Wildlife films [LCSH Genre]
Wildlife management†
NT Video recording in wildlife management
Wildlife motion pictures
USE Wildlife films
Wildlife movies
USE Wildlife films
Wildlife photography
NT Wildlife cinematography
Wildlife television programs (May Subd Geog)
BT Nature television programs
Wildlife television programs
[LCSH Genre]
Wildlife videos (May Subd Geog)
BT Nature videos
Wine in motion pictures (Not Subd Geog)
BT Motion pictures
Wit and humor in motion pictures
UF Humor in motion pictures
BT Motion pictures
Witches in motion pictures (Not Subd Geog)
BT Motion pictures
Witches on television (Not Subd Geog)
BT Television

†**Subject headings noted with a dagger contain additional access points and subheadings that are not pertinent to this text and are not included here.**

Wizard of Oz (Fictitious character)
  (Not Subd Geog)
    UF Oz (Fictitious character : Baum)
Wizard of Oz films *(May Subd Geog)*
    UF Oz films
    BT Fantasy films
Wizard of Oz films *[LCSH Genre]*
Women[†]
    NT Mass media and women
        Motion pictures and women
        Television and women
        Video games for women
        Women's mass media
  —Employment[†]
        UF Women—Occupations
        RT Working women in motion pictures
        NT Women in the broadcasting industry
            Women in the mass media industry
            Working women in motion pictures
        SA *names of specific occupations or
            professions*—Occupations
        USE Women—Employment
Women, White, in motion pictures
  (Not Subd Geog)
    UF White women in motion pictures
    BT Motion pictures
Women authors[†]
    NT Women television writers
Women, Black, in motion pictures *(Not Subd Geog)*
    BT Motion pictures
Women actors
    USE Actresses
Women and mass media
    USE Mass media and women
Women and motion pictures
    USE Motion pictures and women
Women and television
    USE Television and women
Women cinematographers
  (May Subd Geog)
    BT Cinematographers
        Women in the motion picture industry
Women critics[†]
    NT Women film critics
Women detectives in mass media *(Not Subd Geog)*
    BT Mass media
Women employees on television *(Not Subd Geog)*
    BT Television
Women entertainers *(May Subd Geog)*
  —United States
        NT African American women entertainers
Women entertainers, African American
    USE African American women entertainers

Women film critics *(May Subd Geog)*
    UF Women motion picture critics
    BT Film critics
        Women critics
Women film directors
    USE Women motion picture producers and
        directors
Women film producers
    USE Women motion picture producers and
        directors
Women heroes in motion pictures
  (Not Subd Geog)
    BT Motion pictures
Women heroes on television
  (Not Subd Geog)
    BT Television
Women in communication
    NT Women in the mass media industry
Women in mass media *(Not Subd Geog)*
    BT Mass media
Women in motion pictures *(Not Subd Geog)*
    BT Motion pictures
Women in television
    USE Women on television
Women in television plays
    USE Women in television
Women in television broadcasting *(May Subd Geog)*
    UF Women in the television industry
    BT Television broadcasting
Women in the broadcasting industry
  (May Subd Geog)
    BT Broadcasting
        Women—Employment
Women in the mass media industry
  (May Subd Geog)
    Here are entered works discussing women's
    employment in the mass media. Works discussing
    all aspects of women's involvement in the mass
    media are entered under Mass media and women.
    Works discussing the portrayal of women in the
    mass media are entered under Women in mass
    media.
    BT Mass media
        Mass media and women
        Women—Employment
        Women in communication
Women in the motion picture industry
  (May Subd Geog)
  [PN1995.9.W6]

[†]**Subject headings noted with a dagger contain
additional access points and subheadings that
are not pertinent to this text and are not
included here.**

Here are entered works on all aspects of women's involvement in motion pictures. Works on the portrayal of women in motion pictures are entered under Women in motion pictures. Works on specific aspects of women's involvement are entered under the specific subject, e.g., Women film critics.

    BT Motion pictures industry
    NT Women cinematographers
         Women motion picture producers and directors
         Women in the television industry
    USE Women in television broadcasting
         Women in the theater
    USE Actresses

Women jazz musicians in motion pictures
(Not Subd Geog)
    BT Motion pictures

Women journalists in motion pictures
(Not Subd Geog)
    BT Motion pictures

Women lawyers in motion pictures
(Not Subd Geog)
    BT Motion pictures

Women motion picture critics
    USE Women film critics

Women motion picture directors
    USE Women motion picture producers and directors

Women motion picture producers and directors *(May Subd Geog)*
    UF Women film directors
         Women film producers
         Women motion picture directors
         Women moving-picture producers and directors
    BT Motion picture producers and directors
         Women in the motion picture industry
    NT Lesbian motion picture producers and directors

  —Credits
    UF Credits of women motion picture producers and directors
         Film credits of women motion picture producers and directors

  —United States
    NT African American women motion picture producers and directors

Women motion picture producers and directors, African American
    USE African American women motion picture producers and directors

Women moving-picture producers and directors

    USE Women motion picture producers and directors

Women murderers in motion pictures
(Not Subd Geog)
    [PN1995.9.W65]
    BT Motion pictures

Women on television *(Not Subd Geog)*
    [PN1992.8.W65]
    UF Women in television
         Women in television plays
    BT Television

Women presidents in motion pictures
(Not Subd Geog)
    BT Motion pictures

Women presidents on television *(Not Subd Geog)*
    BT Television

Women prophets on television *(Not Subd Geog)*
    BT Television

Women psychics on television *(Not Subd Geog)*
    BT Television

Women, Romani, in motion pictures
(Not Subd Geog)
         Here are entered works on the portrayal of Romani women in motion pictures.
    BT Motion pictures

Women scientists in motion pictures
(Not Subd Geog)
    BT Motion pictures

Women screenwriters *(Not Subd Geog)*
  —United States
    NT African American women screenwriters

Women screenwriters, African American
    USE African American women screenwriters

Women spies in motion pictures *(Not Subd Geog)*
    BT Motion pictures

Women spies on television *(Not Subd Geog)*
    BT Television

Women stunt performers *(May Subd Geog)*
    UF Stunt men and women
         Stunt women
         Stuntwomen
    BT Actresses
         Stunt performers

Women television personalities
    BT Television personalities
  —United States
    NT Cuban American women television personalities

†Subject headings noted with a dagger contain additional access points and subheadings that are not pertinent to this text and are not included here.

Hispanic American women television
personalities
Women television personalities, Cuban American
USE Cuban American women television
personalities
Women television personalities,
Hispanic American
USE Hispanic American women television
personalities
Women television writers *(May Subd Geog)*
BT Television writers
Women authors
Women's liberation films
USE Feminist films
Women's mass media *(May Subd Geog)*
UF Mass media for women
Women's media
BT Mass media
Women's media
USE Women's mass media
Work in motion pictures *(Not Subd Geog)*
BT Motion pictures
Working animals
NT Animals on television
Working class in motion pictures *(Not Subd Geog)*
[PN1995.9.L28]
UF Labor and laboring classes in motion pictures
BT Motion pictures
Working class in television
USE Working class on television
Working class on television *(Not Subd Geog)*
UF Labor and laboring classes in television
Working class in television
BT Television
Working dogs
NT Dogs on television
Working women in motion pictures *(Not Subd Geog)*
[PN1995.9.W6]
BT Motion pictures
Women—Employment
World politics[†]
NT Mass media and world politics
World politics and mass media
USE Mass media and world politics
World Series Baseball 2K1 (Game)
[GV1469.35.W65]
UF Sega Sports World Series Baseball 2K1
(Game)
BT Video games
World War, 1939–1945[†]
—Motion pictures and the war
UF World War, 1939–1945, in motion
pictures

World War, 1939–1945, in motion pictures
USE World War, 1939–1945—In motion
pictures
World Wrestling Federation Smack Down
USE WWF Smack Down (Game)
Worms Armageddon (Game)
[GV1469.35.W67]
BT Video games
Wrestlemania (Game) *(Not Subd Geog)*
[GV1469.35.W73]
UF Wrestlemania 2000 (Game)
BT Video games
Wrestlemania 2000 (Game)
USE Wrestlemania (Game)
Wrestlers in motion pictures *(Not Subd Geog)*
[PN1995.9.W74]
BT Motion pictures
Wrestling video games
USE Video wrestling games
Writing for video
USE Video authorship
Writing in motion pictures *(Not Subd Geog)*
BT Writing in motion pictures
Wu-Tang Shaolin Style (Game)
[GV1469.35.W736]
BT Video games
WWE Smackdown vs. Raw (Game)
UF WWE SvR (Game)
BT Video games
WWE SvR (Game)
USE WWE Smackdown vs. Raw
WWF Royal Rumble (Game)
USE Royal Ruble (Game)
WWF Smack Down (Game)
[GV1469.35.W75]
UF World Wrestling Federation Smack Down
WWF SmackDown (Game)
BT Video games
WWF SmackDown (Game)
USE WWF Smack Down (Game)

X-Men (Game)
[GV1469.35.X25]
BT Video games
X-Men versus Street Fighter (Game)
USE X-Men vs. Street Fighter (Game)
X-Men vs. Street Fighter (Game)
[GV1469.35.X]

[†]**Subject headings noted with a dagger contain
additional access points and subheadings that
are not pertinent to this text and are not
included here.**

UF X-Men versus Street Fighter (Game)
BT Video games
X-rated movie theaters
USE Adult movie theaters
X-rated videos
USE Erotic videos
Xbox video games *(Not Subd Geog)*
UF Microsoft Xbox video games
BT Video games
Xena, Warrior Princess (Fictitious character)
(Not Subd Geog)
UF Warrior Princess Xena
(Fictitious character)
Xena, Warrior Princess (Game)
[GV1469.35.X42]
BT Video games
Xenogears (Game)
[GV1469.35.X45]
BT Video games
Xenophobia in mass media *(Not Subd Geog)*
[P96.X45]
BT Mass media
Xenophobia in motion pictures *(Not Subd Geog)*
BT Motion pictures
XXX films
USE Pornographic films

Yashica camera *(Not Subd Geog)*
BT Cameras
NT Contax RTS camera
Yiddish films *(May Subd Geog)*
This heading is used as a topical heading for
works about films in Yiddish produced from the
1920s to the 1940s in Europe and the United States.
BT Motion pictures
Yiddish films *[LCSH Genre]*
Yiddish motion pictures
USE Motion pictures, Yiddish
Yoshi's Story (Game)
[GV1469.35.Y67]
BT Nintendo video games
Young actors *(May Subd Geog)*
UF Youth as actors
BT Actors
Young adult films
USE Teen films
Young adults[†]
NT Mass media and young adults
Young adults and mass media
USE Mass media and young adults
Youth[†]
NT Mass media and youth
Television and youth

Youth and mass media
USE Mass media and youth
Youth and motion pictures
USE Motion pictures and youth
Youth and television
USE Television and youth
Youth as actors
USE Young actors
Youth films
USE Teen films
Youth gang films
USE Juvenile delinquency films
Youth in mass media *(Not Subd Geog)*
[P94.5.Y72]
BT Mass media
Youth in motion pictures *(Not Subd Geog)*
[PN1995.9.Y6]
UF Youth in moving-pictures
BT Motion pictures
Youth in moving-pictures
USE Youth in motion pictures
Youth in television
USE Youth on television
Youth on television *(Not Subd Geog)*
UF Youth in television
BT Television
Youth street films
USE Juvenile delinquency films
Youth television programs
USE Teen television programs

Zaire in mass media
USE Congo (Democratic Republic)—In
mass media
Zapping (Television) *(May Subd Geog)*
Here are entered works on the use of a remote
control device to change channels on a television, in
order to sample other television programs or avoid
advertisements.
BT Television
RT Grazing (Television)
Zipping (Video recordings)
Zato-ichi films
USE Zatoichi films
Zatō-no-Ichi films
USE Zatoichi films
Zatoichi films *(May Subd Geog)*
UF Ichi films

[†]**Subject headings noted with a dagger contain
additional access points and subheadings that
are not pertinent to this text and are not
included here.**

Zato-ichi films
Zatō-no-Ichi films
BT   Samurai films
Zatoichi films [*LCSH Genre*]
Zeiss cameras *(Not Subd Geog)*
BT   Camera
NT   Contaflex camera
Contax camera
Contax RTS camera
Ikoflex camera
Ikonta camera
Vitessa camera
Zelda (Game)
USE   Legend of Zelda (Game)
Zelda II (Game)
USE   Legend of Zelda (Game)
Zenith camera *(Not Subd Geog)*
[*TR263.Z*]
UF   Cosmorex camera
Prinzflex camera
Revueflex camera
BT   Cameras
Zenith television/video combinations
(Not Subd Geog)
BT   Television/video combinations
Zenith televisions *(Not Subd Geog)*
BT   Television—Receivers and reception
Zenith videocassette recorders
(Not Subd Geog)
BT   Videocassette recorders
Zenza Bronica cameras
UF   Bronica cameras
Zionism[†]
NT   Mass media and Zionism

Zionism and mass media
USE   Mass media and Zionism
Zipping (Video recordings)
(May Subd Geog)
Here are entered works on the use of a remote control device to fast-forward through a video recording, often to avoid advertisements.
BT   Video recording
Zapping (Television)
Zombie films *(May Subd Geog)*
This heading is used as a topical heading for works about fictional films that feature the reanimation of corpses that prey on human beings.
BT   Monster films
Zombie films [*LCSH Genre*]
Zorro (Fictitious character) *(Not Subd Geog)*
Zorro films
[*PN1995.9.Z67*]
BT   Western films
Zorro films [*LCSH Genre*]
Zorro television programs
(May Subd Geog)
BT   Western television programs
Zorro television programs [*LCSH Genre*]
Zulu drama[†]
NT   Television plays, Zulu
Zulu television plays
USE   Television plays, Zulu

[†]**Subject headings noted with a dagger contain additional access points and subheadings that are not pertinent to this text and are not included here.**

About the Contributors

BOBBY FERGUSON is retired from East Baton Rouge Parish (County) Library where she was head of the Technical Services Department. Prior to that she served in the same capacity for the state library of Louisiana, where she learned to catalog by creating MARC records for 16 mm films and sound recordings. She created the *Blitz Cataloging* series of workbooks and published numerous magazine articles and state documents on nonprint cataloging. Ferguson taught cataloging classes and workshops in Louisiana, in library schools, around the country, and in Kazakhstan. She conducted several workshops for the Online Audiovisual Catalogers (OLAC) biennial conventions, as well as state library conventions. She served as treasurer of OLAC, and as a member of several committees in American Library Association (ALA), including the Subject Analysis Committee.

SHEILA S. INTNER is Professor Emeritus at Simmons College's Graduate School of Library and Information Science (GSLIS), where she taught cataloging and collection development for 21 years. Retired in 2006, she was founding director of Simmons' Master of Library Science (MLS) program at Mount Holyoke College, South Hadley, Md. Intner was an ALA councilor at large, president of Association for Library Collections & Technical Services (ALCTS), chair of Cataloging and Classification Section (CCS), chair of OLAC, editor of *Library Resources & Technical Services* and *Technicalities*, and serves now on an ALA Editions Advisory Committee. She is author or principal editor of 29 books, most recently *Beginning Cataloging*, *Standard Cataloging for School and Public Libraries*, 4th edition, and *Cataloging Correctly for Kids*, 5th edition. She received the Margaret Mann Citation Award, the Distinguished Alumna Award of Queens College's GSLIS, the OLAC Award, and the NETSL Award. Sheila teaches cataloging in person at Rutgers' SCI and online for the iSchool at the University of Maryland.

ANDREA LEIGH received her Bachelor's degree in Theater Arts and Master's degree in Information Studies from UCLA. She is head of Moving Image Processing at the Library of Congress Packard Campus for Audio Visual Conservation in Culpeper, Va. Before that, she was the metadata librarian at the UCLA Film & Television Archive. Leigh is active in the Association of Moving Image Archivists and Society of American Archivists where she has made presentations and written articles on topics related to the organization and description of archival moving images.

DAVID P. MILLER is associate professor and head of Technical Services at the Levin Library, Curry College in Milton, Mass. His publications include articles in *Cataloging & Classification Quarterly, Library Resources & Technical Services, Technicalities,* and the *Journal of Library Administration.* He is co-editor of *SALSA de Tópicos = Subjects in SALSA: Spanish and Latin American Subject Access,* the first fully bilingual publication of the Association for Library Collections & Technical Services (ALCTS). He has served as chair of the ALCTS Cataloging and Classification Section (CCS) and of the CCS Subject Analysis Committee, and is a member of the International Federation of Library Associations and Institutions (IFLA) Classification and Indexing Section Standing Committee, as well as its Information Coordinator. He has received awards and honors from the New England Technical Services Librarians, ALCTS, and CCQ, the latter for " 'Such stuff as dreams are made on': How does FRBR fit performing arts?" co-authored with Patrick LeBouef.

EDWARD SWANSON has been active in cataloging for some 50 years. He has extensive experience in the development of cataloging rules, in training for their adoption and use, and in editing of numerous cataloging manuals. He recently retired for the second (but probably not last) time, this time from the position of manager of the Minitex Contract Cataloging Program.